June 14/2009

Leadership and Intercultural Dynamics

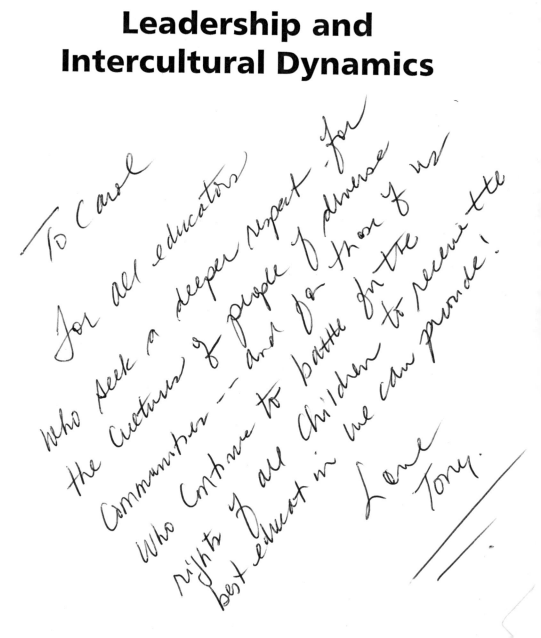

To Carol
for all educators
who seek a deeper respect for
the Cultures & people of diverse
Communities -- and for those of us
who Continue to battle for the
rights of all children to receive the
best education we can provide!

Love
Tony.

Leadership and Intercultural Dynamics

edited by

John Collard
University of Canberra

and

Anthony H. Normore
California State University, Dominguez Hills

Information Age Publishing, Inc.
Charlotte, North Carolina • www.infoagepub.com

Library of Congress Cataloging-in-Publication Data

Leadership and intercultural dynamics / edited by John Collard and Anthony Normore
   p. cm.
   Includes bibliographical references.
   ISBN 978-1-60752-006-1 (pbk.) -- ISBN 978-1-60752-007-8 (hardcover) 1. School management and organization--Social aspects. 2. Educational leadership--Social aspects. 3. Multiculturalism. I. Collard, John. II. Normore, Anthony. III.
   LB2805.L3395 2009
   371.2--dc22

                                                                        2008048552

This volume is jointly sponsored by the Office of Research on Teaching in the Disciplines at the University of Alabama.

Printed in the United States of America

CONTENTS

Foreword
Judith D. Chapman *vii*

Prologue
John Collard *xi*

PART I: THEORETICAL PERSPECTIVES

1. Constructing Theory for Leadership in Intercultural Contexts
   John Collard *3*

2. Research Methods for Leadership in Intercultural Contexts
   John Collard *23*

PART II: WORKING WITH INDIGENOUS CULTURES

3. Culturally Relevant Leadership for Social Justice: Honoring the
   Integrity of First Nations Communities in Northeast Canada
   Anthony H. Normore *47*

4. Leadership in Indian Education: Perspectives of
   American Indian and Alaska Native Educators
   Susan C. Faircloth and John W. Tipperconic *69*

5. Crossing Cultural Boundaries
   Marian Court *83*

6. Conceptualizations of Leadership in Tonga
   Seu'ula Johansson Fua *105*

PART III: WORKING IN MULTICULTURAL SETTINGS

7. American Culture: Latino Realities
   Encarnacion Garza, Jr. and Betty Merchant   *131*

8. A Critical Discourse Analysis of the Meanings of
   Hispanic and Latino in the United States
   Carlos Martin Vélez and John Collard   *151*

9. Muslims in British Schools: Concerns of Learners and Leaders
   Saaeda Shah   *173*

10. Intercultural Leadership in An Australian Binational Setting:
    A Case Study
    Kate Sutherland   *189*

PART IV: WORKING IN INTERNATIONAL CONTEXTS

11. Changing Conceptions of Learning in
    Zhejiang Province, China, 2002–2004
    Ting Wang and John Collard   *211*

12. Chinese Leaders and Western Discourses 2002–2004
    Ting Wang and John Collard   *233*

13. School Leadership in Changing Times: The Case of
    Belarus
    Niklas Eklund, Olof Johansson, and J. Theodore Repa   *259*

14. Riding the Waves: Educators, Leaders Practices in
    Overseas Schools
    Elizabeth Murakami Ramalho and Jill Sperandio   *279*

15. Shifting Landscapes/Shifting *Langue*: Qualitative Research
    From the In-Between
    Maricela Oliva   *297*

PART V: IMPLICATIONS FOR FUTURE THEORY AND PRACTIVE

16. "Isn't it Rich?" From Past Practice to New Horizons!
    John Collard   *327*

About the Authors   *341*

FOREWORD

Judith D. Chapman

This book *Leadership and Intercultural Dynamics*, edited by John Collard and Anthony Normore is groundbreaking in its contribution to the body of theory and research on leadership and intercultural education. The book is crafted from the personal histories, professional experience, intellectual engagements, and moral commitments of the editors and contributing authors. It is grounded in a sense of social justice, deep respect for the cultures of people from diverse communities, and reservations regarding previous "lenses" used to view and attempt to understand the "borderlands" where cultures intersect, particularly in educational institutions serving the needs of people from many cultural, ethnic, religious, and national backgrounds.

As readers of this book we embark on a journey that requires us to engage in thinking about leadership in the future. We are challenged to consider new theoretical perspectives to inform the notions and styles of educational leadership. A model of leadership is put forward, according to which leaders are conceptualized as lifelong learners, reflective thinkers who can understand and respond to changing and complex cultural realities; transformative cultural agents who can mediate and construct appropriate approaches for diverse groups of students and communities; and ethical educators committed to critical and culturally relevant pedagogies responsive to individual student needs and contributing to the formation and development of more just and harmonious societies. Leadership is seen as a "moral art," characterized by ethical practice, guided by an appreciation of the richness offered by diverse student populations, and exercised by educators concerned to ensure that they create meaningful learning opportunities for students who honor the integrity of their culture and traditions. Writers in the various chapters contribute to the laying out of a set of agenda for leaders of educational systems and organizations that has the potential to redress past injustices and create future citizens and leaders for our increasingly diverse and global world.

One of the great strengths of the book lies in its advancing of alternative research methodologies for understanding educational leadership in complex settings. Drawing upon research projects described in various chapters contained in the book, specific recommendations are put forward to assist researchers in recognizing the multiple cultural backgrounds operating in intercultural contexts; designing research studies and developing methods that are inclusive, respectful, and encourage dialogue and reflection; and identifying approaches that enable research findings and outcomes to be analyzed and presented in ways that portray the range of "lenses" and "voices" of all participants in the research process. In so doing the book provides an invaluable resource for researchers and especially for graduate students undertaking research not only in leadership but in intercultural studies more broadly.

From an examination of leadership experiences in diverse settings we see how the complexities associated with preexisting and persisting social structures and practices that privilege one group's "way of seeing and being" over another can undermine innovative and well intentioned attempts to develop more inclusive leadership practices. There is a need for a "revaluing" of cultural difference in school organization, relationships, and structure, just as there is a need for the development of culturally relevant leadership programs and professional learning experiences that change the focus from "what leaders do and how leaders do it," to an emphasis on "what leadership is for," addressing values ends such as social justice, and of the creation of democratic and equitable schools.

Jonathan Sacks (2002) has argued:

> Only when we realize the danger of wishing that everyone should be the same—the same faith on the one hand, the same Mc World on the other—will we prevent the clash of civilizations, born of the sense of threat and fear. We will learn to live with diversity once we understand the God-given, world enhancing dignity of difference. (p. 209)

John Collard and Anthony Normore in their book *Leadership and Intercultural Dynamics* have presented us with a significant work in the field of in the field of educational leadership and intercultural learning. In the words of Jonathan Sacks (2007), they have demonstrated that, "Difference does not diminish; it enlarges the sphere of human possibilities" (p. 209).

REFERENCE

Sacks, J. (2007). *The dignity of difference*. New York: Continuum

PROLOGUE

John Collard

A NEW STANDPOINT FOR LEADERSHIP THEORY

In her classic definition of feminist research methods as "situated knowl-edge" as distinct from "the wandering eye" of mainstream Western social science discourses, Donna Harraway (1988) posed the question "With whose blood were my eyes crafted" (p. 31). In 2005, A Chinese principal in one of my graduate classes commented that "The ideas about student-centered learning have melted thoroughly into my blood now!" She then continued to elaborate upon how constructivist theories of learning had led her to question her heritage of transmission-based pedagogy. Both statements challenge those of us working in intercultural education to define our own standpoint for our research and writing.

While still an undergraduate at Monash University I had the task of co-ordinating a volunteer teaching program for children in orphanages in Melbourne, Australia. My particular site was a Salvation Army Boys Home where most of the children were indigenous members of what we now define as The Stolen Generation in Australia. They had been "removed" from mothers who a patriarchal state deemed "unfit" to raise them. At that time I was asked why I was so committed to improving the lot of such a disadvantaged group. All I could say was "I believe in justice and these boys are the victims of two centuries of white colonialism." And they were indeed victims. As I write this Prologue most of these boys are dead. They died from alcoholism, drug abuse, diabetes, and HIV/AIDS. The idealism of undergraduates was insufficient to redress the structural ravages of colonialism. Of course we also assumed that it was simply a matter of helping them integrate successfully into the mainstream educational system. Our eyes, like those of so many well-intentioned missionaries, were blinded by the culture from which we came!

When I became a secondary teacher I was assigned to schools filled with recent immigrants and became engrossed in developing appropriate curriculum in English and Social Studies for the "multi-cultural society" which Australia, like Canada, declared itself to be in the mid-1970s. My best efforts to improve their literacy were relatively ineffectual until I started to use oral story telling, personal journals, and family history interviews and making film documentaries as strategies. When armed with a tape recorder to capture the history of their immigrant parents students became more engaged and it was relatively simple to use tape transcribing as an instrument to teach sentence structures and grammar. In my frustration, I had stumbled upon pedagogies which departed radically from the curriculum mantras of the age.

I eventually became a principal of an inner urban school where there were a mix of Anglo-Celtic, Italian, and Greek students. By the time I left 8 years later, 25% were Indo-Chinese refugees. The school community responded marvelously to the needs of this group. Inspired by a visionary religious congregation and with parent help a large house was rented and converted to a hostel and each year a staff member would travel to the refugee camps in Thailand and bring back orphans. We would house and educate them and many of these children completed full secondary schooling and continued on to further education in Australia. Of course we still assumed our major task was to integrate these refugees into mainstream society. Then one day a distressed art teacher brought a student's painting of a beheading on a refugee boat to the curriculum committee and challenged us to start dealing proactively with the trauma which was part of the world of many of our students.

Again I was asked why I was committed to such causes. Again my answer was about social justice and the responsibilities of the privileged to assist the dispossessed. When I became an academic specializing in leadership and public policy, I was rapidly deployed into burgeoning international programs by my university. As I began to work with educational and aid programs in developing nations, my experience in schools made me determined that our programs were going to acknowledge and respect the cultures of the groups with whom we were to work. We were not going to foist some contemporary form of Western management cargo upon recipient nations. We were going to try to understand and attempt to meet the needs of the communities we would serve. This led to some innovative off shore program development which utilized bilingual methods of delivery, drew upon the traditions and current issues in the partner cultures and, in turn, generated research interests in the field of leadership in intercultural contexts.

It was only as I began to research and write about the intercultural issues that I came to a full understanding of what had motivated me to be an advocate for social justice and intercultural respect. I came to realize that my entire career had been centered around such issues in varying contexts; from working with dispossessed indigenous youths, to assisting immigrant and refugee families to secure a viable life in an affluent "settler society" and then to sharing our knowledge and skills with others in "developing contexts."

However, when Harraway asked me whose blood had crafted my eyes, I was forced to turn back to my own personal history as an Irish Australian and it was there I found the hard wiring which fueled the intellectual commitment. My ancestors were tenant farmers on a peninsula jutting into the sea in County Cork. My great grandfather was a widower who was dispossessed from his land in 1881 by an English lord who wished to create a seaside estate. Homeless and penniless he raised the funds to send his two daughters, aged 16 and 14 to Australia as countless Irish families were doing at the time. (After 1840 40% of the population in the Australian colonies were Irish). There was the clue! I am a descendant of a colonized and oppressed people and could therefore feel the dispossession, the insecurity and uncertainty in my bloodstream.

On the voyage to Australia, the oldest sister died and my grandmother arrived in Melbourne at the age of 14 by herself. She was a refugee and was promptly apprenticed to an Irish farmer and at 15 gave birth to the first of the 11 children she was to bear him through her lifetime. As a child I listened to the songs of the Irish immigrants. I heard their bitterness and learned to sing their lyrical laments for a land and families they would never see again. As a privileged young adult I made the pilgrimage to the homeland. I stood on the steps of Dublin Post Office on Easter Saturday and felt the resistance of the 16 youths who were gunned down there by English troops in 1916. I recited Yeats' (1916)[1] eulogy for them with passionate conviction. In more recent years I am prompted to capture my ancestral history in poetry and film scripts I write for my actress daughter. This impulse also encompasses a response to the plight of contemporary victims of ethnic cleansing and self righteous regimes:

I met two boys from Sarajevo
Greyhound Terminal, San Antonio,
July 2007.

They had just arrived from Laredo Detention Centre,
three years in the slammer
their reward for refugee status.
Suddenly freed, they seek links with vague relations in New York City.

We shared a meal while waiting for connections,
they struggled with the language
and the staccato messages from black porters
who advised them their bus was delayed.

I learnt they were cousins.
their crime;
witnessing the execution of their fathers when they were six!.

I board my bus to Houston,
look back and wave inadequately
to two boys from Sarajevo
who stare silently in the fluorescent glare,
wondering what wolf pack will invade this night.

And meanwhile,
in another world,
two mothers weep silent tears
into the Adriatic Sea.

So my eyes have been crafted by both personal history and professional experience. My academic credentials and career provide a form of legitimacy for my sustained interest in and commitment to the displaced, the marginalized and the oppressed. At the start of the twenty-first century my nation is an affluent island peopled by immigrants and refugees from many origins. However, it has failed to fulfill its compassionate promise. The majority of our indigenous population (2%) live an existence consistent with desperate third world scenarios. In 2002 our federal government strengthened border security against illegal aliens and "boat people" have been turned back to where they originated or interred in offshore detention centers. The election of a new government committed to structural social justice for indigenous and refugee populations currently promises to turn this around and there is newfound optimism in our nation. However, ethnic and religious intolerance can be found in our cities where Islamic and Sudanese communities are viewed with deep suspicion. Our education and aid programs to "developing nations" come at a price. Our universities are directed to ensure "return on investment," to continue to build "the export dollar" as education becomes one of the key commodities of "the clever country."

Anthony H. Normore is Canadian who currently works in the United States. He has worked extensively with First nations communities in North Eastern Provinces of Canada. He too has a commitment to the dispossessed, the marginalized, and the oppressed. He also comes to have a deep respect for the cultures of the diverse peoples with whom he works. Like me, he is skeptical that the Western lenses through which our leaders and researchers have viewed "other cultures" in the past are accurate or adequate.

Other authors in this book have developed their understandings from working in the borderlands where cultures intersect. These may be reservations, ghettoes, or even prisons within metropolitan states and international development programs. They include schools, universities and shop-fronts where they have taught and learned. For some those borderlands have included refugee camps, internment centers, community aid programs, and educational endeavors. As a group we are committed to fostering deeper insights and understandings into specific cultures and the intersections of cultures. We are committed to the ethics of compassion and social justice and believe that scholarship and research has a moral responsibility to promote such values and to challenge the policies, practices, structures, and inherited cultures which violate fundamental human rights. We invite you, the readers, to join us in our journey towards greater understanding of the aspirations, heritages, and needs of fellow human beings throughout our world.

NOTE

1. Easter (Yeats, 1950) is a poem describing the reaction to f the Easter Rising staged in Ireland against British rule at Easter (April 24). It was unsuccessful, and most of the militant leaders involved were executed for treason. The poem was written between May and September 1916. See The Collected Poems of W. B. Yeats. 1950. Reprint, London: Macmillan, 1982.

REFERENCES

Harraway, D. J. (1988). Situated knowledges: The science question in feminism and the privilege of partial perspective. *Feminist Studies, 14,* 575–599.

Yeats, W. B. (1950). *The collected poems of W. B. Yeats.* London: Macmillan. (Reprint 1982)

PART I

THEORETICAL PERSPECTIVES

CHAPTER 1

CONSTRUCTING THEORY FOR LEADERSHIP IN INTERCULTURAL CONTEXTS

John Collard

INTRODUCTION

Educational leadership in the twenty-first century increasingly occurs in institutions characterized by demographic diversity. The global story has been one of migration and mobility and contemporary nation states are populated by people from many different cultural, ethnic, national, and religious backgrounds (Brown & Davis, 2004: Davis & Cho, 2005; Gay, 2003). Diverse populations are characterized by different cultures and assumptive frameworks. When they meet, whether it is in political summits, the market place or leadership praxis, a process of intercultural interaction occurs.

Intercultural interaction is a dynamic interplay which involves complex forces of differences and similarities. There are multiple definitions of cultural elements and frameworks in leadership discourses. Schein (1985) alerted us to the extent of the complexity when he defined an ascending order from basic assumptions to values to artifacts and creations.

Leadership and Intercultural Dynamics, pp. 3–22
Copyright © 2009 by Information Age Publishing
All rights of reproduction in any form reserved.

Lundberg (1988) sketched a similar framework from core values to symbolic and manifest levels of cultural phenomena. Both agree that values; whether they are assumed or explicit, are central to the life of organizations.

Such conceptions of culture share synergies with recent discourse which recognizes values and morals as core components of leadership praxis (Collard, 2002; Hodgkinson, 1991; Marshall & Rusch, 1995). Leaders are cultural agents who bring values to bear on decision-making and policy decisions (Leithwood, Jantzi, & Steinbach, 1999). They are both the inheritors of established traditions and the transmitters of core values within nations, societies, organizations, and families. Such a concept is also compatible with determinist theses (Parsons, 1952) that culture is both a product and shaper of human social interaction More contemporary theorists dispute unitary and stable conceptions of culture and alert us to the possibilities of myriad crossroads and borderlands within social and national cultures (Rosaldo, 1993).

In the field of educational leadership there is dispute as to what values should drive the actions and philosophies of the actors. Macgregor Burns (1978) and Hodgkinson (1991) support transformational or platonic conceptions of the common good which should override pragmatic considerations and personal power. Begley (1996) has argued that more pragmatic concerns with consensus and conciliation have the strongest influence over the actual praxis of school leaders. His recent characterization of a tendency to "ritualistic rationality" (Begley, 2004, p. 15) in schools alerts us to the influence of traditions of rational thought which have also shaped state bureaucracies and institutional praxis in Western nations (Hearn, 1993). More recently, Blackmore (2004) has stressed the overriding influence of the performative ethics of economic rationalism upon bureaucrats and leaders in the current age.

This debate suggests that educational leaders may actually bring a heterogeneous mixture of assumed and explicit values to their praxis. The issue becomes even more complex when we factor in intercultural aspects such as varied conceptions of human nature, learning, and knowledge. Add to this, different traditions of leadership, gender roles organizational forms, authority and community, and the mosaic becomes more complicated. In the past 2 decades, cross cultural theorists (Hofstede, 1980, 1986; Trompenaars, 1993; Walker & Dimmock, 2000), have mapped specific terrains which illustrate such phenomena.

Schein (1985) placed assumptions about human nature at the base of his cultural pyramid. Those of us studying educational leadership need to extend this to explore conceptions of learning, knowledge, and community. These form epistemological platforms from which much discourse about educational leadership proceeds. Assumptions about human agency are also central. Are organizational leaders simply transmitters of imposed and inherited values whether they are the esteemed traditions of religious authorities, the edicts of political masters or the latest manifestations of bureaucratic and economic accountability? Alternatively, are they reflective practitioners (Schon, 1988) or lifelong learers (Chapman, Aspin, & Taylor, 1998) who respond and adapt to specific contexts and subsequently construct nuanced leadership repertoires?

This issue is fundamental to advancing our understanding of leadership in intercultural contexts. If we view leaders as passive transmitters of dominant leadership cultures and practices, locked into rigid mindframes, the best we can hope for is that cross cultural mapping and the explosion of courses which teach "intercultural competence" will equip them to operate with some sensitivity in alien terrains. However, if we view the leader as a learner constantly constructing and reconstructing a responsive worldview then there is potential for innovation and change. They may be able to adapt to cultural differences more creatively and even build leadership cultures which bridge differences and incorporate the needs of diverse peoples (Merchant, 2004).

The latter concept transcends prescriptive leadership traditions and checklists by conceptualizing leaders as learners, cultural mediators, and constructers of appropriate approaches for intercultural contexts. It shares a synergy with recent thinking about values and ethics which call for "dialogical integrity" among leaders as they critically reflect upon, interrogate and adjudicate between diverse values and their relevance to the sites in which they work (Shields, 2002). This may well be a hallmark of future leaders working as reflective practitioners in intercultural contexts. Outcomes may range from accommodation to adaptation and resistance to varied cultural traditions. Emergent frameworks may also be hybrids which combine elements of preexisting cultures in new and complex combinations (Limerick, Cunnington, & Crowther, 1998).

HISTORICAL PERSPECTIVE

Western traditions of formal education evolved slowly since the Middle Ages. Universities and private schooling were frequently associated with specific elites or religious groups which were predominately monocultural and socially exclusive. The rise of mass public schooling in the nineteenth century was closely linked to the emergence of nation states and allied to the needs of emerging industrial economies. School systems in Britain, France, Germany, and Spain were framed on monocultural assumptions and an imperial ambition to fuel expanding economies and national power. Early leadership praxis frequently embodied the values of other

organizational forms in these nation states. British boys' schools were frequently modeled on military traditions (Protherough, 1984) and public
systems in the United States embodied Taylor's principles for the production line (Tyack, 1974). Although such early praxis has been modified by
an intervening century and alternative discourses, it is still possible to discern such antecedents in leadership praxis in Anglo-American cultures.

As these states colonized other parts of the world, education practices,
like religious heritages, were exported with a blithe assumption that they
were appropriate for other populations. They tended to create a caste system in colonies by becoming a positional good for subordinate elites
(Marginson, 1997) but excluded the vast majority of indigenous
populations from meaningful participation. The failure of paternalistic
educational provision for indigenous populations in settler societies from
Australia to Chile even to this day is a consequence of such practice
(Anderson & Taylor, 2005; Pastrana, Guillermo-Williamson, & Gomez;
2004).

Settler societies such as the United States, Canada, Australia, South
Africa, and New Zealand adopted various cultural frameworks to integrate educational practice into the national state. In the United States a
vigorous nationalism based on assimilation ideologies was intended to
dissolve the ethnic heritage of successive waves of immigrants into a unified national sentiment. The district school displaced the home and
church which had been educational sites of the pioneer nation and, in
doing so, radically constrained forms of cultural diversity (Loveless,
1998). In Canada, the opposing cultural heritage of British and French
populations generated cultural separatism and it was not until the 1970s
that multiculturalism was embraced as a national policy (Tardiff, 2002)
However the consequences of this cultural divide continue to contribute
to provincial disharmony and discrete, bi-cultural school systems across
the nation. Similar tensions emerged between Boer and British traditions
in South Africa.

Australian and New Zealand developments privileged British heritage
and institutional practice over other immigrant cultures. However, the
mass immigration of Irish-Catholic settlers after the 1840s generated a
cultural fault line with far reaching consequences in Australia. They had
already established a fledgling system of "denominational schools" prior
to the efforts of colonial politicians to institute state school systems modeled on British precedent in the 1870s (Austin, 1977; Barcan, 1980). The
1870s rhetoric of "free, compulsory and secular" was met with fierce
resistance as bishops wrote to Ireland to recruit religious congregations to
create what continues to be an extremely robust, yet state funded,
Catholic school system (Fogarty, 1957; Martin, 1986).

Other religious groups and private enterprises also elected to conduct schools which were independent from the state. The consequence was the creation of a tripartite school system; Government, Catholic, and Independent. In the closing decades of the twentieth century new waves of immigrants adapted to this diversity by creating Buddhist, Greek, and Islamic Schools. In 2005 the relative proportions of students in these three systems across the nation were; Government 67%, Catholic 20%, and Independent 13% (Independent Schools Council of Australia Bulletin, 2005). The various sectors vigorously extol cultural and values differences in a manner which makes them very different from government educational institutions (Collard, 2003).

In the 1970s, Australia, like Canada also adopted the rhetoric and policy of the "multi-cultural nation" where cultural differences are valued within a broader framework of national values (Bullivant, 1991). More recently, this has been replaced by a new "muscular nationalism" which has retreated from such diversity However, even the multicultural era did little to produce forms of leadership appropriate for robust provision for the indigenous population (2%). Like many other postcolonial groups throughout the world they remain marginalized on the fringes of mainstream education (Anderson & Taylor, 2005).

European colonialism also influenced higher education practice throughout the world. Colonial elites were educated in metropolitan nations. They then returned to their homelands and perpetuated foreign traditions. Even relatively closed societies like China looked to Western nations for guidance at this level. American practice was a strong influence on the creation of Peking University in the 1920s. In the Cold War era, Russian traditions of pedagogy and scientific positivism left an imprint on Chinese education which is legible to this day (Du, 1992). In the global era we see a burgeoning of international education and aid programs as "advanced western nations" strive to assist or market to emerging economies throughout the world. Most notable are programs hosted by UNESCO, The OECD, The World Bank, and The Asian Development Bank. The most ambitious is undoubtedly UNESCO's Education for All Program which aspires to provide universal education throughout the world by 2015 (Daniel, 2002).

Such programs are frequently based upon contemporary capitalist notions of economic sustainability and yoke educational endeavors to national economic benchmarks. They have been likened to "a tidal wave" of values and beliefs which inexorably draw other cultures into the web of Western values and beliefs (Dale, 1999; Lam, 2001). As such they continue to embed forms of cultural paternalism towards recipient states. The key question becomes whether these endeavors, whether they be aid programs, economic infrastructure projects, or educational leadership programs are in the best interests and built upon an intercultural under-standing of the needs of the target nations.

Another feature of the postcolonial era has been the efforts of advanced Western nations to turn their educational capital into a form of export income. The host programs for overseas students continue to expand in nations like Australia, Britain, Canada, and the United States. However, offshore delivery of programs in recipient nations is a booming industry. It takes many forms from establishing school and university cam-puses in overseas locations, to mentoring new institutions, to short term intensive delivery in universities and the use of digital technology. In the past decade 70% of offshore delivery from Australia has been in the Asian region, especially in Singapore, Malaysia, and Hong Kong and, consider-able expansion has also occurred into China and The Pacific (Australian Vice Chancellor's Committee, 2001, 2005).

From an intercultural perspective, we must ask the question, is the educational practice appropriate to the cultures of the sites in which it is being delivered? Are Western discourses assumed to have a norma-tive validity regardless of local values and traditions? Are the intercul-tural dynamics such that there is opportunity for recipients to mediate and reflect upon the cultural fit between imported intellectual cargo and their own traditions and values? Do agents from the delivery cul-ture have time to understand and reflect and learn from the recipient cultures with which they are dealing? Hallinger (2005) has recently argued the need for Western practitioners to suspend their cultural assumptions if they are to deepen understanding of educational leader-ship in international contexts. He goes even further to add that "when viewed from different cultural traditions and outside of a set of shared universal values," leadership itself "becomes a contested concept" (Hal-linger, 2005, pp. 1–3).

Whether we are dealing with indigenous minorities within postcolonial, Western-centric societies, (Australia, Canada, New Zealand, and the United States) or multicultural populations (Britain, France, India, Malaysia, South Africa, Sweden) we cannot assume that monocultural traditions and values possess a universal currency. If we are conducting leadership training courses in Belarus, Bhutan, China, or Mexico we must question normative discourses and practices from other cultures and nation states. To ignore such considerations is to indulge in a postcolonial form of professional praxis which verges on imperialism and we should not be surprised if our deeply cherished, culturally-derived val-ues encounter resistance or fail to be implemented as we would expect in the West.

CROSS CULTURAL THEORY

Scholars such as Begley (1996), Dimmock and Walker (2000a, 2000b), Heck and Hallinger (1999), Leithwood, Jantzi, and Steinbach (1999), Ribbins (1996) have alerted us to the links between cultural values and leadership praxis and warned of the dangers of continuing to operate from monocultural assumptions and frameworks. They have drawn upon cross-cultural theory and research paradigms of scholars such as Hofstede (1980, 1986, 1995) Trompenaars (1993,) Trompenaars and Hampden-Turner, 1997) to combat cultural blindness and compare cultural landscapes. Others have developed the concept of closed cultural codes and cautioned that "when groups of people from different institutions and countries with different social and political histories, are brought together to perform a task that is differently perceived, there is huge potential for misunderstanding" (Hyatt & Simons, 1999, p. 29). It is therefore timely to explore the potential of cross cultural approaches to redress these issues.

Hofstede (1980, 1986, 1991, 1994) was the first to develop cross-cultural frameworks from his observations in business domains. His concept of culture was akin to the collective programming of the mind which distinguishes one group of people from another. His dimensions are presented as paired choices of empirically verifiable alternatives that allow the emergence of patterns within and between cultures to be discerned. From this he constructed a conceptual map of 40 national cultures and drew distinctions between them. He mapped differences between Anglo-American cultures and those from other realms according to five dimensions. These were power distance, individualism versus collectivism, masculinity versus femininity, uncertainty avoidance, and long term versus short term orientations. His methodology was to study many cultural behaviors as an outsider, compare and contrast them through an analytical framework created by the researcher and to use classificatory criteria which were assumed to be absolute or universal. The outcome is to identify, explain, illustrate or exemplify culture-specific differences with the intention of sensitizing researchers, learners and leaders to them (Humphrey, 2002). Trompenaars and Hampden-Turner (1997) developed this methodology further but never questioned the positivist epistemology upon which it was based.

Once such frameworks are established, the focus of researchers tends to become trained on comparing cultures using predetermined characteristics. For instance, in relationship to leadership, both Hofstede and Trompenaars argued that whereas Western cultures determine status, respect and power according to on the job performance, many Asian cultures were more influenced by position, age or family power. One can immediately recognize the legacy of positivist social science in such an approach. It is no surprise that commentators from the fields of communications and cultural studies have warned of the dangers of describing groups and nationalities in essentialist terms of contrasting beliefs and values as a form of "generalization" which should be treated with skepticism (Humphrey, 2002; Osland & Bird, 2000; Putnis & Petelin, 1996).

The cross-cultural approach is inherently limited by epistemological assumptions which frame culture as a static reality and ignores the possibility of it being a dynamic, fluid and multifaceted phenomena (Collard & Wang, 2005). This can be manifested inside an apparently monocultural reality through generational change or geographical relocation. Within postcolonial, multicultural, or international scenarios there is potential for interactive effects between the values and norms of diverse cultural groups which are not comprehensible through cross-cultural lenses. Nor can we assume that indigenous cultures in post-colonial contexts are static and coherent. They have been destabilized by colonialism and susceptible to practices such as alcohol and drug abuse from which their traditions have failed to protect them. We can also identify how contemporary forces such as digital technology are transforming traditional assumptions about family life in developed and developing contexts.

The practical and research applications of cross cultural theories treat differences as potential barriers and advocate understanding these barriers and respecting the differences. They promote training to bridge the culture gap between agents and this is frequently conceptualized as developing cross-cultural competencies.

A more recent approach involves investigating culture from a perspective which views it as dynamic, ever-changing, multilayered and complex (Gullestrup, n.d); Tardiff, 2002) acknowledges that all cultures are constantly subjected to pressure for change from both internal and external factors. From such a perspective, culture is no longer seen as a monolithic force which scripts the values and behavior of individuals, groups, and organizational leaders in the manner assumed by cross-cultural theory. Communication theorists argue that intercultural studies should be informed by "theories of behaviour that are interaction-oriented rather than culture based. They should emphasise change rather than stability, adaptation and choice rather than cultural determinism" (Putnis & Petelin, 1996, p. 35) This approach acknowledges what each individual brings to their social, educational, organizational, ethnic, national, and even international encounters. It is attuned to postmodern conceptions of learning and knowledge which view individuals as active constructors of their own explicit world views. As such, it avoids simplistic, ethnic, national, and international cultural constructs which can provide only one possible layer in complex, multilayered scenarios (Humphrey, 2002).

Another recent development has been the emergence of intercultural theory (Hart, 1998). It distinguishes between cross-cultural studies which compare and contrast generalized characteristics of two or more cultures and a more dynamic approach which studies what happens at the individual, group or even international levels when cultural agents interact.

Within this theory, intercultural competence refers to a person's capacity to recognize the cultural origins of knowledge and values, incorporate alternative frames of reference into knowledge construction, learn from and with people from other cultures and apply ethical choices which recognize the complexities of cultural interaction (Paige, 2004). Others have defined intercultural competence as "the capacity to change one's knowledge, attitudes and behaviors, so as to be open and flexible to other cultures" and extol "openness and flexibility as the two main components of intercultural competence" (Davis & Cho, 2005, p. 4). They argue the need for learning and growth to occur which facilitates intercultural perspectives into the cognitive schema of cultural agents thereby enabling previous cultural frameworks to be transformed into new perceptions of "interculture" and more flexible responses.

At this point in discussion it is timely to recall Schein's (1985) comment that institutional cultures can become frozen and thereby dysfunctional. His insistence that an organization's culture must be "unfrozen" to enable it to continue to respond to external and internal pressures has been echoed by learning organization theorists who argue that static cultures become dysfunctional in environments characterized by constant and turbulent change (Senge, 1990). Such a process has more generative potential than the typologies of cross-cultural theorists or the communicative technologies taught in intercultural training workshops. Davis and Cho (2005) insist on the need for educational leaders to reflect on their educational beliefs, experiences, and behaviors and to reconstruct them to become competent intercultural agents.

The intercultural perspective has become the dominant paradigm in the Culturelink conferences and networks hosted by UNESCO and The Council of Europe since 1995. The dismantling of the Iron Curtain has generated dialogue about multiculturalism and interculturalism among European states. This led to the definition of The Global Agenda for Dialogue among civilizations adopted by the United Nations in 2001. The description of this process at the Second World Culturelink Conference (2005) suggests that there have been two components of this process. The "recognition of differences between cultures as the key constituent of their identity" is conceptualized as a platform upon which dialogue and cooperation can be based (Second World Culturelink Conference, 2005). Outcomes of this advance in thinking can be seen in the creation of centers and chairs of intercultural studies at the universities of Durham, London,

Manchester (United Kingdom), Osnabruck in Germany, and Vaasa in Finland.

This development now helps us to build an emerging paradigm for cross-cultural and intercultural phenomena in the field of educational leadership. They can be viewed as two stages of a process which has grown in sophistication in both assumptions about culture, learning, knowledge, and praxis. Cross-cultural theory and research has provided roadmaps to help us define the territory. It provides cultural agents with macrolevel templates. Cross-cultural competencies provide a basic technology for working in the territory. However real in depth understanding and cooperation can only occur when these basic knowledge forms are supplemented by deeper research and collaboration. Such knowledge can only be gleaned by intercultural research methods which recognize the individual agency of actors in leadership positions, which recognizes their capacity to reflect and respond to diverse cultural forces and to construct new knowledge which will equip them for the diverse and global interchanges of the future.

CROSS CULTURAL THEORY IN LEADERSHIP DISCOURSE

Pioneer scholars of the past decade recognized that leadership assumptions and beliefs from Western nations did not provide a normative discourse which is appropriate for other cultures. The first wave of this scholarship was cross-cultural in nature. It frequently drew upon Hofstede's (1986) frameworks to highlight the incompatibilities between traditions and social norms. Bush and Qiang (2000) used the concepts of power distance, uncertainty avoidance and long versus short term orientations to explore educational leadership in Chinese societies. Walker and Dimmock (2000) also pointed to the need to recognize distinctive assumptions about authority, collectivism and patriarchy in China. More recently, Hallinger (2005) has argued that the core values of East Asian societies place less value on personal freedom and liberties that predominate in Western societies than on the rights and responsibilities individuals have to families, affiliated groups, and social institutions. He argues that democratic values have lower valence in such cultures than they do in the West and that power differentials are more powerful than would be found between principals and teachers in Swedish or Canadian schools. It is ironic that most of this research occurred in international contexts. There has not been nearly as much sustained work on the interface between mainstream and indigenous cultures or in multicultural contexts.

Hallinger and Kantamara (2000) identified how cultural differences can modify the adoption of contemporary Western discourses about school reform. A similar analysis is provided with regard to concepts of distributed leadership in Chinese contexts (Hallinger, 2005). He explains that traditions of equality and contractual relationships in Western democracies are culturally alien in a society like Hong Kong and constrain actions such as dissent or the expression of criticism in the workplace. Such comments herald the need for caution among Western academics who are employed as consultants or educators in culturally alien contexts.

However, close examination of the text of Hallinger's (2005) most recent writing suggests that his theory is still heavily reliant upon the precepts of Hofstede and his followers. Differences are compared and identified as barriers to intercultural understanding. Cultural stereotypes are assumed and a great divide constructed between Western and "East Asian societies." The very process repeats the positivist fallacies of Hofstede's (1980) thesis. Are we to believe that all East Asian societies are the same? Surely there are important nuances between Islamic states such as Indonesia and Malaysia, Buddhist states like Thailand and Bhutan, socialist market economies such as China and the hybridized, more Western, capitalist cultures of Hong Kong, the Philippines, and Taiwan? To create categories which can in turn mask other important variables such as religious values, economic policies, or the degree of Western penetration into local cultures is to misrepresent reality. An expert on intercultural communication, once related cross-cultural generalizations to the unhelpful trait theories which dominated the social sciences in past generations. He asserted that Japanese diplomats may bow and use intricate forms of polite address in monocultural settings but shake hands in cosmopolitan forums. He went on to add that Muslim women may well be covered and segregated in home states but those who meet diplomats abroad are more likely to be attired in Paris fashions (Fisher, 1989). The key point is that cultures are in constant states of change and adaptation and generalizations which ignore this complexity may ultimately remain unhelpful to researchers and leadership practitioners.

There is evidence in some recent discourse of a move beyond cross-cultural stereotypes towards more nuanced accounts of leadership and culture (Begley, 2004; Walker, 2003). Begley's (2000, 2004) concept of values as cultural isomorphs notes that ethics that appear common to a variety of cultures are actually isomorphic. If, as he contends, value postures appear to share the same shape or meaning from country to country but are really structured of quite different elements, he is contesting the adequacy of the categories used by cross-cultural theorists in the past. If a value such as democracy has a different meaning in Sweden from the United States or even China, then it forces those who wish to study interactions between such nations to use more tightly focused lenses than panoramic stereotypes from the past. If, as he further contends, isomorphs can occur within a single culture or nation, he may also be alerting us to important subcultures within the nation states which Hofstede used as definitive categories. Do indigenous or Islamic Australians share the same concepts of community or customary law as the Anglo-Celtic mainstream and its judicial institutions?

On another level, it suggests that diasporic cultures may also change and mutate according to context. Does the individualized ethic of personal acquisition and power have greater hegemonic power in Taiwan than in the Western provinces of China where survival is dependent on communal cooperation? If so, gross claims about ethnic or national groups become unreliable and leadership scholars are challenged to develop more discrete and detailed knowledge of specific contexts for their praxis.

INTERCULTURAL PERSPECTIVES IN LEADERSHIP DISCOURSE

Recent years have seen fledgling efforts among leadership scholars whose investigative approaches are more attuned to intercultural dynamics (Collard, 2002; Collard & Wang, 2005; Merchant, 2004; Wang & Collard, 2005). They seek to develop more nuanced understandings based upon complex conceptions of culture and the more subtle interactions which occur between agents from different cultures. They have moved from macrolevel mapping exercises to more dynamic research tools based upon constructivist and phenomenological premises. It is advanced as the next step in our journey to enrich leadership theory and praxis in an increasingly diverse world.

At the international level Wang (2004) studied the reactions of a cohort of Chinese leaders in Zhejiang Province to a leadership course provided by an Australian university. She employed cross-cultural theories as a macrolevel framework for her investigation but also used qualitative methods to study the microlevel reactions of the Chinese recipients. Techniques such as interviews and focus groups were used to create a phenomenographic case study of a cohort over 2 years. One of the key foci was the changing conceptions of learning and leadership which accompanied exposure to contemporary Western leadership discourse with an emphasis upon collaborative and distributed frameworks (Gronn, 1998, 2003; Lakomski, 2001). Another focus for investigation was the impact of a participative and constructivist, adult pedagogy (Foley, 2000).

Generalized accounts of Chinese conceptions of learning and teaching frequently focus upon traditions of authoritative, objective, and positivist epistemologies (Gu & Meng, 2001; Zhu, 2002). While participants acknowledge the power of such traditions, there was also evidence of disquiet about them in interviews and a readiness to encounter and respond to contemporary Western pedagogies which cross-cultural stereotypes may obscure. These indicated that Chinese educators are not frozen in a static, inherited culture as cross-cultural theory assumes. Indeed some were extremely critical about "the gap between empty theories and effective solutions" they identified in their cultural inheritance. The microintensive techniques of interview and focus group were able to tap into the subjective realities which lie beneath the panoramic stereotypes and maps and reflect the fluidity and change which is transforming Chinese culture today.

As a whole, the cohort recorded a shift from a dominance of traditional Chinese conceptions of knowledge and learning at the commencement of the course to more extensive beliefs at its conclusion. At the beginning they were skewed towards concepts of knowledge as authoritative and scared and learning as passive reception through formal modes for utilitarian purposes. By the end these conceptions had been somewhat realigned to accommodate understandings that knowledge can be indefinite and contestable, the learner can be an active constructor of knowledge, and that learning can be for a range of personal, organizational and transformative purposes throughout a lifetime. As a group, the cohort experienced a shift in perceptions of knowledge and learning. At the conclusion of the course it is perhaps best described as a hybrid mixture of traditional Chinese and contemporary Western beliefs.

Wang (2004) also traced a similar shift in conceptions of leadership itself in the cohort. At the commencement of the course they thought of leadership as positional power and tended to privilege the values of hierarchical, directive, and moral traditions which have been noted by cross-cultural theorists (Bush & Quiang, 2000; Child, 1994; Wong, 2001). A school system official outlined this inheritance;

> Traditional Chinese leaders are endorsed with official power and authority. They are often autocratic and patriarchal. Their will and decisions are usually imposed on the organizational members through the strict hierarchical structure.... Managers are expected to strictly implement plans according to the set rules and regulations.

While these conceptions were still evident among the cohort almost 2 years later, they had been supplemented by new and broader beliefs that leadership could also be based on nonpositional power, that teamwork within a leadership group was a viable alternative to autocratic directives, that strategic power could be based upon shared vision and that collaborative leadership which consults work groups and constituents has a valid role. A high school principal noted a shift in his conceptions from the leader as a solitary hero, "a firefighter who is at the front to guide followers or urge them with whips at the back," to a collaborative organizational member.

Once again the subjective worlds indicate a level of change that may be obscured by cross-cultural frameworks. Admittedly, the extent of change in conceptions of leadership was not as great in the area of leadership as it was in the realm of beliefs about knowledge, learning, and teaching. This may suggest that change stimulated by direct experience, such as new classroom pedagogies, may be more powerful than change at a conceptual level such as theories of leadership. If this is so it is important to programs which seek to promote cultural change in other nations.

Space prohibits extensive discussion of the research conducted into Hispanic leaders in Texas, (Merchant, 2004) and First Nation communities in North Eastern Canada (Normore, in this volume, pp. 47–68). However Merchant's interview study of a small number of Hispanic leaders provides evidence that leaders in multicultural contexts learn to construct bridges between the communities they represent and mainstream Anglo-American cultures. Her subjects insisted on the importance of role models from within their base culture which made them effective agents when working beyond it. This is especially interesting in the U.S. context where immigrant communities have traditionally been expected to adopt the values and strategies of the Anglo-American mainstream. It suggests elements of resistance and resilience among recent immigrant leaders and provides further evidence that they have the capacity to construct repertoires which transcend cultural boundaries and stereotypes.

The insider, researcher perspective adopted by Normore (in this volume, pp. 47–68) in the interface between indigenous populations and mainstream school authorities in Canada reinforces this perception. He concludes that First Nations school leaders can build and share a common vision which bridges ethnic differences and, in turn contribute fully to the achievement of commonly pursued outcomes. This further implies that reflective leaders can accommodate and adjudicate diverse cultures and in so doing, rescue disempowered native populations from the impoverished margins where colonial conquest has sentenced them.

IMPLICATIONS FOR LEADERSHIP IN INTERCULTURAL CONTEXTS

Leaders working in landscapes characterized by cultural diversity need sophisticated understandings of the concept of culture. They need to see that manifest levels such as roles, rituals and regulations and policies are frequently based on inheritances which may be explicit or assumptive.

There is also a need for awareness that cultures are composed of multiple elements and are fluid and dynamic. Changes in one element of a culture invariably trigger effects in others. When the relationship between indigenous peoples and their land changes, so do the social structures they construct. When a family migrates to a new nation it carries a cultural heritage which mutates in a new environment. When educational leaders study new ideas from abroad their cognitive frameworks shift and they construct new ones which may incorporate elements from both traditional and foreign cultures. As Schein (1985) has argued culture is created through the learning and adaptation of individuals and groups as they respond to contextual changes. In the present age people from all cultures are responding to rates of change which far exceed those of the past and the processes of cultural interaction are becoming more complex.

Such an understanding undermines the validity of essentialist constructs which assume that culture is static and that stable descriptions are enduring. A leader's ability to work with diversity will undoubtedly be assisted by familiarity with cultural maps of ethnic and national groups. They provide the base level of a cognitive schema which is essential for understanding and sensitive intercultural communication. The next ingredient is the knowledge that cultures are fluid and adaptive and what may appear on the surface as an immutable feature has innate capacity to change.

The leaders own concept of him or herself is also vital. Past images of leaders as custodians and transmitters of established values and praxis are no longer adequate. They assume a stable and frequently monocultural reality which is no longer true. Contemporary leaders must be first and foremost reflective learners who can read and respond to changing and complex cultural realities. They continue to be cultural agents but not in a singular and directive mode. Their agency requires them to understand diverse cultural realities, to discern the deep values and assumptions upon which they are based, to mediate between them and to build bridges at cognitive, individual, and institutional levels. As values practitioners they are required to enter into dialogue with individuals and groups from diverse cultural backgrounds. This requires a process of recognizing various frames of reference operating in particular situations. Ethical decision making needs to be informed by cultural sensitivity, the way things were done in the past will no longer suffice.

Leaders are also required to become transformative cultural agents working to create reflexive institutions and systems. There are times when they need to unfreeze established traditions and contest unexamined assumptions. They have a duty to mediate between groups, to help them discern the social and even transcendental good which bridges divisive differences, to be advocates for new cultural norms which accommodate diversity and redress disempowerment. The leader as a transformative cultural advocate also needs an awareness of how to harness diverse forms of cultural capital which clients, workers and communities bring to educational endeavors. This entails valuing diverse epistemologies, acknowledging that there are multiple culturally-based and authentic learning and teaching modes and exploring various institutional frameworks to discover forms appropriate to particular communities. In her presidential address to the University Council for Educational Administration in 2004, Margaret Grogan (2005) called for "an attentiveness that is grounded in care and respect ... predicated on the idea that in every instance we deal with particular others, not representatives of general categories" (p. 8). This is sound advice in contexts characterized by increasing cultural diversity and requiring sophisticated intercultural understanding. It also challenges leadership scholars to explore new research paradigms capable of rendering new knowledge about such phenomena which is the subject of a subsequent chapter.

REFERENCES

Akerlond, G. S. (2003). Growing and developing as a university teacher-variations in meaning. *Studies in Higher Education, 17*(4), 375–390.

Anderson, K., & Taylor, A. (2005). Exclusionary politics and the question of national belonging: Australian ethnicities in "multiscalar" focus. *Ethnicities 5*(4), 460–485.

Austin, A. G. (1977) *Australian Education 1788-1900: Church, State and Public Education in Colonial Australia.* Carlton, Victoria, Australia: Pitman.

Australian Vice Chancellor's Committee. (2001). *Offshore programs of Australian universities.* Retrieved August 28, 2006, from http://www.avcc.edu.au

Australian Vice Chancellor's Committee. (2005). *Offshore programs of Australian universities.* Retrieved August 28, 2006, from http://www.avcc.edu.au

Barcan, A. (1980). *A history of Australian education.* Melbourne, Australia: Oxford University Press.

Begley, P. (1996). Cognitive perspectives on values in administration. *Educational Administration Quarterly, 32*(3), 403–426.

Begley, P. (2000). Cultural isomorphs of educational administration: Reflections on Western-centric approaches to values and leadership. *Asia Pacific Journal of Education, 20*(2), 23–33.

Begley, P. (2004). Understanding valuation processes: exploring the linkage between motivation and action. *International Studies in Educational Administration, 32*(2), 4–15.

Blackmore, J. (2004). The emperor has no clothes: Professionalism, performativity and educational leadership in high-risk postmodern times. In J. Collard & C. Reynolds (Eds.), *Leadership, gender & culture: Male and female perspectives* (pp. 73–194). Philadelphia: Open University Press/McGraw-Hill.

Brown, A., & Davis, N. E. (Eds.). (2004). *Digital technology, communities and education: World yearbook in education.* London: Routeledge.

Bullivant, B. (1991). The evolution of multiculturalism and developments in in-service and cross-cultural training. *Australian Journal of Communication, 18*(1), 67–79.

Bush, T., & Quiang, H. (2000). Leadership and culture in Chinese education. *Asia Pacific Journal of Education, 20*(2), 58–67.

Chapman, J. D., Aspin, D. N., & Taylor, B. (1998). Lifelong learning and the principal. *Leading & Managing, 4*(1), 11–31.

Child, J. (1994) *Management in China during the Age of Reform.* Cambridge: Cambridge University Press.

Collard, J. (2002). Leadership and gender: Time for critical reflection. *Leading & Managing, 8*(1), 100–109.

Collard, J. (2003). Gender, sector and the beliefs of principal. *Alberta Journal of Educational Research, XLIX*(1), 37–54.

Collard, J., & Wang. T (2005). Leadership and intercultural dynamics. *Journal of School Leadership, 15*(3), 178–195.

Dale, R. (1999). Specifying globalization effects on national policy: A focus on the mechanisms. *Journal of Educational Policy, 14*(1), 140-148.

Daniel, J. (2002). *Education for all in The Commonwealth: What are the issues?* Public Lecture, Australian National University.

Davis, N., & Cho, M. I. (2005). Intercultural competence for future leaders of educational technology and its evaluation. *Interactive Educational Multimedia, 10,* 1-22.

Dimmock, C., & Walker, A. (2000a). Developing comparative and international educational leadership and management: A cross-cultural model. *School Leadership and Management, 20*(2), 143–160.

Dimmock, C., & Walker, A. (2000b). *Societal Culture and School Leadership: Charting the Way Ahead. Asia Pacific Journal of Education, 20*(2), 110–116.

Du, R. (1992). *Chinese higher education: A decade of reform and development.* New York: St Martin's Press.

Fisher, G. (1989). *Diplomacy.* In M. F. Asante & W. B. Gudykunst (Eds.), *Handbook of International and Intercultural Communication* (p. 411). Newbury Park, CA: SAGE.

Fogarty, R. f.m.s. (1957). *Catholic education in Australia 1806–1950* (Vol. 1 & 2). London: Melbourne University Press.

Foley, G. (2000). A framework for understanding adult learning and education. In G. Foley (Ed.), *Understanding adult learning and education* (pp. 7–22). Crow's Nest, NSW: Allen & Unwin.

Gay, G. (Ed). (2003). *Planting seeds to harvest fruits.* In *Becoming multicultural educators: Personal journey towards professional agency* (pp. 1–16). San Francisco: Jossey-Bass.

Grogan, M. (2005). *Ethical imperatives for educational leadership: Fifty years beyond Brown. UCEA Review, XLV*(1), 4–9.

Gronn, P. (1998). *Life in teams: Collaborative leadership and learning in autonomous work units.* Burwood: Australian Council for Educational Administration.

Gronn, P. (2003). *The new work of educational leaders: Changing leadership practice in an era of school reform.* London: SAGE/Paul Chapman.

Gu, M., & Meng, F. (Eds.). (2001). *New international education ideas.* Kaikou: Hainan.

Gullestrup, H. (n.d.). *The complexity of intercultural communication in cross cultural management.* Retrieved March 25, 2006, http://www.immi.se.intercultural

Hallinger, P., & Heck R.H. (1996) Reassessing the principal's role in school effectiveness: A review of empirical research, 1980–1995. *Educational Administration Quarterly, 32*(1), 5–44.

Hallinger, P., & Kantamara, P. (2000). Educational change in Thailand: Opening a window intro leadership as a cultural process. *School Leadership and Management, 20*(2), 189–206.

Hallinger, P. (2005) *Educational leadership in East Asia: implications for education in a global society. UCEA Review, XLV*(1), 1–4.

Hart, W. B. (1998). *What is intercultural relations?* The *E-Journal of Intercultural Relations, 1*(8). Retrieved February 2, 2006, http://www.intercultural relations.com

Hearn J. (1993). *Men in the public eye; The construction and deconstruction of public men and public patriarchies.* London: Routledge.

Hodgkinson, C. (1991). *Leadership: The moral art.* Albany: State University of New York Press.

Hofstede, G. H. (1980). *Culture's consequences: International differences in work-related values.* Beverly Hills, CA: SAGE.

Hofstede, G. H. (1986). *Cultural differences in teaching and learning.* International *Journal of Intercultural Relations, 10,* 301–320.

Hofstede, G. H. (1991). *Cultures and organizations: Software of the mind.* London/ New York: McGraw-Hill.

Hofstede, G. H. (1994). Cultural constraints in management theories. *International Review of Strategic Management, 5,* 27–48.

Hofstede, G. H. (1995). Management values: The business of international business is culture. In T. J. Jackson (Ed.), *Cross-cultural management* (pp. 150–165). Oxford, England: Butterworth-Heinemann.

Humphrey, D. (2002). *Intercultural communication: A teaching and learning framework.* Paper presented at conference, Setting The Agenda, University of Manchester, England.

Hyatt, J., & Simons, H. (1999) *Cultural codes-Who holds the key? The Concept and Conduct of Evaluation in Central and Eastern Europe.* Evaluation, 5(1), 23–41.

Independent Schools Council of Australia Bulletin. (2006). Australian Bureau of Statistics, Catalogue NO 4221.0, p. 1.

Lakomski, G. (2001). Organizational change, leadership and learning; culture as cognitive process. *The International Journal of Educational Management, 15*(2) 68–77.

Lam, J. (2001). *Economic rationalism and educational reforms in developed countries, Journal of Educational Administration.* 39(4), 346–358.

Leithwood, K. A., Jantzi, D., & Steinbach, R. (1999). *Changing leadership for changing times.* Buckingham, England: Open University Press.

Liddicoat, A. J. (2004). *Internationalisation as education.* Paper presented at University of South Australia.

Limerick, D., Cunnington, A., & Crowther, F. (1998). *Managing the new organization: Collaboration and sustainability in the post-corporate world* (2nd ed.). Warriewood, NSW, Australia: Business & Professional Publishing.

Loveless, T. (1998). Uneasy allies: The evolving relationship of school and state. *Educational Evaluation and Policy Analysis, 20*(1), 1–8.

Lundberg, C. C. (1988). Working with culture. *Journal of Organizational Change Management, 1*(2), 38–47.

Marginson. S. (1997). *Markets in education.* St. Leonards, NSW, Australia: Allen & Unwin.

Marshall, C., & Rusch, E. (1995). Gender filters in The Deputy Principalship. In B. Limerick & B. Lingard (Eds.), Gender and changing educational management: Second yearbook of the Australian Council for Educational Administration (pp. 79–93). Rydalmere, NSW, Australia: Hodder Education.

Martin F. (1986). Catholic Education in Victoria 1963–1980. In *Catholic Education Office* (Ed.), *Catholic Education in Victoria: Yesterday, today and tomorrow.* Maryborough, Victoria, Australia: Hedges & Bell.

Macgregor Burns, J. (1978) *Leadership.* New York: Harper & Row.

Merchant, B. (2004). Bridge people: agents for social justice. In J. Collard & C. Reynolds (Eds.), *Leadership, gender & culture: Male and female perspectives* (pp. 157–172). Philadelphia: Open University Press/McGraw-Hill.

Osland, J. S., & Bird, A. (2000). *Beyond sophisticated stereotyping: Cultural sense making in context. Academy of Management Executive, 14*, 65–77.

Paige, R. M. (2004). *The intercultural in teaching and learning: A developmental perspective.* Paper presented at University of South Australia.

Parsons, T. (1952). *The social system.* Landon: Tavistock.

Pastrana, J. P., Guillermo-Williamson, G., & Gomez, R. (2004). Learning from Mapuche Communities: Intercultural education and participation in the Ninth Region of Chile. *Journal for Critical Education Policy Studies, 2*(2), 1–29.

Protherough, R. (1984). Shaping the image of the great headmaster. *British Journal of Educational Studies, 32*(3), 239–250.

Putnis P., & Petelin, M. (1996). *Professional communication: Principles and applications.* Sydney: Prentice Hall.

Ribbins, P. (1996). *Producing portraits of educational leaders in context: cultural relativism and methodological absolutism.* Paper presented at Commonwealth Council for Educational Administration and Management Paper, Malaysia.

Rosaldo, R. (1993). *Culture and truth: The remaking of social analysis.* London: Routeledge.

Schein, E. H. (1985). *Organizational culture and leadership: A dynamic view.* San Francisco: Jossey-Bass.

Schon, D. A. (1988). *Educating the reflective practitioner.* San Francisco: Jossey-Bass.

Second World Culturelink Conference. (2005). *Zagreb, Croatia.* Retrieved March 23, 2006, at http://www.culturelink.org/clinkconf.html

Senge, P. (1990). *The fifth discipline: The art and practice of learning organizations.* New York: Doubleday.

Shields, C. M. (2002). *Towards a dialogic approach to understanding values.* Address to the 7th Annual Conference of Values and Leadership, Toronto.

Tardiff, J. (2002). *Intercultural Dialogues and Cultural Security.* Planet Agora, September, 1-9.

Trompenaars, F. (1993). *Riding the waves of culture.* London: Nicholas Brealy.

Trompenaars, F., & Hampden-Turner, C. (1997) *Riding the waves of culture: Understanding cultural diversity in business* (2nd ed.). London: Nicholas Brealy.

Tyack, D. (1974) *The one best system: A history of American urban education.* Cambridge, MA: Harvard University Press.

Walker, A., & Dimmock, C. (2000). Insights into educational administration: The need for a cross-cultural comparative perspective. *Asia Pacific Journal of Education, 20*(2), 11–22.

Walker, A., & Dimmock, C. (2002). *Moving school leadership beyond its narrow boundaries: developing a cross-cultural approach.* In K. Leithwood & P. Hallinger (Eds.), *Second International Handbook of Educational Leadership and Administration* (pp. 167–204). The Netherlands: Kluwer Press.

Walker, A. (2003). *Developing cross-cultural perspectives on education and community,* In P. Begley & O. Johansson (Eds.), *The ethical dimensions of school leadership* (pp. 146–160). Dordrecht: Kluwer.

Wang, T. (2004). *Understanding Chinese Educational Leaders' Conceptions of Learning and leadership in an International Education Context.* Unpublished PhD thesis, University of Canberra, Australia.

Wang, T., & Collard, J. (2005). *Changing conceptions of learning & leadership in Zhejiang Province, China 2002–2004.* Paper presented at 10th annual conference of Values and Leadership, State College, PA.

Wong, K. C. (2001). Chinese culture and leadership. *International Journal of Leadership in Education, 4*(4), 309–319.

Zhu, M. (Ed.). (2002). *Zoujin Xinkecheng: Yukecheng Shishizhe Duihua* [Step into new curricula: A dialogue with curricula implementers]. Beijing: Normal University Press.

CHAPTER 2

RESEARCH METHODS FOR LEADERSHIP IN INTERCULTURAL CONTEXTS

John Collard

The once dominant ideal of a detached observer using neutral language to explain "raw data" has been displaced by an alternative project that attempts to understand human conduct as it unfolds through time and in relation to its meanings for the actors ... there is no way short of a radical rethinking of the research enterprise.

—Rosaldo (1989, p. 37)

INTRODUCTION

Schein (1985) has argued culture is created through the learning and adaptation of individuals and groups as they respond to contextual changes. In the present age people from all cultures are responding to rates of change which far exceed those of the past and the processes of cultural interaction are becoming more complex. A leader's ability to work with diversity is undoubtedly assisted by familiarity with cultural maps of ethnic and national groups. They provide the base level of a cognitive schema, roadmaps of cultural territories, which are essential for

Leadership and Intercultural Dynamics, pp. 23–43

understanding and sensitive cross-cultural communication and appreciation of differences.

To date the dominant research methods in the field have been cross-cultural studies. These have possessed a positivist flavor of allegedly value-free detached observations which seek to identify consistent features of national cultures which offer explanation, research control, and predictability (Clifford, 1983). They are based upon an ontological assumption that there is a fixed external reality which can be studied, captured and defined by allegedly value-free outsiders. This paradigm can be traced to the modernist approach which was ascendant from the early 1900s to the destruction of colonial regimes after World War II when anthropologists and ethnographers produced exotic narratives for privileged White audiences:

> the eye of ethnography ... "is connected to 'the eye of imperialism. Sight and surveillance depend on detachment and distance. Getting perspective on something entails withdrawal from intimacy. Everyday parlance equates objectivity with aloofness. being 'too close' " is akin to losing perspective and lacking judgement. (Conquergood, 1991, p. 357)

The phenomenon of cross-cultural mapping, which emerged in the 1980s, inherited this legacy. The Dutch scholars Hofstede (1980, 1986, 1995) and Trompenaars (1993, 1997) compared cultures using broadly descriptive and stereotypical characteristics. Both have argued that that whereas Western cultures determine status, respect, and power according to on the job performance, many Asian cultures are more influenced by position, age, or family power. The outcome of such typecasting is stereotyped descriptions of national cultures (Hart, 1998). Chinese mandarins are portrayed as aloof decision makers whereas female leaders in British communities are essentially egalitarian and consultative (Adler, Laney, & Packer, 1993; Du, 1992; Ozga, 1993). Such an approach has been subject to criticism for several decades:

> Nothing has done more, I think, to discredit cultural analysis than the construction of impeccable depictions of formal order in whose actual existence nobody can quite believe. (Geertz, 1973, p. 157)

It also carries an inherent danger that researchers impose concepts and categories from their own culture onto foreign terrains and thereby generate distorted images (Dahlin & Regmif, 1997; Osland & Bird, 2000; Putnis & Petelin, 1996). Race theorists have argued that essentialist portrayals of nationality, skin color, or language are convenient and inaccurate fictions which obscure real life complexities (Dyson, 1993).

The macrolevel approach of cross-cultural mapping is accused of only illuminating one layer in complex, multilayered scenarios (Humphrey, 2002). They do not have the depth to report and show the complex life of cultures (Willis, 1977). Contemporary racial theorists draw our attention to the intersections of race class and gender and feminists now do the same (Ladson-Billings, 2003). Cultural theorists warn us of the dangers of assuming specific groups as coherent unities upon which to base explanatory analysis (Frow & Morris, 2003). Young Arabic-speaking men in Sydney manifest a form of "cultural hybridity" as they move between different cultural spaces. Islamic women who board a plane at Heathrow adorned in Western fashions and emerge in burkahs at Amman airport know how to cross cultural boundaries. Some feminist and queer theorists even dispute concepts of a singular or unified self. We are therefore challenged to become more sophisticated in our understandings of mesa or micro level cultures, instead of relying on generic portraits.

Critiques of "situated knowledge" dispute the very existence of an omniscient researcher and argue that research texts embody the standpoint of an author bounded by social, cultural, class and gendered locations and constraints (Haraway, 1998). In the case of cross cultural theory in the closing decades of the twentieth century, we need to acknowledge that the authors were bounded by Western assumptions about national and ethnic cultures and that they were frequently seeking to map alien terrains for international trade and cooperation. As such, they fell prey to the fallacies of previous anthropologists and social scientists who represented complex cultures as coherent, complete and static systems for Western audiences. Their focus on national levels inevitably obscured more complex and dynamic elements from view. Harraway would argue that such motivations may have been "instrumentalist" and stand in opposition to the "power-charged social relation of conversation" where "the agency of the people studied itself transforms the whole project of producing social theory" (Harraway, 1998, pp. 36–38).

Those who have imported cross cultural perspectives into educational leadership discourse have explained how concepts of power, authority, collectivism, patriarchy, workplace freedoms and responsibilities, social and kinship networks, and democratic rights produce different leadership cultures and practices in China and other Asian societies than are common in Western nations (Bush & Qiang, 2000; Hallinger, 2005; Walker & Dimmock, 2000). Such claims resemble past orthodoxies in discourses about leadership and gender where men were categorized as remote, bureaucratic and authoritarian while women were depicted as relational, student centered and consultative (Ferguson, 1984; Ozga, 1993). Research in the past decade has shown that such typecasts are gross descriptions of much more complex phenomena where variables such as school location, organizational scale, student gender and sector identity generate fine grained differences between members of either gender (Collard & Reynolds, 2004).

There are also vast differences between the educational context of a Chinese principal working in an impoverished agrarian community with significant proportions of Muslim students in the Western Provinces and a high status model school in Shanghai or Beijing. Then consider the subtleties enmeshed in the Chinese Diaspora in Hong Kong, Singapore or Taiwan where the Western capitalist virtues of independence and personal wealth have possessed greater valence than the communitarian values of China in the socialist decades. Ethnic and religious schools in multicultural communities often operate from assumptions and values which distinguish them from public or government institutions in nations such as Australia, Britain, Canada, Malaysia, or Mexico. As First Nations communities construct educational communities in synchrony with their indigenous values in Canada, New Zealand or the United States they embed cultural platforms into praxis which differentiate them from more mainstream enterprises.

There are also epistemological reasons to question the ability of positivist research methods to yield objective and neutral knowledge about cultures. Phenomenographic scholars (Marton, 1994) view social realities as constructions, selected, built, and embellished by actors from the situations, stimuli and events of their experience. They are not intent upon discovering a single truth or law but in uncovering the various constructions by individuals and shared by members of social, cultural, familial organizational, and professional groups. These constructions represent the meanings that individuals attach to events, situations, and persons as they attempt to impose order on social interaction. Such constructions are both personal and idiosyncratic and may be as plentiful and diverse as the people who hold them (Lincoln & Guba, 1989, 2003).

Femisists, critical theorists, and liberation scholars have also challenged researchers to become transformative social agents (Lather, 1986). They believe that the study of cultural landscapes should promote cultural literacy: to recognize the strengths, contradictions, and weaknesses of their cultures, and hopefully, become agents of change. The dialogical relationship between the researcher/educator and their subjects is conceived as a catalyst which develops critical consciousness and a capacity to generate ways of ameliorating and improving it (Friere, 1973; Savage, 1988).

RELEVANT APPROACHES FOR EDUCATIONAL LEADERSHIP

The importation of cross cultural theory to educational leadership has lacked sufficient reflection and scrutiny. It has also failed to illuminate dialectic elements of cultural adoption and resistance and the generational changes which impact so directly upon frontline organizations such as schools and universities. Conversely, intercultural theory (Hart, 1998) distinguishes between studies which compare and contrast generalized characteristics of two or more cultures and a more dynamic approach which studies what happens at the individual, group, organizational, systemic, national, or even international levels when agents from different cultural platforms interact. This theory also entails a different conception of culture itself. It is not conceived as a static reality but an unfolding and continuously changing process. In the contemporary global world national and cultural boundaries have become increasingly porous. Rosaldo (1989) insists that we now live in a world where open borders are more real than closed communities. He argues that the research agenda therefore needs to move to exploration of borderlands, the intersections where identities and interests interact with multiple others. The epistemological consequence of displacing "solid centres and unified wholes with borderlands and zones of contest" is to reconceptualize identity and culture "as constructed and relational, instead of ontologically given and essential" (Conquergood, 2003, pp. 1–13).

Postmodern perspectives frame identity as provisional instead of inexorably ordained as cross-cultural theorists assume. It is an ongoing process which is historically incomplete. The refugee, the exile, and the dispossessed, suspended between shattered pasts and insecure futures are the most appropriate symbols of the geopolitical turbulence of today's world. They represent life on the margins of metropolitan states constructed by others from different cultural perspectives. Rosaldo (1989) also reminds us that we do not have to travel to "The Third World" to encounter these borderlands. Western societies increasingly contain minorities defined by race, ethnicity, language, class, religion, and sexual orientation. Subordinated populations in turn create and circulate counter discourses to those of the dominant culture and polity which help them to formulate oppositional interpretations of their identities, interests and needs. These become subcultures which educational leaders need to understand and mediate. As educational leaders we could also add the international professor, the aid worker and the United Nations negotiator to Rosaldo's list. They may possess a different status from the marginalized, but they may encounter common processes as they move between and bridge cultures.

Such observational studies have provided us with macrolevel maps of cultural terrains. Their explanatory power lies in the ability to compare and contrast different landscapes at a macrolevel (Hart, 1998). The outcome is stereotyped descriptions of national cultures; This approach also carries an inherent danger that researchers impose concepts and categories from their own culture onto foreign terrains and thereby generate distorted lenses (Dahlin & Regmi, 1997; Osland & Bird, 2000; Putnis & Petelin, 1996). Such essentialism tends to resemble past orthodoxies in studies of leadership and gender where men were scripted as remote, bureaucratic and authoritarian while women were depicted as relational, student centered and consultative.

The macrolevel approach of cross-cultural mapping is therefore prone to generate simplistic, ethnic, and national cultural constructs which illuminate only one layer in complex, multilayered scenarios (Humphrey, 2002). By way of contrast, intercultural theory (Hart, 1998) distinguishes between studies which compare and contrast generalized characteristics of two or more cultures and a more dynamic approach which studies what happens at the individual, group, organizational, systemic, national, or even international levels when agents from different cultural platforms interact. Such theory recognizes the diverse cultural origins of knowledge and values, incorporates multiple frames of reference into knowledge construction, learns from and with people from other cultures and applies ethical choices which recognize the complexities of cultural interaction (Paige, 2004). When this occurs the cognitive schemata of leaders are expanded and preexisting cultural frameworks are challenged and enriched by diverse possibilities of "inter-cultural understandings" which in turn permit more authentic, flexible, and relevant practice to emerge.

A New Approach?

The time is ripe for more tightly focused, microlevel methodologies to capture the complex, multilayered, and dynamic interplay of cultural values and assumptions at individual, institutional, regional, and systemic levels within nation states. The same is required to comprehend the precise interactions and cognitive reconstructions which occur when agents from different cultures interact in international contexts. In this sense there is a need for "ontological authenticity," for methods which expose multiply-constructed realities within cultures, subcultures and intersections between cultures (Seale, 1999).

Constructivists argue that all knowledge and meanings are constructed between individuals as they engage with and interpret their worlds (Crotty, 1998, pp. 42–43). This also means that transmitted cultural values and beliefs can be reconstructed to cope with changing forces and realities. The emphasis upon the "meaning making activity of the individual mind" suggests that each individual's way of making sense of cultural worlds is as valid and worthy of respect as any other. Individuals may inhabit what appears to be a uniform social culture to an outside observer but may, in fact, see it in various ways. This phenomenon becomes even more complex when individuals find themselves at the intersections of various cultural values and practices. Intercultural research methods therefore need to focus upon the construction of meaning and interpretation of actors responding to and mediating between different worlds.

Theorists from Marx (1867) to Habbermaas (1971, 1983, 1990) and Foucault (1970) have shown us that history and cultures at all levels are determined by dialectical interactions between the forces of established power and the impetus for change. The school reform movements of recent decades make it abundantly clear that there has been constant tension between established educational values and practices and forces for change at national and international levels. Hargreaves and Fullan (2000, p. 5) have argued that contemporary educators need to be transformed into a dynamic learning profession where isolated practice is displaced by collaborative efforts to re-culture schools and systems. Such re-culturing occurs through interactions between players at all levels and learning community theorists have redefined educators as active reconstructors of their professional knowledge and values (Chapman, Aspin, & Collard 2000). Advocates of authentic learning and leadership (Starrett, 2005) emphasize the need for responsiveness to cultural contexts and this requires openness and reflexivity to various beliefs and worldviews. Such thinking positions leaders as "cultural agents" who continuously reconstruct their cognitive schemas (Davis & Cho, 2005). Their conceptions are best captured by qualitative, interpretivist, constructivist and phenomenological research methods which tap into their subjective worlds and culturally based constructs. Research tools such as action research, case studies, focus groups, interviews, journal, or ethnographic and narrative accounts and creative performances are all appropriate sources of data for such studies.

Qualitative inquiry has been described as "a loose coalition of inquirers seemingly united only in their general opposition to … foundationalist-empiricist representationalist nexus of beliefs" (Schwandt, 2003 p. 315). Consequently their research frequently uses multiple methods or triangulation to capture in depth understandings of specific phenomena. It rarely privileges any single methodology and cannot approach the paradigmatic purity claimed by positivist social science. Rather, it is best considered as a set of practices or multiple disciplines, which in turn contain internal tensions and even contradictions. It has been argued that even within a single study, interview and focus group methodologies have generated very different kinds of data (Fine, Weis, Weseen, & Wong, 2003). Multiple sources of data also reflect the socially constructed nature of reality, acknowledging the interactive relationship between the researcher and the researched and the situational and value-laden constraints upon inquiry (Denzin & Lincoln, 2003, pp. 8–13).

If cultural actors are responding to and mediating cultures in a context of social, national or global change reactions and meanings are likely to be constructed over extended periods of time This establishes a need for longitudinal research. First contact and reaction may be a form of culture shock, the type experienced by immigrants and tourists when they find themselves in alien terrain. Adaptation and adjustment takes time and may involve conflict at personal and organizational levels. Immigrant communities in settler societies experience anguish as they realize their teenage children are "losing their home language" or adopting mores which would be frowned upon in ancestral villages. The introduction of digital technology has met considerable resistance among older teachers in schools throughout the Western world but eagerly embraced by Generation X and Y. A cohort in a graduate leadership course in China may appear enthusiastic about Western philosophies of distributed leadership and team building in class but the real test is to implement such practices in worksites governed by more hierarchical traditions. Those of us who have worked in the change industry know that institutionalizing a new culture is a long term project. We need highly sophisticated methods if we are to fulfill Denzin and Lincoln's (2003) rationale that qualitative research involves studying people in their own settings and discovering the meanings they bring to their situations. The following research methods are suggested as appropriate ways of studying the complexities of intercultural interactions.

FOCUSED CASE STUDIES

Researchers use case study designs to gain in-depth understanding of specific situations, cultures and their meanings. Stake (1988, 1994) advocated studies of bounded and coherent systems. Others have shared his faith in the integrity and wholeness of specific contexts (Punch 1998; Sturman, 1997). However, such theorists have often assumed a monocultural and cohesive reality not the multiple values which frequently operate in intercultural contexts. Yin's (1994) emphasis on case study methods in complex real life contexts leads him to talk of the blurring of boundaries. Such perspectives call systems thinking with its rationalist assumptions about individuals and organizations into question and suggest that case studies may uncover some of the irrationality and chaos which Greenfield (1975, 1993) identified when he challenged educational administration's acceptance of organizations as rational entities.

The notion that multiple subjectivities may be in contestation within apparently coherent social units shares common ground with intercultural theory. Competing values codes may exist in multicultural settings with regard to the assumed roles and status of males and females. We have long known that treaty negotiations between mainstream Westerners and indigenous representatives about land are frequently complicated by different assumptive frameworks where one party views land as an economic resource the other as a spiritual hearth. Of course the reality may also be a blending or reconstruction of these values assumptions in process.

The outcome of case study research can be descriptive, interpretative or evaluative. Descriptive data are organized into categories to illustrate, support or challenge theoretical assumptions which preceded the study (Merriam, 1998). For example, Wang's (2004) study of Chinese leaders indicated that their beliefs about learning and leadership were in a state of transitional change after their exposure to Western leadership theory. They no longer corresponded with the cultural polarities which Hofestede had described almost 2 decades before. She thereby moved understandings from observationally-based cross-cultural concepts to more complex insights into their cognitive states as their traditional cultural inheritance was enriched and their reflections stimulated.

INTERVIEWS

Interviews provide a way of studying the underlying meaning of or ways of experiencing phenomena (Gillham, 2000). Open and deep approaches where researchers may have set questions to pursue but are also prepared to follow directions and opportunities raised by the interviewee can lead to fruitful new insights (Booth, 1997). Deep interviews follow certain lines of enquiry until they are exhausted, until the interviewee has nothing left to say or until the researcher and participant have reached common understandings about the topic under discussion (Orgill, 2000). Such approaches provide tools which can explore changes in conceptions before, during and after a specific period of time. They can accommodate complexities such as how individuals in the same context, such as academics, students, parents, system officials and teachers, experience reality differently. They can also provide insight into how an individual's view and conceptions can vary over time.

Open and deep semistructured interviews render different data from the closed questions which we see so frequently in survey responses seeking quantitative patterns. Kvale (1996, p. 11) has likened them to an interpersonal dialogue, a "conversation." This dialogical concept "implies talk between two subjects, not the speech of subject and object. It is humanizing speech, one that challenges and resists domination" (bell hooks, 1989). Marton has argued that the purpose is to explore the phenomenom as experienced and to experience jointly and as deeply as possible:

> The experiences and understandings are jointly constituted by interviewer and interviewee. These experiences and understandings are neither prior to the interview, ready to be "read off," nor are they only situational social constructions. They are aspects of the subject's awareness that change from being unreflected to being reflected. (Marton, 1994, p. 4427)

In this approach, the interview is inter-subjective. Participants discuss and interpret the world they are experiencing and in doing so, the interview becomes more than a data collecting exercise, its dialectical quality transforms it into an active part of intertwined lives (Cohen, Manion, & Morrison, 2000). Personal conceptions, experiences, and interpretations can also become the focus of challenges, reflection, and even reconstruction. The advantage of such an approach is that a rapport is established which facilitates deeper exploration between interviewer and subject. However, like all other interview approaches, potential disadvantages include the dependence on the willingness of the interviewees to report or remember accurately or the danger of them reporting what they think the interviewer is seeking to hear (Collard, 2001; Kayrooz & Trevitt, 2004; Silverman, 2001). This has been found to be relevant in school reform efforts in Thailand culture where polite protocols can encourage respondents to accommodate their answers to the values of the interviewer (Hallinger & Kantamara, 2000).

Analysis of interview data usually attempts to categorize the experience of the subjects by emergent themes. After recordings have been transcribed, the first task is to identify sets of emergent categories which both comprehend and accommodate variations within the data set. Transcripts are read for comparisons and contrasts, for similarities and differences, for minimum and maximum variations within groups and subgroups. This ensures the researcher becomes thoroughly familiar with the data, selects statements which are significant to the focus of the study, delimits parts representing conceptions of significant aspects of the phenomena, and ensures similarity within each category by using the actual words which form the significant statements. Initially such coding will be at a descriptive level whereas later iterations tend to produce higher-order or patterned categories (Punch, 1998) The process needs to be iterative, using repeat cycles whereby the researcher takes the category set back to the transcripts, revises the categories and relationships and continues to iterate between transcripts and categories until stable descriptors are developed and all perspectives indicated by respondents are accommodated (Akerlind, 2003; Martin, Trigwell, Prosser, & Ramsden, 2003). Such a process generates categories which ultimately represent qualitatively different meanings or interpretations of phenomena.

Qualitative researchers frequently use a number of strategies to ensure dependability. These may include low inference descriptors, multiple researchers to categorize and code and peer examination. Another key strategy is respondent validation where the subjects are asked to respond to the categories generated. Inter-rater checks on coding and categorization ensure reliable correspondence between data and results. Where discrepancies arise it is a good idea to scrutinize the different codings and reach a consensus on the most appropriate categorization. The possibility of having respondents verify and discuss categories and interpretations of them can also add to the robustness of intercultural research. It not only ensures accuracy, it provides a way for checking understandings between researchers and respondents from different cultural terrains.

It is important to acknowledge that interview research, like case studies, only provides a limited basis for generalization. Findings cannot be generalized to populations or even national categories in the way proposed by cross-cultural theorists. Highly-focused and limited samples help to understand the subjective worlds of the subjects and articulate patterns and links within a bounded scope. They can also offer critical insights into the class of events upon which they are based. In doing so they can qualify or reenforce generalized theoretical propositions but in the final analysis qualify macrolevel theories rather than actually refute them. The outcomes of such an approach can also be a negotiated text, a site where power, gender, race and class intersect within a culture rather than a sketch of broad contours which obscure such phenomena.

FOCUS GROUPS

Focus groups are a collective activity and are distinguished by the explicit use of group interaction to collect research data on specific issues and experiences (Merton, 1987). They have been used extensively since the mid-twentieth century to explore reactions as diverse as responses to wartime propaganda, marketing initiatives and the advent of HIV/AIDs campaigns (Kitzinger, 1994). It has been argued that they have a special ability to enable people to articulate experiences in ways which break the clichéd conversations of dominant cultural constructions (Geis, Fuller, & Rush, 1986). Focus groups help provide insight into the assumptions, beliefs, ethical perspectives, and knowledge of varying cultural agents.

An exemplary report in the intercultural domain has been the Blake Newton study into the needs of non-White ethnic minorities in Scotland (http://www.scotland.gov.uk/ Publications/2003). It sought to capture the diverse views of a cross section of minority groups and factored in variables such as age, gender, faiths and geographical locations. As such focus groups are consistent with concepts of grounded theory; they enable the generation of new concepts rather than concentrating on exploring predetermined categories.

One danger which arises in focus groups is the tendency for facilitators to use them to confirm preexisting hypotheses instead of exploring the interaction of the participants. Kitzinger (1994) is adamant that groups should be encouraged to engage with one another to challenge contradictions and to surface subtexts. She distinguishes between complementary and argumentative approaches. The former seeks to share common experiences. The latter strives to promote questioning, challenging and disagreement. She argues that both the similarities and the differences contribute to the richness of the data for they can tap into communication forms such as anecdotes, associations, and even jokes which reveal more than the more formalized interview. This could well be an issue which distinguishes intercultural research from cross-cultural predecessors through its capacity to surface differences.

An intercultural approach also has to deal with the concept of representation. If the purpose is to explore cultural diversity, traditional sampling methods may be inappropriate and groups may need to be structured to facilitate the voice of different ethnic or subcultures. There is also a need to provide a range of stimuli other than the set questions of a facilitator. For example, Kitzinger's (1994) exploration of reactions to HIV/AIDS in U.K. populations revealed that stimuli such as grim reaper advertisements, vignettes, and personal narratives was a more powerful source of data than abstract questions.

A common concern with the use of focus groups is the assumption that there is a pressure to generate conformity and consensus. This can be combated by careful structuring of the group itself and facilitation techniques. Deliberate factoring of diversity into groups is a necessity if the aim is to ensure that individuals are forced to explain the reasoning behind their thinking. Their assumptions and values are thrown into relief by the questions they ask, the evidence they provide and the ways in which they challenge each other. When dealing with ethnic and minority groups, the appointment of an assistant facilitator from a member culture may help dissolve communication blocks and distrust of mainstream facil-itators. Such a strategy, if used creatively, can also provide an opportunity for the assistant to supplement the researchers' interpretation of sessions.

Like interviews, focus groups require researchers to take detailed notes during sessions, to tape and transcribe them and to code and categorize the data for interpretation. Identification of similarities and differences in a diversely structured group of representatives from different cultures can be particularly helpful in advancing our understandings of both cultural inheritances and how they operate in inter-cultural sites. They may lead us to see and understand patterns and adaptations which cross-cultural theory obscures.

ACTION RESEARCH

Participative actions research is appropriate for intercultural contexts. Lewin's (1948) foundational work sought to address conflict, crisis, and change within organizations. He was focused on the dialectics of social life rather than broad descriptive categories like cross-cultural researchers. (Clifford, 1983) has argued such research strategies can "derange" pre-conceived expectations of the researcher. Others have argued that action research is particularly appropriate "where you wish to bring about action in the form of change, and at the same time develop an understanding which informs the change and is an addition to what is known" (Dick & Swepson, 1997, p. 2). Intercultural theorists would probably reverse the sequence of these goals to argue that understanding the subjective ter-rains of participants in work sites is a prelude to defining change agendas. Liberationists like Friere (1973) would argue that the dialectic is the means to develop critical consciousness and empowerment.

Action research also involves iterative cycles of planning, acting, observing, reflecting, and subsequent repetition of these steps (Kemmis & McTaggart, 1988). Researchers often use semistructured or open ended interviews and dialogues as a tool to uncover perceptions and meanings. Transcripts are coded whereby raw data is systematically transformed and aggregated into units which allow precise description of relevant concepts (Holsti, 1969). This is followed by a process whereby the unitized or coded data are organized into categories which provide information about the context and its actors (Lincoln & Guba, 1985). At one level, such categories may provide descriptors which can be quantified. At another, they provide the foci for further questioning and interpretation.

However, the use of cycles of reflection and feedback extends the power of this methodology for both researchers and subjects beyond that of the interviewer who departs to a distance to write up an analysis. Dick

(2000) argues that initial "fuzzy" methods become more refined in the process as the researcher becomes a critical reflector and constructer of emergent understandings. A participant researcher is an active learner too. As the researcher moves towards "making sense of what he or she has learned" (Denzin & Lincoln, 2003, p. 37) he or she is creating "grounded theory."

Greenwood and Levin (2003) argue that action research also involves a collaborative-insider relationship between a researcher and the researched which contains potential for empowerment and resolution of social issues. Such approaches differ from the positivist social science traditions where hypotheses, such as cross-cultural descriptions are tested against a controlled sample. The techniques have been widely used to develop understandings of student learning processes in the past but have rarely been used to understand the constructs of subjects in culturally diverse contexts.

NARRATIVE ACCOUNTS

A narrative traces a series of events which unfold through time. The biographical, interpretative method seeks to collect and analyze patterns and turning points in people's lives. They can be garnered through various forms of interviews, biographies and critical incident studies. Chase (1995) has alerted us to their particular power when dealing with culture and the variables which operate in particular circumstances. She argues that people make sense of and interpret experience through narration and that in depth interviews can provide occasions when we ask for life stories. If researchers want to hear stories rather than reports, their role necessitates an invitation to develop narratives and the meanings they carry. In so doing, the "subject" becomes an active participant who helps construct the emergent meanings. Chase argues that there is a qualitative difference between questions which invite narrative response and those which constrain the emergent data to report status. A researcher invites reportage when the weight or import of questions reflect preconceived researcher interests and concerns which position the respondent as a willing informant. Alternatively, more interactive and discursive approaches invite the respondent to take responsibility to construct and interpret the meaning of events. As researchers we are also called to attune ourselves to how narrative accounts may be culturally problematic in that they contain, silences, gaps, disruptions, contradictions, and deeply felt ambivalences. It is our responsibility to ask further questions which help submerged feeling to emerge or even to gently identify inconsistencies and seek the respondent to help us understand their origins and pathologies.

ROLES AND ETHICS FOR RESEARCHERS

Recent controversies about the roles, methods and ethics of researchers in fields of qualitative enquiry also carry implications for inter-cultural research. The positivist traditions of aloof anthropologists and social scientists as omniscient observers of "subject populations" have been "challenged by multiple discourses including subaltern, indigenous, feminist and border voices" (Lincoln & Denzin, 2003, p. 3). They call for empowering, educative ethics that link researchers and subjects in open and collegial relationships. They stress "the importance of community, voice, reciprocity and the building of collaborative, non-repressive relationships based on a concept of the sacred" (p. 218). Such challenges have also raised new questions about the researcher as self and the ethics involved especially when working with marginalized and underprivileged populations. We are challenged to ask whether the research enterprise empowers or continues to disempower marginalized respondents, whether our work fosters emancipation, human dignity, and participation (Friere, 1973). Critical qualitative research must also face the question of whether its methods and outcomes continue to confine specific populations to peripheral zones where they continue to be subjected to the power of others or discover the agency necessary to become active agents of their own destinies (Lincoln & Denzin, 2003).

In the final analysis, the move from cross cultural to intercultural research constitutes a paradigm shift from an outdated colonial past when positivist approaches to social science operated as a handmaiden for domination and distance. In doing so it positioned non-Western cultures and peoples as "others" as exotic primitives or marginalized victims in modern states. Intercultural studies recognizes that there is no privileged, objective stance from which we can draw portraits of others. Instead it is historically self-reflective, critical, interdisciplinary, focused upon the, global and the local and cognizant of the complex variables which shape personal identity, cultures, and places. It disputes deterministic assumptions that how people live and experience the world is solely a product of inherited structures and cultures. It does so in an optimistic belief that individuals can be self reflective learners and agents of hopeful transformation. As an emergent field, intercultural studies is part of the "age of emancipation" where social theorists have been freed from the fetters of "a single regime of truth" and a habit "of seeing the world in one color" (Denzin & Lincoln, 2003, p. 252). We must learn to recognize complex mosaics and listen attentively to multiple voices which represent reality in varied ways. The categorical landscapes drawn by cross cultural theory continue to be useful but must be further interrogated by intercultural researchers to more fully understand what human beings are doing and saying. This approach resembles Kvale's (1996) concept of research as a conversation, a dialogue between equals and privileges a concept of human beings and their cultures as richly complex instead of reducing them to an abstract and objective categories. It also positions the researcher as an explicit voice whether as a narrator, an insider, a participant researcher or an advocate for social justice.

We must also ask how the voices of respondents are heard. Should they be allowed to intrude into the text or to add an epilogue which will moderate, support or even contradict the interpretations advanced by the researcher? Should we invite the researched into joint authorship of the text in the same way that the interview invites them to articulate their experiences and understandings? Only when these voices are heard can the established discourse in educational leadership be challenged and rewritten to incorporate their perspectives. This carries the potential for more inclusive policy and practice between mainstream societies and their multiple minorities. At the international arena it may facilitate understandings and accommodations instead of the mistrust and divisions which characterize our contemporary world.

Regardless of which representational stance we take, intercultural theorists are committed to studying the world from the perspective of the historically situated human being in dynamic interplay with multiple cultural variables. Hopefully we help uncover a variety of voices speaking from specific cultural locations where, race, gender, class, ethnicity, religion and sexuality shape the scripts as they form and change. We have traveled a long way from the Enlightenment dualism where the social researcher stood apart from his subject to paint a generic portrait. Instead we are called to be interactive artists traveling into complex realms inhabited by myriad individuals. Hopefully we bring them to life so they can speak their own truth through us or in multivocal symphonies.

REFERENCES

Adler S., Laney, J., & Packer, M. (1993) *Managing women: Feminism and power in educational management*. Buckingham, England: Open University Press.

Akerlind, G. S. (2003) Growing and developing as a university teacher: Variation in meaning. *Studies in Higher Education, 28*(4), 375–390.

Booth, S. (1997). On phenomenography, learning and teaching. *Higher Education Research and Development, 16*, 135–159.

Bush, T., & Quiang, H. (2000). Leadership and culture in Chinese education. *Asia Pacific Journal of Education, 20*(2), 58–67.

Chapman, J., Aspin, D., & Collard, J. (2000). Lifelong learning in Australia. In J. Field & M. Leicester (Ed.), *Lifelong learning; Education across the lifespan* (pp. 171–190). New York: Routledge/Falmer.

Chase, S. (1995) Taking narrative seriously. In R. Josselson & A. Lieblich (Eds.), *Interpreting experience: The narrative study of lives* (pp. 1–26). Thousand Oaks, CA: SAGE.

Clifford. J. (1983). On ethnographic authority. *Representations, 1*(2), 118–146. (Reprinted in *Turning Points in Qualitative Research: Tying Knots in a Handkerchief,* p. 137, by Y. S. Lincoln & N. K. Denzin, 2003, Walnut Creek, CA: Alta Mira Press)

Cohen, L., Manion, L., & Morrison, K. (2000). *Research methods in education* (5th ed.). New York: Routledge-Falmer.

Collard, J. (2001) Leadership and gender: An Australian perspective. *Educational Management & Administration, 29*(3), 343–355.

Collard, J., & Reynolds, C. (2004). *Leadership, gender & culture; Male and female Perspectives.* New York: Open University Press.

Conquergood, D. (1985) Performing as a moral act: Ethical dimensions of the ethnography of performance. *Literature in Performance, 5,* 1–13.

Conquergood, D. (1991). Rethinking ethnography: Towards a critical cultural politics. *Communication Monographs, 58,* 179- 94. (Reprinted in *Turning points in qualitative research: Tying knots in a handkerchief,* pp. 351-374, by Y. S. Lincoln & N. K. Denzin. 2003, Walnut Creek, CA: Alta Mira Press)

Crotty, M. (1998) The foundations of social research: Meaning and perspective in the research process. Crows Nest , NSW: Allen & Unwin

Dahlin. B., & Regmi, M. P. (1997). Conceptions of learning amongst Nepalase students. *Higher Education, 33*(1), 471–493.

Davis, N., & Cho, M. I. (2005) Intercultural competence for future leaders of educational technology and its evaluation. *Interactive Educational Multimedia, 10,* 1-22.

Denzin, N., & Lincoln, Y. (2003). *The landscape of qualitative research* (2nd ed.), Thousand Oaks, CA: SAGE.

Dick, B. (2000). *A beginner's guide to action research.* Retrieved January 25, 2004, from at www.scu.edu.au/schools/gcm/ar/arp/ppar.html

Dick, B., & Swepson, P. (1997). *Action research FAQ: Frequently asked questions file.* Retrieved January 25, 2004, from www.scu.edu.au/schools/gcm/ar/arp/ppar.html

Du, R. (1992). *Chinese higher education: A decade of reform and development.* New York: St Martin's Press.

Dyson, M. E. (1993). *Reflecting Black: African-American cultural criticism.* Minneapolis, MN: University of Minneapolis Press.

Ferguson, K. (1984). *The feminist case against bureaucracy.* Philadelphia: Temple University Press.

Fine, M., Weis, L., Weseen, S., & Wong, L. (2003). For whom? Qualitative research, representations and social responsibilities. In N. Denzin & Y. Lincoln (Eds.),

The landscape of qualitative research (2nd ed., pp. 167–207). Thousand Oaks, CA: SAGE.

Foucault, M. (1970). *Discipline and punish: The birth of the prison* (A. Sheridan. Trans.) New York: Random House.

Friere, P. (1973). *Pedagogy of the oppressed*. New York: Seabury Press.

Frow, J., & Morris, M. (2003). Cultural studies. In N. Denzin & Y. Lincoln (Eds.), *The landscape of qualitative research* (2nd ed., pp. 489–539). Thousand Oaks, CA: SAGE.

Geertz, C. (1973). *The interpretation of cultures: Selected essays*. (Reprinted in *Turning points in qualitative research: Tying knots in a handkerchief*, pp. 143-168, by, Y. S. Lincoln & N. K. Denzin, 2003, Walnut Creek, CA: Alta Mira Press).

Geis, S., Fuller, R., & Rush, J. (1986). Lovers of AIDS victims: Psychological stresses and counseling needs. *Death Studies, 10,* 43–53.

Gillham, B. (2000). *The research interview*. London: Continuum.

Greenwood, D. J., & Levin, M. (2003). Reconstructing the relationships between universities and society through action research. In N. Denzin & Y. Lincoln (Eds.), *The landscape of qualitative research* (2nd ed., pp. 131–166). Thousand Oaks, CA: SAGE.

Greenfield, T. (1975). Theory about organization: A new perspective and its implications for schools. In M. Hughes (Ed.), *Administering education: International challenge* (pp. 75–99). London: Athlone Press.

Greenfield, T., & Ribbins, P. (1993). *Greenfield on educational administration: Towards a humane science*. London: Routledge.

Habbermas, J. (1971). *Knowledge and human interests* (J. Shapiro, Trans.). Boston: Beacon.

Habbermaas, J. (1983). *Philosophical political profiles* (F. G. Lawrence, Trans.). Cambridge, MA: MIT Press.

Habbermaas, J. (1990). *Moral consciousness and communicative action* (C. Lenhardt & S. W. Nicholson, Trans.). Cambridge, MA: MIT Press.

Hallinger, P. (2005). Educational leadership in East Asia: implications for education in a global society. *UCEA Review, XLV*(1), 1–4.

Hallinger, P., & Kantamara, P. (2000). Educational change in Thailand: Opening a window into leadership as a cultural process. *School Leadership and Management, 20*(2), 189–206.

Haraway, D. (1998). Situated knowledges: The science question in feminism and the privilege of partial perspective. *Feminist Studies, 14*(3), 575-599. (Reprinted in *Turning points in qualitative research: Tying knots in a handkerchief*, pp. 21–46, by Y. S. Lincoln & N. K. Denzin, 2003, Walnut Creek, CA: Alta Mira Press)

Hargreaves, A., & Fullan, M. (2000). *Mentoring in the new millennium*. Retrieved April, 4, 2007. from www.sofweb.vic.eu.au/pd/ies/mentoring_resources.html

Hart, W. B. (1998). *What is intercultural relations? The E-Journal of Intercultural Relations*, 1-8. Retrieved February 20, 2006, from http://www .interculturalrelations.com

Hertzberg, W. H. (1971). *The Search for American Indian identity*. Syracuse, NY: Syr

Hofstede, G. H. (1980). *Culture's consequences: International differences in work-related values*. Beverly Hills: SAGE.

Hofstede, G. H. (1986). Cultural differences in teaching and learning. *International Journal of Intercultural Relations, 10*, 301–320.

Hofstede, G. H. (1995). Management values: The business of international business is culture. In T. J. Jackson (Ed.), *Cross-cultural management* (pp. 150-165). Oxford, England: Butterworth-Heinemann.

Holsti, O. (1969). *Content analysis for the social sciences and humanities.* Reading, MA: Addison-Wellesley.

hooks, bell. (1989). *Talking back: Thinking feminist, Thinking Black.* Boston: South End Press.

Humphrey, D. (2002). *Intercultural communication; A teaching and learning framework.* Paper presented at conference, Setting The Agenda, University of Manchester, England.

Kayrooz, C., & Trevitt, C. (2004). *Research in organizations and communities: Tales from the real world.* Crow's Nest, NSW, Australia: Allen & Unwin.

Kemmis, S., & McTaggart, R. (Eds.). (1988). *The Action Research Planner* (3rd ed.) Melbourne, Australia: Deakin University Press.

Kitzinger, J. (1994). The methodology of focus groups: The importance of interaction between research participants. *Sociology of Health and Illness, 6*(1), 103–121.

Kvale, S. (1996). *InterViews: An introduction to qualitative research interviewing.* London: SAGE.

Ladson-Bilings, G. (2003). Racialised discourses and ethnic epistemologies. In N. Denzin & Y. Lincoln (Eds.), *The landscape of qualitative research (2nd ed.,* pp. 398–432). Thousand Oaks, CA: SAGE.

Lather, P. (1986). Issues of validity in openly ideological research: Between a rock and a soft place. *Interchange, 17*(4), 63–84.

Lewin, K. (1948). *Resolving social conflicts.* New York: Harper& Row.

Lincoln, Y., & Guba, E. (1985). *Naturalistic Enquiry.* Newbury Park, CA: SAGE.

Lincoln, Y., & Guba, E. (1989). Ethics: The failure of positivist science. *Review of Higher Education,12*(3), 221–240. (Reprinted in *Turning Points in Qualitative Research: Tying Knots in a Handkerchief,* pp. 219-237, by Y. S. Lincoln & N. K. Denzin, 2003, Walnut Creek, CA: Alta Mira Press)

Lincoln, Y. S., & Denzin, N. K. (2003). *Turning points in qualitative research: Tying knots in a handkerchief.* Walnut Creek, CA: Alta Mira Press.

Marton, F. (1994). Phenomenography. In T. Husen & T. N. Postlethwaite (Eds.), *The International Encyclopedia of Education* (Vol. 8, pp. 4424–4429). London: Pergammon.

Martin, E., Trigwell, K., Prosser, M., & Ramsden, P. (2003). Variations in the experience of leadership of teaching in higher education. *Studies in Higher Education, 28*(3), 247–259.

Merriam, S. B. (1998). *Case study research in education: A qualitative approach.* San Francisco: Jossey-Bass.

Merton, R. (1987) The focuses interview and focus group: Continuities and discontinuities. *Public Opinion Quarterly, 51,* 550–566.

Mohanty, C. (1984). Under Western eyes. *Boundary. 2*(3), 333–358.

Orgill, M. (2000). *Phenomenography.* Retrieved February 10, 2004, from hemed.chem.purdue.edu/chemed.chem.purdue.edu/chemed/bodnergroup/ frameworks.phenomenography.htm

Osland, J. S., & Bird, A. (2000). Beyond sophisticated stereotyping: Cultural sense making in context. *Academy of Management Executive, 14,* 65–77.

Ozga J. (1993). *Women in educational management.* Buckingham, England: Open University Press.

Paige, R. M. (2004, June). *The intercultural in teaching & learning: A developmental Perspective.* Paper presented at a conference at The University of South Australia.

Punch, K. F. (1998). *Introduction to social research: Quantitative and qualitative approaches.* London: SAGE.

Putnis, P., & Petelin, M. (1996). *Professional communication: Principles and applications.* Sydney, Australia: Prentice Hall.

Rosaldo, R. (1989). *Culture and truth: The Remaking of Social Analysis.* Boston: Beacon.

Savage, M. C. (1988). Can ethnographic narrative be a neighbourly act? *Anthropology and Education Quarterly, 19,* 3–19.

Schein, E. H. (1985). *Organizational culture and leadership: A dynamic view.* San Francisco: Jossey-Bass.

Schwandt, T. A. (2003). Three epistemological stances for qualitative inquiry; interpretivism, hermeneutics and social constructionism. In N. Denzin & Y. Lincoln (Eds.), *The landscape of qualitative research* (2nd ed., pp. 292–331). Thousand Oaks, CA: SAGE.

Scottish Executive. (2003). *Focus groups with minority ethnic minorities.* Retrieved July 7, 2007, from http://www.scotland.gov.uk/Publications/

Seale, C. (1999). Quality in qualitative research, *Qualitative Inquiry, 5*(4), 25–40.

Silverman, D. (2001). *Interpreting qualitative data: Methods for analysing talk, text and interaction* (2nd ed.) London: SAGE.

Stake, R. E. (1988) Case study methods in educational research: Seeking sweet water. In R. M. Jaeger (Ed.), *Complementary methods for research in education* (pp. 253–278). Washington, DC: American Educational Research Association.

Stake, R. E. (1994). Case studies. In N. K. Denzin & Y. S. Lyncoln (Eds.), *Handbook of Qualitative Research* (pp. 236–247). Thousand Oaks, CA: SAGE.

Starrett, J. (2005, October). *Authentic leadership, authentic learning.* Paper presented at 10th annual Leadership and Ethics Conference, Pennsylvania State University.

Sturman, A. (1997). Case study methods. In J. Keeves (Ed.), *Educational Research Methodology and Measurement: An International Handbook* (pp. 61–66). New York. Pergamon.

Trompenaars, F. (1993). *Riding the waves of culture.* London: Nicholas Brealy.

Trompenaars, F., & Hampden-Turner, C. (1997). *Riding the waves of culture: Understanding cultural diversity in business* (2nd ed.). London: Nicholas Brealy.

Walker, A., & Dimmock, C. (2000). Insights into educational administration: The need for a cross-cultural comparative perspective. *Asia Pacific Journal of Education, 20*(2), 11–22.

Wang, T. (2004). *Understanding Chinese educational leaders' conceptions of learning and leadership in an international education context.* Unpublished PhD Thesis, University of Canberra.

Willis, P. (1977). *Learning to labour: How working class kids get working class jobs.* New York: Columbia University Press.

Yin, R. K. (1994). *Case study research: Design and methods* (2nd ed.). Thousand Oakes, CA: SAGE.

PART II

WORKING WITH INDIGENOUS CULTURES

CHAPTER 3

CULTURALLY RELEVANT LEADERSHIP FOR SOCIAL JUSTICE

Honoring the Integrity of First Nations Communities in Northeast Canada

Anthony H. Normore

INTRODUCTION

Nobody today can remain unaffected by social change, but this observation applies to aboriginal people in a very special sense. Research claims that "Aboriginal culture is not a thing of the past, a way of life that is losing its relevance in the face of modernity" (Tanner, McGrath, & Brice-Bennett, n.d., para. 2). For many years, the place of First Nations (Aboriginal) peoples in Canadian culture and history has been undervalued. Indeed, the persistent assertion that Canada is the product of "two founding nations," French and English, is a striking reminder of this lack of awareness (Memorial University of Newfoundland and Labrador, 2008,

Leadership and Intercultural Dynamics, pp. 47–68

para. 3). In the past 3 decades, however, this lack of awareness has begun to change mainly due to the demands of Aboriginal people "that their legitimate claims be recognized" (para. 2).

Under pressure from mainstream Canadian institutions, Aboriginal people sometimes express their particular concern that their cultural knowledge and practices are not being maintained to the extent that they would prefer. This concern is especially common for a minority group, under pressure to change from forces which are seen as controlled by a dominant group. Tanner et al. (n.d.) further assert that because of the "uncertainty of their survival, the ethnic identity of a minority group is of proportionately greater concern to them and is frequently marked by distinctive symbolically-rich historic cultural practices" (para. 2). Under these circumstance, educational systems have a tendency to "essentialize aboriginal cultures by over-emphasizing their uniformity, and representing them as fixed, usually in some past era" (para. 2).

Recent scholars have paid considerable attention to practices and policies that have marginalized students and pose challenging questions to school leaders, educational scholars, and the broader community to engage in discussions about leadership for social justice (Capper, Theoharis, & Sebastian, 2006; Marshall & Oliva, 2006). Leadership theory and practice are responding to societal changes by shifting focus from what leaders do, and how they do it, to what leadership is for. This shift provides leverage for changes in bureaucratic systems that exist to serve the status quo. In this shift the new emphasis becomes leadership praxis for value ends, including social justice, values-orientation, democratic, and equitable schools, in support of learning for all children (Lyman, Ashby, & Tripses 2005). Although important research is increasing around the plight of marginalized populations very little recent research is made available on leadership for indigenous populations such as Canada's First Nations Peoples. Although leadership has been widely studied there is a persistent lack of agreement about what constitutes the most effective leadership styles in educational settings. What is clear however from research is that serving First Nations students requires a unique set of leadership skills and knowledge reflective of and responsive to the cultural and linguistic diversity of the student population (Lynch & Charleston, 1990; Pavlik, 1998).

The primary purpose of the chapter is to deepen our understanding and appreciation of historical and cultural experiences of Northeast Canada's First Nations Peoples: Innu and Inuit. Using these historical and cultural experiences the author builds a foundation for developing a culturally relevant leadership development program in support of social justice while acknowledging and honoring the integrity of Canada's First Nations communities. By bringing the Northeast Canadian

Aboriginal experience to the fore, this chapter helps to illuminate the issues in the context of leadership needed to understand the culture. Although this chapter intends to add value to the field of educational leadership and those who work with First Nations students it is also intended to assist those planning careers in teaching, social services, management, law, administration, healthcare, journalism, forestry, and mining to name a few.

LEADERSHIP AND PRAXIS

Leadership praxis involves self-reflection, critical thinking, and intentional inquiry (Lather, 1986), relationships between thought and action, theory and practice (Freire, 1998), ethics and morals within democracy (Furman, 2002), and social justice and equity as core values (Giroux, 1996). These actions are further supported by a growing number of scholars who have pointed out that in order to address inequities for diverse student populations, educational leaders must have a heightened awareness of social justice issues in a field struggling to meet the needs of all children, particularly given the importance of addressing the needs of traditionally underserved populations (Bogotch, 2005; Furman, 2002). It becomes critical to raise these issues to help educational leaders to advance their understanding of social justice and equity, and how these issues hold up in the world of leadership practice.

Furman (2002) advocates the use of a leadership lens which aims at the construction of meaning and purpose by members of a community through their communicative relationships, or "the reciprocal processes that enable participants in an educational community to construct meanings that lead toward a common purpose about schooling" (p. 29). Research findings from a recent study by Normore and Jean-Marie (2008) revealed that when educational leaders engage in authentic, concrete struggles and practices they find expression in social relations, daily life, and memories of resistance and struggles that shape their leadership praxis. Giroux (1996) emphasizes that praxis in leadership can serve as catalyst for creating conditions and preparing students, staff and community members to become immersed in knowledge and courage in the struggle to "make despair unconvincing and hope practical" (p. 128). The use of courage and hope can serve as extensions of spiritual and religious beliefs and practices. Spirituality is often illuminated at the core of leaders' work for social justice (Normore & Jean-Marie, 2008).

DEFINING SOCIAL JUSTICE LEADERSHIP

The discourses of social justice and leadership are inextricably linked. According to Marshall and Oliva (2006) social justice "has generated a great deal of scholarship over the last decade" which in essence capitalizes on the relevance of such a discourse" (p. 5). However, the notion of social justice is hard to capture. Dantley and Tillman (2006) assert: "It is demanding, fraught with controversy, and highly contextualized ... most people believe it is important but far fewer take the time or energy to actively pursue it" (p. 261). Thinking about social justice from a theoretical or historical perspective is a necessary but insufficient condition for actually achieving social justice. They further claim that discussions about social justice in the field of education have typically framed the concept around several issues including race, diversity, marginalization, morality, ability, gender, sexual orientation, and spirituality (p. 17). Other researchers (e.g., Bogotch, 2005; Normore & Jean-Marie, 2008) assert that social justice has no one specific meaning. Rather, "its multiple *a posteriori* meanings emerge differently from experiences and contexts" (Bogotch, 2005, p. 7.). Bogotch zeros in on a key component by stating that "social justice, like education, is a deliberate intervention that requires the moral use of power" and concludes that it is "both much more than what we currently call democratic schooling and community education, and much less than what we hold out as the ideals of progressing toward a just and democratic society and a new humanity worldwide" (pp. 7–8).

While a review of the literature does not present a clear definition of social justice, there is a general framework for delineating it. Lee and McKerrow (2005) offer such framework by asserting that social justice is defined "not only by what it is but also by what it is not, namely injustice. By seeking justice, we anticipate the ideal. By questioning injustice, we approach it. Integrating both, we achieve it" (p. 1). In practice, individuals for social justice seek to challenge political, economic and social structures that privilege some and disadvantage others. They challenge unequal power relationships based on systems of oppression and educational context.

CANADIAN CONTEXT OF ABORIGINAL EDUCATION

According to Indian and Northern Affairs Canada (INAC, 2008, para. 1–2) the Government of Canada supports education of all Canadians through the Canada Social Transfer to provinces and territories for education, as well as a variety of programs and initiatives. For First Nations (Status Indians) the Indian Act sets out the powers of the Minister of

Indian Affairs and Northern Development to arrange for their education. The department's mandate and responsibilities stem from exercising its authority and fulfilling its obligations under various statutes, treaties, agreements and government policy. Funding instruments relating to departmental responsibilities for First Nations education include contemporary tuition agreements with provincial authorities, funding arrangements with First Nations, comprehensive land claim settlement agreements, self-government agreements, and education policies. Education programming has evolved over time as a result of government policy and is operated under the broad authorities in the Department of Indian Affairs and Northern Development Act (INAC, 2008)

INAC funds band councils and First Nation education authorities for the education of children in Kindergarten to Grade 12 who attend schools on reserves or who attend provincially-run schools off reserve. In 2006–07, the Elementary/Secondary Education Program supported approximately 120,000 students and 515 schools with a budget of $1.2 billion. The program pays for: (1) instructional services in on-reserve schools, operated by the First Nation or by the federal government, (2) the reimbursement to provinces for tuition costs of students who attend provincial schools off-reserve, and (3) support services such as transportation, counseling, accommodation and financial assistance. Approximately 60% of First Nations students are taught on reserve, almost always in schools operated by a band council, another First Nations organization, or a federal school. The other 40% go off-reserve to schools under provincial authority, usually for secondary school (INAC, 2008, para. 1–4).

According to research on Aboriginal languages in North America (Budgel, 1984; Campbell, 1997; Cook & Howe, 2004; Goddard, 1996; Mithun, 2001; Report of the Royal Commission on Aboriginal Peoples, 2006) there are about 45 Aboriginal or First Nation languages spoken in Canada and 11 language families. The most widely spoken Aboriginal languages in Canada are Cree-Montagnais-Naskapi, Ojibwe, Mi'kmaq, Blackfoot, and Maliseet (belonging to the Algonquian family), Carrier, Babine, Dogrib, Chipewyan, Slave, Gwich'in, and Chilcotin (belonging to the Athapaskan family), Assiniboine(Siouan family), Mohawk (Iroquoian family), Gitksan and Nishga (Tsimshian family).

NORTHEAST CANADIAN FIRST NATIONS: INNU AND INUIT

Tanner et al. (n.d.) assert that a "large degree of diversity exists in the way individual Inuit or Innu put the general pattern of their own cultures into practice ... that the past continues to act as an important source of ideas and identification for Aboriginal peoples" (para. 3). It is important to be aware that both of the aboriginal groups—in this case, Innu and Inuit living in parts of Northeast Canada such as Labrador are parts of two geographically larger traditions, each reaching right across Canada and beyond. The Innu, referred to in some earlier sources as Montagnais and Naskapi, are part of the Northern Algonkian tradition which also includes groups like the Cree and Ojibwa. The Inuit are part of the "Eskimo" tradition, which extends from Greenland to Siberia. Presently, some "traditional" aboriginal practices are now being introduced into Labrador from other Canadian aboriginal groups (Pastore, 1997; Tanner, 1987; Tanner, McGrath, & Brice-Bennett, n.d.; Turner, 1894/1979).

INUIT: HISTORICAL CONTEXT

Research indicates that the Inuit are the descendants of the Thule people who migrated to Labrador (Northeast Canada) from the Canadian arctic 700 to 800 years ago (Pastore, 1997, para. 1). Although most Inuit communities are located along the north coast of Labrador many Inuit people are found in a number of other Labrador communities. Those living along the Northern coast of Labrador are the direct descendants of a prehistoric hunting society that spread across Canada from Alaska and centered on capturing massive bowhead whales (Antane, 1984; Brice-Bennett, 1994, 1997; Hiller, 1971; Pastore, 1997). This culture, known as Thule (Brice-Bennett, 1997; Pastore, 1997) first made contact with Europeans in the mid-sixteenth century when the traders established land stations to process whale oil for export to foreign markets during ice free seasons, from summer until late fall (Taylor, 1985; Tanner et al., n.d.). According to Brice-Bennett (1997),

> Europeans and Inuit did not have a language or culture in common and likely avoided face to face meetings. However, Inuit appear to have visited these stations in winter to scavenge for European goods left behind at the sites. In turn, these were distributed along the coast through an inter-group trade network linking Inuit place-groups or bands. These place groups consisted of families who were closely related and used a common hunting area. Band members often identified themselves by adding "miut," meaning "the people of," to a prominent place in the region. (para. 3)

In the early 1600s European whaling activities ended, and more coastal stations were established by French sealers and fishermen during the seventeenth and eighteenth centuries while a simultaneous Inuit demand for European manufactured goods increased during this period (Brice-Bennett, 1997, para. 4). However, approaches seldom occurred because most French outposts feared the Inuit. Consequently, Inuits began "attacking isolated stations to obtain the goods they wanted, which led to counter assaults by French crews" and that "mutual hostility also characterized the relationship of Inuit with British fishermen and New England whalers, who took over French outposts after Northeast Canada was transferred to the jurisdiction of Great Britain in 1763" (Brice-Bennett, 1997, para. 4). English fishing enterprises expanded and a more permanent resident population developed as a result of the diminishing presence of Inuit in southern Labrador. Many fishermen married Inuit women and formed families whose descendants remain in the region to this day (Antane, 1984).

The Inuit population to the north suffered from epidemic diseases during the 19th century "causing high death rates and severe reduction in the size of the mission stations" (Brice-Bennett, 1997, para. 10). Brice-Bennett further reiterates

> The establishment of a military airbase in 1942 in central Labrador, and radar sites which were later erected along the coast, introduced wage employment as an economic option for many Inuit.... During the 1950s two Northeast Inuit communities had no choice but to resettle at other existing communities when church, health and government officials decided that their social and economic welfare would be improved by living in larger centers.... However, this caused serious disruptions to the historical and cultural organization of the northern coast and had long-lasting negative consequences for resettled families. (para. 11)

The Labrador Inuit Association (LIA) was formed in 1973 and currently represents approximately 4,000 members residing mostly in five coastal communities. The purpose of the LIA was to promote the Inuit culture and advance the rights of Inuit to land which they traditionally harvested and occupied. In 1977, the LIA submitted its land claim to the federal and provincial governments and has since sought to negotiate a settlement defining aboriginal jurisdiction in the northern region (Brice-Bennett, 1997, para. 11).

CULTURE, SPIRITUALITY, AND EXTERNAL INFLUENCE

According to Brice-Bennett (1997) customs and beliefs composed Inuit spirituality before direct contact with European missionaries who advocated the adoption of Christian precepts. The spiritual system of the aboriginal people is commonly described as "shamanistic due to the primary role performed by shamans, called *angakut*, in propitiating spirit forces and mediating between them and the Inuit community reliant on success in hunting wildlife for survival" (para. 12). As a result of these ideas the environment was portrayed in a "world view" as populated by a host of spirits with whom people had to appeal, conciliate and defend themselves against harm in order to survive (Tanner et al., n.d., para. 12). This closely interactive system

> governed all aspects of Inuit life from success in capturing game to personal safety, good health, procreation and amiable relations between individuals while simultaneously integrating people with their environment, and provided a complex code for social action that defined the Inuit culture. (Brice-Bennett, n.d., para. 13)

A pre-Reformation Protestant sect known as the Moravian Church missionaries arrived in the late eighteenth century. With their arrival legitimacy of traditional Inuit spiritual beliefs was challenged when the missionaries presented an alternative to their accepted knowledge (Brice-Bennett, n.d.). The Moravians were "determined evangelists of pagan societies around the world who applied their previous experience in converting Greenlandic Inuit to Christianity in their early relations with Labrador Inuit" (para. 5). The first Inuit converts to Christianity challenged and disrupted the solidarity of the aboriginal society by separating themselves from relatives and friends, as the Moravians required, in order to adhere to new standards of religious practices and moral behavior at the mission stations (Brice-Bennett, 1994, 1997). Much of the literature on First Nations affairs in Northern Labrador during the nineteenth and twentieth centuries presents the Inuit adoption of Christianity as an inevitable response to the convincing arguments which the Moravian missionaries brought against the preexisting Inuit spiritual beliefs and practices (Antane, 1984; Brice-Bennett, 1994, 1997; Foster, 1982; McGrath, n.d.; Tanner, 1999; Pastore, 1997; Taylor, 1985; Turner, 1894/ 1979). According to Tanner et al. (n.d.) "the bias suggested by this perspective was that Christianity was actually superior to aboriginal spiritual ideas and Inuit acquiesced by becoming converts" (para. 8). A further implication was that traditional aspects of Inuit spirituality ceased with religious conversion and were completely supplanted by Christian beliefs and rituals (Brice-Bennett, n.d., para. 8).

Research indicates that the Inuit were expected and required by the Moravians to make a "conscious choice in becoming converts and sought to prevent people from blending elements of Christianity with traditional customs" (Brice-Bennett, n.d., para. 8). Christianity referred principally to social relations in a community context, while the primary focus of traditional spiritual practices centered on the harvesting and treatment of wildlife in locations beyond the border of mission stations (Antane, 1984; Armitage, 1992; Brice-Bennett, n.d.). Inuit families resided only in the Moravian communities on a seasonal basis during the nineteenth century and much of the twentieth century. According to Brice-Bennett (n.d.) this pattern was altered after the 1960s,

> when mandatory school attendance for children under 15 years of age began keeping families in the communities from about September until June...once they moved away to remote campsites to hunt and fish, Inuit people resumed command of their traditional lifestyle and culture in a familiar environment that had nourished generations of Inuit proceeding them...They may have been unaware of the subtle manner in which Inuit fused essential principles of their traditional ideology into the socio-cultural framework of post-contact Christian society, thereby ensuring the continuity of their perceptions. (para. 15–16)

These scholars also alluded to anxieties and several ideological oppositions that confronted Inuit society in the past, which possibly serve as a paradigm for comparable stress in the present (Armitage, 1992; Brice-Bennett, 1997; Hiller, 1971; Tanner et al., n.d.).

Primary values have also been retained by the Inuit. These governed their society before the arrival of Europeans and include emphasis on sharing resources, respect for the opinions of elders and proper treatment of wildlife avoiding cruelty and waste. However,

> the lack of use and erosion of the Inuit language by the young generation has contributed to a loss of traditional ecological knowledge. It has also diminished knowledge on matters such as place-names, legends and the oral history of Inuit society kept in the minds of elderly adults, along with social conventions, that formerly governed the coastal communities. (Brice-Bennett, n.d., para. 27)

INNU

Formerly known as the Naskapi-Montagnais, the Innu are descended from Algonkian-speaking hunter-gatherers who inhabited Labrador at the time of European arrival. The major Innu communities in Labrador are located in central Labrador and on Labrador's northern coast. The word "Innu" means "human being" and the Innu language is called "Innu-aimun" (Armitage, 1997, para. 1). Today there are over 16,000 Innu who live in 11 communities in Québec and two in Labrador. The population of the two Labrador communities comprises approximately 1500 (Armitage, 1997). Together, the two communities form the Innu Nation, a regional political organization which represents the Innu people of Labrador to the wider world (para. 2).

Prior to the nineteenth century Europeans had little adverse effect on the life of the Innu of Northern Labrador. Research (e.g., Armitage, 1992, 1997; Podolinsky-Webber, 1974) indicates that an era of great change, much of it harmful, emerged with the arrival of the European trading posts in Labrador and northern Québec in the nineteenth century and the subsequent attempts to draw the Innu into a dependency on European trade goods (Armitage, 1997, para. 5). Increasing competition resulted from white and settler fur trappers, particularly in central Labrador in the late nineteenth and twentieth centuries (Armitage, 1997, para. 5). Other research (e.g., Armitage, 1997; Horwood, 1981; Ryan, 1988; Ross, 1992; Speck, 1935/1977; Samson, 2003; Wadden, 1991) reveal similar findings as Armitage. Armitage (1997) emphasizes,

> that the collapse in fur prices in the 1930s and the reduction in the size of the caribou herds caused great suffering among the Innu including; death and suffering from European diseases; the building of mining towns; the growing population of non-Aboriginal people; the imposition of provincial government hunting regulations; the settlement of the Barren-ground Innu in the late 1960s; the flooding of a huge area of productive Innu land in 1970; and the expansion of NATO military flights over Innu territory in the early 1980s did much to erode the Innu land base and promote culture collapse and its associated social pathologies ... many Innu held on to much of their traditional relationship with the land and its animals despite these assaults on their culture. (para. 6–7)

CULTURE, SPIRITUALITY, AND EXTERNAL INFLUENCE

As Armitage (1992) indicates in his research the culture of the Innu celebrates the division of nondomestic animals into various categories including four legged animals, waterfowl, birds, fish, and insects, with "an additional classification of animal species into kingdoms (*tipentamun*) ... superimposed upon the category of Innu animals" (p. 68). Culturally, each of these categories of animals in the second classification is thought to be ruled by a spiritual "animal master" and occasionally a hierarchical relationship exists between the masters, with caribou and aquatic creatures being the most powerful (p. 69). Podolinsky-Webber (1974) highlighted that the Innu believe in one "supreme being," with bands having different names and attributes for such a being. However, Armitage (1992) points out that this concept should not be equated with "deity" in a monotheistic religion like Christianity. Armitage (1992), Henriksen (1973, 1993, 1994) and McGrath (n.d.) reiterate that

human relationships with other beings in the spiritual world such as canni-
bals, giants and spirits of divination are maintained through observance of
taboos, spiritual ceremonies such as the "shaking tent," the burning of scap-
ular bones, drumming, dreams (all forms of divination), and *"mukaushan"* or
marrow bone feasts. (McGrath, n.d., para. 4)

INFLUENCE OF CATHOLICISM

Like most Canadian Indians, the Innu of Labrador practice Catholicism
(Podolinsky-Webber, 1996). After the Roman Catholic missionaries
arrived some of them took the challenge of converting the Innu much
more seriously than missionaries before them. Henriksen (1973) indicated that the Roman Catholic missionaries learned Innu-aimun and
through confession gathered information about the entire community
that gave them considerable influence. Podolinsky-Webber (1996) argues
that some missionaries;

> never understood that the Innu had their own religion, beliefs and tradi-
> tions which had served them well for a very, very long time and that the
> Christian religion was in many ways alien to Innu beliefs and could not take
> its place but could even become detrimental to their life. (p. 4)

Recent attempts by the Catholic Church to regain its influence in the
community by appropriating Innu traditions has been welcomed by many
elders but resented by many young leaders. Henriksen (1993) believes
that;

> one of the most difficult tasks of the young Innu leaders and elders in the
> near future will be "to sort out the "interface" between the syncretic religion
> of the older people and the younger peoples' yearning for spiritual power
> and the securing of their identity in a decolonized Innu religion. (p. 16)

Substantial diminishing of Catholicism has occurred in some communities in recent years. This is due to too numerous accounts of Innu who
have suffered sexual, physical, and psychological abuse at the hands of
religious workers and teachers. According to Fouillard (1995) Innu testimony at the People's Inquiry of 1992 revealed that the priests suppressed
parts of the Innu culture and customs such as the drum, dancing, and
mukaushan, The current attitude towards Roman Catholicism can be
summed up by two of those who testified at the 1992 People's Inquiry
(Fouillard 1995). According to Fouillard a teenager said of the church and
white society "Their way of living is our way of dying" (p. 59). An older

Innu said "I was baptized and I believe in the Church, but I also believe in our own religion, our own spiritual beliefs ... I respect the Church very much, but we have to go back to our old ways too" (p. 63). Henriksen (1994) maintains that the inconsistency of adherence to two disparate systems of belief is in appearance only and that there is an internal consistency of values that for the older Innu is integrated in the country if not in the village. Podolinsky-Webber (1996) explains that although Christian beliefs are prevalent in villages, most Innu traditions dominate in camp.

Based on research by McGrath (n.d.) "loss of culture, solvent abuse, religious conflict, and family violence are all viewed as illness in the Labrador Innu communities" (para. 23). In times of crises Innu communities engage in "healing processes" through the dramatic productions of its young people. Healing movements are the focus of much of the Labrador Innu community and leadership. According to McGrath (n.d.) "it is in the various forms of healing that current Innu spiritual growth can be found" (para. 18). Healing movements include drumming, traditional clothing, and some dialogue in Innu Aimun. Gatherings, which are organized by the band council twice a year, are an important part of the healing process (Fouillard, 1995; McGrath, n.d.). Traditional Innu healing practices in such cases as solvent and physical abuse emphasize restoration of peace and good relations rather than punishment (McGratch, n.d., para. 21). McGrath further iterates that local rehabilitation centers, as well as well as treatment centers in other Canadian provinces such as Alberta have all provided treatment programs for Innu. However,

> the language barriers, the distance traveled, the separation from family, all limit the effectiveness of these programs. Some Innu feel that the essentially foreign nature of these programs are the reason for the high relapse rate of those who have gone through them and there is a strong demand for a specifically Innu approach to these problems ... the Outpost Program, where families are supported in going by aircraft to live in camps in the bush for as long as three months, is seen as part of the Innu healing process. (para. 19–20)

In summary, Innu and Inuit cultures are rich in history, culture and tradition. Each encompasses matters which are also covered by terms such as "world view"; that is, the core beliefs, culture, values and ethical principles that are characteristic of a particular group. As Tanner (n.d.) so eloquently states,

> both cultures integrate spirituality within everyday activities, like hunting, and with their life in direct contact with the natural environment. In this sense, Inuit and Innu cultures involve beliefs according to which humanity is not seen as separated from, but as an internal part of "nature." This

includes the assumption that humanity, the land and the game animals are not just pragmatically, but also ethically, bound together, in the sense that all are considered part of the same moral universe. (para. 9)

In both the Inuit and Innu cases, the cultural traditions of the past continue to be sources of inspiration in the formation of present-day expressions of ethnic identity, in the context of a modern, multicultural society when dominant cultures impose value systems that infringe upon the past and present values and beliefs of those oppressed. These First Nations Peoples are in a historical period of innovation, change and continuous productivity, a period in which many are searching for certainty and confidence about their place in the world. In the words of Tanner (n.d.), "it is also a period of turning inward, of seeking of ways for the expression of cultural and traditional ideas and values adapted to modern, rapidly changing conditions" (para. 9).

HISTORY AND CULTURE OF FIRST NATIONS: FOUNDATION FOR DEVELOPING RELEVANT LEADERSHIP PEDAGOGY

Based on the historical and cultural contexts of First Nations peoples there is a dire need to redesign pedagogy for its educational leaders. Researchers assert that the development of culturally relevant pedagogy is contingent upon critical reflection about race and culture of educational leaders, teachers, and the students. It is a process for improving practice, rethinking philosophies, raising self-awareness, and becoming effective leaders for today's ever changing student populations (Howard, 2003; Lea & Griggs, 2005). A key contention however is that leadership programs must not only consider promoting and understanding cultural diversity but also acknowledging it. It can be more daunting when the population of potential leaders and their own experiences are themselves quite homogeneous (Capper, Theoharis, & Sebastian, 2006). Many aspiring leaders have too few opportunities to cross school boundaries and form close linkages with surrounding communities in "porous" relationships (Furman, 2002) oftentimes resulting in monocultural experiences. According to Seidl (2007) these experiences can "make it challenging for many White teachers to consider what it means to create education that is relevant for children who are not White and/or middle class" (p. 168). From the perspective of cultural relevance it seems reasonable to recruit more First Nations teachers into leadership programs who may want to lead First Nations schools and who will promote early childhood programs that would provide a safe and challenging early environment for young First Nations children. This is a necessary component of a school's culture if First Nations students are to succeed academically as students and play a meaningful role as local and global citizens. Let us keep in mind however that although many prospective teachers of Indigenous cultures may have experienced diverse cultural contexts, many have been educated within public school systems where they experienced a Eurocentric approach to education and have been provided with few opportunities to consider culturally relevant practices or a multicultural curriculum.

INTERDISCIPLINARY LEADERSHIP DEVELOPMENT PROGRAMS FOR FIRST NATIONS

An effective leadership development program must encompass components for improving teaching and learning of diverse learners from an interdisciplinary perspective. An interdisciplinary school leader is representative of any education discipline such as special education, counselor education, school administration, outreach education, multicultural education, curriculum and instruction or assets-based education, and so forth. The program must focus on the development, preparation and training of educators for various forms of leadership in public schools and in First Nations schools. Such a program must be offered through substantive partnerships and engage with First Nations Peoples in search of appropriate goals for improving educational outcomes that will strengthen the quality, accessibility and cultural relevance of education programs for First Nation students. It will also require active and meaningful parental participation and foster better interconnections and collaboration between First Nation community leaders, First Nations language experts, First Nations artists, First Nations historians, First Nation school leaders, Canadian Indian and Northern Affairs, and other stakeholders.

CHARACTERISTICS OF EFFECTIVE INTERDISCIPLINARY EDUCATIONAL LEADERS FOR FIRST NATIONS

An effective *interdisciplinary* leadership program must be designed to advance skills that effectively build and sustain diverse settings with purposeful constituent relationships. The program must develop leaders with knowledge and understanding, and who acknowledge and are sensitive to social and equity issues, culture, history, and economic challenges of First Nations schools and surrounding communities. These leaders will need to create lifelong learning opportunities that encourage and support the efforts of all First Nations members to improve their quality of life, and to meet their tribal responsibilities through meaningful contributions to the local, national, and world communities in which they live and interact. The greatest educational challenge for many is to build learning environments that allow each of their young children to obtain an education that creates good people that are knowledgeable and wise.

CULTURALLY RELEVANT CURRICULUM FOR FIRST NATIONS

Infusing curricula with multi-approaches to broaden aspiring leaders' experiences beyond their familiarity or limited to their current school setting is an essential goal for relevant leadership. For Canada's First Nations Peoples effective and culturally relevant leadership must encompass opportunities to build a powerful knowledge-base on current research on First Nations issues and be exposed to in-depth knowledge and skills to make meaningful connections between theory and practice for influencing significant education reform efforts that will impact First Nation's schools. For leaders who will work in schools where First Nations students attend it becomes critical to acknowledge the history and culture by infusing elements of both into curriculum. For example, research indicates that within the Indigenous professional community high achievement in academics and motivation depend on the spiritual well-being of Indigenous students, early attention to cognitive development, sense of identity, and social/cultural maturity (Demmert, 1996). Many Innu and Inuit take the position that recognizing one's heritage is necessary to an individual's mental, spiritual, and physical health (Foster, 1982). This belief incorporates the position that improved academic performance will not occur until other factors identified above are included as part of a comprehensive approach for nurturing and educating the whole child.

For these leader development programs it becomes critical to also incorporate tribal language and cultural programs such as short seasonal 'bush' fieldtrips in the curriculum while simultaneously identifying different political or cultural principles involved in developing culturally relevant teaching and curriculum (Ladson-Billings, 1994). The curriculum must support the language and cultural base that helps preserve the identity of First Nations populations. For example, curriculum must acknowledge the importance and role of "the place of First Nations arts and crafts," "tea dolls," "hunting dogs," "tent shaking," "drumming" "throat chanting," "healing movements," "spirituality," "ecological connections," "spirit masters," and "seasonal hunting expeditions to bush camps," "place names," "legends," and "oral history."

MOVING TOWARDS CRITICAL PEDAGOGY

From a traditional standpoint researchers have defined critical pedagogy as educational theory and teaching and learning practices that are designed to raise learners' critical consciousness about oppressive social conditions (Freire, 1998; Ladson-Billings, 1994, 1997; McLaren, 1998; McLauren & Torres, 1999). Freire argues that critical pedagogy focuses on personal "liberatory education" through the development of critical consciousness. Serving as a catalyst to the commitment to social justice liberatory education attempts to empower all learners to engage in critical dialogue that critiques and challenges oppressive social conditions nationally and globally and to envision and work towards a more just society. Such strategies can help current and future leaders to confront transformative and changing social conditions and historical contexts for leading schools where First Nations people attend. Further, it provides the opportunity to analyze and re-examine federal policies and practices that have caused a loss of dignity and ability for many First Nations people to adjust to the demands of modern society, partly because of the failure of schools. As educators move toward a critical pedagogy and a commitment to social justice effective school leaders envision the classroom as a site where new knowledge, grounded in the experiences of students and teachers alike, is produced through meaningful dialogue and experiences (p. 58).

Concepts about knowledge and learning support critical pedagogy and a more social constructivist approach to teaching for social justice. Understanding how knowledge is constructed is critical. Knowledge is not something that exists outside of language and the social subjects who use it. It is a socially constructed process and one that cannot be divorced from the learners' social context. It is constructed by "doing" and from social development experience. First Nations students bring a rich history and prior knowledge related to spirituality, and "healing processes" into a learning situation, which can be incorporated into the curriculum. As Searle (1995) indicates the instructor makes sure she understands the students' preexisting conceptions and guides activities to address and build on them thereby preparing educational leaders who seek to liberate students to make social changes; create space and spaces for trust; and nurture participatory, equitable and just relationships rather than simply managing programs and services. Such strategies facilitate the opportunity for empowerment rather than simply trying to "deliver it." Researchers argue that, critical pedagogy also has a more collective political component, in that critical consciousness is positioned as the necessary first step of a larger collective political struggle to challenge and transform oppressive social conditions and to create a more egalitarian society (Apple, 1995; Carlson & Apple, 1998; Giroux, 1996).

Another important strategy for increased effective leadership development is to focus on the hidden curriculum. According to Lea and Griggs (2005) the "implicit curriculum" in schools is often conducted in the hallways, locker rooms, and at the back of classrooms. Ironically, in the hidden school curriculum often build a replica of the very same power structures from which minorities are excluded in the larger social order. Within a culture of social and cultural oppression, students learn about competition, unequal self-worth and psychological warfare. They also learn that covert relational aggression is a viable and useful strategy to take with them into the adult world. For example, bullying is part of a curriculum of dominance and oppression in which some students, both perpetrators and witnesses, have learned that aggression is an acceptable form of dehumanization, while other students, both victims and witnesses, have learned docility and silence as strategies for survival (Apple, 1990). Leadership development programs are havens that can serve as catalysts of opportunities that address what it means to make teaching and learning more socially conscious and politically responsive in a time of growing conservatism, racism, cultural deficiency, and social injustices locally, nationally and internationally. Effective leadership preparation must provide opportunities to ask hard questions about educational practice, push frontiers about inequities, and solve school problems. Opportunities for aspiring school leaders to work closely with school districts, First Nations leaders, communities, and noneducational organizations in diverse contexts are paramount to do the work that must be done.

FINAL REFLECTIONS

As Bogotch (2005) reminds us, more discussions of educational leadership are in order to deliberately and continuously refocus our educational work in both theory and practice on understanding and becoming more socially just. As scholars and practitioners of educational leadership, we have an obligation to move beyond high-sounding abstractions and turn to research and action. This implies that leadership development programs should promote opportunities for critical reflection, leadership praxis, and develop critical and culturally relevant pedagogy related to social justice. The major goal of this chapter was to describe a process of understanding and acknowledge the culture and history of two Northeastern Canadian First Nations Peoples—Inuit and Innu and the importance of acknowledging this history as an integral component of interdisciplinary leadership that is culturally and pedagogically relevant to their lives. This kind of process can be attempted across many cultural contexts and the ways in which significant cultural and political information is understood and named will depend on the particular cultural context, the people involved, and the ways in which they utilize experience and literature in the process. Creating meaningful educational experiences and lifelong learning environments for both the youth and adults of Canada's First Nations requires a language and cultural context that supports the traditions, knowledge, and languages of the Innu and Inuit as the starting place for learning new ideas and knowledge. There is a firm belief among many First Nations communities and professional First Nations educators that this cultural context is absolutely essential if one is to succeed academically and to build a meaningful adult life. The hope is that the history and culture that is powerful for the author will resonate in ways that support others as they approach what it means to teach, learn and lead across cultures while simultaneously honoring the integrity of those cultures.

An implication from this discussion is the need to conduct further comparative studies on indigenous populations, educational leadership, and social justice in diverse countries outside Canada and United States. While the knowledge base on these issues in North America continues to grow we know much less about those in other countries and the importance of transcending cultural norms, national and international boundaries. In order to fully capture the impact of social justice leadership as it relates to other indigenous peoples, research must involve a greater number of organizations at extreme ends of the value dimensions for measuring culturally relevant leadership. We need more comparative research studies that investigate the contexts, processes, leadership and work experiences, and attitudes of other indigenous school leaders with particular reference to similarities and differences between countries that experience modernization, and industrialization. Attention also needs to be paid to poor, underdeveloped, and developing nations too. Such comparative studies may generate cross-fertilization of ideas and experiences that will provide insight into the social justice leadership-orientations that, to date, have failed to percolate "current Anglo-American literature" Oplatka (2006, p. 615).

We have an aging and culturally biased leadership discourse. Evidence suggests our antiquated styles and methods are creating hindrances in raising the next generation of educational leaders who will promote, understand, and above all else, acknowledge, the culturally relevant pedagogy needed in leadership for social justice. These future leaders need our wisdom; but are our current leadership development plans hip enough to give credibility? Practicing and aspiring educational leaders in all disciplines need to be cognizant of past and current cultural, political, social, and economic landscapes lest they become irrelevant to those whom they lead and serve.

REFERENCES

Antane, S. & Kanikuen, P. (1984). The Innut and their struggle against assimilation. *Native Issues, 4*(1), 25–33.

Apple, M. W. (1990). *The hidden curriculum and the nature of conflict in ideology and curriculum.* New York: Routledge.

Apple, M. W. (1995). *Education and power.* New York: Routledge.

Armitage, P. (1992). Religious ideology among the Innu of Eastern Quebec and Labrador. Religiologiques, 6, 64-110.

Armitage, P. (1997). *The Innu.* Retrieved on May 5, 2008, from http://www .heritage.nf.ca/aboriginal/innu.html

Bogotch, I. E. (2005, November). *Social justice as an educational construct: Problems and possibilities.* Paper presented at the annual meeting of the University Council of Educational Administration, Nashville, TN.

Brice-Bennett, C. (1994). The redistribution of the Northern Labrador Inuit Population: A strategy for integration and formula for conflict. *Zeitschrift fur Kanada-Studien, 2*(26), 95–106.

Brice-Bennett, C. (1997). *The Inuit.* Retrieved on May 18, 2008 at: http://www .heritage.nf.ca/aboriginal/inuit.html

Brice-Bennett, C. (n.d.). *Spirituality among the Inuit and Innu of Labrador.* St. John's, Newfoundland: Community Resource Services Ltd. Retrieved on June 6, 2008, from http://www.innu.ca/tanner1.html

Budgel, R. (1984). Canada, Newfoundland, and the Labrador Indians: Government involvement with the Montagnais-Naskapi, 1949–69. *Native Issues, 4*(1), 38–49.

Campbell, L. (1997). *American Indian languages: The historical linguistics of Native America.* Oxford, England: Oxford University Press.

Capper, C. A., Theoharis, G., & Sebastian, J. (2006). Toward a framework for preparing leaders for social justice. *Journal of Educational Administration, 44*(3), 209–224.

Carlson, D., & Apple, M. W. (Eds.). (1998). *Power/knowledge/pedagogy.* Cresskill, NJ: Westview Press.

Cook, E. D., & Howe, D. (2004). Aboriginal languages of Canada. In W. O'Grady & J. Archibald (Eds.), *Contemporary linguistic analysis* (5th ed., pp. 294–309). Toronto: Addison Wesley Longman.

Dantley, M. E., & Tillman, L. C. (2006). Social justice and moral transformative Leadership. In C. Marshall & M. Oliva (Eds.), *Leadership for social justice: Making revolutions in education* (pp. 16–30). Boston: Pearson Education.

Demmert, W. G., Jr. (1996). *Indian nations at risk: An educational strategy for action. Educating a new majority, Transforming America's educational system for diversity,* San Francisco: Jossey-Bass.

Foster, M. K. (1982). Canada's Indigenous languages: Past and present. *Language and Society, 7,* 3–16.

Fouillard, C. (1995). *Gathering voices: Finding strength to help our children.* Vancouver, Canada: Douglas and McIntyre.

Freire, P. (1998). *Pedagogy of the oppressed* (New Rev. 20th-anniversay ed.). New York: Continuum.

Furman, F. (2002). *School as community: From promise to practice.* Albany, NY: SUNY.

Giroux, H. A. (1996). *Fugitive cultures: Race, violence and youth.* New York: Routledge.

Goddard, I. (Ed.). (1996). *Languages* (Vol. 17 of the *Handbook of North American Indians*). Washington, DC: Smithsonian Institution.

Henriksen, G. (1973). *Hunters in the barrens: The Naskapi on the edge of the White man's world.* St. John's, NF: Institute of Social and Economic Research.

Henriksen, G. (1993). *Life and death among the Mushuau Innu of Northern Labrador.* St. John's, NF: Institute of Social and Economic Research.

Henriksen, G. (1994). The Mushuau Innu of Labrador: Self-government, innovation and socio-cultural continuity by Georg Henriksen. *Proactive, 13*(1), 2–22.

Hiller, J. K. (1971). Early patrons of the Labrador Eskimos: The Moravian Mission in Labrador, 1764–1805. In R. Paine (Ed.), *Patrons and brokers in the East Arctic* (pp. 74–97). Memorial University of Newfoundland, St. John's: Institute of Social and Economic Research.

Horwood, H. (1981) *Tales of the Labrador Indians.* St. John's, Newfoundland: Harry Cuff.

Howard, T. (2003). Culturally relevant pedagogy: Ingredients for critical teacher reflection. *Theory into Practice, 42*(3), 195–202.

Indian and Northern Affairs Canada. (2008). Retrieved on June 15, 2008, from http://www.ainc-inac.gc.ca/edu/res-eng.asp

Ladson-Billings, G. (1994). *The dreamkeepers.* San Francisco: Jossey-Bass.

Ladson-billings, G. (1997). I know why this doesn't feel empowering: A critical race analysis of critical pedagogy. In P. Freire, J. W. Fraser, D. Macedo, T. McKinnon, & W. T. Stokes (Eds.), *Mentoring the mentor: A critical dialogue with Paulo Freire* (pp. 127–141). New York: Peter Lang.

Lather, L. (1986). Research as praxis. *Harvard Education Review, 56* (3), 257–277.

Lea, V., & Griggs, T. (2005). Behind the mask and beneath the story: Enabling students-teachers to reflect critically on the socially-constructed nature of their "normal" practice. *Teacher Education Quarterly, 32*(1), 93–114.

Lee, S. S., & McKerrow, K. (2005). Advancing social justice: Women's work. *Advancing Women in Leadership, 19,* 1–2.

Lyman, L. L., Ashby, D. E., & Tripses, J. S. (2005). *Leaders who dare: Pushing the boundaries.* Lanham, MD: Rowman & Littlefied Education.

Lynch, P. D., & Charleston, M. (1990). The emergence of American Indian leadership in education. *Journal of American Indian education, 29*(2), 1–10.

Marshall, C., & Oliva, M. (2006). *Leadership for social justice: Making revolutions in education,* Boston: Pearson Education.

McGrath, R. (n.d.). *Spirituality among the Inuit and Innu of Labrador.* St. John's, Newfoundland: Community Resource Services. Retrieved on June 6, 2008, from http://www.innu.ca/tanner1.html

McLaren, P. (1998). *Life in schools: An introduction to critical pedagogy in the foundations of education*. London: Longman.

McLaren, P., & Torres, R. (1999). Racism and multicultural education: Rethinking "race" and "whiteness" in late capitalism. In S. May (Ed.), *Critical multiculturalism: Rethinking multicultural and antiracist education* (pp. 42–76). Philadelphia, PA: Falmer Press,

Memorial University of Newfoundland and Labrador. (2008). Retrieved on June 4, 2008, from http://www.mun.ca/interdisciplinary/aboriginal/

Mithun, M. (2001). *The languages of Native North America*. Cambridge, England: Cambridge University Press.

Normore, A. H., & Jean-Marie, G. (2008). Female secondary school leaders: At the helm of social justice, democratic schooling, and equity. *Leadership and Organizational Development Journal, 29*(2), 182–205.

Oplatka, I. (2006). Women in educational administration within developing countries: Towards a new international research agenda. *Journal of Educational Administrtaion, 44*(6), 604–624.

Pastore, R. T. (1997). *Aboriginal peoples*. Retrieved on June 3, 2008, from http://www.heritage.nf.ca/aboriginal/

Pavlik, S. (1988, May). Beyond the common ground: Characteristics of effective Indian school administrators. *Journal of American Indian Education, 27(3)*. Retrieved January 23, 2008, from http://jaie.asu.edu/v27/V27S3bey.htm

Podolinsky-Webber, W. A. (1996). *Place of the boss—Utshimassit*. Unpublished manuscript.

Podolinsky-Webber, W. A. (1974). The healing vision: Naskapi Natutshikans. *Artscanada, 184*(7), 150–153.

The Royal Commission on Aboriginal Peoples. (2006, October). Retrieved June 4, 2008, from http://www.ainc-inac.gc.ca/ch/rcap/sg/sgmm_e.html

Ross, R. (1992). *Dancing with a ghost: Exploring Indian reality*. Markham, ON, Canada: Reed Books.

Ryan, J. R. (1988). *Disciplining the Innut: Social form and control in bush, community and school*. Unpublished manuscript.

Samson, C. (2003). A way of life that does not exist: Canada and the extinguishment of the Innu. St. John's, Newfoundland: ISER.

Searle, J. (1995). *The construction of social reality*. New York: Free Press.

Seidl, B. (2007). Working with communities to explore and personalize culturally relevant pedagogies: Push, double images, and raced talk. *Journal of Teacher Education, 6*(2), 168–183.

Speck, F. G. (1977). *Naskapi: The savage hunters of the Labrador peninsula*. Norman: University of Oklahoma Press. (Original work published 1935)

Tanner, A. (1999). *Innu history*. Retrieved on June 11, 2008, from http://www.heritage.nf.ca/aboriginal/innu_history.html

Tanner, A., McGrath, R., & Brice-Bennett, C. (n.d.). *Spirituality among the Inuit and Innu of Labrador*. St. John's, Newfoundland: Community Resource Services. Retrieved on June 6, 2008, from http://www.innu.ca/tanner1.html

Taylor, G. (1985.). *Inuit post-contact history*. Retrieved on June 6, 2008, from http://www.heritage.nf.ca/aboriginal/inuit_history.html

Turner, L. M. (1979). *Indians and Eskimos in the Quebec-Labrador Peninsula.* Quebec: Presses Comeditex. (Original work published 1894)

Vygotsky, L. (2007). *Social development theory.* Retrieved on June 3, 2008, from http://www.learning-theories.com/vygotskys-social-learning-theory.html

Wadden, M. (1991). *Nitassinan: The Innu struggle to reclaim their homeland.* Vancouver, Canada: Douglas and McIntyre.

CHAPTER 4

LEADERSHIP IN INDIAN EDUCATION

Perspectives of American Indian and Alaska Native Educators

Susan C. Faircloth and John W. Tippeconnic, III

The exclusion of [American] Indians from America's story also excludes them from a prominent place in our collective understanding of the American "we." But that is not because there is no story of consequence to be told. Quite the contrary. American Indian cultures are filled with great thinkers and doers and with histories at least as complex and exciting as those included in the largely Eurocentric body of knowledge acquired by America's graduating seniors. And whether or not we can name Indian contributions to our democracy and our daily lives, they do exist. (Starnes, 2006, para. 5)

INTRODUCTION

More than 473,000 American Indian and Alaska Native students attend elementary and secondary schools in the United States. While the majority of these students attend public schools, approximately 9% attend schools operated or funded by the Bureau of Indian Education (BIE)[1] and tribes.

Leadership and Intercultural Dynamics, pp. 69–82
Copyright © 2009 by Information Age Publishing

American Indian and Alaska Native students experience high drop out rates, academic failure, and special education referral and placement at rates higher than many of their non-Native peers (Freeman & Fox, 2005). These issues pose a number of leadership challenges for individuals working in schools with American Indian and Alaska Native student populations.

In this chapter, we explore the complex nature of leadership in schools serving American Indian and Alaska Native students. We draw upon our experiences as American Indian educators and researchers to explore the extent to which effective leadership in schools serving American Indian and Alaska Native students requires a unique set of knowledge and skills reflective of and responsive to the cultural and linguistic diversity of the student population with which these knowledge and skills are employed. Over the years, we have grappled with this question as we have worked to prepare American Indian and Alaska Native students[2] to assume leadership positions in schools and organizations serving Indigenous students. Give the lack of extant research in this field, much of what we know is based on our personal and professional experiences living in and working with Indigenous communities.

Given the changing nature of leadership, this line of inquiry is germane not only to the field of Indian education but to the field of education at large. Although American Indian and Alaska Native students account for less than one percent of the total school-age population, they represent an increasingly diverse student population composed of 562 federally recognized and 69 state recognized tribes, each with its own unique culture and many with their own language still intact. The perspectives presented in this chapter are representative of this diversity as we draw not only on our own personal and professional experiences, but the experiences and perspectives of current and former participants in Penn State's American Indian Leadership Program (AILP), to explore the characteristics of effective leadership in Indian education.

Background

The establishment of the AILP was made possible in large part by the self-determination movement which began in earnest in the 1960s. During this time, Indian education was at a critical crossroad and in need of drastic reform. National studies (e.g., the Meriam and Kennedy Reports) of the status of Indian education documented the failure of both public and Bureau of Indian Affairs schools to successfully educate Native youth. As a result of these reports, a number of educational reforms were recommended including increased local control of education and the preparation of American Indian and Alaska Native teachers and administrators.

Around the nation, American Indian and Alaska Native communities called for increased local control of Indian education. This movement was marked by the establishment of tribally controlled schools, including Rough Rock Demonstration School established on the Navajo reservation in 1966 and the emergence of tribally controlled colleges and universities. Navajo Community College, later renamed Diné was the first tribal college established by the Navajo Nation in 1968 (Tippeconnic, 1999). This era marked a major shift in the federal government's policy towards American Indian and Alaska Native tribes; a shift from terminating relationships with tribes toward increased tribal self-determination—the right to determine tribal priorities, goals, and objectives. This shift in policy was aided by the Civil Rights movement, Great Society Programs, and the war on poverty which were in full swing in the 1960s and helped to create awareness, provide resources, and facilitate local community action.

Although not located in the heart of Indian country, The Pennsylvania State University was one of the first colleges and universities in the nation to offer administrator preparation programs specifically for American Indian and Alaska Native students. Since its inception in 1970, more than 200 American Indians and Alaska Natives have earned graduate degrees in Educational Administration and Educational Leadership through AILP.[3] This program, housed within the Department of Education Policy Studies, in the College of Education, is directed by Dr. John W. Tippeconnic, III, one of the first graduates of the AILP. Today, the AILP remains the oldest continuously operating educational leadership program for American Indian/Alaska Native students in the United States.

The most recent participants in the AILP represent tribes from across the nation including Pima, Tohono O'odham, Kiowa, Saginaw Chippewa, Seneca Cayuga, Eastern Band of Cherokee, Lakota, Navajo, Turtle Mountain Chippewa, Yavapai, Apache, Hualapai, Mille Lacs Band of Ojibwe, and Chiricahua. The majority of the AILP's past and current participants are enrolled members of Indian tribes and are experienced in the education of American Indian and Alaska Native students. Members of the AILP are recruited nationally from more than 631 federally and state recognized tribes. In addition to support and funding from Penn State, external funding has been provided by grants from the U.S. Department of Education, by way of both the Office of Indian Education and the Office of Special Education and Rehabilitative Services. Both programs have supported the AILP's overall purpose of preparing American Indians and Alaska Natives to assume leadership roles at the local, tribal, state and national levels. Upon graduation, the majority of the AILP fellows have earned a master's degree in Educational Administration/Leadership with an emphasis on Indian education. In addition to the master's degree, many of the participants have complete requirements for principalship certification. Several participants have gone on to earn their doctoral degrees in education at Penn State as well as other colleges and universities around the nation.

Although limited in our ability to deliver a truly Indigenous approach to leadership development in a mainstream institution, a hallmark of the AILP has been its recognition of the cultural and linguistic diversity of each of the students participating in this program. In response, the AILP builds upon the basic tenets of the Educational Leadership program at Penn State while providing opportunities for participants to reflect upon the ways in which these tenets may be applied to the schools and communities with which they plan to work. Our goal is for students to develop and strengthen their own individual models of leadership that are culturally appropriate and educationally sound for use within schools serving American Indian and Alaska Native students. Our students constantly challenge us to think and act outside the proverbial box of traditional educational leadership theory and perspective, as demonstrated by a recent participant who wrote:

> developing a "cookie-cutter" model for Indian Education may prove to be as futile as searching for El Dorado, the Lost City of Gold. In previous classes, we learned how extraneous variables (e.g., school climate, teacher climate, community climate) elicit either success or failure on the part of the school administrator. Research has shown that it takes an average of three (3) years for school programs to be effective. I propose it would require school administrators an equal amount of time to be efficient within a new school setting. A new school administrator will need ample time to 'learn' the politics of the school community. The purpose of school administrator programs should be the transmission of skills, knowledge and creating a networkof Indian educators [who] collaborate in meeting the needs of Indian communities, not the development of a "cookie-cutter" model that will be applicable in all Indian schools. The logical approach to creating individualized Native American systems of education will inevitably depend on the Native American environment.... Creating a shift in the current paradigm from focusing on meeting the requirements as set forth by external educational entities to a paradigm that highlights tribal[ly] defined requirements would be a worthy endeavor.

In addition to the general Educational Leadership curriculum, current members of the AILP enroll in an Indian Education seminar each semester. This course is co-taught by Dr. John Tippeconnic and Dr. Susan Faircloth, faculty members in Educational Leadership and graduates of the AILP. The perspectives presented in this chapter are representative of the types of discussions we engage in during the seminar. A recurring theme in these discussion is the defining characteristics of effective leadership in Indian education.

Defining Effective Leadership

Although leadership has been widely studied there is a persistent lack of agreement about what constitutes the most effective leadership styles in educational settings. According to Hoy and Miskel (2008), there are at least four approaches to the study of educational leadership, including trait, behavior, situational, and contingency. For the purposes of this chapter, we frame leadership as a multifocal construct, based in large part on the tenets of trait-based and situational leadership. This reflects, in part, a renewed interest in the trait-based approach to the study of leadership, and our recognition of the role that individual context plays in shaping the ways in which one leads.

Zaccaro (2007) argues that "a defining core of … leader trait patterns reflects a stable tendency to lead in different ways across disparate organizational domains" (p. 6). Given the wide range of cultural and linguistic diversity among the nation's American Indian and Alaska Native tribes and communities, it seems logical that the schools in which Indigenous students are enrolled vary to a large extent, thus meeting the criteria of disparate organizational domains. Although the study leadership traits or characteristics alone does not constitute a comprehensive view of leadership, the identification of characteristics of effective leaders is an important starting point for studying leadership in Indian education. Such an approach acknowledges and gives weight to the Indigenous Knowledges and ways of knowing that American Indians and Alaska Natives bring to the practice of school leadership. The way in which one opts or is co-opted to lead an educational institution is shaped in large part by one's individual values and attitudes, as well as the contexts or situations within which one leads.

CHARACTERISTICS OF AN
EFFECTIVE LEADER IN INDIAN EDUCATION

The perspectives presented in this chapter are shaped in large part by the voices of current and former members of the American Indian Leadership Program. Participants were asked to identify the characteristics of an effective leader in Indian education. An analysis of responses revealed both similarities and differences in how participants characterized effective leadership in Indian education (see Table 4.1). Both current and former participants indicated that a leader must have integrity and be committed to his or her work in Indian education. Other common characteristics included being a good listener, demonstrating effective communication skills, vision, innovativeness, and serving as a change agent. Participants also cited the importance of community and the local tribal culture. Other common characteristics included understanding the values and issues of the community, connecting to the community, and demonstrating cultural sensitivity and knowledge of the ways and traditions of the community.

Current participants identified political savvy, knowledge of tribal politics, ethical behavior, the importance of relationship building, and knowledge of funding structures as key characteristics of effective leaders. In contrast, former participants indicated that knowledge of Indian education issues, resource utilization, and data driven decision making were important characteristics.

Participants also indicated that leadership is shaped by the contexts within which it occurs. According to Pavlik (1988), "While there are more similarities than there are differences between on and off reservation administrative positions, it is how an individual handles the differences which will ultimately determine if he or she will succeed or fail" (para. 9). Pavlik cited the following characteristics as being unique to leaders in Indian education: (1) people-oriented personality, (2) flexibility, (3) acceptance of the uniqueness of Indian schools, (4) perceives him or herself to be an Indian educator, (5) possesses a specialized set of knowledge and skills, (6) believes in the ability of Indigenous children to succeed, (7) attempts to work with, and when possible, to become involved in the community with which he or she works and (8) dedication and commitment to the education of American Indian and Alaska Native children. According to Lynch and Charleston (1990), "The mark of effective leadership is that it can adapt to changing conditions and create new possibilities for its people. The extent to which Indian leadership in education can accomplish that ...demand[s] creativity and energy in a difficult social environment" (p. 9).

Table 4.1 reflects the wide range of characteristics of effective leaders. As illustrated by Dr. Richard Littlebear (1990), president of Chief Dull Knife College, many of these characteristics are innate and cannot be fully developed in isolation through a formalized leadership preparation program. According to Dr. Littlebear, it is important that we take the knowledge that we gain and strive to make it more applicable to the people with whom we work. This sentiment is echoed by a current participant who wrote,

> it is important to ... [remember] that Native American communities often have a unique social system in place (i.e., clan system, blood relations) that

Table 4.1.   Characteristics of Effective Leaders in Indian Education

Current Participants	*Former Participants/Alumni*
Ability to adapt	Ability to effectively utilize existing resources
Ability to build and sustain relationships	Ability to listen
Ability to work well with the existing political structure	Authentic leadership
Ability and willingness to take risks	Change agent
Attune to the linguistic and cultural diversity of students	Compassion
Aware of community issues and concerns	Commitment
Bravery	Confidence
Change agent (able to institute and sustain change)	Connectedness to tribal communities
Collaborative	Courage
Committed to American Indian and Alaska Native communities	Cultural sensitivity
Creative	Discipline
Effective communicator	Effective communicator
Efficient	Encouraging
Ethical behavior	Fairness
Fortitude	Honesty
Generosity	Imagination
Good listener	Innovative
Innovative	Instructional leadership
Integrity	Knowledgeable of issues relevant to Indian education
Knowledgeable of funding structures at the tribal, local, state, and federal levels	Leads by example
Knowledgeable of the ways and traditions of the community with which he/she works	Resilient
Knowledgeable of tribal politics	Uses data and results to drive decisions
Lifelong learner	Understanding and respectful of Indigenous knowledge systems
Nourished spiritually in order to maintain a proper sense of balance	Visionary
Politically savvy	
Serves the public	
Understands and reflects the values of the schools and communities with which he/she works	
Visionary	
Wise	

permeates the school. Awareness of both the school's and community's ideologies about education, culture, and politics alleviates assumptions and misconceptions of who they are as a distinct group of people.

Although there are a number of ways in which effective leaders in Indian schools and communities differ from their counterparts, there are also a number of ways in which they are quite similar. For example, according to a recent graduate of the AILP, effective leaders are expected to "(a) provide for a safe learning environment for all students; (b) provide a vision or mission for school personnel and community; (c) become an instructional leader (e.g., promote high levels of student learning, support teacher autonomy, provide for professional development opportunities, and recognition of student and staff achievements); (d) [engage in] shared decision-making; (e) [facilitate] team building (i.e., create task forces to tackle issues at the local education agency); (f) be visible throughout the day for students and teachers; (g) provide for effective curriculum development [and] short term/long term strategic planning (i.e., promote language and culture activities on a regular basis); (h) develop consortia with other schools and administrators around the region (i.e., network and build partnerships and relationships including federal and state entities); (i) promote parental involvement activities; (j) effectively communicate with tribal council officials and community members on a regular basis and not [only]on a need-to-know basis; (k) be concise and consistent with everyone when it comes to decision-making; (l) be a risk taker if it benefits the students (i.e., [one] might have to lead a coalition against tribal policy on certain education issues); (m) provide effective assessments and services for [students in special education]; and (n) use effective supervision and staff evaluation techniques."

Defining leadership. A current participant defined leadership as

> the process that empowers members of a group (in a community, organization or institution) to work together toward a common vision or goal. [In contrast], Western leadership focuses on individuals in positions of power [persuading] others to reach a certain goal, whereas Indian beliefs ... are often based on shared leadership and well developed relationships. Indian leadership focuses more on a group of individuals involved in a process that contributes to the good of the community.

He went on to cite an uncle who once said, " 'A native leader is not known for what he has done for himself, but rather what he has done for his people.' "

Implications for administrator preparation programs serving American Indian and Alaska Native students. It is incumbent upon administrator preparation programs to prepare future leaders to work in diverse school settings. As demonstrated in this chapter, effective school leaders must be able to view situations from multiple perspectives, while always striving to act in a manner that is ethical and in the best interest of students. According to one of the current participants, effective leaders in Indian education must be able to look at situations through a dual lens[4] of Native and non-Native approaches to education while moving cautiously, "yet with the integrity and steadfast willingness to stand up for what is right."

One of our greatest challenges as educational leadership faculty is to ensure that our students are adequately prepared to assume leadership roles. For leaders working in Indigenous schools and communities, traditional approaches to leadership development may be insufficient. As one participant wrote,

> In most colleges and universities today, students are taught the American or mainstream style of education, which reinforces Western philosophies. [I have] found this method of education to be effective in educating American Indian students, only about forty to fifty percent of the time. Colleges and universities[5]... need to align with each other and incorporate American Indian thought and philosophies for those students wishing to work in Indian education.

A necessary component of leadership training for Indian educators deals with cultural awareness and sensitivity. One way to achieve this is to involve local experts and community members in professional development and in-service activities at the school and district level. Another approach is to provide opportunities to teach and work in schools serving American Indian and Alaska Native students prior to assuming leadership roles in Indian education. Such experience would help to ensure that future school leaders are knowledgeable of the requirements of federal, state and tribal programs, as well as the unique cultural and social aspects of a particular American Indian or Alaska Native school or community. This would also assist the school leader in interacting more effectively with local tribes and communities.

The need for such preservice experiences was echoed by a participant who also cited the need for community support for school initiatives.

> For tribes to create a positive learning opportunity, the tribal communities must create the opportunity for education "buy-in." For the Navajo Nation, the recent passage of the Tribal Educational Code was a monumental step in taking the reins of Navajo education. This provides the opportunity for a gradual shift in the education paradigm that will focus on the needs of Navajo students as defined by the Navajo Nation.

Implications for tribes and Indian communities. According to one respondent,

> Effective leaders make connections and develop networks with the community, including tribal governments. They know the cultural values, issues, and the different community entities that provide services to community members. They use their communication skills to develop and sustain productive collaborative relationships that benefit both schools and the community.

Collaboration with tribal governments is critical for effective leaders. In recent years, tribal governments have become increasingly involved in the development and delivery of educational programs and services to tribal members.

Collaboration with parents, families, and communities. Although the movement toward Indian control of education helped to facilitate parent, family and community involvement in the development and delivery of educational programs and services, many Indigenous peoples continue to view educational systems as places in which their languages and cultures have been undervalued and in many cases stripped away. This underlying tension requires that educators work to foster a welcoming campus and classroom environment. One way to do this is to actively seek input from families and community members regarding goals and objectives for their students. A welcoming and inclusive learning environment for parents, families, community members and students can also be fostered by the use of curriculum that is representative of Indigenous cultures and languages as well as the contributions of American Indian and Alaska Native peoples throughout history. As one respondent noted, "The door is open for effective Native American leaders to shape and mold a new Native American pedagogy for the millennium." This respondent concluded by writing,

> If one is going to be an effective leader in Indian Education ... he or she is going to have to be attuned to the issues in his or her surrounings. Indian educators must know the culture of the children they are dealing with, if they want to be effective.... Effective leaders ... have to create an atmosphere that is inviting and conducive to [parents who are cautious of the education system]; [one that is] based on a foundation of trust. To be effective, 21st Century Native American leaders ... [one] will have to build trust in a system that has done ... more harm than good. They must keep an open mind and a long term vision that ... incorporate(s) Native American principals and ideals. They need to be conscious of the changes that [will] occur in education in the near future. All of this can be executed effectively by creating a ... trusting environment with an attainable long term vision.

CONCLUSION

As evidenced in this chapter, there are multiple defining characteristics of effective leadership in Indian education. Inherent in these characteristics is the blending of Indigenous and Western educational knowledge and approaches to leadership. Two recurring themes are the centrality of language and culture and the need for leaders who are firmly grounded in who they are as American Indians and Alaska Natives. This grounding enables them to filter their responses to various educational dilemmas and problems of practice through a lens shaped by Indigenous beliefs, values, and practices. Effective leaders not only have the requisite academic and professional knowledge, they are also cognizant of the importance of language and culture to the students and communities with which they work. In sum, the characteristics of effective leadership outlined in this chapter underscore the complex and challenging nature of leadership in Indian education. Among the challenges cited are change, the political nature of education, the need to be innovative and creative, relationship building, ability to see the big picture, and the ability to foster necessary changes in the teaching and learning process.

From our perspective, effective school leadership is shaped in large part by the context in which it occurs. Indian education is in a constant state of flux altered on a daily basis by the political, social, health, and economic realities of a people whose language and culture have for more than 500 years been marginalized by Western systems of education. To combat these forces and promote positive outcomes for American Indian and Alaska Native students, effective leaders must be willing and able to listen, and when appropriate, to relinquish some degree of control to their constituent groups within the local community and to follow the lead of those whom he or she serves. Above all, effective leadership is committed to the continued survivance and flourishing of indigenous peoples across this nation.

Having listened to the voices of current and former members of AILP, we are once again challenged to think and act differently in the preparation of aspiring American Indian and Alaska Native school leaders. It is our belief that a critical part of the teaching and learning process is active and engaged dialogue around the praxis of educational leadership, with praxis defined as an "exercise or practice of an art [or], science" or "customary practice or conduct" (Merriam-Webster, 2006). One of the greatest challenges of the praxis of effective leadership in Indian education is creating and maintaining a balance between the beliefs, customs and practices of the Indigenous communities with which we work and the beliefs, customs and practices of the larger educational community (i.e., local, state, and federal education agencies). The challenge is especially difficult when state and federal mandates leave little or no time for integrating indigenous cultures and languages in schools.

How do we create and maintain this balance while building intellectual and human capital in the field of educational leadership? As we previously noted, this is not a question that can be answered in a simple word, sentence or paragraph. For us, our approach to leadership development is constantly evolving and changing, situational and contextual, based in part upon each new cohort of students and the cultural, linguistic and tribal diversity that they bring to the American Indian Leadership Program, the Educational Leadership Program, the Education Policy Studies Department, the College of Education, the university, and the community at large. Not only does this program speak to the individual needs and concerns of its student members and the communities they plan to serve, it also demonstrates a direct link to national standards for the preparation of educational leaders such as those outlined by the Interstate School Leaders Licensure Consortium (Council of Chief State School Officers, 1996):

> Standard 4: A school administrator is an educational leader who promotes the success of all students by collaborating with families and community members, responding to diverse community interests and needs, and mobilizing community resources. (p. 16)

> Standard 6: A school administrator is an educational leader who promotes the success of all students by understanding, responding to, and influencing the larger political, social, economic, legal, and cultural context. (p. 20)

Members of the AILP have made great sacrifices to further their education; in many cases, leaving their families, friends, communities, and careers hundreds of miles behind as they work to develop and refine their leadership skills. It is hoped that the knowledge gained from their experiences at Penn State will be used to advance Indian education in indigenous communities across the nation. However, it is an ongoing challenge for us, and we are certain, for many others working to prepare cadres of culturally and linguistically diverse educational leaders to deconstruct traditional approaches to the teaching and learning of educational administration and leadership and reconstruct them in such a way that it is more relevant to the linguistically and culturally diverse settings that many of our students return to upon graduation. Although we acknowledge that what makes leadership effective in Indian education varies from tribe to tribe and community to community, we also acknowledge the constants in this equation: knowledge of **and respect** for Indigenous communities; respect for and incorporation of Indigenous languages and cultures; the ability to build and sustain strong relationships with tribal and community members as well as local, state, and national leaders; the ability to communicate effectively; political savvy; an understanding of the complexity of Indian education; and the development of and adherence to a core set of values that places the student at the forefront of his or her work. Effective leaders are motivated foremost by their commitment, vision, knowledge, and passion for Indian education, to provide a relevant education to students. This commitment to the best interests of their students guides their work and reminds them on a daily basis that American Indian and Alaska Native students can and will succeed if their language, culture, values and beliefs are honored.

NOTES

1. The Bureau of Indian Education was formerly known as the Office of Indian Education within the Bureau of Indian Affairs.
2. In this chapter, we use the Indigenous to refer to the collective body of American Indian and Alaska Native students and educators..
3. For additional information, http://www.ed.psu.edu/ailp/
4. When using the term "dual lens," this participant was referring to the sometimes competing demands of non-Native governmental requirements for educational agencies versus the culture of a specific tribe(s).
5. In addition to mainstream colleges and universities, there are more than 30 Tribally Controlled Colleges and Universities, there are approximately 40 Tribally Controlled Colleges and Universities throughout the United State and Canada.

REFERENCES

Council of Chief State School Officers. (1996). *Interstate School Leaders Licensure Consortium: Standards for school leaders*. Washington, DC: Author.

Freeman, C., & Fox, M. (2005). *Status and trends in the education of American Indians and Alaska Natives* (NCES 2005-108). U.S. Department of Education, National Center for Education Statistics. Washington, DC: U.S. Government Printing Office.

Hoy, W. K., & Miskel, C. G. (2008). *Educational administration: Theory, research and practice* (8th ed). New York: McGraw-Hill.

Littlebear, R. (1990). Effective language education practices and native language survival. In J. Reyhner (Ed.), *Effective language education practices and Native language survival* (pp. 1-8). Choctaw, OK: Native American Language Issues. Retrieved April 2006, from http://jan.ucc.nau.edu/~jar/NALI1.html

Lynch, P. D., & Charleston, M. (1990). The emergence of American Indian leadership in education. *Journal of American Indian education, 29*(2), 1–10.

Merriam-Webster online. (2006). *Praxis.* Retrieved July 2, 2006, from http://www.m-w.com/dictionary/praxis

Pavlik, S. (1988, May). Beyond the common ground: Characteristics of effective Indian school administrators. *Journal of American Indian Education, 27*(3), Retrieved January 23, 2008, http://jaie.asu.edu/v27/V27S3bey.htm

Starnes, B. A. (2006, November). Montana's Indian education for All: Toward an education worthy of American ideals. *Phi Delta Kappan.* Retrieved January 23, 2008, from http://www.pdkintl.org/kappan/k_v88/k0611sta.htm

Tippeconnic, J. W., III. (1999). Tribal control of American Indian education: Observations since the 1960s with implications for the future. In K. G. Swisher & J. W. Tippeconnic (Eds.), *Next steps: Research and practice to advance IndianEducation* (pp. 33-52). Charleston, WV: ERIC Clearinghouse on Rural and Small Schools.

Zaccaro, S. J. (2007). Trait-based perspectives of leadership. *American Psychologist, 62*(1), 6–16.

CHAPTER 5

CROSSING CULTURAL BOUNDARIES OR CAUGHT IN POLITICAL CROSSFIRE?

Marian Court

The stories that members of a group pass on to one another are reflective of understandings and practices that are at work in the larger system of cultural understandings that are acted upon by group members. (Denzin, 1989, p. 81)

INTRODUCTION

During the 1990s in Aotearoa/New Zealand there were some fundamental clashes between government and business groups driven by desires to increase school effectiveness in terms of developing a more competitive nation in the global marketplace (Boston, Martin, Pallot, & Walsh, 1996; Peters & Marshall, 1996) and those who looked at school improvement and effectiveness as a fundamental way of coping with personal and social development and equity issues in a growing conflicting world (Codd, 1993; Middleton, 1992; Olssen & Morris Matthews, 1995). Taking the latter view, this paper explores some of the complexities that can blight innovative attempts to develop more inclusive leadership structures and

Leadership and Intercultural Dynamics, pp. 83–103

practices. It demonstrates the point that these need to be built on deep appreciations of the aspirations, values, curriculum and pedagogies of different ethnic groups and cultures, through re-telling and reflecting on the experiences of Mere Katene[1] a young Māori *kaiako* (teacher) of a bilingual, then full immersion Māori language class.

Mere's aspirations for her students should have been able to be successfully achieved at Telford School, a very innovative and seemingly open small New Zealand primary school. Its co-principal partners were aiming to build participatory leadership structures and practices that reflected and respected the values and aims of each of the three strands in the school; the original state strand of two classes, a Montessori strand of two classes and the full immersion Māori class (Court, 2001). Mere's story makes painful reading, however, in its illustrations of how some deep-seated issues around cultural differences and inequalities of power can confound such a well-intentioned innovation. I illuminate these issues by viewing them through the lenses of discourse analysis and some Māori analyses of bicultural relations in school organizations (Durie, 1993, 1997; Johnston, 1999; Smith, 1997).

The research that this paper draws on involved longitudinal case studies of three primary school co-principal initiatives. Fieldwork carried out between 1995 and 2000 included repeat interviews and observations with co-principals, board chairpersons and school staff in each school. Interviews were also undertaken with parents, students, and representatives of state education agencies, national governing boards, principals' associations, and teacher unions, alongside analysis of school and state policy documents. The resulting case study narratives described how each co-principalship was initiated and either established or disestablished. A discourse analysis of these narratives then examined how links between discourse, knowledge and power were being negotiated and challenged, as the new subject position of "co-principal" was being constructed in New Zealand (Court, 2001).

As the researcher, I am, of course, embedded in this study, both in terms of its design and its "findings," which have been constructed within and filtered through my own subjectivity as a middle class, Pākehā academic researcher, who has grown up and been schooled in the mainstream education system in Aotearoa New Zealand. In undertaking a qualitative case study that also drew on discourse analysis, I tried to cross boundaries between "realist" and poststructuralist research approaches to understanding people's everyday experiences. I have described elsewhere (Court, 2004) the dilemmas that this poses for feminist researchers who are working in what Lather (1997, p. 283) has called "the ruins of a feminist ethnography." These include issues around authorial distance and representation and participant voice and confidentiality. Suffice to say here that the following account reflects my own interpretations of what I observed and what my research participants told me during the time I was visiting their school.

TELFORD SCHOOL

Let me now introduce Telford School and the background to its innovative structure and co-principalship. In 1993, Telford School "broke" some traditional school organizational "rules" and boundaries, grasping opportunities made available during the introduction of the national educational administration reforms for local school self-management (Department of Education, 1988). It expanded its traditional state school structures to include three "schools within a school": its original state strand of two classes, a Montessori strand of two classes and a full immersion Mäori language class.

Parents who were in the school in the early 1990s, told me about the background to how this occurred. Marg Tua, a Mäori parent who later became a board member, said that "the school roll was then over 50% Mäori," but after the removal of school zoning as part of the introduction to a market approach to education provision, the school's roll had gone into a rapid decline, indeed, some parents thought that the school was under threat of closing. Marg and Rawinia Hunt, another of the Mäori parents, watched some "white flight" occurring,[2] but said that some Mäori parents were also taking their children elsewhere, because "they couldn't see anything Mäori happening in the school." Phillipa Beecham, one of the Päkehä parents who later became the board chairperson, remembered that it had been a "real effort to keep our little school going, with only a few people with the time and resources to focus on its continuation."

In 1992, as a way of increasing Telford's roll, the then principal, Peter MacDonald, met with the Montessori Association to explore the possibility of establishing a Montessori unit in the school. Ann Howells, who had trained as a teacher in the state system and later as a Montessori teacher, was asked if she would be interested in leading this development and she agreed. She told me that:

> It all happened very quickly—I was appointed on a Thursday, teacher only day was on the Friday and we had to open on the Monday with a class of three children. Ann thought that the principal's view was that Montessori were upper socio-economic people who would come in with all this money and this would help the school.

She found though, that the Montessori group had "come into a hornet's nest that we weren't really aware of. The *whänau*[3] were furious, understandably I think, because setting up the Montessori class had preempted the establishing of a bilingual unit."

Rawinia agreed that was the case:

> Mäori parents had been struggling for years to get a bilingual class up and running, but it had been very difficult to get any Mäori activity going in the school. We wanted kapa haka for our children, we wanted their needs met, but that had been overlooked for a long time—we weren't taken seriously by the management in the school.

Marg also felt that the principal was:

> not very sympathetic to things Mäori. You'd be trying to talk to him about the class and he'd just stand there and listen to you, but the next minute he'd be saying something to someone else while you were trying to have a conversation with him. He'd write something down as if he meant to take action on it—but nothing ever happened.

Not surprisingly, the Mäori parents were "really upset when Montessori was invited in, but we were not going to give in easily," Rawinia said. A public meeting was called, and in Marg's view, "the principal was pushed into setting up the bilingual unit—he couldn't get out of it."

So it was out of these struggles that Telford was reborn at the beginning of 1993, as a three stranded school. Ann remembered that as she was establishing her Montessori class, working from scratch with parents who set up a trust to buy equipment for their classroom. Mere Katene was working alongside the Mäori parents who had formed themselves into a *whänau* support and management group, to establish a bilingual class. From Ann's perspective, the two groups encountered similar problems. She saw both groups as "having a vision of where we were going, but meeting difficulties as well as advantages in being separate units in a state school." Rawinia said, however, that while she found Ann helpful when she spoke with her sometimes about what was happening in each of their strands:

> When we got our bilingual unit established we were almost isolated. We didn't have the skill level or the knowledge level to do what we wanted to do in the class or to understand the whole system.

Neither did the *whänau* have the financial resources of the mainly better off Montessori parents. These differences persisted, causing some tensions between the three strands in the school.

A CO-PRINCIPALSHIP IS ESTABLISHED

In August 1994, the principal left the school and Kate Nicholson was appointed as relieving teaching principal for the rest of that year. This meant that all five teachers in the school were then women, four being Päkehä (White Anglo/European) and one Mäori. They taught 106 children, 63 of whom were Päkehä, 41 Mäori, and two Pacific Islanders. These factors, of a predominantly White female staff, teaching children of mixed ethnicity, in a relatively small primary school, are common in New Zealand.[4] Although the school's organization into three different educational "valuational communities" (Furman, 1998, p. 314) was unusual, this also reflected, in a particularly visible way, New Zealand's wider ethnic and class divisions and inequalities. The original state strand and Montessori strand parents were mainly Päkehä and middle class, while the *whänau* strand parents were Mäori, who held mainly working class jobs.

After her appointment, Kate quickly established that she could work well with each of the strands, but she was concerned about the tension and distrust between them that she had noticed when she arrived. She also soon became concerned about the huge paperwork demands of the teaching principalship and their encroachment on available time for her family. These two factors, along with her commitment to professional collaborative practice, motivated her to ask Ann Howells to apply with her for the permanent principal's position when it was advertised towards the end of the year. She suggested that they could share the position as co-principals, splitting the paperwork between them and working together to build more unity across the three strands in the school through introducing school wide shared decision making and participatory management practices. Kate thought that although she was a Päkehä woman, as she spoke *Te Reo* (Mäori language), she could represent both the state and the *whänau* strands, while Ann, also Päkehä but trained and experienced in Montessori teaching and management, could represent that strand.

Ann initially felt a little nervous about this idea, but after thinking about it, she agreed and together, the two women developed a combined application and co-principal proposal, which they presented to their board. The board, which was made up of representatives of each strand, were delighted with their application and suggestions, and appointed them to start as co-principals at the beginning of 1995.

Underpinning Kate's and Ann's co-principal proposal was a desire to cross and break down some boundaries that have persisted within the bureaucratic organization of schooling. In terms of crossing the traditional principal/teacher management divide, although they could not include all the teachers in a leadership collective, because two were beginning teachers and the other was a relieving teacher, they set out to "involve all in shared decision making and in regular review of decisions affecting pupil welfare, property, spending in curriculum and staff development." When they put their proposal to the staff, Frances, who taught in the original state strand alongside Kate, Deborah, the other teacher in the Montessori strand and Abbie, who was the principal release teacher, accepted that in small schools like Telford all the staff had to cooperate. They were attracted to the idea of a co-principalship as a supportive, collegial model, seeing it also, Abbie said, as "a good model for the children, particularly in a school like this where you have such diversity. It is good for them to see the sharing of responsibility."

However, Mere was concerned about becoming more fully involved in school wide decision making and administration responsibilities. She felt that as a beginning teacher, she needed to be putting a lot of time into her class teaching and as she said, "There was no reading material or specific Māori resources in the school." Kate and Ann felt a little worried about Mere's stance, but agreed that they "would have to work round this situation." Their dilemma here was one commonly experienced by principals who are committed to distributive participatory leadership practices. How much can be "demanded" of teachers in terms of expecting them to be involved in school-wide decision making, when accountability lines, salary, and status differentials between teachers and principals legitimate teachers who say "You are paid to make the decisions so don't require me to be involved?"

In terms of crossing professional/lay divides, the co-principals also wanted to encourage more active participation by the board in not only policymaking but also in the shared administrative tasks of the co-principals. More importantly, with no regard to the themes of this paper, Kate and Ann wanted to cross the "divides" of educational philosophy and values that underpinned the division of the school into its three strands. The first step they took here was to work with Phillippa, the board chairperson, to involve the whole school in reviewing the existing school charter. A series of meetings were held with the teachers and parents in each strand to identify firstly their educational philosophies for the children in their own classes, and then their aims for a set of values, beliefs and vision for the school as a whole. Phillippa facilitated individual and whole school discussions of the latter and after several redraftings, most felt proud about the resulting revised charter, which described their school as "unique" and stated that:

> It incorporates three strands, each delivering the national curriculum through its own method - two of these are strands of special character. As well as the original part of the school which provides a typical New Zealand

state education, the school has a Māori language immersion unit and a unit
in which the children are taught in accordance with the Montessori philosophy and teaching method. (Telford School Charter, 1995, p. 2)

Despite this encouraging beginning, as I have explained elsewhere, the
co-principals encountered a range of difficulties over the next 2 years
(Court, 2003, 2004). These included problems emerging from Ann's lack
of experience in management in the state system and some exhausting
demands on both women in terms of having to negotiate and deal with
some significant material and cultural inequalities of resourcing and
power between the teachers and parents of each of the strands. I do not
want to repeat my analyses of those issues here, nor focus unduly on a
range of associated leadership dilemmas that the co-principals' tried to
deal with, such as how much authority or decision veto power a principal
should retain within espoused participatory decision making. Rather, the
next part of this article centres on Mere's story about her experiences in
this innovative school, describing her difficulties and dilemmas as she
juggled her commitments to her students with the multiple and conflicting expectations of others.

MERE'S STORY

In 1994, when Mere was appointed as the first *kaiako* (teacher) of the bilingual class, this was also her first teaching position. She had just graduated as a Māori speaking teacher trained to work in bi-lingual and
immersion classes. When I began my research in the school in the third
term of that year, a *kaiārahi reo* (language teaching assistant) had just been
appointed to help her development of the bi-lingual unit into a full
immersion Māori language class. They were working with their students
to transform their classroom into a *marae*[5] space and a *whare nui tipuna*
(house of the ancestors, meeting house). Mere, the *kaiārahi reo* and the
children were painting *kowhaiwhai* (patterns) on the *heke* (rafter beams).
They had pasted black paper over the walls and windows, so that they
could paint on the *poupou* (carved figures) and *tukutuku* (woven wall panel
patterns) that adorn the inside of a *whare nui*. Mere told me later, "the
children helped us lay down the *tikanga* of the room- by the time we were
finished they knew the true meaning of the marae." She was excited about
what was being achieved.

As time went on however, Mere found it increasingly difficult to juggle
the work she was doing with her class and the expectations of the board
and the co-principals that she should be providing *kapa haka*[6] for all the
Māori students in the school. In her view she had been employed "to

teach Māori to the immersion class children." Rawinia agreed with her, saying:

> We want our kids to learn Māori. We like to share our knowledge but, you know, all our energies need to go into getting this (class) up and running and we can't do that if we have to keep giving out all the time to others in the school.

However, Kate thought that Mere and the *kaiārahi reo* should be working

> with all the Māori children. The application for funding that I put in to the Ministry in 1994, that had been developed with input from the whānau, outlined that view and it was on those grounds that we got the funding.

This requirement gave rise to a range of dilemmas for Mere. In particular, she said that when she had to speak English with other adults or children while doing *kapa haka* with them,

> I found that really hard, because I spoke Māori with my kids, but I had to swap in front of them for other adults and the kids were sitting there saying, "Oh but you said you had to talk Māori to us all the time!"

Another pressure was being put on Mere, from some of the *whānau* parents themselves. They were asking her to ensure that their children achieved equally in *Te Reo* and English, in *tikanga* Māori and the mainstream curriculum, but they were querying the time given to *mihimihi* (greetings) or *karakia* (prayers). When she reflected later on this Mere said:

> Really some of the educated parents were looking at it in what I would call a Pākehā way. They did not have a full understanding of what we were doing.... Like they would come in and we would be having karakia or mihimihi and they would say, "Why does it take so long to do that? In the mainstream it only takes ten minutes." I was having to explain myself all the time. Whānau hui (meetings) were really horrible for me because it was always, "Why haven't you done this? Where's this?" And I thought, "I've explained to you what we are doing, where we are going," but it wasn't good enough—that's how I felt, it wasn't good enough for a lot of them.

Some of her own students' parents also objected to her use of *Te Reo* at times, such as on the children's reports. Mere described her reaction when some said,

> "My child does immersion, not me." That was a big knife in my heart after a while. I would be teaching their kids all about whānau and how we need to

have all the Māori values and it wasn't happening in front of them at home— only at school, nine till three.

As 1994 drew to a close, Mere also found that increasingly she was getting "caught in the middle of all the politics of the three strands in the school." She described the Montessori parents as:

> very business orientated and knowing how to do that management sort of stuff, and our parents were saying, "Well why can't we get those resources and things?" I thought, well if the Montessori parents offered the school a whole new building, for example, they have the money and can afford it, so that's good—let them do it. But some of my parents worried about the political side of things, sort of asking, "What are they wanting from us?"

In 1995, the issue of Mere taking *kapa haka* with the whole school came to a head, when it was brought up at a board meeting. A resolution, proposed by the *whānau*, was that the board employ someone else to take responsibility for cultural and language maintenance for the rest of the school, and this was done. Privately Kate thought however, that this "undermined the authority of the principals, because we shouldn't be told by a group of parents that particular teachers shouldn't do this or that." Kate's opinion was supported by the board chairperson, who acknowledged that "Mere was a great teacher and her kids' self esteem was great," but in terms of the rest of the school, "it was really quite difficult because Mere seemed to be wanting to be not involved."

This perception was not entirely wrong. Kate and Ann had been encouraging Mere to participate in the school wide shared leadership processes, such as in chairing staff meetings occasionally. But Mere told me:

> I didn't think I was capable enough to go into those other management sides of the school because I was only getting certificated as a teacher.... I was more worried about the kids I had and what I had to do as a teacher to fulfil my curriculum stuff.

Partly as a way of keeping focused on her class, Mere had begun doing things with her students during lunch breaks. Partly to avoid the school politics, she had also stopped going to the staff room for morning tea. She said that she and the *kaiārahi reo* "sort of lost contact with what was happening in the rest of the school in a way, not by choice, but because we didn't want to get involved in the politics and in the running of it all."

It is probably not surprising that by the end of the second term in 1995, the relationship between Mere and the co-principals had become rather strained. Kate felt that although she did attend staff meetings,

Mere was participating only on her own terms, "with no input into discussions on the vision of the school whatever." Kate was disappointed and thought that it had "a kind of demoralising effect on everyone else" and both she and Ann were worried that Mere was becoming "politically separatist," as Kate put it, and committed to establishing the immersion class as a separate entity on the Telford School site. Kate decided to raise this at the next *whānau hui* and she told me later that, "the whānau made it absolutely clear that they did not want two separate entities in the school. They really wanted to be very much part of the school." This was corroborated by Rawinia when she said that some of the whānau did feel that Mere seemed to want to "take them away from the school, like to set up a kura kaupapa, and this was hard, because we did not want that."

The other teachers also felt that Mere was withdrawing from them and from their collective work in the school. This judgement was reinforced by their reading of Mere's actions in covering the windows of her classroom with black paper. From within Mere's cultural world-view, this was part of creating of a *whare nui* within a *marae* space—it was exciting, empowering for the children and sacred. Within one Pākehā teacher's world-view however, different interpretations were being made—she tentatively told me, "It was *black* paper, you know."

It seemed to me at the time that there was some classic "talking past each other" occurring between different individuals and groups. In particular, while Mere was being seen by several people as becoming politically separatist, Mere saw herself as "just keeping on doing what I was employed to do- teach Māori."

At the end of 1995, Mere and the *kaiārahi reo* resigned. Mere was burnt out from the struggles over negotiating conflicting expectations for her work and ongoing struggles over finding or making resources. She was pregnant and wanted and needed time out.

EPILOGUE

At Telford, when Ruth was interviewed for the vacant *kaiako* position, the expectation that she would be involved in some school wide activities and shared decision making was explored with her. Ruth was happy for this to happen, and the new *kaiārahi reo*, a fluent speaker of *Te Reo*, was also supportive of the idea that at times Ruth might work with the other strands in the school. And Mere? Two years later, she accepted a teaching position in a *kura kaupapa*, a full immersion Māori language school, where curriculum and pedagogies were consistent with *tikanga* Māori. When I spoke with her, she was excited about her job and what was being achieved in what she described as a very happy school.

REFLECTIONS

In the following reflections, I use a discourse analysis that draws on some Mäori analyses of teaching and organizational practices, to unearth how politics of cultural recognition and misrecognition were in play in the shared leadership initiative at Telford School. My purpose here is to illuminate how well intentioned efforts to effect school leadership changes can be undermined by pre-existing and persisting social structures and practices that benefit one group's ways of seeing and being in the world over "others."

Despite what could be read as a later happy ending, Mere's story is saddening in its illustrations of the marginalizing of dilemmas and difficulties many Mäori teachers encounter when trying to work within their own cultural world views and practices within mainstream schools. Mere's experiences resonate strongly, for example, with some of Waitere-Ang's findings in her 1999 study of a group of Mäori women educators who were working in bi-lingual and full immersion classes. These women found that they were "placed at odds with a system" and they had to find strategies to cope with multileveled "borderlands" and binaries that could constrain and delimit their agency (Waitere-Ang, 1999, p. 235). In their different work sites, the women were using "a mix of holding silence and breaking silence" as a strategy of resistance and change (p.235). "By being silent, safe spaces were created in which contrary views and their oppositional forms of social critique could be safely held without evoking the antagonism of those in influential positions of power" (p. 242). Mere's strategy of withdrawing from the staff room and focussing on her work in her own classroom is illuminated by this analysis.

It seemed particularly ironical to me, though, that her strategy was necessary in a school which, of the three New Zealand examples of primary school co-principalships that I studied, was making the most effort to be inclusive of Mäori aspirations and values. In Telford School's charter, for example, the parents and teachers had stated:

> We want a school that has three strands contributing equally to the school as a whole, and each meeting the particular needs of its community of children, parents and caregivers. We want these strands woven together by co-operation and tolerance to create a school in which diversity is valued and all children can develop to their full potential. We want a school that honours the Treaty of Waitangi.[7] (Telford School Charter, 1995, p. 2)

Some further Charter goals articulated the school's aims "to ensure that Mäori children have their ethnic and cultural heritage affirmed" and that "the entire school community learns about and respects the diverse cultural heritage of New Zealand people by acknowledging the unique place of Māori; New Zealand's role in the Pacific; and the value and diversity of other cultures in the world." These seem at first glance to be openly valuing Māori people and culture, and about building tolerance, respect, and care for others. These are important aims for the building of a democratic community that treats others as equals and values difference and in articulating them, Telford School could be described as a bicultural, "Māorifriendly" school (Johnston, 1999, p. 78). Indeed, most of its Pākehā teachers and board members did appear to be very supportive of Māori aspirations and the school was going some way towards improving educational practices for Māori.

Johnston (1999) has argued however, that Pākehā "Māori-friendly" attitudes and practices are focused on biculturalism as a way of reducing prejudice, rather than on changing dominant power relations. Indeed, she points out that this approach is "unable to address the unequal power relations between Māori and Pākehā because Pākehā are effectively able to control the level and manner of Māori involvement" (p. 78).

The presence of these power inequalities is revealed in a discourse analysis of the language of the Telford School Charter. Like Kate's and Ann's proposal for a co-principalship, which aimed to effect *acknowledgement* of the differences within the school and to ensure that the school's emphasis was on *reflecting* the values of each of the three strands, the school Charter statements were about *including* existing cultural affiliations. That is, the cultural aims for the school were being articulated within a liberal discourse of *toleration* of difference—rather than a more radical *revaluing* of cultural differences (see Court, 2003 for a more detailed analysis of this point; Fraser, 1997). The effect is to re-embed New Zealand's existing White-centric discursive power relations. This is because the liberal discourse of toleration is constructed within the worldview (beliefs, values, and practices) of the Pākehā dominant group, which takes on the status of the unspoken norm (Johnston, 1999). This is unremarked as neutral, while culturally different beliefs, values, and practices, in this case, of Māori, are treated as "different' in ways that subordinate and devalue them (Foucault, 1980).

A Māori-centred (Durie, 1997) approach, however, "aims at addressing unequal power relations ... by incorporating appropriate decision-making forums ... by Māori for Māori" (Johnston, 1999, p. 78). These more genuinely empowering Kaupapa Māori (Smith, 1997) organizational approaches address political claims for self determination and autonomy through structural changes that enable Māori participation in decision making on their own terms. Was such an approach possible in Telford School's shared leadership structures and practices? It is helpful to think about this question in relation to Durie's (1993) bi-cultural continuum, reproduced in Figure 5.1.

A Bicultural Continuum (Durie 1993)

	Unmodified Mainstream Institutions	Introduction of a Maori Perspective	Maori Involvement in Mainstream Institutions	Parallel Maori Institutions	Independent Maori Institutions
Principles	▪ Homogeneity	▪ Cultural Pluralism	▪ Participation	▪ Partnership	▪ Rangatiratanga
Aims	▪ Uniform approach	▪ Cultural Sensitivity	▪ Maori Dimension with Corporate Identity	▪ Integrated Maori Development (Social Cultural Economic)	▪ Mana Maori Motuhake ▪ Maori Management of Maori Resources
Goals	▪ Simplicity ▪ Institutional Focus ▪ Consumer Adaptation	▪ Greater Understanding ▪ Cultural exchange ▪ User friendly	▪ Institutions Representative of community ▪ Effective Maori Participation	▪ Shared Decision-making ▪ Contractual relationships ▪ Shared objectives	▪ Retention Maori structure, processes ▪ Maori control ▪ Tikanga Maori
Limitations	▪ Cultural Oppression ▪ Institutional Racism	▪ Superficial ▪ Cultural Erosion	▪ Conflict of Tikanga ▪ Assimilation	▪ Duplication ▪ Double Standards ▪ Organisational confusion	▪ Economies of scale ▪ Separate Development

Figure 5.1.   Durie's (1993) bicultural continuum.

The co-principals' efforts to build shared, shared objectives, and contractual relationships, through agreed statements recorded in the school's charter do seem to reflect some of the partnership principles that Durie identifies in institutions that feature parallel Māori/Pākehā structures. The school was not aiming, though, for fully integrated Māori development in terms of goals for social, cultural, and economic development, as Durie identifies in parallel institutions. For example, while the *whānau* could and did identify their own philosophy for their strand, including their educational values and aims, final decisions about staffing and resource acquisitions had to be approved by the co-principals and board, as they do in all state schools in New Zealand.

Could Telford be placed then, at the level of supporting Māori involvement in a mainstream institution? It *was* aiming for Māori participation, yes, but from both Mere's and Marg's perspectives, it was not enabling "effective" participation. Marg told me that although she was able to be a voice for the *whānau* on the board, Māori participation in decision making at that level was compromised by the fact that they did not have a Māori co-principal. Although Kate could speak *te reo* and was sympathetic to things Māori, she was, as Marg put it, "still wearing two hats."

Moreover, the board wanted Marg to "give the Māori viewpoint" on issues, but as she pointed out, "I could not do that. Individuals within the *whānau* held different perspectives on different issues, and I needed to have time to go back and consult with them." The issue here is not only about allowing enough time for this to happen, but also that the Pākehā habit of treating Māori individuals as a homogeneous group needs to change. As Durie (1995, p.1) has pointed out, "Maori are as diverse and complex as other sections of the population, even though they may have certain characteristics and features in common."

Given these points, would it be more accurate to place Telford School at the level of introducing a Māori perspective? (See Figure 5.1). As the school was exhibiting principles of "cultural pluralism," with aims for "cultural sensitivity" and goals for "greater understanding" and "cultural exchange," its approach does seem to fit here. Concomitantly, as my earlier analysis suggests, it could also be described as reflecting the characteristics of a liberal, bicultural reformism, as identified by Durie in Figure 5.2.

That is, Telford's approach to bicultural relations did have its origin in invocations of the Treaty of Waitangi and it was aiming to increase

Partnership and Biculturalism (Durie 1993)

	PARTNERSHIP	BICULTURAL REFORMISM	BICULTURAL DISTRUBTIVISM
ORIGINS	1. Treaty of Waitangi 2. Tribes & Crown share in National development.	1. Treaty of Waitangi 2. NZ heritage based on two main cultures	1. Treaty of Waitangi 2. Continuing Maori Sovereignty
OBJECTIVES	1. Equity and Social Justice for tribes & other NZers.	1. Cultural sensitivity & awareness in State institutions 2. All NZers able to understand some Maori & Pakeha.	1. Iwi Nationhood 2. Maori control over things Maori
EXAMPLES	▪ Maori Fishing Commission ▪ Mana, Maccess	▪ Taha Maori in schools] ▪ Maori units in Government Departments ▪ Cultural Advisory Officers	▪ Kura Kaupapa Maori ▪ Runanga-a-iwi ▪ National Maori Congress
FOCUS	▪ Negotiation with government ▪ Maori delivery systems	▪ Introduction of a Maori perspective ▪ Attitudinal Change	▪ Exercise of tino rangatiratanga ▪ Development of Maori institutions operating within tikanga Maori.
COMPLICATIONS	▪ Inequity prevents genuine partnership ▪ Tribes become State agents ▪ Crown usurps role of the other partner.	▪ Maori expertise eroded ▪ Maori culture compromised ▪ Cultures thrown into conflict	▪ Maori isolation from mainstream ▪ Alienation of non-aligned Maori ▪ Parallel development becomes separate development.
ADVANTAGES	▪ Increased Maori participation. ▪ Equitable distribution of goods and services ▪ Maori initiative allowed to flourish.	▪ Improved access to goods and services ▪ Institutions user friendly ▪ Better understanding between Maori and Pakeha	▪ Maori solutions for Maori situations ▪ Strengths of Maori society enhanced ▪ Equality of power

Figure 5.2.   Durie's (1993) partnership and bicultural continuum.

understandings of "New Zealand heritage as based in two main cultures." The school was aiming to build "cultural sensitivity and awareness in a State institution" and to ensure that its students were "able to understand some Mäori" as well as "some Päkehä (Durie, 1993, p. 31). Was it, then, also running the risk of the complications that Durie identifies: erosion of Mäori expertise, compromise of Mäori culture and having the two cultures being thrown into conflict? Mere's story indicates that each of the latter complications was occurring at Telford. While the school's approach could be described as tolerantly Mäori-friendly, with well-intentioned aims of improving Mäori/Päkehä understandings and relations, the school seemed to be making only superficial moves towards shifting inequalities of power (see Figure 5.1). This analysis is becoming rather depressing! What can be done to help change the persistence of these kinds of unfair and inequitable social power dynamics?

DISCOURSE ANALYSIS AND POWER

In thinking about these issues, I have found Foucault's (1980) analyses helpful for considering how my own use of language can insidiously re-inscribe the very power relations that I may be trying to change. Foucault argued that by going to the extremities of where power is exercised we will be able to identify how social relations of power "cannot be established, consolidated, nor implemented without the production, accumulation and functioning of discourse" (p. 93). That is, individual and group exercising of power cannot occur without the evoking of particular discursive configurations of "truth" that shape what can and cannot be said in particular situations, who is authorized to speak and who is excluded. I have already illustrated how a liberal egalitarian discourse of toleration can be a powerful "truth" discourse that maintains Päkehä as "normal" and Mäori as "other" in Aotearoa/New Zealand. The Päkehä teacher's comment about Mere's classroom windows being "black, you know" is worth thinking about further here, in the light of Pecheux's (1975) notion of "pre-constructed" discourse.

The concept of pre-constructed discourse is a tool that can assist us to "dig beneath the surface" of apparently innocuous everyday "bits of chat," to reveal how dominant social power relations can be perpetuated in language practices. Pre-constructed discourses are the "always already there" or the "what everyone knows" about how things are in societies. They evoke long established and hierarchically ordered oppositions that persist as base patterns of meanings and understandings, which listeners can be "hooked into" through the use of universalizing phrases like "as everyone knows," or "as anyone can see" (Hennessy, 1993, p. 77). The comment about the paper over the windows being "*black*, you know" could be interpreted as offered within a Päkehä pre-constructed discourse about race relations, in which Whiteness is un-remarked and normalized as "neutral," while blackness is marked and re-marked as not only different, but also "not normal." The tagged on "you know" was functioning to hook me, the listener, into further sets of underlying oppositions that "we all know about": between White/Anglo-European/civilized, and Black/native / savage/violent.

Whatever interpretation is made of the comment "it was black, you know," the much more explicit naming of Mere's actions by Kate and others, as *politically separatist*, were negatively positioning Mere as a threatening outsider, associating her with radical Mäori revolutionary aspirations and practices. It could be argued that lying beneath the surface of these two phrases, is a "memory" or trace for Pakeha listeners of incidents such as when the Prime Minister, Helen Clark, broke into tears at a national ceremony commemorating Waitangi Day, when her right to speak was challenged by Titiwhai Harawira, a radical Mäori activist, or when some other Mäori radicals have thrown mud (literally) at some Päkehä people of national standing. Within the context of Mere's story, the comments "'it was black, you know" and "political separatism" evoke unspoken links with issues of racial apartheid and our country's struggles over unjust race relations. I suggest that what is lying being the surface here are some fears about potentially painful, or even dangerous social divisions and disorder occurring right in the school's own backyard. In this case, the power of a White "regime of truth" about race relations in New Zealand.

The Päkehä colonizers' role in subjugating Mäori is not remarked in this "truth" discourse, but instead the spotlight is focused on Mäori, as "other"—different, deficient, needing assistance to progress within mainstream schools for example, and, in Mere's case, defiant and possibly dangerous. It could be suggested then that within their everyday language practices, some of the teachers at Telford School were re-constructing and transmitting the values, beliefs, categories and meanings of the dominant Päkehä version of race relations, to Mere's detriment. Consider, for example, if Mere had been white, how her actions of transforming her classroom into a *marae* space and staying there with her students during morning interval would have been judged by the rest of the teachers? Would they not have said she was conscientious and hard-working, rather than assuming that she was building a destructive separatism?

Mere's comments also indicate that some of the *whänau* parents were implicated in these discursive power relations. Her description of those parents as "the educated ones ... thinking in a Pakeha way" suggest her own analysis of what was happening reflected a colonized consciousness of separation from mainstream power. The meanings that Mere was constructing around her actions went largely unheard in this environment, if, indeed, they were even spoken to other teachers in the school. The effect was to position her as being in opposition to and obstructive of the school's aims, rather than as having legitimate aspirations that should have been, and could have been supported and applauded, given this school's aims to value diversity and each strand equally.

MOVING ON

Mere's story highlighted for me how some taken for granted assumptions about race and ethnic differences and unequal power relations can persist beneath the surface of radical innovations, blighting the best intentions of educational change agents. I wondered whether any different outcomes would have eventuated if the shared leadership initiative at Telford had included a fully registered, experienced Mäori teacher within a co-principal triumvirate? Indeed, I began to wonder whether a bi-cultural partnership, in Durie's (1993) sense of parallel development with equal decision-making power, was even possible in mainstream schools.

There are a few Mäori/Päkehä bi-cultural co-principalships in some primary and secondary schools in New Zealand. One, at Mountain View Primary School in Auckland, has been lauded in Education Review Office (ERO) reports and in the media as successfully turning around a school that was failing to provide adequate educational programmes. In its 2001 report on this school, ERO noted:

> The March 1998 report identified the appointment of the co-principals as the major impetus for positive change. This led to the improvement of curriculum management systems and a strong commitment to Mäori education The motto "Kia puäwai" (to nourish and nurture) is enacted within the school. Students learn to care for people, plants and property, and the school demonstrates a strong wairua of value and respect for its students. Children are provided with learning experiences that assist them to achieve their best and to maintain a strong sense of their own cultural beliefs, background and identity.... A sense of family (whanaungätanga) pervades the operation (kaupapa) of the school.... Te reo me öna tikanga (language and culture) are central. These features are a major contributory factor to the increased success and participation of Mäori students).... The inclusive nature of the school ensures that children with special learning needs and from non-English speaking backgrounds are well integrated. (pp. 2–8)

The same document also reported that the school's "co-principals' leadership style is visionary, dynamic and inclusive. (It) contributes to the unique Mountain View School culture and the strong sense of *whänau* within the school." This report is very encouraging in terms of what a bicultural Mäori/Päkehä co-principal partnership approach could offer schools. It throws some light on how a different approach to a "culturally inclusive" shared leadership may have been more enabling of Mere's aspirations at Telford School.

Deciding that these issues needed further exploration, I invited my Mäori colleague and friend, Hine Waitere, to develop with me a study of bi-cultural leadership partnerships. We called it "Nau te raurau, naku te raurau, ka ora ai te kura; Building Bi-cultural Leadership in Schools" (Court & Waitere-Ang, 2004). In this study, we set out to explore how Mäori and Päkehä co-principal partners and other bi-cultural teacher leader partnerships understand themselves as Mäori and Päkehä and how they position themselves in relation to bi-cultural identity politics in Aotearoa New Zealand (Bell, 2004). We wanted also to look at practices of cultural school leadership collaborations within shifting notions of and commitments to bi-culturalism. We carried out a number of interviews and observations in one school, but then one of the co-principal participants retired and this, combined with our own other work demands interrupted the study. However, and probably more significantly, we had realised that before continuing to research other people's bi-cultural relationships and partnerships, we needed to clarify and enhance our own understandings and practices of bi-culturalism within our own research relationship.

This work, begun through many conversations about our families and communities and our experiences in the academy, continues, as we reflect on our own relationship and those with others, as we talk and think together about our teaching, supervision, reading, researching, and writing. It has been at times a challenging journey, but always an exciting and richly rewarding one. An important milestone has just been reached. Over the last year we have researched and written together a reflective discussion of Mäori education as alternative/alter-native /(alter)native. This chapter, written for *Alternative Education in the 21st Century* (Waitere & Court, 2009) talks back to, while talking through, hegemonic sites of power. We explore Mäori and Päkehä politics, policy, and practices as evidenced historically and currently in education, and as evidenced in Nga Manu Korero, the state initiated but Mäori coopted, developed, and celebrated secondary schools Mäori speech competitions (Waitere & Court, in press). Significantly for the point being made here, the chapter also records in images and in analyses, some of our reflections on questions we asked of ourselves in relation to what it means to be Mäori and Päkehä in a research and writing relationship.

ACKNOWLEDGMENT

A previous version of this chapter appeared in the *New Zealand Journal of Educational Leadership*, *20*(1), 47–64 (2005). Copyright permission granted by publisher.

NOTES

1. All names of individuals and places in this account are fictitious.
2. For discussions of this issue, see Gordon, 1994; Lauder, Hughes, & Watson, 1999.
3. *Whānau* means extended family. This is the name the Māori parents chose for their management group supporting the bilingual class.
4. *Kapa haka* was originally the name given to a Māori culture club. In schools these focused originally on teaching singing, dancing, and *haka* skills, but they developed into being an important part of Māori language and cultural maintenance and advancement.
5. New Zealand has an unusually large number of small primary schools, with around 60% having a roll of less than 200.
6. *Marae* means in simple terms, home and tribal meeting place. However, it is more than just a set of buildings (including traditionally the whare nui – central meeting house, whare kai—dining house, church and urupa—cemetery. It has been described as the whi rangatira mana me rangatira wairua (place of greatest prestige and spirituality); the whi Mori rangatira iwi (place that heightens people's dignity) and the whi rangatira tikanga Mori (place where Mori customs are given ultimate expression) (Turoa & Turoa, 1986, p.6).
7. The Treaty of Waitangi is the founding document for New Zealand as a dual culture nation. When it was signed in 1840, the British Crown promised to honour the right of Māori people to retain their way of life and language, and to give them equal status as citizens. These promises were not kept, however. Assimilatory state policies and large-scale land purchases and confiscations followed. Consequently, Māori have struggled against political marginalization and economic disadvantages to ensure the survival of their language and culture and to achieve "official" status as the *tangata whenua*.

REFERENCES

Bell, A. (2004). *Relating Maori and Pakeha: The politics of indigenous and settler identities*. Unpublished PhD thesis, Massey University, Palmerston North, New Zealand.

Boston, J., Martin, J., Pallot, J., & Walsh, P. (1996). *Public management: The New Zealand model*. Auckland, New Zealand: Oxford University Press.

Codd, J. A. (1993). Equity and choice: The paradox of New Zealand educational reform. *Curriculum Studies, 1*(1), 75–90.

Court, M. R. (2001). *Sharing school leadership: Narratives of discourse and power.* Unpublished PhD thesis, Massey University, Palmerston North, New Zealand.

Court, M. R. (2003). Towards democratic leadership. Co-principal initiatives. *International Journal of Leadership in Education, 6*(2), 161–183.

Court, M. R. (2004). Using narrative and discourse analysis in researching co-principalships. *International Journal of Qualitative Studies in Education, 17*(5), 579–603.

Court, M. R., & Waitere-Ang, H. J. (2004, November). *Nau te raurau, naku te raurau, ka ora ai te kura: Building bi-cultural leadership in schools?* Paper presented at the New Zealand Association for Research in Education Conference in the symposium "Turning the Co-principalship Kaleidoscope: Past, Present and Future Developments," Wellington, New Zealand.

Denzin, N. K. (1989). *Interpretive biography.* Newbury Park, CA: SAGE.

Department of Education. (1988). *Tomorrow's schools: The reform of education administration in New Zealand.* Wellington, New Zealand: Government Printer.

Durie, M. (1993, September). *Maori and the state: Professional and ethical implications for the public service.* Paper presented at the Public Service Senior Management Conference, Wellington, New Zealand.

Durie, M. (1995, February). *Nga matatinii Maori: Diverse Maori Realities.* Paper presented at the Maori Health Framework Seminar, Turangawaewae Marae, Ngaruawahia, New Zealand.

Durie, M. (1997, December). Identity, access and Maori development. *New Zealand Journal of Educational Administration, 12*, 41–45.

Education Review Office. (2001). *Accountability Review Report: Mountain View School.* Wellington, New Zealand: Author.

Foucault, M. (1980). *Power/Knowledge: Selected interviews and other writings 1972–1977.* London: Harvester Wheatsheaf.

Fraser, N. (1997). *Justice interruptus: Critical reflections on the "Postsocialist" Condition.* New York: Routledge.

Furman, G. C. (1998). Postmodernism and community in schools: Unravelling the paradox. *Educational Administration Quarterly, 34*(3), 298–328.

Gordon, L. (1994). Is school choice a sustainable policy for New Zealand? A review of recent research findings and a look to the future. *New Zealand Annual Review ofEeducation, 4*, 9–24.

Hennessy, R. (1993). *Materialist feminism and the politics of discourse.* New York: Routledge.

Johnston, P. M. G. (1999). "In through the out door": Policy developments and processes for Maori. *New Zealand Journal of Educational Studies, 34*(1), 77–85.

Lather, P. (1997). Drawing the line at angels: Working the ruins of a feminist ethnography. *Qualitative Studies in Education, 10*(3), 285–304.

Lauder, H., Hughes, D., & Watson, S. (1999). The introduction of educational markets in New Zealand: Questions and consequences. *New Zealand Journal of Educational Studies, 34*(1), 86–98.

Middleton, S. (1992). Gender equity and the school charter. In S. Middleton & A. Jones (Eds.), *Women and education in Aotearoa: 2* (pp. 1–17). Wellington, New Zealand: Bridget Williams Books.

Olssen, M., & Morris Matthews, K. (1995). *Education, democracy and reform.* Auckland: New Zealand Association for Research in Education in conjunction with the Research Unit for Maori Education Education Dept. The University of Auckland.

Pecheux, M. (1975). *Language, semantics and ideology.* New York: St. Martins.

Peters, M., & Marshall, J. (1996). The politics of curriculum: Busnocratic rationality and enterprise culture. *Delta, 48*(1), 33–46.

Smith, G. H. (1997). *The development of Kaupapa Maori: Theory and praxis.* Unpublished PhD thesis, University of Auckland, New Zealand.

Turoa, H., & Turoa, P. (1986). *Te Marae: A guide to customs and protocols.* Auckland, New Zealand: Reed Methuen.

Waitere-Ang, H. J. (1999). *Te kete, the briefcase, te tuarau: The balancing act—Maori women in the primary sector.* Unpublished MEdAdmin thesis, Massey University, Palmerston North, New Zealand.

Waitere, H., & Court, M. (2009). "Alternative" Mäori education? Talking back/talking through hegemonic sites of power. In P. Woods & G. Woods (Eds.), *Alternative education for the 21st century: Philosophies, policies, practices.* Palgrave: Macmillan.

CHAPTER 6

CONCEPTUALIZATIONS OF LEADERSHIP IN TONGA

Seu'ula Johansson Fua

INTRODUCTION

Leadership in Tonga has always been the business of kings and nobles. Their leadership has come to define not only Tonga but also what it means to be Tongan. Their leadership has been ascribed and based on their title and later followed by their achievements and skills. Today, leadership in Tonga is a business shared by commoners, albeit elite commoners. Commoner leaders, without titles, draw their leadership from their achievements and skills. But what are these skills and how can commoner leaders exert the same influence as traditional leaders? Where kings and nobles rule over islands and estates, commoner leaders are leading organizations of various types and forms. Are there skills that commoner leaders can learn from traditional leadership?

The Pacific Leadership Program[1] advocates looking at traditional leadership as a point of reference for defining a contemporary approach to organizational leadership. To do this, we need to have a better understanding of the forms of traditional leadership as well as the concepts that guide traditional leadership.

This chapter will discuss the traditional forms of leadership by highlighting some of the key concepts that guide traditional leadership. In the second part, I will focus the discussion on educational leadership. In this part I will discuss certain concepts from traditional leadership that I believe need to be adopted and developed as an approach to contemporary educational leadership. The final part of this paper will put forward some key recommendations on developing educational leadership in Tonga.

TRADITIONAL FORMS OF LEADERSHIP IN TONGA

Traditional leadership in this discussion refers to indigenous and cultural understandings of what leadership means for a society. In contemporary Tonga, it refers to such leadership as personified in the monarch as supreme ruler of Tonga and the nobles of the realm. Traditional leadership also refers to leadership within *kainga* (clan/tribe) as shown through the *'ulumotu'a* (head of a clan) and to some extent the *mehekitanga* (father's sister). The position of leadership within traditional understandings is based on rank, support of the *kainga*, and individual ability (Bott, 1981; Herda, 1987; Wood-Ellem, 1987). Thus, traditional leadership is not only based on kinship and blood ties but is maintained through negotiations of power relations and cultural recognition of the leader by followers (Helu-Thaman, 1991). This cultural recognition is symbolically exhibited through such values as *'ofa* (love), *mateaki* (loyalty) and *faka'apa'apa* (respect) (Latukefu 1974; Wood-Ellem, 1999). In more recent times, church leaders as well as prominent family heads have acquired respect and are often referred to as leaders within villages. Table 6.1 gives an illustration of the major traditional leadership roles within various societal units in Tongan society.

The key to understanding traditional leadership in Tonga lies in the understanding of several concepts. One of these concepts is rank, which is a key feature when examining the nature of relationships within groups. Relationships within traditional leadership are hierarchical, strongly rooted in tradition, sometimes autocratic, and protective. Every person in Tonga is ranked from birth into a position of inferiority as well as superiority. Ceremonies such as funerals, birthdays, and weddings affirm and often correct one's ranking. One's rank is always defined within *famili* (family) and/or *kainga* context. While an individual might hold a superior position during a birthday for his/her maternal relations, the same individual will hold a much more inferior position during a similar ceremony

Table 6.1. Traditional Positions of Leadership in Tongan Society

Societal Positions of Leadership	Familial Positions of Leadership
Hau 'o Tonga (King of Tonga) ↓	**'Ulumotu'a** 'oe kainga (Head of extended family) ↓
Nopele ma'u tofi'a (Noble of each estate) ↓	**Mehekitanga** (Father's sister) ↓
Matu'a tauhi fonua (Landed gentry) ↓	**Tamai** 'o e famili (Father) ↓
Matapule ma'u tofi'a (Landed gentry)	

for his/her paternal relations. Similarly, superiority within one's *famili* does not mean that it extends to functions of the nobles and society at large. That individual's can hold a superior rank within their maternal relations and that sisters are always of higher rank is a reflection of the respect and high status accorded to women in Tongan society. In their position as a sister and *mehekitanga,* women are always ranked higher than their brothers and their children. However, as a mother and a wife, women are of lower rank than their husbands. Gender and age are two major identifiers for ranking within Tongan social units (Aoyagi, 1966; Bott, 1981; Herda, 1987; Wood-Ellem, 1987; Helu-Thaman, 1988).

The concept of power ultimately comes into the conversation when rank and leadership are discussed. The use of power and authority in this discussion refers to the "nature of influence" dimension. Power/*mafai* is translated by Bott (1981) to be "the de facto capacity to lead a group and direct its activities" (p. 10). The term "power" in a Tongan context is to be differentiated from the word "*pule*," which Churchwood (1955) translates as "authority." Although Helu-Thaman (1988) also translates *pule* to mean "authority," she also defines *pule* within the context of kinship:

> to refer to power or influence, as is implied in a position of higher rank: the power to influence those "lower" than oneself. If this power to influence is recognized by those being influenced, thus legitimizing the power, then we can say that such persons (the influencers) have authority or "pule"] over those being influenced. Authority or "pule" as used here then, might be taken to mean legitimized, recognized power to govern in the context of modern government. (p. 43)

Helu-Thaman's (1988) definition reflects contemporary use and understanding of the term "power." The term *pule* and *mafai* can be used interchangeably when *pule* becomes *pule'i*. For purposes of this discussion *pule* refers to authority, while *mafai* is used for power. I want to make this differentiation, as a person of *pule* (authority) does not necessarily hold *mafai* (power). An example of this is the much-debated power of the *mehekitanga* and her apparent lack of *pule* (Helu-Thaman, 1988; Herda, 1987). Within traditional leadership, *mafai* is also divided into *mana* (mystical powers) associated with *mehekitanga* and secular power (not necessarily associated with men) (Herda, 1987; Rogers, 1977).

The issue of power often becomes multifaceted and confusing when one considers the position of the *mehekitanga* within *famili*, *kainga*, and nobles and in relation to the monarch. The powers held by *tamai*, *'ulu-motu'a*, nobles, and the monarch are easily understood when the basis of their power is within the land that they hold. The King owns Tonga as a kingdom and by law he allocates estates to the 33 nobles of the realm from which they divide land to each *kainga* and to each Tongan male. Women in Tonga are not allowed to inherit nor own land other than through lease permits (Latukefu, 1975). However, power associated with women as *mehekitanga* and holders of *koloa fakatonga* (fine mats and tapa cloth) as well as "mystical powers" of the *mehekitanga* are more complex to understand. Despite this complexity, it is widely understood in Tongan society that *mehekitanga* has "power." Bott (1981), through her discussions with the late Queen Salote and through Wood-Ellem's (1987) own work, has argued that traditional female authority in Tonga is associated with rituals (weddings, funerals, etc.) and mystical powers. The power of the *mehekitanga* to cast curses has been a much-debated topic by past and present anthropologists (Douaire-Marsaudon, 1996; Helu, 1999; Rogers, 1977; Taumoefolau, 1990).

Wood-Ellem's work (1987) is perhaps the most comprehensive scholarly work to date on traditional leadership in Tongan society. She presents a model of traditional leadership that was the basis of Queen Salote and Tungi's leadership during their reign. As she describes:

> There arose what was in traditional terms a quite extraordinary partnership between wife and husband. And there was only one model of female-male partnership for Salote and Tungi to follow: the traditional dual leadership of a male chief and his "eldest sister." (p. 219)

Traditional leadership can be summed up to be a joint effort, where the *'ulumotu'a* oversees all responsibilities associated with the land and all secular affairs while the *mehekitanga* oversees all responsibilities associated with *koloa fakatonga* and all that is sacred in Tongan rituals. When traditional leadership is examined under the dimension "nature of influence" it is defined by power/*mafai* and authority/*pule* that are contextual, negotiated and largely determined by the "nature of relationships" which is further defined by a hierarchical structure of rank that is based on the notion of 'Eiki, or divine leadership. When considering tradition and the function of culture within the Tongan context, the influence of over a century of contact with western civilization has lead to what Marcus (1981) has referred to as "a compromise culture" or Helu-Thaman's (1988) preferred metaphor of "a composite culture." The preceding definition of traditional leadership within a contemporary setting is a reflection of this "composite culture."

CULTURAL CONTEXT

Perhaps Helu-Thaman (1988) best describes contemporary Tongan culture when she coined it as a "composite culture." It is a composite culture as it has and continues to select and adopt foreign customs that best serve societal purposes and are "acceptable" to established customs and beliefs. Most notable in Tongan culture is the place of Christianity, introduced by foreign missionaries in the early seventeenth century. Christian values are the basis of the Tongan Constitution and have come to be internalized as part of "Tongan custom." Further to this, as foreign missionaries, particularly British missionaries, were instrumental in establishing formal schooling in Tonga, much of their own values and beliefs about work, school and life in general have also been adapted to become part of *anga fakatonga* or the Tongan way.

Helu Thaman (1995) draws attention to the symbolic importance of the land (*fonua*) to the identity of Tongan and Oceanic people. *Fonua* does not only refer to the land itself, but also to the people who populate the land. The cultural identity of Tongan people, like other Oceanic people, is closely associated with *fonua*. Helu Thaman also emphasizes that "culture is something that is lived and continually demonstrated as a matter of behaviour and performance" (p. 723). In Tonga, culture is alive not only through dances, *kava* rituals, weddings, funerals, and other customary rituals, but also through Tongan peoples' experiences in their daily lives.

Helu (1999) describes Tongan culture as "more of a shame culture," where people value interpersonal and group relationships and strive to avoid shame and public disapproval. The focus is on maintaining relationships within small communities. This is particularly true within a society that is centralized and hierarchical, where it presents "honourable" values on the surface, under which lie complicated networks of relationships. When a Tongan is asked to define his/her culture, such values as *'ofa* (love), *faka'apa'apa* (respect), *fevahevahe'aki* (sharing), *fetokoni'aki* (helpful) are often mentioned. Further to this, most Tongans, whether abroad or in Tonga, will proudly tell of their monarch, the nobles, and the place of commoners within the social hierarchy of the society.

Tongan culture is also noted for the nature of its chiefly authority; the orientation towards extended families; the place of religion, as well as the role of the supernatural, within the everyday lives of people; and values such as respect, love, hospitality, friendliness, love of ceremony, conformity, social relationships, kinship relationships, restrained behavior, and a tendency to discourage overt criticism.

Basic to understanding Tongan culture is the hierarchical nature of its society, from ranking within family units, to *kainga* (extended family) to the wider societal structure. The concept of rank permeates every foci of Tongan society. In discussing rank, the subject of power and authority cannot be excluded. In Tongan society the basis of power usually rests on the person's rank as being *'eiki* (noble, higher ranked) while the basis of authority rests more on titles, positions and access to resources.

TRADITIONAL MODES OF LEADERSHIP

The Tongan Constitution (Latukefu, 1875) has to a large extent defined traditional leadership in contemporary Tongan society. Formal education and, more recently, an increasingly commercialized economy has also contributed to further defining traditional leadership in Tongan society.[2]

The Constitution states in the 34th clause that "The form of government for this kingdom is that of a Constitutional Government under His Majesty, King George Tupou, his heirs and successors." This clause not only defines the nature of the government but also legitimizes and grants authority of leadership to the monarch. In the 47th clause of the constitution it states that "The King is the Sovereign of all chiefs and all the people. The kingdom is his." In this clause, the power of the monarch as the highest ranked chief *'eiki* in the country is confirmed. Through carefully arranged marriages and linking of high-ranking families, the present monarch is the highest ranked chief in the country, as he holds all kingly titles. The respect and loyalty accorded to the present monarch is not only based on this constitutional authority but also on the power that he holds as supreme chief of all Tongans. *Kava* ceremonies for the installation of noble titles and other customary rituals continue to reinstate the supreme power of the monarch over all other titles and positions of traditional leadership. Furthermore, the authority of the monarch as government head is played out in the day-to-day political arena of Tongan legislative assembly and cabinet. The authority vested in the monarch as granted by the Constitution is supported and maintained by the power of being the highest ranked chief.

The Constitution not only defines the authority of the monarch, it also limits and defines the authority and responsibilities of nobles. The first article in the Declaration of Rights (Latukefu, 1875) declares the freedom of all Tongans to "use their lives and persons and time to acquire and possess property and to dispose of their labour and the fruit of their hands and to use their own property as they will." What this means for nobles is that they can request, on the basis of their power as the 'eiki (highest ranked) in the village, resources, and other favors from the people. And although the village itself is located on the noble's estate, and nobles have authority over their estates, the Constitution also grants commoners legal rights to own land.

The introduction of formal Western education has been seen as the great leveler for all Tongans, commoners, nobles, and kings. One of the most noticeable social phenomenon emerging in Tonga since the mid-twentieth century is a new social class—Tonga's middle class. Education and religion have played crucial roles in the creation of this new class. And it is from this new middle class that a group of new leaders is emerging.

Bott (1981, p. 69) recorded that Tongan society in the late 1950s had "social classes [that] consisted of the nobles, a heterogeneous middle class and peasants" (p. 69). He argued that:

> the production for export, overseas work, and the changes in the system of titles and landholding have led to the development of a new middle class based partly on income, but, even more on education and occupation with a heavy bias towards the church, teaching, medicine, law and Government posts involving technical skills. (p. 69)

Bott described the middle class to includie clergy, teachers, medical practitioners, lawyers, shopkeepers, and government employees of varying degrees of skill and education. She also observed that the value being placed on "education was the common feature, but in other respects the middle class was heterogeneous and did not think of themselves as a power group" (p. 77). Bott also argued that "education has to some extent replaced the building up of local *kainga* as the first step in gaining political power." She believed that the traditional class "with its independent but interpenetrating and overlapping bases of stratification is changing into a social class system in which rank, power in the form of access to the Government, economic resources and education are tending to coincidee" (p. 76).

Bott (1981) believed that, although this group of new middle class had not begun to see themselves differently from other commoners, more was to come out of this group in the future. During this period (1950s–1960s), Bott observed, as did Marcus (1977) that nobles as ruling elites and the gentry were still at the top of the modern class structure of Tongan society. Bott described the "ruling elite" as being composed of aristocratic title-holding families, and a few highly educated commoners holding senior positions in government and often married to high-ranking women.

Almost half a century later, James (1997) observed;

> it is increasingly apparent that not all of the chiefs are regarded as effective leaders by the people, especially the nobles, who neither sit in Parliament nor take an active interest in the well-being of the people on their estates. In current times, positions of leadership are increasingly being assumed by a range of people who are prominent in the fields of education, church and public administration, and commerce. (p. 49)

Thus, what Bott (1981) described to be a new emerging middle class in Tonga during the 1950s, had, by the end of the twentieth century, become a visible group of some authority within modern Tongan society.

The middle class that had firmly established itself by the end of the twentieth century is characterized by several "modern" features just as several "traditional" features of Tongan culture limit them. The new middle class that is now holding various positions of leadership ranges from government departments to religious organizations and commercial and other private organizations in Tonga. With the emergence of leaders from commoners, power bases and relationships change, and hence promote changes to conceptualizations of traditional leadership.

For the first time in the history of Tongan politics, there are more commoners than nobles who are now holding ministerial positions within government. In an interview with Pesi Fonua in a local Tongan magazine *Matangi Tonga* (July-September, 1997), the King expressed the view that he preferred to select his own ministers from the best in the community. The King believes that good leaders are people "who have been trained and educated, and have good manners and are honest" (p. 13). The appointment of seven ministerial positions from among commoners suggests that the King prefers to select leaders on the basis of their education and professionalism. This is indeed a move away from traditional leadership where rank and ascribed status were the basis for leadership. More recently (2005), the King selected two ministerial positions from the people's representatives, a proposal that the People's Representatives in government have been lobbying for over the last decade. This indeed signified a turning point, not only in Tongan politics but also in thinking about conceptualizations of leadership, particularly when thinking about the "nature of influence" and what negotiated power means.

Ministers of the Crown, whether commoner or noble, are treated, to a certain extent, in a similar way as nobles. They are bestowed the title of "Honourable" and addressed in respectable language and in the same manner as nobles. Ministers then, particularly those who are commoners, have authority based on achieved status, through their education and skills. On the other hand, their fellow ministers who are nobles and hold princely titles, not only have authority based on their own achieved status and education, but they also have traditional power based on their rank. The difference between commoner ministers and noble ministers is that in *kava* ceremonies to install titles, commoner ministers have no place in this *kava* circle, as the *kava* circle belongs only to traditional leaders of rank and ascribed status.

At the community level, there is an emerging position of leadership found among town officers and district officers. In an interview with Fonua (1992), one particular noble said that the "new generation of young nobles are greatly concerned that their leadership role in their villages is slowly being taken over by government administration and other emerging figures in the villages and that the nobles' influence has withered beyond repair" (pp. 14–15). These emerging figures in the villages include other "noticeable contenders for influence like farmers, businessmen, church ministers, scholars and politicians" (pp. 14–15).

James (1997) agrees that

> most of the nobles today are no longer effective leaders because they are less closely associated with their people and less incorporated in local communities than were the titled chiefs who ruled before the constitutional changes of the last centur. (p. 52)

In Fonua's (1992) interview, one noble explained that "the land was our power base, and we used to have the respect of the people because we owned the land, but now … there is no good reason for them to remain our obedient partners in the villages" (p. 14). The Constitution not only defined the authorities of nobles, but it also gives every Tongan male of 16 years old a right to receive and register land from noble or government estate. James (1997) points out that villagers' independence from their noble landlords is most evident in places where all the land from the estate has been allocated and registered by the tenants, as was intended by Tupou I's 1882 Land Act (p. 61).

It is not only the allocation of land to commoners that is causing nobles to lose some power over their villagers. Most nobles now reside in the capital Nuku'alofa, rather than on their own estates, thus only visiting their estates for major social events. Further to this, younger nobles are seen by most of the elderly villagers as being too far removed from 'their world'. In this "power vacuum" town officers and district officers step in as government administrators.

In an interview with Fonua (1992) 'Eseta Fusitu'a, Secretary to Cabinet, agreed that town officers and district officers are now closer to the community than nobles. She believes that this is part of the modernization process that was set in place with the Constitution in 1875. She said "the point is that town and district officers are employees of the government; they are our men in the field" (p. 15). James (1997) explains that with the diminution of the authority of traditional leaders', the influence of town officers is increasing. She gives the example of one noble who complained of trying to implement development programs in the village with much difficulty and resistance, while on the other hand, some town officers are successfully able to implement programs to aid general development in the village.

James (1997) and Fonua (1992) highlight the importance of relationships between a leader and his followers. In the case of the noble, his absence from his village makes it more difficult for his village to relate to him. Further to this in the interview (with Fonua, 1992), one noble believed that there is a growing "anti-nobles sentiment." This noble said that he has:

> heard of a noble being the last person to be served in shops, and derogatory remarks being made against nobles. [He doesn't] know for sure how this anti-nobles sentiment came about, but [he] suspects that it is due in part to some nobles abusing their authority and being dishonest to their people. (p. 13)

In place of the noble's absence is the strong and visible presence of the town officer and the district officer. James (1997) described the reason behind a village's election of one particular man for the position of town officer for consecutive terms amounting to a total of over 15 years. James said that

> the people respected him and found him to be always honest in his dealings with them. When they chose to follow him, it was because they liked him rather than because of his government position and he was always careful to ask his fellow islanders to do things rather than to order them. (p. 64)

One of the main differences between people's relationships with town officers and with nobles is that, people find it easier to approach town officers about their concerns since they are commoners. People find town officers more approachable not only as town officers but also as commoners because the officers live in the same village and have similar concerns and living conditions. Further to this, as town officers are well aware, if they do not carry out a "good" job in the eyes of their fellow villagers they can very well be voted out in the next election.

Their *'eiki* or high rank of the nobles, inhibits commoners from out-right disagreement or questioning their orders, requests or wishes. In cases where commoners do disagree with a noble, they often listen to the noble's wishes but simply do not carry out the orders given to them. There are few incidents where commoners have disagreed openly with nobles and challenged their wishes. Traditional leadership as in the role of the noble is that his orders are on the basis of status as *'eiki*/noble of the estate and through authority as defined by the Constitution of a noble. But much of people's respect for the noble is based upon his *'eiki* title—being the highest ranked person in the village. On the other hand, the town officer, or *pule kolo* has no rank to draw traditional power from and has to rely on his authority (*pule*) and, more importantly, his ability to con-vince his fellow villagers of the appropriateness or rightness of the task at hand.

This "co-existence" of traditional leadership in the position of nobles and that of the emerging "commoner-leaders" as in the position of town officers and district officers presents new challenges to leadership in the community. As the Secretary to the Cabinet stated in her interview with Fonua (1992) "it appears that there are leadership problems in the vil-lages [therefore] it maybe wise to redefine the role of the town and district officers" (p. 15). Although she did not venture further to explain how the role of the town and district officers might be redefined, this points to a recognition that there are points of contention in the micropolitics and sphere of authority and power within community settings in contempo-rary Tongan society.

As early as the 1960s, Bott (1981,) observed that, with the transforma-tion to a class system as shown by the emergence of the new middle class, encouraged by economical developments, "is opposed by the system of personal rank, by the Tongan propensity for expressing different princi-ples of social differentiation in separate context" (p. 77). James (1997) agreed, stating that new leaders in the form of church ministers, business people and educators are stepping into the leadership roles left vacant by many nobles and that these leaders are earning a form of respect and per-sonal following through their own efforts. However, James (66) believed that

> because of the deference still accorded to rank and title in Tongan society, the newer people filling leadership positions often lack legitimacy in the eyes of the people. Their assumption of authority is tentative and ambigu-ous, fraught with social contradictions, and tempered by the tension sur-rounding commoners who 'get above their station' (fie 'eiki). (p. 66)

Perhaps one of the most telling features of this "conflict" are the words *pule* and *kau taki*, used to define commoner leaders as opposed to *'eiki* in reference to nobles and also to ministers of the Crown. *Pule* or authority is used in several ways to describe a position of leadership within an organization or other group, such as *pule kolo* for town officer, and *pule ako* for school principal. *Kau taki* is used to describe commoners holding senior leadership positions in government or in churches. The term *kau taki* suggests that these leaders lead as one leads an animal, such as a horse. James (1992) points out the fact that "modern Tongans do not easily find a term for these new people of influence suggests the anomaly and ambiguity of their role" (p. 68).

Thus, at the beginning of the twenty-first century, traditional leadership in Tonga is still held in the positions of the monarch and nobles of estates throughout the country. With an increasingly educated and financially independent population, a new middle class is emerging to take hold of new positions of leadership in villages, government, and private organizations and churches. Church ministers, educators, business people, farmers and town, and district officers are some of the leaders who are emerging from the middle class commoners. Nobles retain their authority and power on the basis of their *'eiki* title and authority granted to them through the Constitution of 1875. They continue to hold on to their ascribed status as traditional leaders through power as defined by rank and title, while new leaders from the middle class commoners through achieved status, gained through education, commerce and industry, are defining new leadership roles that rely more on authority and their ability to lead.

The emerging role of town officers with reliance on their close relationships with villagers is to a large extent reflected in school principals' effort to foster closer working relationships with their staff. Town officers, principals and commoners holding leadership roles are slowly realizing the importance of relationships as the source of influence when they lack the high rank and traditional power of nobles. The importance of relationships within communities and organizations confirms what Helu (1999) believes, that Tongan people value interpersonal and group relationships and strive to avoid shame and public disapproval.

LEADERSHIP CONCEPTS FOR SKILLS DEVELOPMENT

I propose two key concepts that can be adopted from Tongan traditional leadership, Tongan core values and relationships. This proposition is supported by my studies of Tongan leadership (Johansson Fua, 2001; Johansson Fua, 2003) and other Tongan scholars who have delved into the intricacies of Tongan culture (Helu, 1999; Helu Thaman, 1991, 1995; Kavaliku, 1966) and leadership (Paongo, 1990; Samate, 1995; Vete, 1990).

These two concepts are crucial to understanding traditional leadership and the contemporary very fabric of Tongan society. How people behave, express themselves and ultimately make decisions are based on their values and how these values through manifest themselves in their relationships. As our concern is with educational leadership, I will specifically focus on how school principals may expand these leadership concepts as key skills in their leadership development. Generalizations can be inferred for other positions of leadership.

Values

The study of values in educational leadership is an expanding field that until recently has been dominated by western perspectives. Studies from eastern perspectives (Cheng, 1998) are gaining momentum but fewer have been carried out in the Pacific region (Helu-Thaman, 1988; Johansson Fua, 2001, 2003, 2005a; Tavana & Randall, 1997). However, as our concern is with developing leadership that is true to whom we are and respects the people we lead it is essential that we gain a better understanding of values and how they influence the way we lead.

Values and principles are concerned with people's belief systems, their cultural identity, ideas and behaviors that are intrinsically desirable. Our values define how we see the world, how we relate to those around us, and how we perceive ourselves in our various social roles. Subsequently, certain values come to define social, political and economic structures in our broader societies. Education is one such arena that is loaded with values, from its organizational structures, to its philosophy, to the curriculum that we teach our children.

The centrality of values to understanding educational administration requires leaders to understand their own values as well as the value processes and arenas that come into play in their surroundings. School principals operate within layers of value arenas. For one, they have their own personal values, according to which they live. Second, as principals, they have professional values that they adhere to as professionals. Third, they work as part of a larger organization with a distinctive culture and values. Finally that organization operates within a wider societal unit that also operates according to its own philosophies, values, and culture. Consequently, the processes that occur within each value arena also influence how principals perceive and practice their leadership. Figure 6.2 illustrates the value arenas within which principals find themselves working.

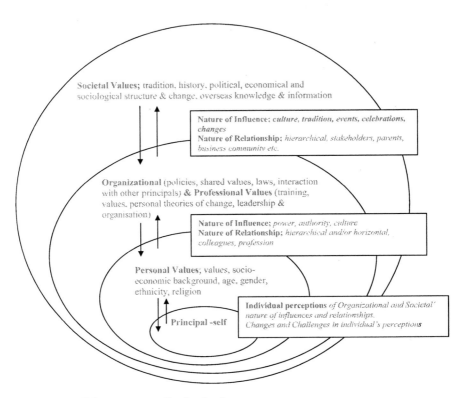

Figure 6.2.   Value arenas of principal.

Findings from my study of educational leadership in Tonga (Johansson Fua, 2003) clearly illustrate the interaction and dynamics between these value arenas; personal, professional, organizational, and societal. An example of this is the professional values of school principals who participated in the study. The professional values described by participants include dedication, hard work, loyalty, and commitment to their school and organization. These professional values are closely related to participants' personal values of Christian faith. I suspect that participants' motivation for being committed, loyal, and dedicated to their job lies in their belief that their appointment as principals is their "calling." Further to this, societal culture encourages values of dedication, commitment and loyalty to country, to community and to family. Kavaliku's (1966) description of the *tangata poto* (the ideal person) is one who uses his/her skills and knowledge for the betterment of others including, family, community and country. Principals' commitment and loyalty to their job may be attributed to other personal reasons but, based on their social and cultural contexts, it is fair to suggest that principals themselves are striving to be "*tangata poto.*"

In describing their professional values, participants also expressed the importance of relationships in their leadership practice. Contemporary principals are increasingly valuing relationships with their stakeholders. The increasing value of relationships between educational leaders and those they lead is reflective of not only changes in leadership practices but also changes in conceptualizations of traditional leadership between nobles and villagers. Fonua (1992) describes the changing nature of traditional leadership in the villages, where nobles are struggling to maintain traditional power over villagers. Behind this change in traditional power dynamics is the relationship between nobles and their people. Relationships between leaders and those they lead are slowly being recognized as essential components of contemporary leadership in Tonga. The hierarchical nature of traditional relationships between nobles and their people is slowly changing.

When participants described their practice, relationships, and values, several core societal values were easily identified. Societal values which were evident in the leadership practices of contemporary Tongan principals included; respect, acceptance, societal moral codes of ethics (Christian and culturally based), obedience, patience, and maintenance of tradition and customs. These values were evident in their relationships with stakeholders and in their own espoused personal and professional values. These societal values were also evident in organizational values and in relationships between educational authorities and their schools, principals and stakeholders. While these values are easily identifiable, they are, however, difficult to separate from personal, professional, and organizational values. The relatively homogenous nature of Tongan society enables core societal values to fuse with other value arenas.

I want to highlight two findings from this study; relationships are primary to the practice of commoner leaders; and societal values are evident throughout all value arenas and particularly evident in professional values.

Relationships

At the core of Tongan people are their relationships—their "*va.*" Core values such as *'ofa* (love), *mateaki* (loyalty), *fetokoni'aki* (reciprocity) and *faka'apa'apa* (respect) all define appropriate relationships within the Tongan context. When examined carefully, these values reflect relationships that are mutual and negotiated. Often, Tongan leadership has been accused of being autocratic and non-negotiable and sometimes it is. However, I wish to argue that when the core values of *'ofa, mateaki, fetokoni'aki* and *faka'apa'apa* are properly observed in relationships, relationships are then harmonious, mutual and the work gets done. I think that it is when these values are confused, misinterpreted, and sometimes disregarded altogether that relationships are broken, distanced and disengaged.

These core values also strongly suggest a sense of negotiation between one person and another. I have mentioned earlier in this chapter the negotiated nature of traditional leadership; power and authority are not necessarily absolute. And this is even more so for commoner leaders. My studies of Tongan principals (Johansson Fua, 2001, 2003) strongly suggest that leadership for commoner leaders relies heavily on their ability to relate to people. Whereas the power (*mafia*) of the noble is within his title (*'eiki*) the power base of the commoner leaders is within his/her relationships with stakeholders.

Building Relationships

I have proposed elsewhere (Johansson Fua, 2005a) that we consider "relationship" as one of the fundamental concepts of educational leadership in The Pacific. I have proposed that we consider building organizational relationships as a key tool in our leadership. Transferring the fundamental conceptualizations of societal relationships into our organizations can help build organizational relationships in our educational systems. By such a task, I suggest that we transfer the values that underpin our societal relationships namely; love, loyalty, respect, reciprocity, and tolerance into our educational organizations.

Building relationships begins with leaders defining what values, attitudes, behaviors, and cultures are acceptable in a workplace. My interest in educational leadership came about when working with a Tongan principal at one of the Ministry of Education's schools. To me, she lived her values through and through. One of the practices that I admired most was that she was always respectful towards her staff. She understood when a teacher needed to go home to take care of her sick child and when a teacher needed just a quiet moment. Through her relationships with her staff, she gained loyalty and respect beyond her authority. In turn, it helped to build a distinctive culture for the school, one that I always look back to with admiration.

Leaders also need to build relationships with outside stakeholders; parents, communities and others. In one of my studies in Tonga, I came across a principal who for months struggled to get parents to attend parent/teacher meetings. Finally, she decided to take the parent teacher meeting out into the communities. She held *fono* or traditional meetings in each community hall, inviting parents and their children to attend. In this *fono*, she and her staff were present sitting around a mat to *talano*a with parents about their children and their education. This is an example of how a principal has taken a Tongan concept of consultation known as "*fofola 'a e fala ka e fai 'a e alea*" to build relationships with her community.

When relationships within any organization are harmonious, information is shared easily and quickly. Similarly, consultation processes, decision-making processes and problem-solving processes are more efficient and effective. Relationship-building within organizations is crucial to vision-building, organizational analysis, implementation and monitoring, and the evaluation phases of any plan. Relationship building is also key to conflict resolution, team-building, community connectedness and communication strategies. Building organizational relationships that reflect cultural values is an investment that cannot be ignored.

Decision Making Processes

Leadership is primarily engaged in two main arenas: decision making and problem solving. Simon (1965) argues that experts solve problems by drawing on their recognition capabilities and that analytical capabilities are used when problems are not recognized by the memory. Leithwood and Stager's (1989) study of how principals solve problems highlights five components of problem solving; the interpretation of the problem, the goals to achieve by solving the problem, the principles used to guide the thinking process, possible constraints, and the solution processes adopted to solve the problem. Their study found that expert problem solvers are more likely to interpret the problem more clearly, more carefully, and more succinctly. Experts are also more likely to use principles to guide their decisions, find ways around constraints, plan their solution process, show concern for the consequences of action to others, and remain more calm and confident when confronting problems.

Studies which have looked at the application of values theory to the practices of school administrators generally find that most educational leaders use Type I value (principles) only under particular conditions and are more likely to use Type II (consequences and consensus) to solve value conflicts (Begley, 1988; Begley & Johansson 1998; Campbell-Evans, 1991). My study of Tongan principals and their decision-making processes (Johansson Fua, 2001) reveals the importance of values in the process. The secondary school principals who were involved in this study preferred to use Value Type II,[3] consequence and consensus in dealing with administrative matters; in their relationship with their staff; in resolving issues faced by students; and working with the community. Value Type III preferences were used occasionally, especially in dealing with the staff and with students. Participants in all facets of their role as administrators used Christian principles. The values preferred by Tongan principals (Johansson Fua, 2001), generally confirm findings from other values and leadership research elsewhere.

When principals centre their decision-making process around the values of consequences and consensus, they take their relationships with others into consideration. Decisions based on this way of thinking reflect a more rational approach; the principal has taken time to "think things over." In my studies of principals in Tonga (Johansson Fua, 2001, 2003). I have found that expert decision makers tend to "think things through." They tend to take time to gather information from staff, reflect on possible consequences, talk with their management teams, and consult other stakeholders before making their decision. I also found that principals who were clearest about their values and the value arenas that they worked within tended to make decisions that they could justify. I also found that principals who had good working relationships with their staff and stakeholders had greater support and respect from their staff when making decisions.

RECOMMENDATIONS FOR LEADERSHIP DEVELOPMENT IN TONGA

Based on the results of my studies (Johansson Fua, 2001, 2003) I offer several recommendations for Tongan educators to consider in their efforts to address the changing needs of Tongan education.

Professional Training for Principals

Current "training" of Tongan principals occurs on a professional socialization level, where principals are selecting what they think are the best practices and use them in their work. Based on the results of my studies, I would suggest to policymakers as well as principals that they consider formal mentoring programs for principals. Informal mentoring processes are already happening, as participant principals have identified learning the role of principalship through observing their "mentors." The literature on cognitive apprenticeship (Begley, 1995; Leithwood & Hallinger, 1993; Prestine & LeGrand, 1991) supports the application of mentoring programs as it encourages being social, contextual, flexible, and diverse. Through mentoring programs, principals learn on site, and they are socially acculturated in the school, the organization, and surrounding communities.

The Ministry of Education and private educational authorities must look within current trends to find better ways of providing professional development for principals. Principals are already using various personal approaches to identifying mentors and emulating their practices. Through better organizational support from educational authorities, systems can be set up to restructure this already informal process into a more sustainable formal process of learning. I propose the use of professional mentoring programs that are based on applying *cultural and cognitive perspectives* to the preparation of administrators. Such programs will strategically place future principals with experienced principals as a way of professional training. In such a program, future principals will also be helped to understand problem-solving processes and decision-making processes and how they can be translated through relationships that are rooted on Tongan core values.

Organizational Support for Principals' Leadership Practices

Findings from my studies suggest that all too often the Ministry of Education and private educational authorities are not giving their principals the support that they need to pursue best practices in their leadership. The apparent lack of defined organizational policies should be one of the key areas for educational authorities to address. An example from the Latter Day Saints' educational authority in terms of clearly outlined organizational visions and defined school objectives is very encouraging. Job descriptions and broad organizational mission statements are clearly not enough for principals to aid them in their leadership practices. Clearly defined, relevant, and meaningful organizational policies are needed more than ever before as principals are struggling to forge leadership practices in a changing environment.

The traditions of a school frequently extent, define its very culture and values yet these are often only defined through unwritten or implicit policies. The Ministry of Education as well as educational authorities need to work seriously in cooperation with principals and teachers when designing policies that do not just look good on paper but are also applicable to everyday practices of a Tongan principal. Tongan culture shapes the people who work within schools and policymakers and educational organizations need to recognize that people within these organizations cannot peel off their culture and hang it by the door as they enter the organization. Therefore, policies that should aid and support social dimensions and relationships within Tongan educational organizations should honour and reflect the values and culture of their members. Failing to do so only creates conflicts and contradictions in principals' leadership practices and in their relationships with teachers and educational authorities. In the changing environment of Tongan society, contextual, applicable, acculturated, and defined organizational policies are needed.

Principals' Leadership Practices

One of the core findings of my studies shows that principals recognize the importance of relationships in exerting social influence over teachers, students and stakeholders. This is a key area of professional development that principals may like to explore in depth. Participants in the study recognized that fostering close working relationships with teachers helps them to gain their respect and support. Such principals are recognizing that "authority" might be based on their position as principal, but their 'power' to influence the lives and activities of people in their schools depends primarily on their ability to maintain appropriate relationships with these key stakeholders.

My study (Johansson Fua, 2003) also shows that principals are aware of their personal and professional values and recognize that these values do affect their leadership practices. This is an encouraging sign indeed when participants argued that *principals must have principles* in their approach to educational leadership. The place of values and ethics in the leadership practices of incumbent principals is another key area for principals to consider in their professional development. Contemporary approaches to educational leadership needs to seriously consider the place of values and ethics in professional relationships and in decision-making processes. Principles need to be in the forefront of principals' leadership practices.

In light of uncertain policies from educational authorities and The Ministry of Education, and the prevailing nature of professional development programs, principals must take it upon themselves to initiate and demand organizational support for their practices. The Principals' Association is a good starting point for principals to place initiatives for professional development programs based on their needs.

ACKNOWLEDGMENT

This paper is based on findings from my doctoral thesis: *Pule Ako: Educational Leadership in Tonga.* Unpublished doctoral thesis, University of Toronto, Canada, 2003.

NOTES

1. Leadership Pacific Program—is an NZAid funded activity run by the University of the South Pacific and the University of Victoria, Wellington. The program takes an indigenous approach to understanding leadership within the context of South Pacific countries. It begins by asking questions such as "what does leadership mean in your cultural context?" some of the key focus areas in the program include; conceptualizations of leadership; ethics and relationships in Pacific communities; resource management; problem solving and decision making. The program is specific to the context of each of the Pacific countries that participate in the program.

2. the leadership for commoners at the early years were based on qualifications and merit. This was demonstrated clearly in the line up of government ministers in the 1980s and 1990 who were technocrats and were appointed by the King based on their expertise and qualifications for the given portfolio. An example, was the appointment of Dr Kavaliku as the Minister of Education, he being the first commoner to obtain a PhD. In the beginning of the twenty-first century, there is increasing evidence of new line of elites—who are becoming leaders based on their economic standing rather than qualifications. In 2008, the Prime Minister for Tonga is a prominent business man, who also holds a PhD in Economics. There are other Ministers and Parliamentarians who are also business people. Obviously, issues of misuse of funds and corruption among these new leaders have become great concern for the public service. While education was seen in the past as the qualifier for leadership, Tonga at the turn of the twenty-first century is increasingly embracing—for better or for worse—a new qualifier for leadership—finances. The new commoner elite for Tonga are the business people.

3. I used Hodgkinson's (1991) value typology where value Type I: principles, value Type II: consensus and consequences, and value Type III: preferences.

REFERENCES

Aoyagi, M. (1966). Kinship organisation and behaviour in a contemporary Tongan Village. *Journal of Polynesian Society, 75*(2), 141–196.

Begley, P. T. (1988). *The influence of personal beliefs and value on principals' adoption and use of computers in schools.* Unpublished PhD thesis, University of Toronto.

Begley, P. T. (1995). Using profiles of school leadership as support to cognitive apprenticeship. *Educational Administration Quarterly, 31*(2), 176–202.

Begley, P. T., & Johansson, O. (1998). The values of school administration: Preferences, ethics and conflicts. *Journal of School Leadership, 8*, 399–421.

Bott, E. (1981). Power and Rank in the Kingdom of Tonga. *Journal of Polynesian Society, 90*(1), 7–81.

Campbell-Evans, G. H. (1991). Nature and influences of values in principal decision making. *The Alberta Journal of Educational Research, 37*(2), 167–178.

Cheng, K. (1998). Can educational values be borrowed? Looking into cultural differences. *Peabody Journal of Education, 37*(2), 11–30.

Churchwood, C. M. (1955). *Tongan Dictionary.* London: Oxford University Press.

Douaire-Marsaudon, F. (1996). Neither Black nor White: The father's sister in Tonga.' *Journal of Polynesian Society, 105*(2), 135–164.

Fonua, P. (1997, July-September). Searching for good and honest leaders. *Matangi Tonga,* 10–13.

Fonua, P. (1992, July-August). Leadership crisis in the villages. *Matangi Tonga,* 14–15.

Helu, F. (1999). *Critical essays: Cultural perspectives from the South Seas.* Canberra, Australia: ANU.

Helu-Thaman, K. (1988). *Ako & Faiako: Cultural values, educational ideas and teachers' role perceptions in tonga.* Unpublished doctoral thesis, University of the South Pacific.

Helu-Thaman, K. (1991). *Ako and Fai ako: Cultural values, educational ideas and teachers' role perceptions in Tonga.* Unpublished PhD thesis, University of the South Pacific, Suva, Fiji.

Helu-Thaman, K. (1995). Concepts of learning, knowledge and wisdom in Tonga, and their relevance to modern education. *Prospects, 25*(4), 723–733.

Herda, P. (1987). Gender, rank and power in 18th Century Tonga. *Journal of Pacific History, 22*(4), 195–208.

Hodgkinson, C. (1991). Educational leadership: The moral art. Albany, NY: SUNY.

James, K. (1992). Tongan Rank Revisited: Religious hierarchy, social stratification and gender in the ancient Tonga polity. *Social Analysis, 31.*

James, K. (1997). Rank and leadership in White. In M. Geoffrey & L. Lindstrom (Eds.), *Chiefs today, traditional pacific leadership and the post-colonial state.* Palo Alto, CA: Stanford University Press.

Johansson Fua, S. (2001). *Values and leadership practices of secondary school principals in the Kingdom of Tonga.* Unpublished MA thesis, University of Toronto, Canada.

Johansson Fua, S. (2003). *Pule Ako: Educational leadership in Tonga.* Unpublished PhD thesis, University of Toronto, Canada.

Kavaliku, S. (1966). *Educational reorganisation for national development in Tonga.* Unpublished PhD thesis, Victoria University of Wellington, New Zealand.

Latukefu, S. (1975). *The Tongan Constitution: A brief history to celebrate its Centenary.* Nuku'alofa: Tonga Traditions Committee Publication.

Leithwood, K., & Stager, M. (1989). Expertise in principals' problem solving. *Educational Administration Quarterly, 25*(2), 126–161.

Leithwood, K., & Hallinger, P. (1993). Cognitive perspectives on educational administration: An introduction. *Educational Administration Quarterly, 29*(3), 296–301.

Marcus, G. (1977). Contemporary Tonga—The background of social and cultural change. In N. Rutherford (Ed.), *Friendly islands: A History of Tonga* (pp. 210–227). Melbourne, Australia: Oxford University Press.

Marcus, G. E. (1981). Power on the extreme periphery: The perspective of Tongan elites in the modern world system. *Pacific Viewpoint, 22*(1), 48–64.

Paongo, K. (1990). *A vision for the call: A conceptualisation of educational administration for the improvement of the free Wesleyan education system in Tonga.* Unpublished PhD thesis, University of Queensland.

Prestine, N. A., & LeGrand, B. F. (1991). Cognitive learning theory and the preparation of educational administrators: Implications for practice and policy. *Educational Administration Quarterly, 27*(1), 61–89.

Rogers, G. (1977). The father's sister is Black: A consideration of female rank and powers in Tonga. *Journal of Polynesian Society, 86*(2), 157–182.

Samate, A. F. (1995). *Education and national development in Tonga: A critical policy review.* Unpublished PhD thesis, University of Queensland.

Simon, H. (1965). *Administrative behaviour* (2nd ed.). New York: Free Press.

Taumoefolau, M. (1990). Is the Father's sister really "Black?" *Journal of Polynesian Society, 100*(1), 91–98.

Tavana, G. H., & Randall, E. V. (1997). Cultural values and education in Western Samoa: Tensions between colonial roots and influences and contemporary indigenous needs. *International Journal of Educational Reform, 6*, 11–19.

Vete, V. (1990). Professional development and training needs of school principals in Tonga. Unpublished MEd thesis, Edith Cowan University.

Wood-Ellem, E. (1999). *Queen Salote of Tonga, The story of an era 1900–1965.* Auckland. New Zealand: University Press.

Wood-Ellem, E. (1987). Queen Salote Tupou of Tonga as Tu'I Fefine. *Journal of Pacific History, 22*(4), 209–227.

PART III

WORKING IN MULTICULTURAL SETTINGS

CHAPTER 7

AMERICAN CULTURE

Latino Realities

Encarnación Garza, Jr. and Betty Merchant

HISTORICAL PERSPECTIVE

From its inception, the position of school administrator was designed to attract individuals who were willing to comply with a view of schooling that validated, rather than challenged, existing norms (Callahan, 1962; Tyack & Hansot, 1982). With the rapid growth of cities in the mid-nineteenth century, both the principalship and superintendency became increasingly important mechanisms for imposing order on a large and diverse student population (Pierce, 1935).

Because of their historic focus on management, departments of educational administration have not typically been associated with social justice issues, and consequently, most of the research in this area has originated outside of the field of educational administration. When policy studies is incorporated into educational administration departments, social justice advocates and critics of the status quo such as critical race theorists tend to be identified with other departments, such as cultural studies or educational foundations. Such divisions may be perpetuated by faculty members who seldom, if ever, interact across these boundaries. In recent years, however, there has been a growing interest in incorporating a strong social justice component into the formal preparation of principals and superintendents at the university level. This is evidenced in the writings of increasing numbers of educational administration scholars (Capper, 1993; Donmoyer, Imber, & Scheurich, 1995; Gonzalez, Huerta-Macias, & Tinajero, 2002; Johnson & Shoho, 2002; Lomotey, 1995, 1989; Lugg, 2002; Marshall & McCarthy, 2002; Merchant, 1999a, 1999b; Merchant & Shoho, 2002; Reyes, Scribner, & Scribner, 1999; Rorrer, 2002; Scheurich, Skrla, & Johnson, 2000).

The past 20 years have witnessed a shift in the hiring and outreach practices of colleges and universities, increasing the number of females and scholars of color who are faculty members (Hargens & Long, 2002; "A JBHE Report Card," 2001–2002; Lindholm, Astin, Sax, & Kron, 2002; Pounder, 1990; Turner, 2000). Many of these new faculty members bring with them a rich set of experiences with diverse populations across a variety of local, state, national, and international contexts. Part of the legacy of these new scholars is their deep commitment to applying the principles of equity and social justice to educational reform, so that public schools can become places in which all children are provided with the opportunities and resources to succeed academically and socially.

LATINO REALITIES

The educational statistics for Latino students reveal disproportionate academic underachievement in comparison with their Anglo counterparts (Cummins, 1989; Valencia, 1991; Valenzuela, 1999). Such research has typically defined the students, their families, and their neighborhoods as "culturally deprived" or "disadvantaged." As a result of these deficit-oriented definitions, the public school system has continued to design programs to remediate or compensate for these students' "deficiencies." The administrators running these programs, using a therapeutic discourse, commonly view the children as *pobrecitos* (poor little children) who need to be saved (Garza, Reyes, & Trueba, 2004).

Texas possesses one of the highest percentages of Latinos in the United States. Seven years ago, the Intercultural Development Research Association conducted a comprehensive longitudinal statewide study (1986–2001) in an effort to critically review the drop out data and during that time, the attrition rates for Latino students increased from 45% to 52%. (Cárdenas, Robledo, & Supik, 2001). A wide array of additional data (Texas Education Agency [TEA], 2001) indicate that the achievement gap between Latino and Anglo children continues to be an area of concern.

STUDENTS AND EDUCATORS: DIVERGENT DEMOGRAPHICS

While the students in U.S. schools are increasingly poor and of color, the majority of their teachers are White, monolingual, middle-class women (Zeichner, 1993). According to the National Center for Education Statistics (1996), the number of students majoring in education in that year was 493,606. Of these, 86.5% (426, 748) were White, 6.8% (33,436) were African American, and 2.7% (13,533) were Latino. These figures clearly illustrate that a growing percentage of predominantly White student teachers are being prepared to educate a population of public school students who are growing increasingly different from them, racially, ethnically, linguistically, and economically. That is, whereas approximately 88% of the teaching force in the United States is White, the non-White student population will soon be over 50%.

According to 2005 data from the TEA, student demographics in the state at that time were consistent with national trends (45% Latino, 38% White, 14% African American). As was the case nationally, teacher demographics at that time did not reflect those of their students (70% White, 20% Latino, 9% African American) (TEA, 2005). Since the pool of principal candidates comes from the teacher ranks, it is not surprising that the demographic patterns are similar for school principals in Texas. Data from the TEA reveal that, in 2002, 72% of the principals were White, 18% were Latino, 10% were African American (TEA, 2002). These divergent demographics will not be shifting drastically in the coming years. In fact, the data show that the number of Latino students is growing at a faster pace than expected. In Texas, the Latino population now represents over 50% of the population (U.S. Census Bureau, 2005).

The increasingly diverse student population in today's public schools, particularly the significant and growing numbers of Latinos, requires that we take a critical look at the university-level programs that prepare educational administrators to work with these students. One of the most striking aspects of such programs is the low numbers of Latino professors in departments of educational administration. Data from the National Center for Educational Statistics (2002), indicate that of the total number of doctoral degrees in education (7,088) conferred by degree-granting institutions in academic year 2003–2004, 67% (4,747)of the degree recipients were White, whereas 4% (307) were Latino. While the data on master's degrees were incomplete for the 2003–2004 academic year, the data for 2002–2003 reflect a similar pattern to that of the doctoral degree. That is, 116,305 White students compared to only 8,802 Latinos received a master's degree in educational administration that year.

A second characteristic of most university-based programs in educational administration is the lack of books and journal articles in course syllabi that focus on effective educational leadership with diverse populations of students, particularly second English language learners. What does exist is written largely by researchers who are members of the groups about which they write such as racial, ethnic, linguistic, socioeconomic minorities, or by White scholars whose work focus on issues of social justice and equity. The research of these individuals provides considerable insight into the characteristics of schools that effectively serve diverse learners. For the purposes of this chapter, we focus our attention on the literature that is relevant to improving the academic and social success of Latino students.

EFFECTIVE SCHOOLS FOR LATINO STUDENTS

A review of the research indicates that there are many schools that are effectively serving Latino students. Some of this literature is framed by models of successful practices in the corporate world, such as the recent study by the Center for the Future of Arizona and the Morrison Institute for Public Study at Arizona State University (Waits, Campbell, Gau, Jacobs, Rex, & Hess, 2006), that draws on the business leadership practices articulated in Jim Collins' (1999) *Good to Great: Why Some Companies Make the Leap and Others Don't*. This study examined 12 elementary and middle schools that served a high percentage of Latino students in Arizona that "beat the odds." The data indicate that six factors were crucial to the success of these schools: (1) clear bottom lines, (2) ongoing assessment, (3) a strong and steady principal, (4) collaborative solutions, (5) stick with the program, and 6) built to suit. Although these practices are not culturally specific, the Latino students in these schools did well because their principals and teachers refused to let them fail.

While some of the research on successful schools is based on leadership models from the corporate world, our understanding of such schools has been greatly enhanced by educational researchers whose work is informed, in part, by their previous experiences as principals and superintendents. Maria Luisa Gonzalez (2002) provides "sketches" of three successful principals of schools in which the majority of the students were Latinos of Mexican descent.

She found that the principals' everyday practice was driven by their philosophy of social justice. They honored and dignified the lifestyles, language, and culture of their students, viewed their differences as assets and held high expectations for themselves, the students and teachers. The principals sought the support of the parents, conducted frequent home visits, and were successful in creating an inviting atmosphere that made the parents feel comfortable and valued. They practiced a collaborative model of leadership and the teachers felt empowered as participants in the decision making process. According to Gonzalez (2002), "the principal was the major player in this outcome ... the main ingredient in their [the Latino students'] school success is the culturally competent principal" (p. 26).

A third approach to understanding the factors that contribute to the school success of Latino children involves the study of a number of purposively sampled, high-performing Latino schools by teams of university educators. One such example of research was conducted in the mid-1990s by a team from the University of Texas at Austin led by Reyes, Scribner and Paredes Scribner (1999). The study looked at eight schools on the Texas-Mexico border; three elementary, three middle schools, and two high schools. All were serving Latino students effectively and were outperforming most schools on state assessment standards. Over 95% of the students enrolled in these schools were Latino and over 80% were economically disadvantaged. Based on their findings, the researchers concluded "that there are no excuses for anything other than high-impact schools and high-performing Hispanic students" (Reyes et al., 1999, p. 208).

These researchers found that all of the participating schools had established learning communities that were committed to creating a shared vision and a successful learning environment for all children. These communities reflected four dimensions: collaborative governance and leadership, community, and family involvement, culturally responsive pedagogy, and advocacy-oriented assessment. While this study does not specifically address the role of the principal in developing high-performing schools for Latino students, the impact of the principals' leadership is evident in the findings.

AN ALTERNATIVE MODEL OF SCHOOL LEADERSHIP

The purpose of this section is to describe a "different" model of leadership preparation that was designed and customized to prepare school leaders to practice in schools where the student population is predominantly Latino. It is a preparation program that is designed to advance interactive collaboration between students, professors and school district administrators. As researchers, we have been involved since the inception of the program. Our main sources of data for this project are the students. We rely heavily on the experiences of the members of the first and second cohorts to describe the collaboration between The University of Texas in San Antonio (USLC) and the San Antonio Independent School District (SAISD). This partnership, the Urban School Leaders Collaborative

(USLC), was designed to facilitate and enhance the opportunities for practitioners and scholars to work collaboratively in a meaningful and effective manner in the preparation of aspiring school leaders.

The USLC is a different model of preparation in several distinct ways. First, it is driven by a philosophy of social justice advocacy. The focus of preparation is initially on attitudes and mindsets, and then on skills. Second, it is a truly collaborative partnership. The school district and university are actively involved in the selection, planning, teaching, and evaluation processes. Third, it is a closed cohort model: only for employees of the partnering school district, and leadership preparation is customized to meet the needs of the children of this school district. Fourth, professors are field-based; all classes taught by department faculty are held in campuses throughout the school district. And finally, support continues even after the students graduate and assume leadership positions.

In this study, the racial identity of the educators in the USLC was considered to be of high value and we have focused on how their racial identities intersect with their future positions as leaders for social justice and diversity. The cultural relevance of this preparation program is captured through the narratives of the participants who are part of this cultural fabric. The majority of educators in the program are Latino or African American, serving a population with a majority of Latino children. A qualitative analysis of the participants' narratives provides strong evidence of students' culturally relevant practices, especially those related to the needs of families and students in the district. Because of the focus on social justice leadership, this analysis also considers the emerging leaders' perceptions of how their ethnicity influences their mission, and their commitment to improving the preparation of the Latinos.

A CHRONOLOGICAL REPORT—COHORT 1

The investment of the leaders from SAISD (superintendent, assistant superintendents, director of special programs) and UTSA (dean of education, chair of the department of educational leadership and policy studies) in conceptualizing and designing the program was critical in the creation of this preparation program. Furthermore, the long-time personal and professional relationship between the dean and the superintendent and the trust that evolved between them and the department chair were essential to the formation of the USLC. Without their collaboration, this partnership may never have been conceived.

Although the planning began in 2002, it was not until spring 2003 that the first 14 students began their program (8 Latino, 3 African American, and 3 White; 12 females and 2 males). They enrolled in two courses that were taught together by the dean and department chair. From the beginning, it was obvious that developing trust was a major focus to the success of the first SAISD Cohort. Students strongly agree that the professors facilitated powerful activities that compelled them to look deeply into their souls. Each member of the group was asked to bring an artifact to share that would describe him/her. Written student reflections validated the impact of this activity. This assignment was the starting point for most cohort members. In the formative stages of an organization or group, it is important for members to examine their strengths and weaknesses. It was important for the professors to model a trust-building exercise at this stage of the cohort. "The trust and climate that permeated after that exercise had a positive effect on our commitment, our personal motivation, and most definitely our confidence. The exercise sparked conversation, inquiry, and with time, meaningful relationships" (Pesina, Reed, Schulte, Whited, & Woodberry, 2004, p.5). As each of us revealed the inner layers of our lives, the ground was soft for trust to form within the group. "Our instructors in the spring … were dynamic, supportive, caring and encouraged us to be risk takers, those who will develop and create our schools to foster the risk of investing in ideas to think about different alternatives" (Galinzoga, Morado, & Vargas, 2004. p. 3). We recognized that this activity was obviously an epiphany not only for the students, but also for our professors as stated by Dr. Merchant:

> I actually think the first "a-ha" moment, at least for me, was the artifact exercise … the collective artifact exercise was extremely powerful. And I think what everyone got out of that, including Dean Cardenas and myself, was the fact that everyone of the people in the cohort embodied the passion for social justice. (Galinzoga et al., 2004, p. 3)

The spring sessions set the stage and expectations for the rest of the faculty and the students for the two classes during the summer. I (Garza) was assigned to teach one of those courses. Another professor facilitated a course in supervision and evaluation which was also carefully designed to elicit deep reflection and personal growth. One participant noted"

> EDL 6973 was not just another class. Rather, it was a life-changing experience, an authentic experience, causing one to look inward, to reflect, to think, to empathize, to self-monitor and to personally adjust. I learned so much, and grew personally. Dealing with controversial issues caused us to grow together, not apart. (Lynn)

The cohort came to a point of transformation and growth through reflection, bonding and trust; "Reflection was the avenue we used in order for us to strengthen our core beliefs about social justice and validate each member's unique contributions. Individuals whose voices were barely heard last semester became louder" (Galinzoga et al., 2004, p. 3).

The assignments for this class required students to look deeply inside themselves. First, they were asked to develop a set of core beliefs about children. They had been able to articulate their values and beliefs verbally, but none of them had ever put these in writing; "We, in essence, looked into "our box" so that we could start thinking out of the box." (Virginia). One group emphasized the importance of reflection in this process:

> As educational leaders we knew our vision and goals and yet could not pinpoint the experiences that had lead each of us to these non-negotiable beliefs about education and our role as leaders. Through deep, meaningful discussions we were able to dig, find and reflect on those "educational moments" that defined us as the educators we are. Reflection allowed us to turn inward and evaluate ourselves with questions like, "Who am I?" "What are my core beliefs?" and "What is the baggage that I bring to the table that affects my educational perspective. (Galinzoga et al., 2004, p. 4)

Several students observed that this exercise was deceivingly difficult. It made them feel more accountable to themselves because it served as a written contract which became a document that bound them to their commitment to social justice. Using these core beliefs, they also wrote a philosophy statement. They were able to explain how they had developed some of their non-negotiables and how their lived experiences had influenced their philosophy. They were also asked to write their life story in the form of a self-presentation. As their professor, I (Garza) gave them copies of my set of core beliefs, philosophy statement and life story. My own self-disclosure was a form of modeling and it facilitated the building of a trusting relationship.

In the fall of 2003 the next professors taught the research and proseminar courses as a team. By this time, the students came to expect all professors to integrate reflection in all their courses. So reflection was embedded in these classes too. During this class the students experienced another moment of revelation. A student speaking on behalf of the group expressed the following:

> We kind of came to the conclusion that we knew too much to go back. We couldn't define it, but we understood that because there were fourteen of us and we are all working in the same district, there was no way that we could actually stray away from our vision or stray away from what's right for kids without somebody calling us on it later on down the line. (Ruben)

Students' work was designed as action research and special attention was given to scholarly, yet practical, meaningful work in the field. Student reflections validated this practice. Many of the course assignments were relevant to the cohort member's daily work and all served as learning experiences for future work. The cohort appreciated the efforts of the faculty to create relevant learning experiences as evidenced by their reflections (Pesina et al., 2004).

By spring 2004 it had been a year since the students had started the program and their personal and professional growth was incredibly evident. During the fall we met to discuss the possibility of combining the principalship and the internship courses. Class assignments and readings were integrated with and relevant to the practical field experiences of the internship. The two classes merged into one seamless course. Reflection focused primarily on the internship experiences in an effort to connect "theory" with practice:

> The manner in which the course was conducted was very valuable. Reflection (once again) was incredibly powerful. We were asked to examine what was going on in the course, in our schools, in our internship and quite possibly in our lives and interrelate it to the content. (Melissa)

The internship was designed to help students understand the roles and responsibilities associated with the principalship. Students spent a minimum of 50 clock hours interacting with a principal/mentor throughout the semester. This interaction was a combination of shadowing/observation, interviewing/discussion, co-leading, assigned projects, and related activities. Students kept a journal/fieldnotes as a means of gathering and documenting data. They prepared a final report using the Texas Test Framework for Principals as a conceptual model for analyzing their data. The final report included the data analysis, a summary of the findings, implications, and a conclusion. In addition, students were required to bring their mentors to one class meeting to participate in a panel discussion:

> Dr. Garza also invited guest speakers to share their careers and real-life experiences. The best part of the internship was the Principal Panel. The members invited their principal [sponsor] to class. We shared the day-to-day life of a principal.... The best part of the internship was the Principal Panel. The members invited their principal [sponsor] to class. We shared the day-to-day life of a principal. (Karen)

Student feedback reflected their appreciation of these features, "if I had to name this course I would call it 'Principal Confidence Course' because my confidence soared as a result of this course (JC).

The summer of 2004 was a test of perseverance as the students were determined to finish the program and to walk across the stage in December. This required them to take three courses (none credit hours) in the summer and six in the fall or vice-versa. They decided upon the former but wanted to complete their courses by the end of July so that they could have some time off before they returned to work. We knew that it would be very difficult for them to take three courses in 4 weeks. This required a non-traditional approach to scheduling. It was decided that they would take one course at a time in 2-week intervals beginning in mid-May. After an intensive and grueling 6 weeks they were done with General Finance and Taxation, Administration and Function of Special Programs, and Psychological Basis of Learning.

By the fall 2004 the cohort was in their final semester. Although they were enrolled in only two courses, the intensity did not diminish. Besides their coursework, they had to take and successfully negotiate the required comprehensive exam in order to graduate. In addition, they were preparing to take the state principal certification exam (TExES). During this last semester, the cohort was enrolled in a special topics class as a culminating activity for their preparation. The main purpose of the course was to have the students reflect on their experiences of the 2-year program. To capture and document their stories, the students produced a video documentary that was presented at the annual convention of the University Council for Educational Administration (UCEA) in Kansas City, Missouri (2004). In addition, they presented four papers titled; *Understanding Alternative Viewpoints as a Means for Transformation, Social Justice and the Cohort Experience, Building Leader's Visions and Self-Efficacy, and Analysis of Relationships within a Cohort Model for Educational Leaders*. To produce the documentary, the students video taped many hours of interviews with each of their professors, the SAISD superintendent, other SAISD administrators, and other district administrators. Three main themes emerged from their analysis: relationships, transformation, and social justice.

The professors closely observed how this semester-long reflection exercise influenced them. The students learned a great deal more about each other, but mostly importantly, more about themselves. Asking and answering critical and thought provoking questions during these interviews resulted in considerable self-disclosure. This was the ultimate degree of the reflective pedagogy.

All Cohort 1 students completed their program in December 2004, all of them took the state principalship certification exam, all 14 passed and all were in attendance at their graduation ceremony. Their appointments are diverse and at all three levels: one is an elementary principal, three are high school assistant principals, three are middle school assistant principals, one is an elementary assistant principal and one is a district level special education coordinator. The other six cohort members have not yet decided to apply for administrative positions; three are curriculum coordinators and three are classroom teachers and one is a full-time doctoral student.

Some evidence suggests that cohort experiences extended beyond the graduate program by building professional networks and altering other workplace behaviors. The university acknowledges that preparation does not end with formal coursework and recognizes the importance of support for students as they begin to assume leadership positions. Although Cohort 1 students have completed their preparation, their relationship with the university continues. The university has made special efforts to continue a close relationship with Cohort 1 students. For example, they have been assigned as mentors to the new cohort students. They have attended class with their mentees and they have participated in several class activities. The Cohort 1 mentors have served as case studies for the new cohort and we continue to gather post program data them.

COHORT 2

It was expected that we would proceed to identify the students for Cohort 2 to begin the program in the Spring 2005. SAISD began to accept nominations in the fall of 2004 and finalized their selection in October 2004. After the applications were screened, 22 candidates were invited to participate. The candidates knew that selection did not guarantee admission; only 16 of the 22 candidates decided to accept the invitation to the USLC.

We were assigned to team teach the first to two classes for Cohort 2. It was immediately obvious that the new group was different from Cohort 1 in several ways. The most obvious difference was gender representation, 8 females and 6 males. In general, Cohort 2 was younger, and thus, less experienced. Cohort 1 students had more time in the SAISD system; 8 were Campus Instructional Coordinators (CICs) and 4 were classroom teachers. In contrast, in Cohort 2 only 2 were CICs and 14 were classroom teachers. Eight of the cohort members were Latino, 3 were African American, and 3 were White.

We integrated our course syllabi and taught the classes as a team. One of the main purposes for these combined courses was to introduce and socialize them into the program and our main goal for this semester was to begin to build cohesiveness within the group. Our syllabus was carefully crafted to include activities that kept Cohort 1 students involved as mentors. This was mutually beneficial to both groups. We matched mentors and mentees based on similarities and differences. The first activity was to arrange a formal meeting between mentors and mentees. It was held during one of our initial class meetings at the home of one of the Cohort 1 students.

Collaboration between UTSA and SAISD went beyond program planning and student selection. It was important to establish relationships and networks with school administrators. Two SAISD central administrators were therefore assigned to teach a curriculum course. Working collaboratively with the field also encourages academics to leave the sanctuary of the university to work with practitioners in the naturalistic setting of the school campus. Most of the classes were held on school district campuses and while this may seem insignificant, it is important to students. "I really enjoy the classes and especially that they are held on our turf in the schools" (Stefanie).

The second course the students took was Contemporary Educational Philosophy. Cohort 1 had taken this course at the end of their program, but recommended that it should be at the beginning.

The fall and spring courses (Research and Pro-Seminar, Legal Foundations in Education, Administration and Function of Special Programs and School and Community Relations were taught by a mix of individual and team approaches.

The summer courses (Psychological Basis of Learning and General Finance and Taxation) were again taught by SAISD administrators. Their last two courses were also team taught and like the previous cohort, they took and passed the comprehensive exam and also presented at the UCEA conference that was held in San Antonio, Texas (2006). Twelve of the 16 members of Cohort II graduated in December 2006 while the remaining four self-selected out of the program. Of these two enrolled in the department's traditional master's program in educational leadership. The third left without providing an explanation, and the fourth left for financial reasons. Two of the four were Latino, one was an African American female and the other was a White male. We are unable to draw definitive conclusions about the factors that resulted in the withdrawal of the first three students (African American female, Latino male, and White male). However, we speculate that their departure from the program was motivated, at least in part, by their discomfort with our focus on constructivist teaching, self-reflection, exploration of biases, and critical examination of the personal, and professional factors that shape beliefs about self and others. The White male specifically expressed his discomfort with these approaches as well as his conviction that these exercises were not a good use of his tuition money.

RACIAL IDENTITY, SOCIAL AGENCY AND, LEADERSHIP FOR SOCIAL JUSTICE

The knowledge gained from the cohort experience has not only contributed to the individual development of each aspiring school leader, but it has provided us with important insights into the value of reflective practice as a tool for training school leaders to recognize how their racial and cultural identities intersect with their position as leaders for social justice. "From the very beginning the of the partnership between the University of Texas at San Antonio and San Antonio Independent School District, cohort members became cognizant of the diversity of their life experiences and the importance of social justice" (Kuyoth, Olvera-Cruz, & Karen, 2004, p. 11). Most of the educators in this collaborative acknowledged that the program's focus on social justice was significant in their future career plans. "When I heard that the program focused on social justice, my antennae wiggled," stated one student. She decided to join the cohort mainly because of this focus. Once in the program, students deepened their reflections on this theme. One commented how she made sense of the new information:

> The cohort helped me realize what diversity as connected to social justice was. I was not aware of the term until the cohort began exploring the issue. I was not aware that I was an advocate until the class reflections brought it to my attention. So this in itself prepared me to be an advocate and activist. It gave method to my madness. I now have a justification for my cause.

The program also provided a safe place for students to reflect on their own experiences of marginalization:

> I have been given the opportunity to express my views in a safe forum. My colleagues have been given the same opportunity. The topics discussed were appropriate, and timely. We attempt as educators to address variables that affect student learning, but only scratch the surface. (Ruben)

These opportunities helped students develop skills to connect (Merchant & Shoho, 2002) their own identity with their decision to adopt social justice as a mission. However, it was evident that it was difficult to translate their lived experiences into social agency when they had to confront their own racial identity. One of the students stated:

> Our conversation in class was stimulating. How do we label ourselves? There are a multitude of options for Latinos to use: Chicano, Hispanic, Latino, Mexican, Mexican-American, etcetera. During my college years, I thought of my race and ethnicity daily since I went to school in a predominantly

Anglo school and town. I personally never thought about my race as an identifying factor in my current school because as an administrator in a predominantly Latino school, I am part of the majority ... I don't want my skin color or my last name to dictate and influence what others think of me.

Reflection was painful; it opened up the wounds of cruelty and humiliation they had experienced in lives. Students shared their experiences openly and with great emotion:

When I got into a new school after the age of 12, I was being singled out. I was told to return across the Rio Grande. I had never even heard of the Rio Grande. So, I asked my father what that meant. I recall that day very well, for it would be the day that I would be stereotyped and made to assimilate into the white way of life. I was deprived of my culture in school. It was bad to speak Spanish. I learned the English language at the expense of losing my own identity. I was being asked to no longer be proud to be a Mexican American.

While ethnicity was always at the center of the students' reflections, issues of gender and leadership were also part of the discussions. One student shared that she prepared herself through self-discovery; "sometimes through painful reflection, to what it means to be a woman ... leader ... a Latina leader!" Students were in conflict about losing or having lost their racial and cultural identity. They were keenly aware of Valenzuela's (1999) notion of subtractive schooling. They realized that their own schooling had erased their culture and identity and that no matter how much they tried, others would still determine where *one belongs* based on race or gender:

None of my teachers looked like me, acted like me, or had any sense of my culture. There was never a sense of cultural congruence in my high school years. The only class that had a teacher that looked like me was Spanish. Even in that class I was seen as different because I did not speak Spanish. Many times other students would ask me, "How did I get a higher grade than you? I mean, you are Mexican. I felt like a failure all the way around, I was unable to perform well in academic classes and the only class where the instructor looked like me, and where I was "supposed" to perform well, I performed at an average level. When my Spanish teacher spoke to me in Spanish, I felt like a failure because I was unable to answer her back in Spanish.

The lived experiences of the students were strongly connected to their commitment to social justice and their potential for advocacy was evident in their reflections:

I know the meaning of suffering, and do whatever I can to help end it. Students misbehave in classes because they are dealing with issues no child or adult should have to experience," stated one of the educators. "The program helped me to stand up for the people who are unable to speak for themselves," affirmed another educator, "especially children who are unable to verbalize their troubles—that's why I want to be a voice for them

However, it is important to note that learning about social justice does not necessarily inspire or result in social agency, unless diversity issues are adopted in their mission. As one student stated, "embracing diversity requires courageous decision making to address the status quo." Reflection about the challenge ahead in becoming future school leaders was expressed as realizing that "sometimes the things you don't do ... also send a strong message."

LESSONS LEARNED

We learned several lessons with our experiences with Cohort 1. The most striking observation was the realization that we had plenty to learn about collaborative preparation programs. We learned that we did not know all the answers with Cohort 1 and we still do not know all the answers with Cohort 2. Our experience with Cohort 1 was very positive and rewarding. As individuals, members of Cohort 1 pulled together to negotiate and navigate through the program. This was a highly successful group of students who depended upon each other for support. They established high standards and very high expectations for future cohorts.

These positive experiences led to our first mistake with Cohort 2. It was difficult to avoid a comparison between the two groups. Fortunately, as we discussed the differences among ourselves, we realized that it was not fair to Cohort 2. We came to realize that we must consciously avoid this unfair comparison. Every individual is different and every combination of individuals makes every group unique. We learned that it is our responsibility as professors to facilitate a process that builds meaningful relationships with our students and among themselves. We learned that group cohesiveness and strength is possible only when the cohort members feel respected as individuals. We learned that comparing Cohort 2 to Cohort 1 was not respectful to the individual student or to the group in this regard.

We learned some logistical things as well. Feedback from Cohort 1 was important and taken very seriously. We learned that certain courses were more useful at the beginning and we adjusted the sequence of courses accordingly. Also, expert and willing faculty were specifically assigned for the 2-year program. We have learned that feedback from students about their progress and experience in the cohort was critical.

With Cohort 2, we met with students early to discuss their progress. This was useful because students were asked to assess themselves individually and as members of the cohort. Although this was done in an informal and non-threatening way, the information was useful because it helped us make changes to improve the program.

It also became obvious to us that, unless we formally include our former students in our teaching and preparation programs, they will not feel connected to the university beyond the completion of their programs. One student offered the following reflection:

> Requiring us to meet and log our experiences was difficult, but necessary. If we weren't forced to do it, the likelihood of our getting together would be minimal. I intend to maintain our friendship for as long as possible and only hope that I in turn can provide to [mentor] something of value in return.

Finally, we have learned that gaining experience is important, but this experience can also get in the way. One year of experience with our partnership with SAISD helped us gain new knowledge about collaboration and program implementation. However, this experience also created some issues because our expectations for the members of the second cohort became barriers rather than tools to develop their unique skills.

It is evident that collaboration has been critically important for both institutions; both the school district and the university manifest a mutual commitment to the students and their success. This partnership approach has helped to facilitate and support students through the program. Students have expressed their appreciation for the opportunity to learn from each other and their professors. Equally important is the support and recognition from the school district. Student persistence and success is the product of the genuine collaboration of the partnership.

Although we are pleased with our analysis of the early stages of the USLC, there is much more work to be done. The principle ingredients of a successful partnership are in place to maintain credibility with district leaders and cohort members. As this endeavor proceeds, the Educational Leadership and Policy Studies department faculty anticipates that other partnerships will be formed, and resulting modifications made in both the on-campus master's degree and principal certification programs.

The knowledge gained from the cohort experience has not only contributed to the individual development of each aspiring school leader, but it has provided us with important insights into the value of reflective practice as a tool for training school leaders to recognize how their racial identity intersects with their position as leaders for social justice. As professors, it is our responsibility to set the stage for critical thought about social justice and to better prepare our graduates to be effective leaders of schools with diverse populations of students, particularly Latinos and English language learners who comprise the majority of students in the public schools in which we work

REFERENCES

A JBHE Report Card on the Progress of Blacks on the Faculties of the Nation's Highest-Ranked Colleges and Universities. (2001–2002, Winter). *The Journal of Blacks in Higher Education, 34*, 10–14.

Callahan, R. (1962). *Education and the cult of efficiency.* Chicago: University of Chicago Press.

Capper, C. (1993). Administrator practice and preparation for social reconstructionist schooling. In *Educational administration in a pluralistic society* (pp. 288–315). Albany: State University of New York Press.

Cárdenas, J. A., Robledo, M., & Supick, J. (2001). *Texas school dropout survey project.* San Antonio, TX: Intercultural Development Research Association.

Collins, J. (1999). *Good to great: Why some companies make the leap ... and others don't.* New York: Harper Collins.

Cummins, J. (1989). *Empowering minority students.* Sacramento: California Association for Bilingual Education.

Donmoyer, R., Imber, M., & Scheurich, J. (1995). *The knowledge base in educational administration: Multiple perspectives.* Albany: State University of New York Press.

Galinzoga, S., Morado, A., & Vargas, V. (2004, November). *Understanding Alternative Viewpoints as a Means for Transformation.* Paper presented at the University Council of Educational Administration annual conference, Kansas City, MO.

Garza, E., Reyes, P., & Trueba, E. (2004). *Resiliency and success: A case of migrant children in the United States.* Boulder, CO: Paradigm.

Gonzalez, M. (2002). The pivotal role of the principal. In M. Gonzalez, A. Huerta-Macias, & J. Tinajero (Eds.), *Educating Latino students: A guide to successful practice* (pp 3–28). Lanham, MD: Scarecrow Press.

Gonzalez, M., Huerta-Macias, A., & Tinajero, J. (Eds.). (2002). *Educating Latino students: A guide to successful practice.* Lanham, MD: Scarecrow Press.

Hargens, L., & Long, J. S. (2002). Demographic inertia and women's representation among faculty in higher education. *The Journal of Higher Education, 73*(4), 494–506.

Johnson, B. C., & Shoho, A. R. (2002). *Social justice in educational administration preparation programs.* Paper presented at the meeting of the University Council for Educational Administration, Pittsburgh, PA.

Kuyoth, L., Olvera-Cruz, I., & Karen, R. (2004, November). *Social justice and the Cohort experience.* Paper presented at the University Council of Educational Administration annual conference, Kansas City, MO.

Lindholm, J., Astin, A., Sax, L., & Korn, W. (2002). *The American college teacher national norms for the 2001–2002 HERI faculty survey.* Los Angeles: Higher Education Research Institute.

Lomotey, K. (1989). Cultural diversity in the urban school: Implications for principals. *NASSP Bulletin, 73*(521), 81–85.

Lomotey, K. (1995). Social and cultural influences on schooling: A commentary on the UCEA Knowledge Base Project, Domain I. *Educational Administration Quarterly, 31*(2), 294–303.

Lugg, C. A. (2002, October). *Social justice and educational administration: No longer mutually exclusive?* Paper presented at the meeting of the University Council for Educational Administration, Pittsburgh, PA.

Marshall, C., & McCarthy, M. (2002). School leadership reforms: Filtering social justice through dominant discourses. *Journal of School Leadership, 12*(5), 480–502.

Merchant, B. M. (1999a). Ghosts in the classroom. Unavoidable (?) casualties of principals' commitment to the status quo. *Journal of Education for Students Placed at Risk, 4*(2), 153–171.

Merchant, B. M. (1999b). Now you see it; now you don't: A district's short-lived commitment to an alternative high school for newly-arrived immigrants. *Urban Education, 34*(1), 26–51.

Merchant, B. M., & Shoho, A. R. (2002, October). *Bridge people: Leaders for Social Justice.* Paper presented at the meeting of the University Council for Educational Administration, Pittsburgh, PA

National Center for Education Statistics. (1996). *Urban schools: The challenge of location and poverty* (NCES 96-184). Washington, DC: U.S. Department of Education.

National Center for Educational Statistics. (2002). *Digest of educational statistics. Chapter 2: Elementary and secondary education.* Retrieved March 23, 2003, from http://nces.ed.gov/programs/digest/d02/tables/dt101.asp

Pesina, R., Reed, E., Schulte, S., Whited, D., & Woodberry, J.C. (2004). *Analysis of relationships within a Cohort model for educational leaders.* Paper presented at the University Council of Educational Administration annual conference, Kansas City, MO.

Pierce, P. (1935). *The origin and development of the public school principalship.* Chicago: The University of Chicago Press.

Pounder, D. (1990, October). *Educational megatrends and increased female leadership in schools.* Paper presented at the annual meeting of the University Council for Educational Administration, Pittsburgh, PA.

Reyes, P., Scribner, J. D., & Paredes Scribner, A. (1999). *Lessons from high performing Hispanic schools: Creating learning communities.* New York: Teachers College Press.

Scheurich, J., Skrla, L., & Johnson, J. (2000). Thinking carefully about equity and accountability. *Phi Delta Kappan, 82*(4) 293–300.

Texas Education Agency. (2001). *Academic excellence indicator system.* Austin: Author. Retrieved March 1, 2007, from http://www.tea.state.tx.us

Texas Education Agency. (2002). *Academic excellence indicator system.* Austin: Author. Retrieved March 15, 2007, from http://www.tea.state.tx.us

Texas Education Agency. (2005). *Academic excellence indicator system.* Austin: Author. Retrieved March 15, 2007, from http://www.tea.state.tx.us

Rorrer, A. (2002, October). *District leadership: Reinstitutionalizing equity in American public education.* Paper presented at the meeting of the University Council for Educational Administration, Pittsburgh, PA.

Turner, C. (2000). New faces, new knowledge. *Academe, 86*(5), 34–39.

Tyack, D., & Hansot, E. (1982). *Managers of virtue: Public school leadership in America, 1820–1980.* New York: Basic Books.

U.S. Census Bureau. (2005). Retrieved April 15, 2007, from http://www.census.gov/Press-Release/www/2005/dp.comptables.html

Valencia, R. R. (1991). The plight of Chicano students: An overview of schooling conditions and outcomes. In *Chicano school failure and success: Research and policy agendas for the 1990's* (pp. 204–251). London: Falmer Press.

Valenzuela, A. (1999). Subtractive schooling: U.S. Mexican youth and the politics of caring. Albany: State University of New York Press.

Waits, M. J., Campbell, H. E., Gau, R., Jacobs, E., Rex, T., & Hess, R. K. (2006). *Why some schools with Latino children beat the odds … and others don't.* Tempe, AZ: Morrison Institute for Public Policy& Center for the Future of Arizona.

Zeichner, K. M. (1993). Educating teachers for cultural diversity (Special report). East Lansing, MI: National Center for Research on Teacher Learning.

CHAPTER 8

A CRITICAL DISCOURSE ANALYSIS OF THE MEANINGS OF HISPANIC AND LATINO IN THE UNITED STATES

Carlos Martin Vélez and John Collard

INTRODUCTION

Both the terms that people use to identify themselves and the reasons for adopting them are varied and complex, and their meanings are continuously contested.... Thus, exploring the meanings and social values embedded in these terms is essential for these labels play a significant role in the struggle for citizenship rights and social justice in U.S. contemporary society. (Oboler, González, Aparicio, Torres, & Torres-Saillant, p. 511)

How valid, reliable and useful are ethnic descriptors as stereotypes in contemporary U.S. society and popular culture? This study reports upon a broad scale investigation into the use of these terms in journalistic reports, a gubernatorial debate, and in depth interviews with academics and journalists. The study uncovered an array of consistent meanings and

Leadership and Intercultural Dynamics, pp. 151–171
Copyright © 2009 by Information Age Publishing
All rights of reproduction in any form reserved.

preference for the Hispanic/Hispano label over the Latino in *New York Times*, *San Antonio Express News*, and *La Prensa* newspaper reports. Journalists were found to associate "Hispanic" with political issues and use "Latino" to describe cultural realities, especially in the music industry. Both terms were also used interchangeably in a number of news reports. Academics tended to attach the terms to local and institutional realities.

The study reveals how both personal and public utterances falsely categorize and obscure differences among minorities of Mexican, Latin American, and Spanish descent in the U.S. today. It illustrates how the superficial use of the descriptors fails to comprehend the actual complexity of ethnic cultures and linguistic and social identities within them. The hegemonic usage of ethnic labeling in public and institutional discourses is treated as problematical and an argument is advanced to dispense with generic typologies and to replace them with grounded understandings of particular forms of Hispanic and Latino identities in specific places and times.

A subsequent argument is that the use of ethnic labels in educational leadership discourse needs to be treated with great caution. If such labels tend to obscure the heterogeneity of Hispanic/Latino groups in public discourse, but are better understood in specialist ethnic studies programs, they are also likely to become confused in educational discourses. How do such contradictions effect the development of children, adolescents and adults who are trying to construct a coherent and viable identity as Hispanic/Latino Americans? What cognitions are in operation when teachers and academics work with members of these ethnic minorities? These questions prompt us to develop more nuanced understandings (Collard & Wang, 2005; Lincoln & Denzin, 2003) capable of recognizing and attending to the aspirations and needs of specific individuals and populations. Such discourses also need to address the intersection of specific ethnicities with variables such as age, family cultures, gender, individual histories, sexuality, and social class. Only then will educational leaders begin to deal with the reality that individuals are culturally and historically situated requiring nuanced strategies of care and responsibility.

The U.S. Census uses ethnic/racial labels to produce statistics on the socio and economic advancement of various ethnic groups (Yanow, 2003), including those of Hispanics/Latinos. Scholars tend to favor the use of Latino over Hispanic in their academic work. The idea that Hispanics/Latinos are people who claim present or previous heritage in a Spanish speaking nations in Latin America or Spain is common in most discourses in the United States. It is also common knowledge that Hispanic, Hispano, and Latino are generally used to lump U.S. Latino groups for specific marketing or political purposes in news reports, Web sites, or TV news.

Hispanic and Latino conceptions are closely connected to the imaginary cultural and social identity of a racial/ethnic "minority group" in the social structure in the United States. In this regard, the U.S. Census Bureau produces and reproduces Hispanic and Latino identities through the classification of people and dissemination of information about this ethnic/racial group (Gimenez, 2006). In 2000, the U.S. Census Bureau added Latino to Spanish/Hispanic to the official ethnic classification of people who indicate their origin as Mexican, Puerto Rican, Cuban, Central, or South American, or some other Hispanic origin (Guzmán, 2001), and who lived in the United States. Similarly, recent U.S. Census information (see Table 8.1) shows the increase of Hispanic origin groups in the United States from 1990 to 2000 indirectly produces an association of these groups with nationality groups from Spanish speaking nations in Latin America and Spain. Table 8.1 also shows a very high increase of people who self-identified as Latino in 2000 as compared to 1990. However what regiments these labels? Who is considered Hispanic or Latino in the news? What are the purposes of using these labels? Who benefits, and who loses out because the use of these labels? Moreover, what are the subjective and situated dimensions of the local meanings[1] of Hispanic (Hispano) and Latino?[2]

We rarely examine the powerful effect of the media in shaping people's knowledge of those categorized as Hispanics/Latinos. Thus we need to research the meanings and social values of the terms *Hispanic* and *Latino*. We also need to research the subjective understandings held by diverse members of U.S. Hispanic/Latino groups, from native to foreign born to legal and illegal immigrants, if we wish to advance the social and educational conditions of these diverse U.S. minority groups.[3] The multilayered social, cultural, and sociocognitive dynamics that inform the local meanings of Hispanic and Latino among segments of this heterogeneous population needed incisive understanding if we are to achieve equal for citizenship rights and social justice for them in the United States.

HISTORICAL FACTORS

The interchangeable use of Hispanic and Latino in public discourses can be associated with ongoing immigration from Latin America, especially from Mexico. Immigration grew in the 1970s, gathered momentum in the 1980s, and surged in the mid-1990s. The Hispanic population more than doubled between 1980 and 2000, increasing from 14.6 to 35.3 million (Pew Hispanic Center, 2005). Current reports indicate people of Mexican origin are the highest proportion (18 million) among foreign born populations from Latin America The number of illegal immigrants is around

Table 8.1. Hispanic Origin Population by Detailed Group: 1990 and 2000

Population by Origin Response	Census 1990 Total Number	Census 1990 (%)	Census 2000 Total Number	Census 2000 (%)	Change 1990 to 2000 Total Number	Change 1990 to 2000 (% +/-)
Total	**21,900,089**	**100.0**	**35,238,481**	**100.0**	**13,338,392**	**60.9**
Mexican	13,393,208	61.2	20,900,102	59.3	7,506,894	56.1
Puerto Rican	2,651,815	12.1	3,403,510	9.7	751,695	28.3
Cuban	1,053,197	4.8	1,249,820	3.5	196,623	18.7
Dominican	520,151	2.4	799,768	2.3	279,617	53.8
Central American	1,323,830	6.0	1,811,676	5.1	487,846	36.9
Costa Rican	57,223	0.3	72,175	0.2	14,952	26.1
Guatemalan	268,779	1.2	407,127	1.2	138,348	51.5
Honduran	131,066	0.6	237,431	0.7	106,365	81.2
Nicaraguan	202,658	0.9	194,493	0.6	-8,165	-4.0
Panamanian	92,013	0.4	98,475	0.3	6,462	7.0
Salvadoran	565,081	2.6	708,741	2.0	143,660	25.4
Other Central American	7,010	0.0	93,234	0.3	86,224	1,230.0
South American	1,035,602	4.7	1,419,979	4.0	384,377	37.1
Argentinean	100,921	0.5	107,275	0.3	6,354	6.3
Bolivian	38,073	0.2	45,188	0.1	7,115	18.7
Chilean	68,799	0.3	73,951	0.2	5,152	7.5
Colombian	378,726	1.7	496,748	1.4	118,022	31.2

Ecuadorian	191,198	0.9	273,013	0.8	81,815	42.8
Paraguayan	6,662	0.0	8,929	0.0	2,267	34.0
Peruvian	175,035	0.8	247,601	0.7	72,566	41.5
	21,996	0.1	20,242	0.1	−1,754	−8.0
Uruguayan	47,997	0.2	96,091	0.3	48,094	100.2
Venezuelan	6,195	0.0	50,941	0.1	44,746	722.3
Other South American	519,136	2.4	112,999	0.3		
Spaniard	1,403,150	6.4	5,540,627	15.7	−406,137	−78.2
General Hispanic	390,945	1.8	2,316,515	6.6	4,137,477	294.9
Hispanic	1,577	0.0	411,559	1.2	1,925,570	492.5
Latino	444,896	2.0	765,879	2.2	409,982	25,997.6
Spanish	565,732	2.	2,046,674	5.8	320,983	72.1
Other Hispanic					1,480,942	261.8

Source: U.S. Census Bureau, Census 2000 and Census 1990.

11 million and more than 6 million are also of Mexican origin (Passel, 2005).

Quantitative studies in the previous decade associated factors such as age and generation to the use of Hispanic or Latino among survey respondents (de la Garza, De Sipio, Garcia, & Garcia, 1996; Jones-Correa & Leal, 1992). However, qualitative and theoretical studies have offered different analyses of the ideologies, meanings and contextual factors related to the use of Hispanic or Latino labels in the United States (Chabram-Dernersesian, 2003; Gimenez, 1992; Mignolo, 2002). These have deepened our understanding of factors that affect the meanings of Latino or Hispanic as ethnic labels which have been used to create a sense of pan-ethnic community among various Latino groups in the United States (Jones-Correa & Leal, 1996).

Theoretical interpretations suggest that hegemonic ideologies and the official imposition of the Latino or Hispanic label erases the racial, historical, and cultural differences between the various U.S. Hispanic or Latino groups (Forbes, 1992; Gimenez, 1992; Hayes-Bautista & Chapa, 1987). Other studies imply that there are hemispheric neo-liberal economic motives for the recent preference of the Latino term (Chabram-Dernersesian, 2003; Mignolo, 2002). Mexican-American perspectives since the late 1960s which the use terms such Chicano, Hispanic, reflects active re-negotiation of ethnic labels. They argue that the Chicano label emerged as a form of political identification in the late 1960s for Mexican, but was displaced by the Hispanic label some years later by a number of politicians (Muñoz, 1989). The use of the latter label is favored among middle-class Mexican Americans (Acuña, 1996; Foley, 1997), or politicians (De León, 1999; García, 1996). These studies therefore suggest that the term Chicano was a generational political identity among Mexican Americans and that the use of Hispanic, especially of Texas, symbolized an acceptance of a less progressive and perhaps conservative ideology.

Ethnographic studies among immigrant and established Latino groups have found that social actors use the Latino label when diverse groups work towards a common political goal (Padilla, 1985). Other studies suggest that Hispanic or Latino are employed as racial labels that go beyond Black and White (Flores-Gonzalez, 1999; Itzigsohn & Dore-Cabral, 2001). Further studies suggest that Chicano professionals' use of Hispanic or Latino depends on political decisions to include Latin American professionals in their job-related networks (Hoover Rentería, 1998). Finally, other studies imply that adult Latin American immigrants may adopt these labels based on their social class background (Oboler, 1995).

Many scholars have suggested that the subjective meanings and relevant contextual factors which effect these meanings should be investigated (Gómez, 1992; Itzigsohn & Dore-Cabral, 2001; Oboler, 1995; Schecter & Bayley, 2002; Stephens, 2003). Others scholars have suggested that political alliances for social justice goals among different Latino groups could be advanced by acknowledging the structural differences between the groups but keeping Latino as an umbrella label to unite them (Barbosa-Carter, 1999).

The power of media discourse in modern information societies is undeniable (Cotter, 2002; van Dijk, 2000). This power is "discursive" (expressed, enacted, and confirmed by text and talk) and "symbolic" since media discourse is the main source of people's knowledge, attitudes, and ideologies (van Dijk, 2001, p. 36). Recent empirical studies of the discursive nature of Latino representation in U.S. public discourse in California, argue that the U.S. media shapes public opinion and aligns it with the ideology of the dominant culture and society at large (Darder, 1998; Santa Anna, 2002).

These cognition-and-language-based studies shed light on the representation and racialization of U.S. Latinos in immigration and education-related news (Urciuoli, 2003), and point to the need for more research in this area. Specifically, scholars have advanced our understanding of Latino representation using textual analysis of large quantities of national and regional newspaper articles. Findings suggest that Latinos are seen as foreigners in the California in the 1990s (Santa Ana, 2002) or as an underclass in North Carolina in the same decade (Vargas, 2000), Representations of Latinos' s in printed media are thereby seen contribute to the distancing or exclusion of Latinos from the fabric of the U.S. mainstream. Latino and minority media research have also contributions to our understanding of Latino representation in U.S. mainstream television news (Subervi, 2004) and in U.S. newspapers written in Spanish (Benitez, 2003).

Academics and programs in ethnic studies, tend to use the labels Latino, Chicano, and Mexican American in addition to Hispanic to explore the meanings associated with these terms. Latino has been the focus of attention among Chicano scholars (Chabram-Dernersesian, 2003), and this category is a useful category for charting areas of intellectual inquiry and political advocacy (Flores, 2003). Chicano studies have matured over time appears to embrace Latino in institutions embedded in specific regional and historical areas in which Mexicans Americans are a majority of the Latino population. Recent research shows that Chicano and Mexican American studies programs are more common than Latino studies programs in the United States (Macías, 2005).

THE STUDY

This strand of the research critically considered the use of ethnic labels in major media outlets and how they are subjectively reflected by those people they aim to represent in U.S. public and institutional spaces. It was by Chicana activist Gloria Anzaldúa. She posits that the collapse of cultural binaries and the continued use of related categories by those in power contains possibilities for challenging established categories obsolete labeling (Anzaldúa, 2002a). Such a stance can be viewed as a Chicana activist's invitation "to move beyond separate and easy identifications creating bridges that cross race and other classifications among different groups via intergenerational dialogue" (Anzaldúa, 2002b, p. 2).

This study adopted a critical discourse approach which Van Dijk has argued that is a *movement* of scholars who focus on social issues and not primarily on academic paradigms. Critical Discourse Analysis (CDA) scholars typically study the use and abuse of power in language and communication in domains such gender, race, ethnicity, and class. Such scholars want to know how discourse enacts, expresses, condones or contributes to the reproduction of inequality (van Dijk, 2004, p. 18). As such CDA offers an approach to accepting Anzaldúa's invitation to move beyond obsolete labels and to study how they contribute to the oppression of groups in societies and institutions like schools and welfare agencies.

The study therefore sought to investigate the local meanings of Hispanic and Latino labels in newspapers texts and personal interviews with academics and journalists in New York City and San Antonio, Texas. The agency of individuals in negotiating and contesting hegemonic and obsolete labels was also explored.

Van Dijk (1993) argues that sociopolitical analyses of language use, needs to explore the cognition of individuals as well intersect this dimension with the social conditions in which language is used in communicative situations. This help us to understand the labels *Hispanic* and *Latino* contribute to the construction of subjective identities and to manage group identities, attitudes, knowledge, opinions. In addition this study also used content analysis to counteract the critiques from media research scholars about how representative texts used in CDA research projects tend to be. A coding-scheme was used for this. Second, linguistics tools were used to describe and analyze the words associated with Hispanic and Latino labels in the newspaper corpora used in this investigation. This enabled combining the findings of the content analysis with a representative sample of articles from the corpora. The descriptions provided by these methods can helped situate the discourse analysis of representative articles into van Dijk's sociocognitive discourse approach.

DISCOURSE DATA

Five different types of data and three research tools were used to compare and contrast the meanings of Hispanic and Latino in various language texts. These included the editorial policies on the use of Hispanic and Latino in The *New York Times* (*NYT*), *San Antonio Express News* (SAE) and *La Prensa* (*LAP*) (Data Set 1). Next 3,115 newspaper texts published in 2002 that contained Hispanic, Hispano, or Latino labels in these three papers from electronic data sources were analyzed (Data Set 2). Nine representative news reports drawn from this data set became Data Set 3. In addition, 21 news reports on the Texas Gubernatorial Spanish/English Debate in March 2002 were also examined (Data Set 4). Finally four interview transcripts with academics and journalists in San Antonio and New York City were also analyzed (Data Set 5).

The media content analysis identified major themes associated with Hispanic, Hispano, and Latino labels in editorial policies and the 3,115 news reports. Next macropropositions were developed that summarized the texts: identification of group schema categories associated with Hispanic/Latino group ideologies, the knowledge types used, opinions, and discourse structures. Macropropositions were inferred from the local (micro) structures of meaning. They provided a first summary of the texts and helped develop topics and group ideology schema. Van Dijk's (1998) schema categories were adapted for Hispanic/Latino groups (see Table 8.2).

EDITORIAL POLICIES

The audiences of the three different newspapers were national, regional and local. The *NYT* is widely recognized as one of the most important newspapers of record in the United States (Cotter, 2002). The *SAE* targets the city's English language readers and is the most important local and regional English paper in South Texas. *LAP* is a family-owned and

Table 8.2. Schema Categories Used to Explore Hispanic/Latino Groups

Membership criteria: Who is Latino? Who is Hispanic? Where are they from? What do Hispanics/Latinos look like? Who belongs to these groups? Who can become a member of these groups?

Activities: What do Hispanics/Latinos do? What is expected of Hispanics/Latinos
Goals: What goals do Hispanics/Latinos want to realize?
Values/norms: What are Hispanic/Latino main values?

operated bilingual newspaper in English and Spanish which targets local bilingual or Spanish or English monolingual readers in San Antonio.

Content analyses indicated the variability that the meanings of Hispanic, Hispano and Latino have in the *NYT*, *SAE* and *LAP* news reports. Editorial policy, regarding the usage of these terms was most clearly stipulated by the *NYT*[4], less clearly defined by the *SAE*, and the *LAP* only articulated a personal policy when interviewed. The editorial policies of three newspapers differed in the meanings associated with these labels.

The *NYT Manual of Style* (Siegal & Connolly, 1999) defined Hispanics as people descended from a Spanish-speaking land or culture. Latino was defined identically. It was noted that although the two terms could be used interchangeably, Hispanic was considered more widespread and Latino was seen to be more common in the West and Southwest states. The *SAE Cyber-Stylebook Book* (2007) maintained that: Hispanic is used when referring to people with Latin American or Spanish roots; Latino or Latina could be used based on a personal choice basis by news actors; Hispanic and Latino/Latina could not be used interchangeably.[5] Policies for the use of Hispano, Hispanic, and Latino were based on the personal decision of the general editor at *LAP*. He paper Hispanic because of its use by the U.S. government.

The media conceptions of Hispanic in general (and Latino in particular) referring to people with roots in Spanish-speaking countries in Latin America and Spain were therefore very similar to that used by The U.S. Census Bureau (Guzmán, 2001). The *LAP* editor had already indicated this and a *SAE* journalist stressed; "I know the difference between all those words.... Uh, but you have to follow your newspaper style and things, but at least, I let the person self identify." In this regard the interviewees in this study differed from the editor of *The Los Angeles Times* who indicated a willingness to use Chicano in addition to Hispanic and Latino in news reports with care and accuracy "to convince all those potential consumers of news that we respect them, and are trying to better understand their diverse culture and national origins" (del Olmo, 2001, p. 12). In relation to the major themes and category texts the terms *Hispanic or Hispano* tended to appear in articles about politics, city life, sports, law, and media (*NYT*); politics, city life, business, health and higher education (*SAE*); and politics, health, aliens, business, and city life (*LAP*). Politics and city life were similar themes in all three papers albeit in different orders of importance. This first level of media content analysis therefore confirmed the practice of labeling diverse ethnic groups as Hispanic in U.S. media discourse. (See Figures 8.1 & 8.2 in Appendices, p. 166)

The term *Latino* had less political and more cultural dimensions. It was primarily associated with politics, city life, and music in the three papers. It also tended to be associated with food in the *NYT* Only the *LAP* linked it with political activism. When the combination Hispanic/Latino label was used it was usually in relation to politics and city life predominated in all three newspapers.

We are therefore able to conclude that the media themes are more inclined to link Hispanic/Hispano to politics whereas Latino is more associated with the arts. This indicates a disassociation of the two terms in U.S. media discourse. We should also bear in mind that (Subervi, Torres, & Montalvo, 2005) analysis of political discourses in national TV networks between 1995–2004 were predominantly focused upon "crime, illegal immigration, and election politics." As 2002 was an election year in the United States, the finding that Hispanics/Latinos were associated with politics is not surprising in this context.

NEWS REPORTS

The characteristics of the three Hispanic/Latino news reports are analyzed in Table 8.3.

The first text 1 (*NYT*) The ambivalence focused upon differences within the population based upon nationality and place of birth citizenship. Immigrant Latinos, were depicted as more socially conservative than those born in the United States. It indicated that a specific candidate was

Table 8.3. Characteristics of Three Representative News Reports

Source/ Date/Author	Theme/ Section/Words	Headline	Summary
NYT, 07/26/02 Mireya Navarro	Politics/B 1594 words	Speaking the language, and the issues, Putaki makes inroads with Latino voters	Governor Pataki is trying to speak fluent Spanish, looking better to many Latinos and has taken specific steps to appeal to Hispanic constituencies although these efforts may be criticized
SAE, 10/04/02 Gary Martin	Politics/A 750 words	Latino vote bloc hard to pin down Neither party has a lock on electorate	President Bush celebrates ethnic diversity with Hispanic leaders. Some findings on a Latinos political attitudes survey are presented.
LAP, 10/10/02 Anonymous	Business/D 519 words	El poder de compra latino es el de mayor crecimiento	Latinos' buying power is growing more than any other minority group and that suggests newer products for these groups

finding strong support among elderly Latinos and newer immigrants in Hispanic enclaves. It indicated that such areas (*SAE*) reported that in the 2000 presidential election, Latinos voted 2-to-1 for Democrat Al Gore over Bush. Among registered Latinos, about half (49%), identified as Democrats, with 20% declaring themselves to be Republican or independent (19%). However, Bush's leadership in the war on terrorism has subsequently helped him to improve his standing with Hispanics and other voting blocs. The poll also found foreign-born, registered Latino voters tended to be more conservative than native-born Hispanics. For example, 46% of foreign-born Hispanics said having a child out of wedlock was unacceptable, compared to 33% for native-born Latinos. The third text (*LAP*) reported that the purchasing power of California Latinos' was the highest in the country, and almost the double of the purchasing of those in the Texas, Florida, New York, and so forth.

The macroproposition ("El Poder de Compra," 2002; Martin, 2002; Navarro, 2002) about the use of Hispanic/Latino in these texts indicates that Hispanic/Latino can was used interchangeably and associated with a political group in English language texts while they tend to be associated with a consumer group in the Spanish language text.

The three writers of the reports provide different slants on Hispanic/Latino topics. The *NYT* writer reports on how the Republican candidate attempts to lure Latino voters, referencing information from a recent Pew Hispanic poll on Latino voters' characteristics. She uses Latino more frequently than Hispanic delineators. The *SAE* writer documents new information gained from a visit to the White House. He quotes segments of President Bush's speech on the opening night of Hispanic Heritage Month. This writer used the terms Latinos and Hispanics more interchangeably than the *NYT* author. He also provided information from the same Pew Hispanic poll on Latino voters as the *NYT* writer. However, the *LAP* writer focused on Latinos'/Hispanos' buying power. Although Latino is favored in the headline, it was also used interchangeably with Hispano.

In addition to the content knowledge the writers have contextually managed the meanings associated with Hispanics and Latinos in their texts, they could have contextually managed the characteristics Latinos/Hispanics under an ideology or group schema.

Analysis of the *NYT* text may suggest that the writer constructs to readers from a Latino immigrant community who can be labeled either Hispanics or Latinos. However, the *SAE* writer assumes an audience who do not differentiate between Hispanic and Latino. Instead he constructs a potential voters' group which blends the two. The *LAP* writer does something similar when he that positions Latinos/Hispanos as a buyers' group in the United States. In all three cases we see how the terms are conflated in public discourse. Of course a subsequent question is whether they are also conflated in professional discourses in areas such as education, health, and welfare.

INTERVIEW WITH AN ACADEMIC

The subject of this interview was born and raised in the US, and is of Puerto Rican ethnic origin. Her age is between 40 and 45 years old and works for a state university in New York city. The interview lasted more than an hour and was in the Professor A's office in May 2006

The macroproposition for the interview was "the institution, an Ethnic Studies Department, has a strong influence on the ideological meanings of ethnic labels." It was associated with the following three topics "Latino constitutes an inclusive term for our ethnic origin (membership criteria); it is a political term (personal knowledge) and it is important to be aware of issues associated with the Latino term (opinion)."

The subject argued that "Latino constitutes a more inclusive label for diverse ethnic origins" because:

- the term Hispanic only refers to that which belongs to Spain
- the term Hispanic ignores the African and indigenous roots Latin American descendants in this country need to acknowledge ... who we are as a people; why we look so different, ... why we have so many different elements from various cultures.
- we don't want to use Hispanic because we favor the term Latino, which is short for Latino/Americano ... more and more people are using the term Latino, it is more inclusive than the term Hispanic.

She stated that her Ethnic Studies Department also adopted the Latino term because many people were using it. She also acknowledged that the term Latino, as opposed to Puerto Rican in her own case, was "a conscious symbol of solidarity with other Latinos in Southwest and Northeast USA."

The subject continued to elaborate her understandings from her period as ar graduate student in a Northeastern university of Latino as a political term as follows:

so you can call yourself Hispanic, I'm not going to look down on you. If I understand you to say that you are Latino, I sort of hear something else. And, what I hear is that you are more politically aware of the political term to identify yourself. Whereas as Hispanic is more of an Anglicized version of the term Hispano, and it was from outside the community, we didn't call ourselves Hispanics.

With regard to how mainstream Americans understand the issues of language use and cultural identity she continued:

> we know, that say for the Mexicans who have been here for seven or eight generations, some ... don't even speak Spanish. Does that make them not a Latino? So, the language issue, in terms of us speaking Spanish, not all of us speak Spanish, but we are still Latino or Hispanic, which ever you prefer, because of our ancestry our culture. It's not that whether we speak Spanish or not.... That is one of the challenges of the term Latino. That people tend to think that we all speak Spanish, when we don't.

She then argued "mainstream society tends to forget that we are very distinct from one another, even our Spanish is distinct." This means that Latinos are not one monolithic group but composed of between 19 and 26 ethnic groups. She emphasized that:

> even in one Latin American country, you have the different indigenous groups that have their own ethnicity, and their own culture, expressions, food and languages ... even in ... in the same country, you might have, Latinos who are more towards the Spanish in terms of the Spaniard culture, and others who are more oriented around the indigenous culture.... We may be able to understand each other, but some words, because our dialects are different, because of indigenous, African influences. The way we speak is different and distinct.

From this perspective she disputed the definition of Latinos as a race in The Census. Latinos, *tend to identify with their nation with their culture.* She viewed this as a *cultural identification*, preference, rather than a *racial one.* However, she also saw the political advantages in the use of this *umbrella term ... if we sort of unite because we can sort of understand each other, we can communicate if we sort of unite as a whole, then we can be a force to be reckoned with.* She saw that this *strength* could also be *capitalize(d)* on in other arenas such as *business* and *education.*

We can summarize this professor's viewpoint to be a preference for the term Latino as opposed to Hispanic because it includes diverse cultural groups. She has a sense of membership based on the different U.S. Latino groups with a heritage link to any Latin American country. Second, she uses Latino as a political label. However, also sees that the label can be a source of limitations in academic settings. Her preference for Latino needs to be contextualized within the desire of New York city institutions to include Latino groups in their curricula. If we juxtapose her position with the historical processes associated with the development of Chicano and Latina studies (Macías, 2005), her interview provides a localized use of the meanings of the labels of Hispanic and Latino. The postcolonial U.S.-Latin American relations as a historical dimension on the meanings of Hispanic and Latino were not mentioned during the interview. Nevertheless, the information provided by offers important understandings of how the meanings of Hispanic and Latino are situated within academic and political experiences.

IMPLICATIONS FOR EDUCATIONAL LEADERSHIP DISCOURSE

The quantitative analyses indicate the meanings of Hispanic/Hispano and Latino in the newspaper data indicates how the terms continues to be confused in public discourse in the United States. The cognitive discourse analysis of three Hispanic/Latino news reports indicates that writers even use these labels interchangeably. They obscure the heterogeneity of U.S. Hispanic/Latino groups by locking them up generally in nationality groups. I t is therefore highly likely that such confusion permeates many educational institutions. Do teachers and leaders really understand the nature of the populations they are dealing with/ Do they have a repertoire of responses appropriate for the diverse groups with which they every day? If not they cannot deal adequately with "the particular others" Grogan mentioned in her 2005 address to the University Council for Educational Administration. Even more importantly, is there a recognition that students, parents and even teachers may by struggling to hold a coherent view of their own identities when there is such confusion in the public realm? What curriculum and pedagogic innovations are needed to deal with such phenomena?.

The responses of a professor from a specialized institution which serves both Hispanic and Latino populations acknowledge the complexity of the issues by stressing the use of Latino as a political tool, but regards Hispanic as part of people's repertoires of identification. As a professional working in a diverse context she developed strategies for the selection and use of these labels. Do other teachers and leaders in educational institutions require the same degree of sophistication as they mediate between subjective worlds and political realities? Her interview presents a richer and more reflective layer which helps us to understand the social, cultural, institutional, and subjective dimensions associated with the local meanings of Hispanic and Latino than evident in the public media and public discourse. Her discourse is more nuanced (Collard & Wang, 2005; Lincoln & Denzin, 2003) and points to new directions needed in educational leadership discourses.

First, theorists need to become aware of labels that essentialize and marginalize ethnic or other minorities and to struggle for more precise and sophisticated descriptors of the populations they study. Second, they need to recognize the value of cognitive discourse analysis as a tool capable of yielding precise insights into knowledges, opinions, and group ideology schemas. The interactive roles of essentialized labels in institutional lives and subjective identities also needs to be researched if we are to understand the worldviews from which students, parents, and teachers are operating. It is important to research how opportunities to negotiate and reflect on the use of these labels by different actors can enhance the quality of their professional work. Furthermore, how does awareness of local meanings associated with the labels under study help enrich educational practice? and varied factors and experiences, people using these labels attach to these terms.

Critical studies on ethnic labels, whether in international, national or local fields also need to acknowledge the interaction of other cultural variables such as gender, sexuality, and abilities if they are to comprehend the full complexity of how these ethnic labels are socially and discursively constructed. A number of recent studies on cognitive-oriented discourse analysis as an interdisciplinary enterprise, sociolinguistic ethnographies, social theory, and Chicano and Latino studies (Blommaert, 2005; Flores, 2003; Gimenez, 2006; Givón, 2005; Heller, 2006; Torres-Saillant, 2005; van Leeuwen, 2005) can help us to expand the research agenda on group and social labels not only in the United States but throughout the world.

The public misuse of terms like Hispanic and Latino has erased the differences that a historical, cultural, and racial hegemonic system has assigned to these heterogeneous groups. Hispanics and Latinos are continuously imaged as political allies and their specific histories, unique experiences, processes, and daily lives become invisible to the general public and even to those working closely with them in educational institutions. As educators we need detailed understandings about how social cognitions such as knowledge and opinions are negotiated and co-constructed and how knowledge strategies are employed and expanded among different groups. The local meanings associated with Hispanic/Hispano and Latino, as detailed in this chapter, are not only contextually managed by writers, news actors, and academics but are the fabric of daily existence. Future research projects in educational leadership need the co-participation of researchers with diverse research orientations if we are to improving the social advancement of minority groups in various nation states. This research and future discourses also needs to address the intersection of specific ethnicities with variables such as age, family cultures, gender, individual histories, sexuality and social class. Only then will educational leadership theory begin to deal with the reality that individuals are culturally historically situated requiring nuanced strategies of care and responsibility.

NOTES

1. We investigate the textual uses and meanings of both the Hispanic and Latino labels/terms. *Latino* is used as an umbrella label to include Hispanic and Latina or other labels. *Hispanic/Latino* are used interchangeably when quoting or referring the work of other authors.

2. Local meanings are the result of the selection made by speakers or writers in their mental models of events or their more generally socially shared beliefs. They are the kind of information that (under the control of global topics) most indirectly influences the mental models, and hence the opinions and attitudes of recipients (van Dijk, 2001).

3. There are tremendous social disparities between Hispanic/Latino groups and other ethnic groups in the U.S. drawing from national statistics certain Hispanic/Latino populations seem to have the lowest level of educational attainment and poverty (Pew Hispanic Center, 2006). For example, one in three of native Hispanics aged 25 and over tends to have a high school diploma while one on three of foreign born Hispanics in the same age group tends to have only attended school to less than the ninth grade standard (see Table 19 in Web site). Foreign born Hispanics under 18 years old tend to be less economically disadvantaged than native born Hispanics (see Table 30 in Web site).

4. Communication the *NYT Public Editor* (March 31, 2006) provided the relevant data about Hispanic and Latino usage. The *NYT Manual of Style and Usage* (Siegal & Connolly, 1999) was consulted later.

5. The *SA's* electronic stylebook was based upon the *Associated Press Style Book* (Goldstein, 2004). It contained a three line entry for Hispanic and a one line on Latino/a. http://www2.mysanantonio.com/aboutus/expressnews/style/ (Retrieved March 31, 2006). An overall finding on the use of similar ethnic/racial categories (in plural) was performed before the coding. Under African Americans, Anglos, and Hispanics, it was found that Hispanics is mostly used in the *SAE*, *NYT*, and *LAP* (in this order), followed by African Americans in the *NYT*, *SAE*, and *LAP* (in this order) and Anglos used in *SAE* and *NYT* (in this order) and no use was found in *LAP*. The quantitative results of the associations of these labels with their major themes (see Table 8.1 for more specific details) represent more than the 40% for *SAE* and *LAP* and around 30% for *NYT* when the total number of texts for each newspaper was considered.

APPENDICES

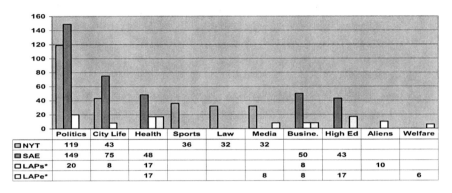

	Politics	City Life	Health	Sports	Law	Media	Busine.	High Ed	Aliens	Welfare
□ NYT	119	43		36	32	32				
▣ SAE	149	75	48				50	43		
□ LAPs*	20	8	17				8		10	
□ LAPe*			17			8	8	17		6

Notes: s*: *: texts in Spanish; e*: texts in English in the *LAP* corpus.

Figure 8.1.   Distribution of Hispanic and Hispano texts and five major themes.

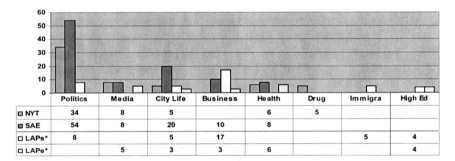

	Politics	Media	City Life	Business	Health	Drug	Immigra	High Ed
□ NYT	34	8	5		6	5		
▣ SAE	54	8	20	10	8			
□ LAPs*	8		5	17			5	4
□ LAPe*		5	3	3	6			4

Figure 8.2.   Distribution of Latino texts and five major themes.

REFERENCES

Acuña, R. (1996). *Anything But Mexican: Chicanos in contemporary Los Angeles*. New York: Verso.

Anzaldúa, G. E. (2002a). Now let us shift ... the path of conocimiento ... inner work, public acts. In G. E. Anzaldúa & A. Keating (Eds.), *this bridge we call home: Radical visions for transformation* (pp. 540–578). London: Routledge.

Anzaldúa, G. E. (2002b). Preface: (Un)natural bridges, (Un)safe places. In G. E. Anzaldúa & A. Keating (Eds.), *This bridge we call home: Radical visions for transformations* (pp. 1–5). London: Routledge.

Barbosa-Carter, E. (1999). Multiple identity and coalition building: How identity differences within us enable radical alliances among us. *Comparative Justice Review, 2*(2), 111–126.

Benitez, J. L. (2003). *Research paper: The framing of Latino immigrants' issues from a Latino journalistic angle*. Retrieved May 03, 2005, from http://list.msu.edu

Blommaert, J. (2005). *Discourse: A critical introduction*. Cambridge, England: Cambrdge University Press.

Chabram-Dernersesian, A. (2003). Latino/a: Another site of struggle, another site of accountability. In J. Poblete (Ed.), *Critical Latin american and Latino studies* (pp. 105–120). Minneapolis: University of Minnesota Press.

Collard, J., & Wang. T (2005) Leadership and intercultural dynamics. *Journal of School Leadership, 15*(3), 178–195.

Cotter, C. (2002). Discourse and media. In D. Schiffrin, D. Tannen, & H. E. Hamilton (Eds.), *The Handbook of Discourse Analysis* (pp. 416–436). Malden, MA: Blackwell.

Darder, A. (1998). The politics of bilculturalism: Culture and difference in the formation of Warriors for Gringostroika and The New Mestizas. In A. Darder & R. D. Torres (Eds.), *The Latino Studies Reader Culture, Economy & Society* (pp. 129–142). Malden, MA: Blackwell.

de la Garza, R. O., DeSipio, L., Garcia, F. C., Garcia, J., & Falcon, A. (1992). *Latino voices: Mexican, Puerto Rican, & Cuban perspectives on American politics*. Boulder, CO: Westview Press.

De León, A. (1999). *Mexicans Americans in Texas: A brief history* (2nd ed.). Wheeling, IL: Harlan Davidson.

del Olmo, F. (2001). Hispanic, Latino or Chicano?: A historical review. In N. A. O. H. Journalists (Ed.), *Latinos in the United States: A resource guide for journalists* (pp. 9–12). Washington, DC: National Association of Hispanic Journalists.

El poder de compra latino es el de mayor crecimiento. (2002). *La Prensa*. Retrieved March 17, 2006, from http://proquest.umu.com

Flores-Gonzalez, N. (1999). The racialization of Latinos: The meaning of Latino identity for the second generation. *Latino Studies Journal, 10*(3), 3–31.

Flores, J. (2003). Latino studies: New contexts, new concepts. In J. Poblete (Ed.), *Critical Latin American and Latino studies* (pp. 191–205). Minneapolis: University of Minnesota Press.

Foley, N. (1997). Becoming Hispanic: Mexican American and the Faustian pact with Whiteness. In *New Directions in Mexican American Studies* (pp. 53–70). Austin, TX: Center for Mexican American Studies University of Texas at Austin.

Forbes, J. D. (1992). The Hispanic spin: Party politics and governmental manipulation of ethnic identity. *Latin American Perspectives, 19*(4), 59–78.

García, I. M. (1996). Backwards from Aztlán: Politics in the age of Hispanics. In R. M. De Anda (Ed.), *Chicanas and Chicanos in contemporary society* (pp. 191–204). Boston: Allyn & Bacon.

Gimenez, M. E. (1992). U.S. ethnic politics: Implications for Latin Americans. *Latin American Perspectives, 19*(4), 7–17.

Gimenez, M. E. (2006). With a litlle class: A critique of identity politics. *Ethnicities, 6*(3), 423–439.

Givón, T. (2005). *Contexts as other minds: The pragmatics of sociality, cognition and communication*. Amsterdam/Philadelphia: John Benjamins.

Goldstein, N. (Ed.). (2004). *Associated Press Stylebook and Briefing on Media Law*. New York: Basic Books.

Gómez, L. (1992). The birth of The "Hispanic Generation": Attitudes of Mexican-American political elites toward the Hispanic label. *Latin American Perspectives, 19*(4), 45–58.

Grogan, M. (2005) *Ethical imperatives for educational leadership: Fifty years beyond Brown.* UCEA Review, *XLV*(1), 4–9.

Guzmán, B. (2001). *The Hispanic population: Census 2000 brief.* Retrieved March 5, 2004, from www.census.gov/prod/2001pubs/c2kbr01-3.pdf

Hayes-Bautista, D. E., & Chapa, J. (1987). Latino terminology: Conceptual basis for standarized terminology. *American Journal of Public Health, 77*(1), 61–68.

Heller, M. (2006, July). *Communities, identities, processes and practices.* Paper presented at the Sociolinguistics Symposium 16, Limerick, Ireland.

Hoover Rentería, T. (1998). *Chicano professionals: culture, conflict, and identity.* London: Garland.

Itzigsohn, J., & Dore-Cabral, C. (2001). The Manifold character of panethnicity: Latino identities and practices among Dominicans in New York city. In A. Laó-Montes & A. Dávila (Eds.), *Mambo montage: The Latinization of New York* (pp. 319–335). New York: New York University

Jones-Correa, M., & Leal, D. L. (1996). Becoming "Hispanic": Secondary panethnic identification among Latin American origin population in the United States. *Hispanic Journal of Behavioral Sciences, 18*(2), 214–254.

Lincoln, Y. S., & Denzin, N. K. (2003). *Turning points in qualitative research: Tying knots in a handkerchief.* Walnut Creek, CA: Alta Mira Press.

Macías, R. F. (2005). El grito en Aztlán: Voice and presence in Chicana/o studies. *International Journal of Qualitative Studies in Education, 18*(2), 165–184.

Martin, G. (2002). Latino vote bloc hard to pin down Neither party has a lock to electorate. *San Antonio Express News.* Retrieved March 16, 2006, from http://infoweb.newsweek.com

Mignolo, W. (2002). Globalization and the borders of Latinity. In M. Saénz (Ed.), *Latin American perspectives on globalization: Ethics, politics, and alternative visions* (pp. 77–101). Lanham, MD: Rowman & Littlefield.

Muñoz, C., Jr. (1989). *Youth, identity, power: The Chicano Movement.* London: Verso.

Navarro, M. (2002). Speaking the language, and the issues: Pataki makes inroads with Latino voters. *New York Times.* Retrieved March 14, 2006, from http://proquest.umi.com

Oboler, S. (1995). *Ethnic labels, Latino lives: Identity and the politics of (re)presentation in the United States.* Minneapolis: University of Minnesota Press.

Oboler, S., González, D. J., Aparicio, F. R., Torres, M. d. l. A., & Torres-Saillant, S. (2005). Latino Identities and Ethnicities. In S. Oboler & D. J. González (Eds.), The Oxford Encyclopedia of Latinos and Latinas (Vol. 2, pp. 510-518). Oxford & New York: Oxford University Press.

Padilla, F. M. (1985). *Latino ethnic consciousness: The case of Mexican Americans and Puerto Ricans in Chicago.* Notre Dame, IN: University of Notre Dame Press.

Passel, J. S. (2005). *Estimates of the size and characteristics of the undocumented population.* Washington, DC: Pew Hispanic Center.

Pew Hispanic Center. (2005). *Hispanics: A people in motion.* Washington, DC: Author.

Pew Hispanic Center. (2006,). *A statistical portrait of Hispanics at mid-decade: Tables 1-32*. Retrieved March 15, 2007, from http://pewhispanic.org/reports/middecade/

San Antonio Express News. (2007). *The Cyber-Style Book*. Retrieved March, 5, 2007, from http://www2.mysanantonio.com/aboutus/expressnews/style/mainh.htm

Santa Ana, O. (2002). *Brown tide rising: Metaphors of Latinos in contemporary American public discourse*. Austin: University of Texas Press.

Schecter, S. R., & Bayley, R. (2002). *Language as cultural practice: Mexicanos en el Norte*. Mahwah, NJ: Erlbaum.

Siegal, A. M., & Connolly, W. G. (1999). *The New York Times: Manual of Style of Usage*. New York: Three Rivers Press.

Stephens, T. M. (2003). *The changing face of ethno-racial constructs and language in the Americas*. Lanham, MD: University Press of America.

Subervi, F. (2004). *Network Brownout 2004: The portrayal of Latinos & Latino issues in network television news, 2003: Quantitative and qualitative analysis of the coverage*. Washington, DC: National Association of Hispanic Journalists.

Subervi, F., Torres, J., & Montalvo, D. (2005). *Network Brownout Report 2005: The Portrayal of Latinos & Latino Issues on Network Television News, 2004 With a Retrospect to 1995*. Austin and Washington, DC: National Association of Hispanic Journalists.

Torres-Saillant, S. (2005). Racism in the Americas and the Latino scholar. In A. Dzidenko & S. Oboler (Eds.), *Neither enemies nor friends: Latinos, Blacks, and Afro-Latinos* (pp. 281–304). New York: Palgrave Macmillan.

Urciuoli, B. (2003). Book review. Brown tide rising: Metaphors of Latinos in contemporary american public discourse. *Latino Studies, 1*(1), 198–200.

van Dijk, T. A. (1993). Principles of critical discourse analysis. *Discourse & Society, 4*(2), 249–283.

van Dijk, T. A. (1998). *Ideology: A multidisciplinary approach*. London: SAGE.

van Dijk, T. A. (2000). New(s) racism: A discourse analytical approach. In S. Cottle (Ed.), *Ethnic minorities and the media: Changing cultural bundaries* (pp. 33–49). Philadelphia: Open University Press.

van Dijk, T. A. (2001). Multidisciplinary CDA: A plea for diversity. In R. Wodak & M. Meyer (Eds.), *Methods of critical discourse analysis* (Vol. 95–120). London: SAGE.

van Dijk, T. A. (2004). *Critical context studies*. Retrieved December, 1, 2005, from http://www.discourse-in-society.org

van Leeuwen, T. (2005). Three modes of interdisciplinarity. In R. Wodak & P. Chilton (Eds.), *A new agenda in (critical) discourse analysis: Theory, methodology and interdisciplinarity* (pp. 3-18). Philadelphia: John Benjamins.

Vargas, L. (2000). Genderizing Latino News: An analysis of a local newspaper's coverage of Latino current affairs. *Critical Studies in Mass Communication, 17*(3), 261–293.

Yanow, D. (2003). *Constructing "race" and "ethnicity" in America: Category-making in public policy and administration*. Armonk, NY: M. E. Sharpe.

CHAPTER 9

MUSLIMNESS IN ENGLISH SCHOOLS

Concerns of Learners and Leaders

Saaeda Shah

The education of diverse groups of students from different cultural, religious and ethnic backgrounds has become an increasingly complex, controversial and problematic challenge across the world (Bank & McGee Banks, 2003; Griffin, 2007; Griffiths, 2003; Meer, 2007; Parker-Jenkins, 2007). The progressive integration of the global economy and migration from less to more prosperous regions and countries are producing rapid changes in the social, cultural, and religious structure of communities and schools (Shah, 2006b). An increasing number of schools in the United Kingdom and elsewhere are emerging as multiethnic, multicultural, and multifaith (Shah, 2006a). There is a heightened awareness of diversity and of the difficulty of developing and sustaining inclusive policies that are sensitive and responsive to issues of ethnicity and identity (Abbas, 2005; Anwar, 1998; Brah, 1996; Feagin Vera, & Imani, 1996; Shah, 2007; Vincent, 2003). Although schools, especially in urban areas, are often experienced and successful in providing for diverse needs, there are long-

Leadership and Intercultural Dynamics, pp. 173–187

standing concerns about the relative underachievement of ethnic minority students, inclusion, and engagement, and the extent to which relevant policy has been translated into effective practice (Macpherson, 1999). Many studies make strong claims that education has failed some groups of young people (Abbas, 2004; Anwar & Bakhsh, 2002; Muslim Council of Britain, 2007). These concerns are voiced more strongly with regard to Muslim students, and are often underpinned by the perceptions of *Muslimness*.

The paper explores the experiences of *Muslimness*, and debates the key issues relevant to managing it in English maintained schools with substantial numbers of Muslim students. It draws on data from a pilot study of two schools with substantial numbers of Muslim students. The ways in which Muslim students understand and interpret their identity and their experiences of schooling, and how these are interpreted and managed by educational leaders/teachers are significant for the debates on inclusion and engagement. The study focused on issues of Muslim identity and its interplay with schooling. It sought to identify perspectives from teachers/ leaders and Muslim students in order to explore and highlight implications for managing multiethnic schools. The chapter also draws upon data from two earlier studies of multiethnic schools in England (East Midland Leadership Centre, [EMLC] 2004; National College for School Leadership [NCSL], 2004). In each case, the data was collected from leaders/teachers (Muslim/non-Muslim) and Muslim students. The main tool of data collection was in-depth interviewing. The discussion draws on direct data but is also supported by wide ranging international literature.

EXPERIENCING *MUSLIMNESS* IN ENGLISH SCHOOLS

Muslim students are a unique multiethnic group, defying the accepted race/ethnicity categories (Afridi, 2001), with claims to a transnational (Muslim Parliament of Great Britain, 1992; Siddiqui, 1992), cosmic (Mernissi, 1991), or superordinate identity (Hopkins & Kahini-Hopkins, 2004). There is abundant literature on identity in sociology, social psychology, and feminist theory (Bhabha, 1994; Brah, 1996; Braidotti, 1991; Giddens, 1991; Gilroy, 1997; Hall & de Gay, 1996; Hopkins & Kahani-Hopkins, 2004; Vincent, 2003), presenting different theories, and analyzing the factors involved. However, recognition of religion as a category of influence for identity construction and self-projection in the recent scenario is not a fully explored phenomenon (Modood, 2005). The revival of religions in the post-modern world (Ahmed, 1992; Ahmed & Donnan, 1994; Bauman, 1997a, 1997b; Esposito, 2002a; Kepel, 1997, 2003), and the heightened "political" conflicts in the wake of 9/11 with reference to Islam and Muslim identity underline the importance of investigating this sensitive area and its implications for learners and leaders.

Muslims in Britain have emerged as a politically visible community specifically in the post-Satanic Verses context. The Muslim/non-Muslim divide has been a historical phenomenon, underpinned by numerous dynamics including factors such as the conflicts in Spain/Jerusalem, The Crusades, Western Imperialism, the demise of the Ottoman Empire, (Ahmed, 1992) and the ensuing rise of Islamic movements. Some major Islamic movements such as Khilafat, the Muslim Brothers, and the Jamaat-e-Islami in particular contributed to the development of the concept of *Muslimness* and Muslim identity in an oppositional position to non-Muslim. More recently the plight of Muslims in Palestine, Kashmir, and other parts of the world, the role of the West (especially the United States) in the Gulf War, the Iran/Iraq war, Afghan *Jihad* against Russia, the Middle-East oil, the struggle for control over international resources and the perception among Muslims of being targeted have added to the tensions (Ahmed, 1992; Esposito, 2002a).

It was in this backdrop, that the stand taken by the West over the Satanic Verses inflamed Muslims. The protests against Rushdie and the burning of his *Satanic Verses* (1989) fueled the drive to be recognized and respected as Muslims (Ahmed, 2003; Kepel, 2003). Later international events such as the Al-Qaeda factor, the 9/11 terrorist acts, the invasions of Afghanistan and Iraq, and more recently the stand taken by the West on publishing of the Prophet's cartoons and knighting of Rushdie have further left their mark both on in-group and out-group identity formations of young Muslims. Such events have increased the challenges for school leaders and teachers in multiethnic schools.

Muslimness is emerging as a coveted identity among the Muslim youth in particular. The concept is reinforced through images and social/political forces operating from outside Muslim societies. It is not a single, homogeneous identity, but certainly appears to be an important self-projection. 1.6 million Muslims in the United Kingdom comprise the largest religious group after Christians (British National Statistics, 2001), who increasingly tend to project themselves as one group or *Ummah* in spite of wide ranging, multilevel variations and differences. This in-group coherence has political underpinnings. Broadly speaking *Ummah* includes all those who define themselves as Muslims, or who are born into families where Islam is the household faith (Richardson, 2004). Socially, Muslim *Ummah* is hugely diverse with regard to ethnicity, language, culture, and other indicators. With regard to religion, Muslims differ in the level of their adherence to religion and also in matters of belief and practice. On the international scene, many Muslim countries, communities, and sects have serious conflicts and disagreements. In spite of all that, *Muslimness* is emerging as a global phenomenon, conveying a message of a cosmic Islamic identity. A commission for racial equality (CRE, 2005) study highlighted eight shared dimensions of a common representation of Britishness, but explicitly acknowledged that "religion was a dominant source of identification for Muslim participants," explaining that "It would seem that the emotional significance attached with Islam has grown in strength over the recent past" (p. 38). In the present study, Islam emerged as the primary self-descriptor for all the research participants:

> I'm a Muslim, just a Muslim, not anything else. And then I am British. Don't know why media, TV lead me to think I'm Bangladeshi, not English. I feel rejected—generally, everything the way it's done, media, government, and policies.

There appears to be an attempt to accommodate *Muslimness* and Britishness in the concept of British-Muslim identity, but rejection and racism directed at Muslims (Modood, 2005; Parekh, 2000; Richardson & Wood, 2004) appear to pose challenges to this hyphenated identity (Verkuyten, 2004). Another CRE (2005) study investigating the causes of decline in *Britishness*, emphasized that the main barrier to integration is not so much self-segregation on the part of ethnic minority communities, but the subtle and everyday "policing" of the boundaries of Britishness by many White British people and their demand for complete assimilation. One key finding was that "Anti-Muslim sentiments were expressed frequently and forcefully, mainly by white participants" (p. 28). The profusion of anti-Muslim sentiments in the media and society can be a strong factor in strengthening identification with *Muslimness*. Giddens (1991) explains that "A self-identity has to be created and more or less continually reordered against the backdrop of shifting experiences of day-to-day life and the fragmenting tendencies of modern institutions" (p. 186). In the case of Muslims, experiences in the schools and society appear to influence creating and re-creating of identities:

> I don't have a sense of belonging to England—being a Muslim is the most important identity for me. I feel I belong in Bangladesh—because I'm a Bengali. I do want to belong to UK and to mix in with others, but...

The unfinished sentence has significance in signalling rejection and marginalization. Werbner (1997) argues that "exclusion, silencing, any act of discrimination is an act of violence," emphasizing that "violence begets violence, and violence need not be physical" (p. 228). Being imagined and created by media and masses as "potential terror suspects" (Ahmed, 2003; Hagopian, 2004; Hardy, 2005) and being at the receiving end of "institutional racism" (Macpherson, 1999) has generated significant insecurity among Muslim students, forcing them to re-think and re-create identities, which certainly have implications for education and inclusion:

> When others make fun of you or pass comments—you know—it makes you feel an outsider. I have been born and brought up here. I have been to Pakistan only once in my life and I don't fit there. I am walaiti [from the West] there. So where do you belong? Who do you hang around with? I used to have White friends but now all my friends are boys from our community.... We go to mosque and community gatherings, and attend talks about Islam and Ummah.

International political events have added to this polarization and fragmentation. Kabbani's (2002) comments in the post-*Satanic Verses* situation provide an example:

> We were caught between two tyrannies: Khomeini's impossible death sentence against a writer (fallible or foolish though he may have been) and the harsh "liberal" fatwa against our religious identity, with its blanket dismissal of us as alien, barbaric. Such was the polarisation, that even those who had hardly perceived of themselves as "Muslim" before, except in family ritual or personal reference, were suddenly forced to stand up and be counted as "warriors" for subtlety in either side's position. (para. 2)

This push factor seems to be stronger in developing in-group identity. Many Muslim training teachers and teachers new to post in Osler (2003) confirm similar experiences of being pushed to the peripheries which led to their moving closer to community, culture, and religion. It is thought provoking for policymakers and practitioners why young Muslims feel marginalized and excluded, and its possible implications for their self-perception and schooling. Bauman (1997a) explains exclusion as "Anthropoemic, 'vomiting the strangers, banishing them from the limits of the orderly world and barring all communication with those inside ... a strategy of exclusion" (p. 47). These can be difficult experiences for young learners:

> My primary school was mostly Asians, but when I came to this school often White boys would call me Paki in a very bad way. Many days I wouldn't want to come to school, and then my Dad would sing benefits of being in England - that we were very poor, and this country has given us good life, a nice home and security of meals. I don't care. We have got these things because my family worked for it, perhaps harder than the White people. We did not get things in charity, so why are we made to feel as if we are less than Whites? (Student participant)

The feeling of being discriminated against is exacerbated by a sense of ongoing discrimination:

> My elder brother went to the university—was the first one in our family. My family had huge celebrations after his graduation, his graduation picture with family came in an Urdu newspaper which Mom and Dad would show to all visitors and relatives. This was three years back and he is still jobless ... I mean, no professional work. He is driving a taxi like my Dad has been doing. So what is there in education for us?

Unemployment among graduate Muslims is higher not only as compared to Whites but even other BME groups (British National Statistics, 2001). Muslim learners feel that they are specific targets of discrimination, and they explain it as hostility directed towards their faith. Richardson (1997) explains "unfounded hostility to Muslims" as Islamophobia, leading to the exclusion of Muslims from mainstream social and political affairs (p. 4). A grave consequence of this "unfounded hostility" is reflected in the experiences of exclusion and discrimination by young Muslim learners in the schools. A year 7 research participant liked the school but resented being called Bin Laden:

> I am new to this school. I like it, but there are times when I just want never to come to school. A White boy called me Bin Laden—it was probably my first week in the school - and now many have joined him. I once complained to the teacher and she said it was silly of him, just ignore it. But I don't like being called Bin Laden.... I don't look like him, and I have no beard!

Exclusion signals a culturally hostile environment and undermines any positive sense of self. For young people this could lead to exploring alternate identities and self-projections which may contribute to empowerment through belonging. Merry (2007) argues that a positive sense of self and a culturally coherent environment are very important for healthy learning outcomes. A coherent environment encourages a positive sense of self, promoting coherence across multiple identities. Conflicting identities heighten the challenges for the leaders and learners alike by disrupting inclusion and engagement.

CHALLENGES FOR LEADERS

According to British National Statistics (2001), more than 30% of Muslims in Britain are of school age, and an estimated "at least 500,000 British Muslim students are in compulsory education" (Anwar & Bakhsh, 2002, pp. 2–3). Muslim students in British schools, mostly come from poorer communities such as Bangladeshi and Pakistani groups, perform below average on public tests, and for these reasons constitute a cause for concern (Haque & Bell, 2001, p. 366; see also Abbas, 2004, 2006; Anwar & Bakhsh, 2002; Modood, 2003; Department for Education and Skills [DFES], 2003b; Office for Standards in Education, 2004). A high majority of Muslims in the United Kingdom come from working class backgrounds and many studies argue that factors linked to immigration (Haque & Bell, 2001) and socioeconomic class have implications for their schooling (Abbas, 2004). However, the current young learners, the majority of whom are second or third generation immigrants, appear to be experiencing more complex issues than those associated with immediate immigration or problems of language, dress, halal food, prayer rooms, and others as highlighted by some earlier studies (Parker-Jenkins, 1995). The issues are more about belonging and identity. Heightened political tensions and conflicts in the wake of 9/11, the London bombings (7/7) and the apparent alienation of a significant number of second generation Muslims (Hardy, 2005) suggest that their sense of inclusion in British life, or lack of it, has become problematic posing grim questions regarding their schooling as well as societal cohesion. The situation constitutes a potentially serious challenge to multicultural strategies for achieving inclusion, and raises important questions for the leadership of multiethnic schools.

Studies focused on leadership of multiethnic schools that identify broad strategies for successful leadership and management of multiethnic schools (Dimmock, 2005a, 2005b; EMLC, 2004; NCSL, 2004), also recognize that appropriate strategies have often been insufficiently developed and applied, and have not provided a satisfactory resolution of the progressively more acute anxieties that have emerged (Anwar & Bakhsh, 2002; Hardy, 2005; Macpherson, 1999). The launch of the government's Commission for Integration and Cohesion (Woodward, 2006) illustrates the increasing sensitivity to the debate about community relations and the extent to which liberal assumptions about pluralism and the multicultural society are being questioned (Joppke & Lukes, 1999; Malik, 2002; Parekh, 2000). These issues have been exacerbated by accelerating demographic change, international events, and varied domestic responses to the national and international policy towards Muslims and Muslim countries (Jacques, 2004).

In this age of cyberspace, young people have higher exposure to information and media. Educational institutions are no longer discrete learning zones with control over student learning. The media has higher probability of affecting the young students' wider knowledge, responses and attitudes. The perceived Muslim/non-Muslim tension, uninformed practices, and related media hypes create discourses of conflict and exclusion. There is an increasing perception among the

Muslim students that it is the faith dimension of their identity which White community in schools and society has problems accommodating. This challenges their sense of self, which is reflected in the explicit emphasis on their faith identity and associated symbols, causing worries among teachers and leaders:

> You see more and more girls wearing hijab in school now. There is an increasing interest in faith and faith-related activities and debates. What worries us is that there is always a risk of these debates leading to conflict among young people or groups.

Multiethnic schools have diverse communities with different in-group loyalties. In addition to that, within-group differences and tensions (Ahmed, 1992) complicate the situation for the teachers and leaders. Many participants pointed out very practical issues with regard to Muslim learners:

> Muslims are such a diverse community that it is often challenging to understand their needs or anticipate their responses. Parents have such different positions on dress, swimming, music, sex education, and all in the name of religion. Even the religious day such as Eid falls on different days for different Muslim families and you don't know how to respond to that.

This might not be very different from other major religions of the world such as Christianity, Hinduism, Judaism, or others. No faith community is homogeneous. However, the data signals a need to enhance awareness and understanding of diversity for the purposes of inclusion. The perceptions of many participants indicate persistent concerns about inclusion and equal opportunity, despite the work of many heads and teachers who dedicatedly pursue the Every Child Matters (DFES, 2003a) agenda and who are "genuinely committed to the principles of social justice and redressing inequality at all levels" (NCSL, 2004, p. 8). The participating teachers and leaders expressed strong commitment for equal opportunities and inclusion:

> We have clear policies in place to report and control racism. However, with young people it is always a challenge…. There are occasional incidents and we take action according to our policy.

In spite of this commitment at the leadership level to discourage and eliminate racism, there does not seem to be enough knowledge and relevant training to prepare staff to handle such problems, as reflected above in the teacher's response to the student's complaint when called Bin

Laden by a White student. Richardson and Wood (2004) reported a similar incident:

> I'm the only Asian teacher at my school. During the war in Iraq a pupil who's also Asian told me that she was being teased by other pupils. "We killed hundreds of your lot yesterday ... Saddam's your dad, innit ... we're getting our revenge for what you Pakis did to us on 11 September...." I asked her if she had told her class teacher. Yes, she had told her teacher, and her teacher had said: "Never mind, it's not serious. It'll soon pass. You'll have to expect a bit of teasing at a time like this." (p. 64)

These attempts on the part of particular staff to keep the things quiet by silencing can cause serious problems in longer term. They can encourage racist attitudes, and embolden the offenders in their racist practices. Recent studies have found that the experience of racial discrimination and harassment features at a significantly higher level among ethnic minority young citizens (Basit et al., 2006; Shah, 2006c). Young Muslims, in particular, are said to feel that "they are not being treated equally and that they are in practice second-class citizens" (Anwar & Bakhsh, 2002, p. 71). The hostile media against Muslims (Ahmed, 2006), experiences of racial discrimination and harassment in the schools (Richardson & Wood, 2004; Tyrer & Ahmad, 2006), and lukewarm anti-racism practices create a culturally incoherent environment (Merry, 2007), with negative implications for the learners' self-perceptions, inclusion and educational engagement. The participating teachers/leaders in this study recognized the gravity of the issue but explained their conciliatory attempts as efforts to avoid volatile situations:

> Muslim students' response to culture/faith-related issues is very emotional. Teachers avoid treading into these difficult areas. They avoid saying anything which might be misunderstood or misconstructed, leading to complaints from learners and community.... We try to maintain a positive and peaceful learning environment, and yes, at times we do encourage conciliation.

Some participating students saw such strategies as ad hoc, failing to promote inclusion and engagement. These complex issues and contending positions need to be understood and managed with knowledge and sensitivity. The perspectives and experiences of Muslim students themselves in relation to their identity, inclusion, and schooling, and their teachers' perspectives on these issues, signal the urgent need to include Muslims in contemporary conceptions of democratic citizenship (Modood, 2005) as well as to prepare leaders and teachers to understand the diversity of needs with focused efforts to improve inclusion and coherence.

CONCLUSIONS

According to the British National Statistics (2001), more than a quarter of the British population is of diverse ethnic origins and faith orientations, with different sociocultural and knowledge heritages. In an increasingly multiethnic/multifaith society. The need for a better knowledge and understanding of diverse communities, including the faith communities, has gained high significance, particularly to maintain social stability, harmony, and educational engagement.

It is highly important in a diverse society to investigate the forces driving towards identity formations, and their impact on the individuals and the society as a whole (Griffiths & Troyna, 1995). This small study into Muslim students' perceptions of their identity in educational contexts affirmed that their primary descriptor of identity was *Muslimness*. The issues around identity, inclusion, and educational engagement encapsulate major problems and issues germane to the Muslim perspective on schooling and society in Britain at the present time. There appear to be interconnections between all three—a sense of identity having implications for a feeling of inclusion/exclusion, and both having implications for educational engagement. The perception amongst Muslims, and young Muslims in particular, of "institutional racism" and discrimination could have uncharted consequences for their learning, inclusion, and commitment to the wider society. There is an urgent need to understand how students experience *Muslimness* at a time of crisis and potential polarisation, and how these experiences contribute to their schooling as well as wider societal cohesion.

Within a wider social and political debate, *Muslimness* is emerging as a complex phenomenon with urgent relevance for those who wish to understand the new social diversity of many urban communities and to improve the quality of education in multiethnic schools (Archer, 2003; Jacobson, 1998; Modood, 2005). The search for "integration and cohesion" is further complicated by the shift from a "uniform consensus on the value of multiculturalism" (Kelly, as cited in Woodward, 2006, p. 180) to a period when the multicultural approach is perceived to have failed, and "sustained, focused work on community cohesion" is believed to be the "key to ensuring that communities successfully integrate" (Phillips, quoted in Woodward, 2006, p. 7).

Before the establishment of the Commission on Integration and Cohesion (Woodward, 2006), policies for managing diversity and inclusion encouraged schools "to offer a range of extended services that help pupils engage and achieve," and to help "communities to value education and be aware that it is the way out of the poverty trap" (DFES, 2004, pp. 1–2). The assumption was that a diverse society should agree on a set of "shared values" that transcends "deep-seated conflicts between cultures embodying different values" (Malik, 2002, p. 7). The current attack on multiculturalism now challenges liberal pluralism and opens a philosophically difficult debate on sensitive ground. As the search for "practical solutions, based on local ideas that have potential" (Singh, 2006, p. 182) unfolds, it becomes doubly important to understand the experience and perspectives of young Muslim students and how these may in future contribute to new styles and forms of inclusive education.

Government agencies seek to resolve threats to social cohesion by emphasizing an apparently value-neutral, results-centred performativity (Gleeson & Husbands, 2001), that is expected to ensure success for all. However, Muslim parents and organizations continue to express concern about educational issues, with complaints that there is inadequate provision for distinctive Muslim needs (Anwar & Bakhsh, 2002; Parker-Jenkins, 2005). In spite of a recent review by the comptroller and auditor general presenting a more positive picture of ethnic achievement in general (House of Commons, 2003, p. 6), the education system is perceived to be failing Muslim pupils (Anwar & Bakhsh, 2002, p. 15). The educational achievement levels of Muslim students in Britain are on average lower than white and some other ethnic groups.

School leaders make efforts to consciously construct an inclusive school culture, supported by relevant government policies. However, the challenge has intensified, with growing numbers of ethnic minority students from diverse backgrounds in British schools and with increasingly unhelpful, polarizing influences reflected in the media (Ahmed, 2003; Esposito, 2002b). Many schools, therefore, might be unable to respond with sufficient strength of purpose to the multifaceted demands they face.

Muslims constitute more than a quarter of the world population and are spread across the world. In Britain also, Muslim presence in schools is a country wide phenomenon, with higher concentration in urban areas. Modood (2005) argues that while different minorities need to be accommodated in different ways, a single template is not appropriate. He suggests that such differential accommodation cannot be the task of the state alone but must be shared across different civil society sectors. This points to the need to review and revise existing strategies and approaches to managing inclusion at regional and local levels. The views and perspectives of Muslim students and the teachers/leaders in schools with substantial numbers of Muslim learners need to be considered to gain understanding of the strengths and limitations of current policy and to also inform the future policy and practice at school, local and national levels.

ACKNOWLEDGEMENT

The author was a member of the research team.

REFERENCES

Abbas, T. (2004). *The education of British South Asians: Ethnicity, capital and class structure.* New York: Palgrave.

Abbas, T. (Ed.). (2005). *Muslim Britain: Communities under pressure.* London: Zed Books.

Abbas, T. (2006). *Muslims in Birmingham, UK.* Background paper for the University of Oxford Centre on Migration Policy and Society, England.

Afridi, S. (2001) *Muslims in America: Identity, diversity and the challenge of understanding.* New York: Carnegie Challenge.

Ahmed, A. S. (1992). *Post-Modernism and Islam: Predicament and promise.* London: Routledge.

Ahmed, A. S. (2003). *Islam under siege: Living dangerously in a post-honor world.* Cambridge, England: Polity Press.

Ahmed, F. (2006). British Muslim perceptions and opinions on news coverage of September 11. *Journal of Ethnic and Migration Studies, 32*(6), 961–982.

Ahmed, A. S., & Donnan, H. (Eds.). (1994). *Islam, globalization and postmodernity.* London: Routledge.

Anwar, M. (1998) *Between cultures: Continuity and change in the lives of young Asians.* London: Routledge.

Anwar, M., & Bakhsh, Q. (2002). *State policies towards Muslims in Britain* (A research report). Coventry, West Midlands, England: University of Warwick, Centre for Research in Ethnic Relations.

Archer, L. (2003). *Race, masculinity and schooling: Muslim boys and education.* London: Open University Press.

Banks, J. A., & McGee Banks, C. A. (Eds.). (2003). *Handbook of Research on Multicultural Education.* San Francisco: Jossey-Bass.

Basit, T., Roberts, L., McNamara, O., Carrington, B., Maguire, M., & Woodrow, D. (2006). Did they jump or were they pushed? Reasons why minority ethnic trainees withdraw from initial teacher training courses. *British Educational Research Journal, 32*(3), 387–410.

Bauman, Z. (1997a). The making and unmaking of strangers. In T. Modood & P. Werbner (Eds.), *The politics of multiculturalism in the New Europe: Racism, identity, and community.* London: Zed Books.

Bauman, Z. (1997b). *Postmodernity and its discontents.* Cambridge, England: Polity Press.

Bhabha, H. (1994). *The location of culture.* London: Routledge.

Brah, A. (1996). *Cartographies of Diaspora: Contesting identities*. London: Routledge.

Braidotti, R. (1991). *Patterns of dissonance: A study of women in contemporary philosophy*. Cambridge: Polity Press.

British National Statistics. (2001). *Online Office for National Statistics*. Retrieved May, 7, 2003, from http://www.statistics.gov.uk

CRE (2005). Citizenship and belonging: what is Britishnes? *ETHNOS Research and Consultancy by the Commission for Racial Equality (CRE)*. Retrieved from http://www.cre.gov.uk/downloads/what_is_britishness.pdf

Department for Education and Skills. (2003). *Every child matters: The Green Paper*. London: Author.

Department for Education and Skills. (2003) *Aiming high: Raising the achievement of minority ethnic pupils*. London: Author.

Department for Education and Skills. (2004). *National curriculum assessment and GCSE/GNVQ attainment by pupil characteristics in England, 2002 (Final) and 2003 (Provisional)*. London: Author. Retrieved May 2004, from www.dfes.gov.uk/rsgateway/DB/SFR/

Dimmock, C. (2005a). Leading the multi-ethnic school: Research evidence on successful practice. *The Educational Forum, 69*(3), 291–304.

Dimmock, C. (2005b). The leadership of multi-ethnic schools: What we know and don't know about values-driven leadership. *Education Research and Perspectives, 32*(2), 80–96.

East Midland Leadership Centre. (2004). *Developing successful leadership in multiethnic schools: Implications for leadership, training and development*. Unpublished Research Report, University of Leicester.

Esposito, J. L. (2002a). Foreword. In Y. Haddad (Ed.), *Muslims in the West: From Sojourners to citizens* (pp. vii–viii). England: Oxford University Press.

Esposito, J. L. (2002b). *Unholy war: Terror in the name of Islam*. England: Oxford University Press.

Feagin, J., Vera, H., & Imani, N. (1996). *The agony of education: Black students at White colleges and universities*. London: Routledge.

Giddens, A. (1991). *Modernity and self-identity*. Cambridge, England: Polity Press.

Gilroy, P. (1997). Diaspora and the detours of identity. In K. Woodward (Ed.), *Identity and difference*. London: SAGE.

Gleeson, D., & Husbands, C. (Eds.). (2001). *The performing school: Managing, teaching, and learning in a performance culture*. London: RoutledgeFarmer.

Griffiths, M. (2003). *Action for social justice in education: Fairly different*. England: Open University Press.

Griffiths, M., & Troyna, B. (Eds.). (1995). *Antiracism, culture and racial justice in Education*. Stoke-on-Trent, England: Trentham Books.

Griffin, R. (Ed.). (2007). *Education in the Muslim world: Different perspectives*. Providence, RI: Symposium Books.

Hagopian, E. C. (2004). *Civil rights in peril: The targeting of Arabs and Muslims*. Chicago: Haymarket Books.

Haque, Z., & Bell, J. F. (2001). Evaluating the performance of minority ethnic pupils in secondary schools. *Oxford Review of Education, 27*(3), 358–368.

Hardy, R. (2005). *UK multiculturalism under spotlight*. Retrieved July 14, 2005, from www.news.bbc.co.uk/1/hi/uk/4681615.stm

186   S. SHAH

House of Commons. (2003). *National Audit Office Report* (HC 1332 2003-04): Making a difference: Performance of maintained secondary schools in England. Retrieved August 2006, from http://www.nao.org.uk/publications/nao_reports/02-03/02031332es.pdf

Hopkins, N., & Kahani-Hopkins, V. (2004). The antecedents of identification: A rhetorical analysis of British Muslims activists' constructions of community and identity. *British Journal of Social Psychology, 43*(1), 41–57.

Jacobson, J. (1998). *Islam in Transition: Religion and identity among British Pakistani Youth*. London: Routledge.

Jacques, M. (2004). Our moral Waterloo. *Guardian Unlimited*. Retrieved May 15, 2004, from http://www.guardian.co.uk/comment/story/0,1217365,00.html

Joppke, C., & Steven Lukes, S. (1999). Introduction to multicultural question. In *Multicultural questions* (pp. 1–26); Oxford, England: OUP.

Kabbani, R. (2002). Dislocation and neglect in Muslim Britain's ghettos. Monday June 17, 2002. *The Guardian*. Retrieved in August 2006, from http://www.guardian.co.uk/world/2002/jun/17/religion.politics

Kepel, G. (1997) *Allah in the West: Islamic movements in America and Europe*. Oxford, England: Polity Press.

Kepel, G. (2003). *Jihad: the trial of political Islam*. London: I. B. Tauris.

Macpherson, W. (1999). *The Stephen Lawrence inquiry: Report of an inquiry*. London: TSO.

Malik, K. (2002, Summer). Against multiculturalism. *The New Humanist*. Retrieved August 2006, from http://www.kenanmalik.com/essays/against_mc.html

Meer, N. (2007). Muslim schools in Britain: Challenging mobilisations or logical developments. *Asia Pacific Journal of Education, 27*(1), 55–71.

Mernissi, F. (1991). *Women and Islam: A historical enquiry*. Oxford, England: Blackwell.

Merry, M. S. (2007). *Culture, identity and Islamic schooling: A philosophical approach*. London: Palgrave MacMillan.

Modood, T. (2005). Ethnicity and intergenerational identities and adaptations in Britain: The socio-political Context. In M. Rutter & M. Tienda (Eds.), *Ethnicity and causal mechanisms* (pp. 281–300). Cambridge, England. Cambridge University Press.

Muslim Council of Britain. (2007). *Towards greater understanding: Meeting the needs of Muslim pupils in state schools*. Retrieved from http//www.mcb.org.uk/downloads/Schoolinfoguidancev2.pdf

Muslim Parliament of Great Britain. (1992). *Race relations and Muslims in Great Britain*: A discussion paper, Muslim Parliament, London.

National College for School Leadership. (2004). *Effective leadership in multi-ethnic schools*. Retrieved from www.ncsl.org.uk

Office for Standards in Education. (2004) *Managing the ethnic minority achievement grant: Good practice in secondary schools*. London: Department for Education and Skills.

Osler, A. (2003). Muslim women teachers: Life histories, identities and citizenship. In T. Benn & H. Jawad (Eds.), *Muslim women in the United Kingdom and beyond: Experiences and images women and gender: The Middle East and the Islamic World, 2. Netherlands:* Brill.

Parekh, B (2000). *Rethinking multiculturalism: Cultural diversity and political theory.* Basingstoke, England: Palgrave.

Parker-Jenkins, M. (1995). *Children of Islam: A teacher's guide to meeting the needs of Muslim pupils.* Stoke-on-Trent, England: Trentham.

Parker-Jenkins, M. (2005) *In good faith.* Williston, VT: Ashgate.

Parker-Jenkins, M. (2007). *Aiming high.* SAGE.

Richardson, R. (Ed.). (2004). *Islamophobia: Issues, challenges and action.* Staffordshire, England: Trentham Books.

Richardson, R., & Wood, A. (2004). *The achievement of British Pakistani learners.* The report of the RAISE project, 2002-04, funded by Yorkshire Forward. Staffordshire, England: Trentham Books.

Rushdie, S. (1989). *The satanic verses.* New York: Viking Penguin.

Shah, S. (2006a). Leading multiethnic schools: A new understanding of Muslim youth identity. *Journal of Educational Management, Administration and Leadership, 34*(2), 215–237.

Shah, S. (2006b). Educational leadership: An Islamic perspective. *British Educational Research Journal, 32*(3), 363–385.

Shah, S. (2006c). Leading multicultural schools: A concept of *Adab* for managing diversity. in J. K. Richards (Ed.), *International perspectives on education and training* (pp. 439–456). Athens, Greece: ATINER.

Shah, S. (2007). Managing Muslim identity in schools: Understanding the challenge. *Race Equality Teaching, 2*(25), 10–14.

Siddiqui, K. (1992, January 4). *The Muslim Parliament: Political innovations and adaptations.* Inaugural meeting of the Parliament, London.

Singh, D (2006, August 24). *Speech by Darra Singh as Chair of the Commission on Integration and Cohesion (CIC) at the launch of the Commission.* Retrieved September 2007, from http://www.communities.gov.uk/index.asp?id=1502287

Tyrer, D., & Ahmad, F. (2006). *Muslim Women and higher education: Identities, experiences and prospects; A summary report.* Liverpool, England: John Moores University and European Social Fund.

Vincent, C. (Ed.). (2003). *Social justice, education, and identity.* London: Routledge Falmer.

Werbner, P. (1997). Essentialising essentialism, essentialising silence: Ambivalence and multiplicity in the constructions of racism and ethnicity. In P. Werbner & T. Modood (Eds.), *Debating cultural hybridity: Multi-cultural identities and the politics of anti-racism* (pp. 226-254). London: Zed Books.

Woodward, W. (2006, August 25). Kelly vows that new debate on immigration will engage critically with multiculturalism. *The Guardian*, p. 7

Verkuyten, M. (2004). *The social psychology of ethnic identity.* London: Routledge.

CHAPTER 10

INTERCULTURAL LEADERSHIP IN AN AUSTRALIAN BICULTURAL SETTING

A Case Study

Kate Sutherland

INTRODUCTION

It is easy to assume, from an Australian educator's point of view, that all Western educational leaders would operate the same way; utilizing shared assumptions, values, and beliefs which have been developed and exercised through organizational experience and professional learning. After all, we operate in liberal democracies; access for all to universal education is highly valued and we are engaged in pursuing it to its highest quality for our young people. One could also assume that, being members of the "West" we would therefore lead our schools in similar ways. However, I discovered through an intercultural leadership experience, that leadership is a culturally bound concept. To work successfully, in a collaborative

Leadership and Intercultural Dynamics, pp. 189–208
Copyright © 2009 by Information Age Publishing
All rights of reproduction in any form reserved.

way, with colleagues from another culture requires the leaders themselves to operate from an intercultural framework. What follows is my learning journey, from an Anglo-Saxon (as opposed to Gallic) perspective, towards developing an intercultural leadership approach. The narrative reflects a constructivist approach where my own experience and reflections become the source of data on which knowledge of intercultural leadership is built. The analysis also draws on the work of intercultural and cross-cultural researchers who have already begun exploring intercultural dynamics from different perspectives in response to the globalization of business and education.

In May 2005 I accepted an appointment as deputy principal at a binational, bicultural, bilingual French-Australian government school in Canberra, Australia. It was an exciting prospect because the opportunity provided a complex education environment, working alongside professionals from another culture, in an international context. This appointment followed on from an exciting and dynamic leadership position where I had helped change staff attitudes to professional and student learning environments utilizing contemporary theories of Anglo-American organizational leadership.[1] This experience and a background working in a highly participative employment culture[2] were the frame of reference on arrival at Telopea Park School. I soon realized that assumptions and associated practices of this manner of leadership did not easily translate to this hybrid education environment. So began a phase of deep critical reflection and a learning journey within an international intercultural leadership environment. As such, it called for the exercise of lifelong learning principles required for a rapidly changing world (Chapman, Aspin, & Collard, 1997).

THE SETTING

Telopea Park School/Lycée Franco-Australien de Canberra (TPS) was established by inter-government treaty in 1983.[3] The purpose of this cultural agreement was to establish a French-Australian government school in Canberra that would provide bilingual education in English and French as well as foster respect for other cultures. The school would also provide a French education setting for local French nationals and at the same time disseminate and promote understanding of French language and culture.

TPS was created at a time when France was creating similar education links with Germany whereby French-German schools were created at Versailles (*Lycée de BUC*) and in Freiburg and Saabrücken in Germany. More recently, cultural links have been forged with Greece, Scotland, and

England. These schools form part of a network of French schools around the world that provide French education to both French nationals and local students. Indeed, the French Agency for Teaching of French Overseas (*Agence Pour l'Enseignement Français à l'Etranger*) operates to support education programs in the network. Consequently, TPS could be considered an Australian government school, a French school abroad as well as an international school: a complex and rich education environment; which is truly intercultural.

The intergovernment treaty established that the principal would be an Australian but a French assistant principal (head of French studies) would oversee French curriculum, pedagogy, and administration. The leadership structure (French-Australian) is similar to the French-German lycees in which French and German leaders work interculturally to lead their school communities. French trained and licensed teachers work at the school, including educational advisers (*conseiller pédagogique*[4]), and are employed by either ACT Department of Education and Training, or through the French Embassy or French Department of Foreign Affairs. The school currently has a student population of 1,100 students from kindergarten to year 10, the final year of compulsory schooling and a teaching staff of one hundred. Thirty-five of these are French nationals.

Within this structure, my brief, as deputy principal, was to lead and manage the bilingual primary school of 18 French staff and 17 Australian staff with the head of French studies and the *conseiller pédagogique*. A major objective was to harmonize or merge the French and Australian curricula. To achieve this was to ensure synergy within the bicultural professional environment fostered through harmonized practices and processes, at the same time, meeting educational and administrative requirements of both Australian and French governments. What follows is an exploration of the evolution of a developing intercultural leader within this context;. It analyzes what processes and frames of reference have been utilized to lead with education leaders from two professional cultural backgrounds.

METHOD AND MEANING MAKING

In the early twenty-first century culturally defined conceptions of leadership are under scrutiny. The work of researchers, such as Hofstede,[5] who sought to explain cultural interactions within business organizations, provides lenses through which cross-cultural leadership can be analyzed. Two major and recent international leadership studies undertaken on behalf of the European Union and the Wallenberg Foundation in Sweden led by Professor John MacBeath at the University of Cambridge[6] not only highlight culturally divergent nature of school leadership but also, the central role language, the use of educational terms and their meanings has in creating mutual understanding.

Intercultural leadership is a new field demanding attention as education and educational leadership is drawn into the forces of globalization. This is especially so in an TPS where the school leadership team is a binational one comprised of an Australian principal, a French head of French studies/*proviseur*, Australian deputy principals at primary and secondary levels and a French pedagogical advisor/*conseiller pédagogique* who also functions as quasi-deputy principal to the *proviseur*. Social research in both Europe and North America[7] indicates a dearth of intercultural research and the need for more understanding in this field. Collard and Wang (2005) have recently observed that "scant attention has been paid to interactions between diverse cultural traditions both within and between nations (p. 179).

Researchers have worked at defining "intercultural leadership" in fields as diverse as communication and education (Collard & Wang, 2005; Dahl, 2007; Lewis, 2007; Dimmock & Walker, 2005). They define " 'culture' variously, but essentially as" ' (Abercrombie et al., as cited in Dimmock & Walker, 2005 p. 63). "Intercultural" perspectives examine the interaction between cultures as opposed to a cross-cultural analysis, which highlights differences. But, importantly, it needs to be noted that to operate interculturally one must employ cross-cultural perspectives. That is, in an intercultural environment it is counterintuitive to adopt a cross-cultural approach when you desire to find common ground to forge an intercultural way of working. However, on a personal level, you have to utilize cross-cultural perspective initially to identify where you stand culturally in relation to the "other," in this case the French. This is a necessary step to know who you *are*, because by knowing who you are culturally paradoxically enables you to identify common ground on which to begin building intercultural leadership. Once operating interculturally, I used my cross-cultural perspective as a frame of reference: a strategy to calibrate our cultures. This occurs typically at times of misunderstanding and dissonance to try to identify, once again possible points of commonality and a way forward. In fact, if I operated from a cross-cultural perspective routinely, it is very easy to adopt almost a deficit model when looking at the "other"; a destructive approach when the goal is to work interculturally.

Therefore, within this binational context intercultural leadership becomes a reflection of the interactions between French and Australian education leaders and the resulting outcomes. It is a complex and difficult process that produces positive outcomes that move the school forward and contribute to the binational project, as well as other outcomes that were both unexpected and challenging. I recognize that the following intercultural construction (Collard & Wang, 2005) and its analysis is from an Anglo-American perspective and some may consider this a limitation.

Initially, identification of a method for analyzing what was occurring in this instance was difficult. In the first instance I drew heavily on concepts from critical reflective practice and concepts from contemporary leadership theories and practice. The former facilitated intrapersonal exploration and the latter provided a frame of reference for understanding some interpersonal and organizational dynamics within an educational setting. Later, research and visits to a similar bilingual French-German school in France, as well as regular French schools, provided other lenses through which to view this Australian experience.

I have used methodologies developed by Chase (2003) and Oliva (2000) as points of reference to help construct this narrative. Chase (2003) promotes narrative as a valid means of analysis:

> Taking narrative seriously means directing our attention to that process of embodiment, to what narrators accomplish as they tell their stories, and how the accomplishment is culturally shaped. (p. 274)

Her analysis recognizes the importance of immersion and one's own culture within the experience and explanation of the story. Oliva (2000) provides another dimension for the analysis of this kind of research environment where, in an intercultural context not only is the researcher integral to the making of the story but also that language (*langue*, as well as *parole*) becomes fundamental to creating meaning; the author becomes part of, and is instrumental in the transaction within a bilingual environment as she proposes "a new method for qualitative research that explicitly heightens the importance of a researcher's 'dwelling' in the transactive space (p. 35).

Oliva (2003) subscribes to the use of the "third place" to engage in intercultural interaction. The same idea is also reflected in the Australian Government's Asian Languages Professional Learning Project.[8] "The third place is a position between the two cultures from which one can interact comfortably with people from the other culture while maintaining one's own identity" (Australian Government Quality Teacher Program, 2005, p 17)

The "third space" is a key aspect of my approach to intercultural leadership; it is the location of intercultural discourse and leadership interaction and creation. This narrative is, therefore, generated from experience within the "third space," where a professional and learning environment is created that is neither French nor Australian but a marriage of the two, respecting both cultures' educational perspectives. The "third space" epitomized what I wanted to do and be in order to work with my French colleagues to create a dynamic hybrid leadership environment, which was neither purely French nor purely Australian. It held the promise of creating a harmonized/merged professional environment of TPS. I came to this concept in 2006 and it continues to remains a point of reference, used to define the space in which intercultural leadership occurs. I had tried other strategies as I will outline later but it was within the "third space" that intercultural leadership occurred and insights emerged. What follows is a narrative presented on two levels: personal and professional.

INTRAPERSONAL PERSPECTIVES

On arrival at TPS the landscape was initially confronting because my pre-existing leadership schemas did not immediately apply. French colleagues personified an unknown set of assumptions, beliefs, and values: Who were they?, what motivated them as school leaders?, what attitudes to education and school leadership did they have?, what did they value in education and learning?, what is their role here and in French schools?, what did they want of me as a colleague?, how could I build a trusting connection with them?, how could I understand them when they speak French? These questions are where intercultural leadership started, within myself, on a very personal level. To effectively operate in an intercultural leadership capacity within the "third space" it has been necessary to perpetually work from within oneself and, at the same time, identify and develop strategies for functioning with French colleagues.

In the first instance, I had to rely upon my inherent interest in other cultures, my experience of living with non-Anglo-Celtic ethnic groups within in the Australian community, including within my immediate family, to engage with my French colleagues, leaders or not. While wanting to achieve a connection quickly, I knew I would have to draw upon some of my personal qualities to engage with a familiar, yet different culture. Being a perceptive person I would also need to exercise my empathy, tact, understanding, subtlety, and positive reaction (Lewis, 2006) to work effectively in this bicultural environment. Each of these came into play, but only after a faltering start. An experience from my first week at the school, which remains a significant learning point, relates to a reaction of my French colleague, the *conseiller pédagogique* who misread my reflective approach to engaging with my new position. I had spent time in my office in a concerted effort to come to grips with the scope of what was required in this new position. After a visit from the principal to inquire why I was not speaking with my French colleague, I was shocked to realize the perception of my French colleague was that I did not want to speak with him.

This was a shocking experience because I discovered that innocent behaviors could be misconstrued. Following this important lesson, I always ensured that I considered how my behavior may be perceived by my French colleagues and I worked consistently to avoid misconceptions. I then considered that learning French would be a visible sign of my commitment to the binational agreement and on a personal level, to my French colleagues. I joined *Alliance Française de Canberra* and took French classes for 2½ years. This provided opportunities to gain insights to the power of language as a vehicle for disseminating culture. I began to recognize that their language and culture were extremely important to my French colleagues and began to consider how this could be respected in the workplace.

In the process of learning French I also began to recognize my own mental models as an Anglo-Australian, in a multicultural Australian society. Making connections between the two professional cultures by utilizing cross-cultural comparisons was a significant step. Initially, this was done through observation and gathering information through professional conversations with French colleagues, who pointed out Anglo-Saxon approaches. Indeed, it was during these initial conversations where my approach or view point was, politely pointed out to be "Anglo-Saxon," that I began to realize the pervasiveness of my Anglo-Celtic heritage on my thinking as well *as* realizing that in this educational setting there was another important lens through which to consider anything—the Gallic lense. It became apparent that research was necessary to assist in making more meaningful connections.

Curiosity about the French and France grew as knowledge of the language and culture also increased, especially about the French professional and school cultures and their place within the globalized world. It was satisfied later through visits to schools, in mainland France and New Caledonia (*Nouvelle Caledonie*). The visits provided a sense of the learning and professional environments: roles of French leaders, school operations, dynamics between staff, school leaders, students and parents, and even the aesthetics of school environments. I observed that *teacher focus* was squarely *in the classroom* and *parents remained outside the school*.

Motivated and determined to be successful in this international environment I reflected on my own professional experience to see what skills could be transferred to this context. My preferred leadership style is inherently inclusive and respectful in nature. As a collegial and collaborative leader of teams I had a range of skills that would underpin and facilitate intercultural interactions. My leadership platform included:

- Positive and respectful relationships between all members of the school community.

- Inclusive practices involving students, staff and parents.
- Openness to new ideas and the voice of "other."
- Taking responsibility for building teams and the notion of shared leadership.
- Commitment to excellence and improvement through building capacity.
- A commitment to lifelong learning.

These reflect contemporary Anglo-American leadership discourses. These emerged through the latter part of the twentieth century in tandem with school reforms, and at a time when globalization led to greater movement of peoples around the world and the further expansion of international education. Of course the situation at TPS was related to these developments, it was an aspect of French government efforts to expand its network of schools worldwide.

Leadership in French schools developed differently from that in Australian schools where leaders have required skills to enable them to juggle a multidimensional school leadership role. My observation of French leadership is that the administrative structure seems to define the style. The resulting leadership style, whilst tempered by the character and personality of the individual leader, is more managerial. It appeared to limit opportunities for collaboration, teaming, and inclusive practices. It also generated somewhat more formal and distant relationships with teaching staff. These characteristics need to be considered when plans of action and processes are being designed in abi-cultural institution.

In France there is a duality[9] in the loci for leadership in schools. The administrative, managerial, and sometimes bureaucratic role of French school leaders sits alongside the essentially educational leadership role of French inspectors, who operate from a regional perspective. This is the frame of reference which French leaders and their staff carry to their new appointments at TPS. The nature of French school leadership is thrown into relief in one recent leadership overview, *Leadership and Educational Change [sic]* (Service de Veille Scientifique et Technologie, 2007), that highlights areas for change and development to support education reform in response to the growth of the European Union and the impact of the forces of globalization. Indeed the paper discusses at length the virtues of participative and shared leadership, the structures required, and the processes to develop. It confirms my observations that French education leadership structures and practices are somewhat different from those of Australia and particularly, the Australian Capital Territory. It sheds some light on why French staff have a rather more distant relationship with their leaders as compared to the closer and more accessible relationship Australian staff have with theirs. French staff are trained impeccably in implementation of French government education policy and the relations with hierarchy supports this mode of operation. This particular characteristic underscores the importance of modelling accessibility and approachability by a deputy principal and the employment of inclusive practices where possible.

Distinctive differences appeared in leadership style and processes, creation of the curriculum[10] and pedagogy, teacher assessment, the role of parents, participative management, and the inclusion of teacher voice. Participative management and decision making in ACT schools is integral to the structure and operations of school communities. This professional culture means that:

- Leaders are central figures in the dynamic,
- Staff, parents and students work in partnership to achieve student outcomes
- Collaborative teams are used to design curricula
- Democratic meeting structures and procedures characterize decision making
- Interactive professional learning sessions are a feature of professional development
- Democratic decision-making processes and collaboration extend to consultations with parents and even community groups.

These are all second nature to members of school communities in the ACT. This expectation of complete immersion in the corporate life of the school is at odds with the French teachers whose culture is to be predominately classroom-based and focused. This difference has had significant implications for intercultural leadership as creative tensions existed when I attempted to developing collegial capacity to cooperate A similar tension exists in the French-German context at BUC, France where German teachers, who have similar work culture to Australian teachers, involve themselves in aspects of the corporate life of the school, whereas French teachers do not. For example, German teachers are prepared to remain after classes and be involved in meetings and curriculum writing, whereas French teachers come and go as their teaching commitments require. At TPS there has been a successful merging or harmonizing of the two cultures in this regard partly through a culture that has been developed over time. It has been facilitated, in part, because the majority of French staff are employed under ACT government conditions.

Teacher accountability and assessment also reflects two quite different sets of assumptions. Professional pathways, the ACT method of enabling and guiding professional growth in line with system, school and personal goals, is underpinned by trusting professional relations and the capacity of supervisors to conduct professional conversations and exercise mentoring and coaching to achieve results. While professional conversations are undertaken by French colleagues with their staff their assessment happens in two loci reflecting the leadership of schooling: regionally with the inspector (implementation of the curriculum and pedagogy) and, in the school with the *proviseur* for their administrative performance. Each gives a mark out of twenty. There is a sense of a different type of professional relationship between teachers and leaders and this plays out in other ways, particularly when French teachers are teamed with Australian supervisors for professional pathways. Australian leaders tend to induct French teachers into the purpose of these interactive professional conversations that are to guide and challenge professional growth. For the most part the dynamic is very productive, but sometimes French staff do not understand and appreciate the process since they place higher value on the "marking system" they are used to.

Social interactions are very important to French colleagues, so being aware of and using polite salutations and responding to their sensibilities has been paramount in building trusting relations and showing respect and acceptance. One must always allow time for a French colleague to recount their experience of the weekend. Opportunities, such as weekly morning teas, whereby French and Australian staff come together have been in existence for sometime to foster such relationships. These have also been extended with binational social events in private homes and luncheons at school.

Although relations are given priority some French staff struggle with the hybrid nature of the school and much energy has to be given to staff welfare by both French and Australian leaders in this regard. Indeed, for French staff living in a foreign land, at great distance from mainland France, staff welfare becomes of paramount importance. Although power distance in this culture complicates relations, the strength of the bicultural leadership and collective staff team is a major factor in successful management of difficult cases.In one instance, when a staff member was particularly unhappy support was given by continuing to speak with the teacher on a daily basis, to reduce the sense of isolation and by facilitating required leave, access to other support and the termination of the contract. Other staff gain confidence in the school and its leadership when such matters are resolved tactfully. Indeed, when they are not the inverse occurs.

Reflecting on the responsibilities a leadership position in this context carried it became apparent that very clearly it is a complex educational setting where one's knowledge of oneself becomes paramount if one is to relate and connect with "others." Mental models around the centrality of education in building society and culture, particularly bilingualism, became a key area for collegial focus. The recent pedagogical theories promoting teacher as facilitator have a prominent role requiring constructivist approaches. One cannot be in didactic or authoritarian mode in a context like TPS.

Ultimately, and inadvertently, I had satisfied Chen's and Van Velsor's (see Dimmock & Walker 2005) model identifying intercultural competencies for effective leadership in culturally diverse contexts. These include:

> interrelated skills: motivational (a value orientation towards others and a willingness to work towards building harmonious relationships); cognitive (the acquisition of knowledge and an understanding of the cultural values and norms of diverse groups); and behavioural (the skills of working with others from diverse backgrounds and value orientations). (p. 73)

It was now a matter of transforming this intercultural awareness into practice.

INTERCULTURAL LEADERSHIP: WORKING IN THE "THIRD SPACE"

The viability of intercultural leadership in the "third space" relies on the healthy operation and exercise of several components:

- a willingness to pursue, nurture and maintain positive relationships
- respect for, awareness of, and a motivation to understand 'others'
- awareness of the centrality of language and other forms of communication
- motivation for and skill in leading diverse teams
- principles and practices for collaborative workplaces
- a willingness to build an effective binational education organization (*éstablissement*) together.

In such contexts, knowledge of and skills in diplomacy and the virtue of constructive international relations are also paramount. The intrapersonal work I undertook and continued from the beginning, combined with a willingness to continue in the mode of life-long learner contributed to the creation of a platform on which intercultural leadership could be developed and nurtured.

The efficacy of any human interaction is a reflection of the personal relationships operating. So too, in an intercultural context positive relations are paramount and are developed and fostered in various ways. The basis on which the "third space" is always approached is one of respect, respect for the participants and their culture as well as the entity that is being fostered, which is binational education at TPS. Without this, intercultural leadership could easily break down and slip into cross-cultural leadership privileging differences rather than constructing common ground. It demands an approach of openness and awareness of other, the other's point of view is always valid.

Within a bilingual environment where French and English are the languages of engagement, language itself becomes pre-eminent in enabling the "third space" to function. Oliva (2000) makes an obvious distinction that our understanding of language, even common words, is informed by our gender, race, cultural differences and that this impacts on *parole* or use of language in communication (Oliva, 2000). Furthermore, she utilizes *dialogism*, or the *interaction that values all the discourses in communication* (Oliva, 2000, p. 38) to expand our understanding of spheres of interlocking influence between cultures resulting from respectful dialogue. Through respectful dialogue the intercultural leadership team creates a trusting place that "facilitates the meeting of minds" (MacBeath, 2006) in which shared meaning can be created. Without shared meaning dissonance occurs and this creates fractures in intercultural leadership, which necessarily then require repairing.

Responding to damaged interactions takes time and draws heavily on previously built relationships as well as the belief in the purpose of the institution. For example, at the beginning of 2006 a failure on both sides to maintain open communication created a period of dissonance. Joint projects and access to advice stopped and had a direct impact on operations and conclusion of projects. This can be illustrated through explaining the impact of the dissonance on Francophone Week, an annual event which usually includes bicultural and bilingual activity. The previous year a creative activity, in collaboration with Alliance Française de Canberra, had been very successful as a result of bicultural cooperation in the leadership team. But the dissonance between some leaders curtailed willingness to even engage in a joint project and created an unsustainable and destructive environment the following year. This created a negative impression of the leadership team amongst the staff. It had a strong impact on relations within the primary school teaching team who felt the dissonance and uncertainty in relationships. In a school, time spent in repairing dislocated relations detracts from the educational purpose. It is far more purposeful to be proactive in one's approach so that opportunities for dissonance are minimized.

Indeed, it behoves the intercultural leader to keep all parties engaged in the process of intercultural leadership, especially in planning, formation of policy and practice. This is achieved by ensuring they are engaged in *parole* and that the level of trust is such that French colleagues feel comfortable in putting their views, even if they are contrary to the mainstream discourse. This is necessary for constructive and meaningful dialogue to take place. It is often on the basis of these conversations that plans, policies and procedures are designed and developed. Therefore, by facilitating the use of both languages (French and English) in discourse, meetings, social settings, and in professional conversations one is demonstrating an awareness, respect and acceptance rather than dismissively expecting French colleagues to conduct transactions in their second language and simply adapt to mainstream practices. This dynamic is a common and powerful one that is used the world over to either include or exclude "others." Language then, becomes a means of respecting or disrespecting "others." In intercultural leadership language must be used to both respect "others" as well as facilitating communication for the benefit of the organization.

What both Australian and French colleagues had in common was navigating the bilingual education terrain. The brief of the cultural agreement is *to promote progressive bilingualism in its educational program and to enhance access by students to quality bilingual education.*[11] This becomes a common focus around which joint projects and ways of managing evolve, to preserve the efficacy of the bilingual program. In a sense, the bilingual program is the child of French-Australian leadership reality. Therefore, the binational team makes many decisions informed by impacts on the bilingual program such as staff and resource selection, formulation of the yearly calendar, and class programs.

Allied to this have been efforts to extend the degree to which communications in the school are bilingual. The limiting factor has been access to translators, which are expensive. While essential communications such as key sections of the newsletter, the Web site, and parent letters have been translated "in house" for some time this approach has become a substantial drain on staff time.[12] Despite this, major documents that are fundamental to the work of the primary school brief; delivery of a harmonized curriculum and pedagogical approaches have not been translated as yet! The current school plan identifies translation of documents as central to the bicultural ethos. Substantial school resources have therefore been recently committed to translating *Every Chance to Learn* (ACT curriculum framework released in 2007) so the French staff are able to contribute more meaningfully to the curriculum development process. An English version of the French curriculum framework was released by the French government in 2007. The school has also identified a staff member who undertakes day-to-day translations such as newsletters, parent correspondence, student welfare and management documents. This commitment to translation of major school documents is a symbolic affirmation of the binational French-Australian school.

Intercultural cooperation and understanding are required to implement Australian and French Government education policies and practices in this setting. While some policies to only the French or Australian curriculum are implemented without adaptation, neither side expects policy cloning on the part of the other. However, where policies need to be applied across the whole school and for them to operate effectively reflection, dialogue and preparedness to change and adapt them to the setting are required. Through this process emergent understandings (Collard & Wang, 2005) are created and on the bases of the understanding a TPS approach can be devised. A clear example of this is harmonization of the curriculum, the merging French and Australian curricula. This cannot be done external to the school or removed from French leaders or the teachers who would deliver it. Rather, a collaborative binational team approach is used with a bilingual mode of communication to identify essential outcomes and competencies, common aspects of the curriculum and a sequence that will accommodate both French and Australian needs. The TPS curriculum documents are created with reference to both French and Australian government sources. However, it is achieved with some difficulty because Australian staff bring a tradition of school-based curriculum development where curricula for individual schools are created using a policy framework to meet the learning needs of the individual school community. As such they have a range of skills and frames of reference to draw upon. Alternatively, with a few exceptions, French national curriculum is developed centrally in Paris and is implemented at local level using supporting curriculum resource materials and the expertise of the *conseiller pédagogique*. So French staff are less likely to have had the degree of experience in designing school-based curricula as their Australian colleagues.

In this domain, intercultural leadership requires a jointly devised plan of action, that included an explanation of harmonization, drawing links between ACT and French curriculum frameworks, modeling the process by creating scope and sequence instruments from science and technology and then forming binational teams that can be led by French and Australian staff. The planning phase is extremely important because it affords time when the *conseiller pédagogique* and I can work on developing a shared understanding our own assumptions, values and beliefs. We share our frames of reference in relation to curriculum writing and program planning, which include examining our two new curriculum frameworks. We have discovered that even though the ACT framework had more detail there were many commonalities with the French parallel. They both:

- define the scope of what is to be learnt in compulsory years of schooling
- identify what the nation sees as important to learn for the twenty-first century
- have overarching outcomes to be achieved (The French "Pillars" and ACT Essential Learning Achievements)
- prioritize literacy and numeracy, science, civics, and information and communication technology
- highlight the importance of understanding French and Australian cultures
- have a focus on developing lifelong learning skills and competencies
- believe in the development of the affective domain
- recognize that our countries exist in interrelationship with others

I have found the need to explain the philosophy of school-based curriculum development; its intent, expectations and process. Most importantly, we have to identify what is important for our governments and ensure that these are addressed. What we have discovered is commonality between our two curriculum frameworks and that this can be used as the point of departure, which will engage staff in seeing the possibilities for harmonization Also, the concept of harmonization needs to be explained to teachers as it underpins much of what we do, not just in curriculum development but in structures, processes, and practices. It is modeled throughout the whole action plan including the bilingual delivery of professional learning and the translation of documents. In effect the dialogue between the *conseiller pédagogique* and myself has to be replicated on a larger scale with the staff. Consequently, intercultural leadership in this instance involves operating at a metalevel to plan with my French colleague, but at the same time educating him and then the staff. Throughout, I continue to learn myself.

Mediating the "third space" is a measured process that moves at two paces. Established routines and practices can move at a pace that *langue* can manage. Achieving common understandings and maintaining positive relations is a much slower process that takes time but is essential for constructive intercultural relations. It is in this area that time is spent on a daily basis, so that matters which a leader might set aside time for in a monocultural school, will take much longer in this intercultural setting.

A good example is a staff matter where a resolution may require an Australian approach a difficult interaction with a parent. This is a point of potential repetitive tension. At TPS, the majority of parents are Australian and used to the a participatory approach set down in legislation. Parents are considered partners in the education process and are welcome to contact the school about any matter. Australian staff are experienced in managing parent interactions and usually have a repertoire of approaches. However, parents in France do not have the same access to schools and staff. This means that French staff do not have such a wide range of strategies for dealing with parents and their concerns. Indeed, this area, constantly generates disharmony between teachers and parents and requires sensitive leadership. It has required modeling by Australian leaders as to how to approach the interview so that the matter is resolved satisfactorily for all stakeholders but demonstrating the integration of the "French voice," Where these conditions exist so does intercultural construction where the participants are the agents for leveraging the creation of an intercultural leadership environment;

> Intercultural dynamics permit adaptation, fluidity, nuanced change, and even resistance ... agents and recipient become partners in intercultural construction. (Collard & Wang, 2005, p. 181)

Intercultural leadership requires drawing on strengths from both sides. The adoption of Australian shared leadership and other participatory management strategies not only facilitates intercultural leadership it ensures involvement of all parties. The focus on teaming facilitates and nurtures collaboration between leaders as well as teachers at class and grade levels. Teaming ensures collegial approaches in developing bilingual teaching programs, activities, and projects. The combination of the Australian capacity for problem solving by creating and developing solutions along with the French capacity for precision and quality in implementation of plans provides a potent mix for creating exciting and productive learning environments.

Managing change is a constant at TPS and it is the role of the intercultural leadership team to manage this through binational planning and negotiation. Not only is change a product of contemporary school reform in the wider globalized education environment, it is also integral to this context as French staff arrive and leave mid-year. Relationships end and others beginning with a new cohort. Australian turnover occurs typically at the beginning of the year in February. These periods of uncertainty draw heavily on established patterns of interaction within the intercultural leadership team. They are put under even more strain and uncertainty when the leaders themselves change. At these times routines are emphasized and interruptions and new projects are minimized while new relationships and patterns of intercultural interaction are established.

An aspect of intercultural leadership is managing the connectedness of French staff to the hybrid binational environment. The nature of TPS is neither fully French nor fully Australian, although French staff perceive it as Australian because it is so different from the conventional French schools from which they have just come. It takes newly arrived French staff some months to internalize the nature of the school; this is easier for some than others. Staff who adapt to the hybrid education environment are those who adopt intercultural approaches similar to those described above. They are motivated, flexible, willing to suspend judgement as they negotiate the new professional terrain and bring considerable interpersonal skills to the environment. Where the integration does not occur and a French staff member feels disconnected, this can happen on different levels both French and Australian leaders work in cooperation looking after different aspects of the matter.

CONCLUSION: LESSONS FROM THE JOURNEY

Through leading with French colleagues within a government school setting in Australia it has become apparent that, while many fundamental elements of leadership are shared, Anglo-American interpretations of leadership of organizations do not have universal currency throughout the Western world. For example, we share a desire for high standards, attainment of optimum outcomes for all children, respect for our staff and their professionalism, a motivation to provide world class education that nurtures our future citizens with French professionals. We can both argue that we exhibit qualities desired within the five domains of the ACT Educational Leadership Framework;[13] *Leading Teaching & Learning, Leading Strategic Resource Management, Learning-Centred Leadership, Leading a Quality Organisation and Leading and Working With Others.* But, it is the participative nature of the ACT school system and its decentralized processes that create a sharp contrast to the more bureaucratic and centralized French one. Each of these environments has generated extremely different leadership styles.

It is my belief that values of Anglo-American concepts of organizational learning and leadership practices generated by the knowledge economy that have the capacity to part, enable intercultural leadership. This has been combined with a strong focus on diplomacy and international relations by French leaders in their role as school leaders appointed through the French Ministry of Foreign Affairs. Without the mindset of shared leadership, participative practices, and international consciousness, intercultural transaction would be much more limited.

Intercultural leadership processes are ongoing! There is not a point at which they have been completed because there is a constant state of change in this context, just as change is a constant in the globalized knowledge economy. The environment requires leader participants to engage in ongoing reflective practice, including a willingness to engage in reflective dialogue:

> They are required to become reflective practitioners (Schon, 1988) who understand the traditions that have shaped their own perceptions and beliefs and recognise equivalent processes in the people with whom they are working. (Collard & Wang, 2005, p. 181)

Collard (in this volume) again highlights the role of intercultural competence:

> intercultural competence refers to a person's capacity to recognize the cultural origins of knowledge and values, incorporate alternative frames of reference into knowledge construction, learn from and with people from other cultures and apply ethical choices which recognize the complexities of cultural interaction. (p. 11)

Intercultural leadership is also constructed from a cultural perspective. It would be of great interest to formulate a French definition of the concept. Indeed, a bicultural, collaboratively generated, perspective on intercultural leadership would be of great value. This is a limited study and further detailed research is necessary. Not withstanding this, this limitation my narrative is offered as a contribution to understanding intercultural dynamics and the leadership that is generated in a contemporary binational and bilingual leadership context.

The context demanded operating through multiple lenses, creating inclusive environments and modelling desired ways of working. A creative tension is a constant as one oscillates between Australian and French perspectives in a myriad of transactions, finding collegial and collaborative solutions, the results of which should build the binational project within a wider context of school reform. There is a responsibility to maintain an on-going commitment to critical reflection, respectful dialogue, aspirations for improvement, respect for others, and a capacity to adjudicate on transactions in the interests of all. In fact, it requires us reconceptualize leadership to fit the settings in which we work in an increasingly diverse world.

NOTES

1. Anglo-American theories and practice relating to leading change (Hargreaves & Fink, 2006), leading learning organizations (Senge, 1990;

Limerick, Cunningham, & Crowther, 1998), creating professional learning communities and communities of inquiry (De Four & Eaker, 1998).

2. The Education Act of the Australian Capital Territory (ACT Government, 2004) establishes that governance of local schools is a participative process involving school professionals, parents, students, and the government. School and system structures and processes have been created and maintained over a long period to facilitate this fundamental feature of the jurisdiction.

3. Telopea Park School, existed as a local Australian school from 1927. An intergovernment bicultural agreement between the Australian and French Governments (Commonwealth of Australia, 1983) created the current bicultural and bilingual French-Australian school in 1983. The 25th anniversary of the agreement is 2008.

4. In France, the *conseiller pédagogique* assists regional Inspectors with implementation of curriculum and pedagogy. At Telopea Park School the role also encompasses staff welfare, administrative support to the head of French studies and aspects of coordination of the primary school

5. Hofstede was the first person to undertake cross-cultural research in organizations. Although his work is considered limited by some his work is widely cited along with that of Trompenaars and Hampden-Taylor (in Dahl, 2007).

6. Professor MacBeath outlined the project and the results in *Leadership as a Subversive Activity* ACEL Monograph 39 Australian Council of Educational Leaders, 2006.

7. For an overview of intercultural research see Stephen Dahl (2007).

8. Australian Government Quality Teacher Program. (2005). *Getting started with intercultural language learning: A resource for Schools.*

9. The French head of French studies (*proviseur*) also works to the French Embassy, which adds another dimension to their administration.

10. In the Australian Capital Territory school-based curriculum development has been in place since the inception of the education system in the 1970s. School structures and processes support this, including the provision of curriculum frameworks from which individual schools develop their curriculum. This is the opposite of the centrally imposed curriculum which French staff are used to.

11. Article 2, point b, Australian Treaty Series 1983 No 8

12. At Lycée de BUC translation was also an issue. their solution has been to have translations done by the *proviseur* and her deputy *proviseur* who are both bilingual (French-German).

13. The ACT Educational Leadership Framework is currently being revised.

REFERENCES

ACT Department of Education. (2007). *ACT Educational Leadership Framework.* Unpublished manuscript.

ACT Government. (2004). *ACT Government ACT Education Bill.* Canberra, Australia: Author.

Australian Government Quality Teacher Program (2005). *Getting Started with intercultural language learning: A resource for schools.* Canberra, Australia: Government Department of Education Science and Training.

Chase S. E. (2003). *Taking narrative seriously: Consequences from method and theory in interview studies.* In Y. S. Lincoln & N. K. Denzin (Eds.), *Turning points in qualitative research* (pp. 273–296). Walnut Creek, CA: AltaMira.

Chapman, J. D., & Aspin, D. N. (1997). *The school, the community and lifelong learning.* London: Cassell.

Collard, J., & Wang, T. (2005). Leadership and intercultural dynamics. *Journal of School Leadership, 5,* 178-195.

Commonwealth of Australia. (1983). *Australian Treaty Series 1983 No. 8. Agreement between the Governments of Australia and the Government of the French Republic concerning the establishment of a French-Australian School in Canberra,* Canberra: Australian Government Publishing Service.

Dahl S. (2007) *Intercultural research: The current state of knowledge.* Retrieved May 12, 2008, from http://papers.ssm.com/sol3/papers.cfm?abstract_id=658202

Dimmock, C., & Walker, A. (2005). *Educational leadership culture and diversity.* London: SAGE.

Du Four R., & Eaker, R. (1998). *Professional learning communities at work: Best practices for enhancing student achievement.* Reston, VA: ASCD.

Hargraves, A., & Fink, D. (2006). *Sustainable leadership.* San Francisco: Jossey-Bass.

Hayden, M., Thompson, J., & Walker, G. (2002). *International education in practice dimensions for national & international schools.* London: RoutledgeFalmer.

Lewis R. D. (2006). *When cultures collide leading across cultures* (3rd ed.). Boston: Nicholas Brealey International.

Limerick D., Cunnington, B., & Crowther, F. (1998). *Managing the new organisation collaboration and sustainability in the post-corporate world* (2nd ed.). Warriewood, Australia: Business & Professional Publishing.

Oliva M. (2000). Shifting landscapes/shifting langue: Qualitative research from the in-between. *Qualitative Inquiry, 6*(1), 33–57.

MacBeath, J. (2006). *Leadership as a subversive activity.* ACEL Monograph Series Number 39 Australian Council of Educational Leaders, Winmalee.

Senge P. M. (1990) *The fifth discipline: The art & practice of the learning organisation.* Sydney, Australia: Random House.

Service de Veille scientifique et technologique. (2007, January). Leadership and educational change. *La Letter d'Information, 24.* Retrieved May 18, 2008, from http://www.inrp.fr/vst

PART IV

WORKING IN INTERNATIONAL CONTEXTS

CHAPTER 11

CHANGING CONCEPTIONS OF LEARNING IN ZHEJIANG PROVINCE, CHINA, 2002–2004

Ting Wang and John Collard

INTRODUCTION

This and the following chapter report upon an international program in educational leadership at Hangzhou, Normal University between 2002 and 2004. It involved a master of educational leadership degree delivered in bilingual mode by the University of Canberra, Australia. The authors were involved in the design, delivery, and evaluation of the program. The research involved an intensive case study which utilized semistructured interviews with 20 members of a cohort of 52 students. These interviews were conducted at the beginning and conclusion of an 18 month delivery schedule. Focus groups were conducted with the interview sample at the mid point of the program.

Australian academics who taught the course tended to hold and privilege contemporary Western conceptions of learning and leadership. Their teaching methods placed high priority upon participatory and constructivist pedagogy which characterizes work with adult learners in

Leadership and Intercultural Dynamics, pp. 211–232

Australian higher education (Foley, 2000). These were different from the more transmission-based traditions of instruction in Chinese universities (Zhu, 2002). The Australians were also more inclined to operate from assumptions that knowledge is provisional and subjective and that there can be multiple knowledge frames interacting in any one teaching situation (Akerlind, 2003).

The Chinese participants were drawn from a variety of educational institutions and levels in Zhejiang Province, an affluent area of China near Shanghai. The sample was selected to represent as much variation as possible. They came from varied disciplines, ages, genders, and with different levels of experience as teachers. Participants had worked in diverse settings such as primary and secondary schools, higher education institutions, and local educational authorities.

The profile of the research participants was consistent with the entire cohort. Males constituted 77% and 23% were females. School principals, university administrators, and system officials each accounted for approximately one third of the cohort. The research sample comprised 20 participants, 15 (75%) males and 5 (25%) females. School principals (8) accounted for 40% of the respondents while university administrators (6) and system officials (6) each accounted for 30%. The ages ranged from 31 to 52 and the mean age was 38 years. Twelve interviewees were from Hangzhou, the capital city of Zhejiang Province while 8 were from other cities in the Province. All had bachelor degrees and about two thirds had participated in graduate study and obtained postgraduate certificates. Their academic backgrounds drew upon a wide range of disciplines ranging from mathematics, psychology, physics, physiology, chemistry to history, Chinese, and English. More than half had science teaching backgrounds. Such a proportion is unusual in western institutions and may have contributed to adherence to scientific and positivist assumptions in China where education is frequently conceived as a science (Gu & Meng, 2001; Zhu, 2002).

THE GRADUATE COURSE

The University of Canberra (UC) entered into a partnership with Hangzhou Normal University in the relatively affluent and developed Zhejiang Province in Eastern China. The agreement involved UC undertaking responsibility for six subjects from a Master of Educational Leadership program and the local university taking responsibility for an additional four subjects requested by Chinese authorities. The participants who met the entry criteria and finished the coursework were awarded a master's degree from UC, which was also recognized by Degree Awarding Office of the State Council in China. The six subjects offered by the University of Canberra were as follows:

- *Leadership in Learning Organizations* explored leadership and management roles within a variety of learning organizations and focused upon core concepts such as leadership, learning cultures and organizational development. Global, national and micro-organizational issues were studied intensively and assignments provided opportunities for students to analyze and develop interventions in work sites with which they were familiar. Particular attempts were made to respond to the emerging leadership needs of educational institutions in China.[1]

- *Educational Futures* explored the concept of educational futures in Chinese and international contexts. It covered critical perspectives about educational provision at primary, secondary, postsecondary and higher educational settings. It utilized the concept of lifelong learning as an integrative paradigm. It identified challenges which confront policymakers and practitioners in a world characterized by rapid globalization, technological innovation, changing workforce needs, and growing inequality.

- *Professional Development in Educational Organizations* explored major concepts underlying professional education theory, analyzed the relationship between professional development and organizational effectiveness, and broader structural issues of teacher career structures, promotional processes, accountability, and professionalism in the Chinese context.

- *Training, Development and Knowledge Transfer* studied the nature of learning organizations, identified adult learning approaches, and the processes of knowledge acquisition and transfer. It required students to apply an understanding of knowledge transfer to a professional setting or training and development program.

- *Educational Policy and Planning* explored the key influences and concepts underlying contemporary educational policy in domains such as schooling, vocational training and higher education. It paid particular attention to the economic and social assumptions which inform policy making from a range of levels. Specific attention was paid to various levels of policy making within Chinese education. The role of international policy agencies and policy history in developing nations was also examined. Students were expected to develop critical analytical frameworks to examine policy matters through the concepts of power, participation, conflict and accountability. They were required to plan a policy implementation process in a worksite.

- *Educational Effectiveness and Evaluation* explored the concepts of organizational effectiveness, the role of evaluation in a broad range of public and private settings, the characteristics of effective evaluation methodologies and their roles in building learning capacity, and cultures in organizations. Case study analysis and the design of an evaluation for a specific setting was incorporated.

The four subjects offered by Hangzhou Normal University included: Educational Philosophy, Educational Economics, Education Management, and Information Technology. The six core subjects were delivered by UC academics in Hangzhou in three intensive teaching blocks in a face-to-face context over 12 months. Each teaching block usually lasted 2 weeks. It was followed by an extended period of self-study, call-back days and an assignment stage supervised by Chinese co-teachers.

The participants were part-time students with full-time work commitments. They were high caliber educational leaders in Zhejiang Province but most possessed limited proficiency in English. Indeed many had enrolled in the course to improve their English. Therefore, a co-teaching and bilingual model of delivery was adopted.

Lectures were delivered in English and Mandarin using Powerpoint presentations simultaneously. Chinese academics translated course materials, were co-teachers in the classes, provided support to complete assignments after the intensive phase, and marked assignments which were subsequently moderated in Australia. Of the 52 students who commenced the course, 51 were awarded a master's degree from UC in December 2003.

The overall design of the course reflected a strong commitment to characteristics known to facilitate adult learning (Brookfield, 1986; Foley, 2000; Knowles, 1978, 1980; Knowles, Holton, & Swanson, 1998; Kolb, 1984; Mezirow, 1991). These included:

- a high degree of choice, self-direction, and participation;
- opportunities to relate the core concepts of the subject to workplace realties;
- utilization of group learning processes consistent with theories of learning cultures;
- criterion-based and honest feedback from teaching staff and fellow students;
- opportunity for field-based exploration of and application of learning

The Australian academics generally employed constructivist, dialogical and inquiry approaches which focused upon the prior experience of learners' prior experience. They emphasized participation through lectures with group and report back sessions where students were encouraged to construct their own critical understandings based upon their knowledge of Chinese cultural values and educational traditions plus input from the Australian academics. They were encouraged to keep learning journals and assignments required them to analyze local situations and workplaces and then apply their acquired knowledge through personal reflection and planning change interventions.

METHODOLOGY

The study examined the experiences and understandings about learning and leadership of 20 participants in the Hangzhou cohort. They were interviewed twice over a 12-month period. It sought to compare the respondents' conceptions of learning and leadership prior to and after undertaking the course. Potential differences between school based, system and university personnel were also considered in the analysis. The research design followed the phenomenographic tradition which was considered appropriate to allow full descriptions and allow coherent meanings to evolve (Boulton-Lewis, Wilss, & Lewis, 2003). This tradition has been used previously to study student conceptions of knowledge. However, we are not aware of it having been used to study leadership cognitions previously. It was primarily qualitative and longitudinal although we frequently report the concepts and changes in them as proportional figures.

The interview sample of 20 students, was selected duplicate the variation in the full from cohort to surface different perspectives of learning and leadership (Trigwell, 2000). They came from varied disciplines, ages, and both genders; 15 were male and 5 were female. They possessed varying levels of experience as teachers and came from distinct educational sectors such as primary and secondary schools, higher education institutions, and local educational authorities. School leaders, university administrators, and system officials each accounted for approximately one third of the interview sample. All except two participants had teaching experience before they undertook their administrative positions. Three participants had formal qualifications in educational administration or management. The majority of participants had training and professional development experience in education or specific disciplines.

Interviews sought to capture the individuals' conceptions about learning and leadership. They were "open" in the sense that although the interviewer had a list of questions or concerns, there was also opportunity to follow any unexpected lines of reasoning that the interviewee addressed that were not anticipated by the researcher (Booth, 1997). They were also "deep" in that they could follow a certain line of questioning until the researcher and participant reached some kind of common understanding about the topics of discussion (Orgill, 2000). They averaged 60 minutes in duration. Questions were designed to elicit authentic personal responses. They probed personal understandings and experience of leadership and learning and asked for contextual examples to illustrate abstract claims. The experiences and understandings were jointly constituted by interviewer and interviewee. They were neither prior to the interview, ready to be "read off," nor were they only situational social constructions. They became aspects of a dialogue in which the subject's awareness changed from being unreflected to being reflected (Marton, 1994, p. 4427).

Responses were recorded, transcribed into Mandarin, validated by respondents and subsequently sorted into conceptual categories on the basis of similarities and differences both before and after the course. What emerged were two group portraits and individual cameos. The second set highlighted changes in conceptions between March 2002 and April 2003.

The initial coding of the transcripts was descriptive and of low inference, whereas subsequent coding integrated data by using higher-order concepts (Punch, 1998). Transcripts were also summarized as a series of vignettes of specific individuals. The analytical process was iterative. In the first stage, the researcher identified sets of categories of variations within the set of transcripts as a whole. These were then reviewed and revised and transcripts were revisited until stable sets of categories and relationships were developed (Martin, Trigwell, Prosser, & Ramsden, 2003). Previous phenomenographic studies have identified a hierarchical structure in conceptions of learning and leadership (Fairholm, 1991; Marton, Dall'alba, & Beaty, 1993), so consideration was given to whether hierarchical categories could be found in both areas of this study.

The possibility of consistent links between the conceptions of learning and leadership was explored as well. Attention was paid to similarities and differences in forms of excerpts, expressions, and words. The data analysis was also conducted by moving between the full transcripts and the vignettes. The entire analytical process was carried out by the researcher and validated by another researcher. In a second stage higher-order inference pattern codes emerged (Punch, 1998). The outcome was classifications of first-order and second-order concepts of learning and leadership.

In qualitative research reliability can be regarded as "a fit between what researchers record as data and what actually occurs in the natural setting that is being researched" (Bogdan & Biklen, 1992, p. 48). Qualitative research, strives to record the multiple interpretations of, intention in, and meanings given to situations and events (Brock-Utne 1996). Dependability is related to the care and sensitivity in the research process, as well as with precision in results. In this study, dependability of interviews was enhanced by inter-rater checks on the coding of answers to open-ended questions (Silverman, 2001). Around two thirds of interpretations between the two coders were the same. Where discrepancies arose, the researchers reexamined the responses, discussed their different interpretations and finally reached a consensus on the appropriate classification.

Issues of credibility were addressed by making the analysis as contextual as possible. Respondents were asked to illustrate their understandings of phenomena through examples and descriptions of concrete experiences. Rather than solely looking for meaning in discrete words, sentences or phrases, the analysis concentrated on a pool of information.

Some scholars argue that it is difficult to generalize findings from case studies to different settings. It is true that they cannot provide scientific generalizations in the positivist tradition. However, the aim of this study was not to infer global findings from a sample to a population, but rather to understand the phenomena of learning and leadership, and to articulate patterns and linkages of theoretical importance within a bounded sample. A case study may refute a universal generalization such as those propagated by cross-cultural theorists. It can also be used to confirm, challenge, modify, or extend theoretical perspectives. This case study sought to make a significant contribution to theory about conceptions of learning and leadership operating in intercultural contexts, and assist in refocusing the direction of future investigation in the area. It may be a source of hypotheses for future research by showing that such an interpretation is plausible in a particular case and therefore might be so in other cases. Once such a case is studied it can provide insights into the class of events from which the case has been drawn.

INITIAL CONCEPTIONS OF LEARNING

Four dominant conceptions emerged which bear some resemblance to those identified by Marton et al. (1993). They were:

- Learning as acquiring knowledge and skills
- Learning for instrumental purposes
- Learning as applied knowledge
- Learning as understanding the world

These conceptions prevailed across school, system and university sectors. For instance, a principal defined learning as "closely related to knowledge acquisition." A system administrator maintained that learning was "gathering information or absorbing knowledge, mostly passively." A university administrator spoke in terms of "individual study or acquiring knowledge and skills from teachers." Another equated learning with "gaining knowledge from books or others' experience, especially from experts." This last point is important because it reflects traditions of transmissive teaching and passive learning. It also links with the traditional Confucian conception of the teacher as an expert authority figure who cannot be questioned. One insisted that in schools and higher education Chinese students assume that "learning is predominantly knowledge transmission by teachers" and that teachers believe "that students are like empty containers or storerooms."

Many respondents tended to hold absolute beliefs about knowledge as static and universal truths which can be readily transmitted to learners. It was construed to be sacred and authoritative rather than indefinite and contestable. An academic commented:

> Knowledge is regarded as sacred and authoritative. Theories are considered as important bodies of knowledge which should be mastered by the students. It is especially true in the field of education. Theories or definitions of concepts should be memorized. There is only one correct answer to a problem.

In summary, most comments from respondents suggested that receiving, gaining, absorbing, gathering and being told were the dominant ways they construed learning at the start of the course. It was seen predominantly as a passive and reproductive act and there was little recognition of a need for individuals to construct their own understandings. However, some were critical of this inheritance and commented that "little attention was paid to applying the knowledge or promoting creative thinking." Such comments provide some evidence that the cultural assumptions were not absolute, that there was some momentum for change among the cohort which belies cross-cultural paradigms of static cultures.

Another conception of knowledge or skills was essentially pragmatic. They were seen as important because they could be put to some use, such as preparing for examinations, completing assignments, obtaining degrees, or accomplishing certain work tasks. In this sense learning was simply a means to accomplishing immediate tasks. Respondents generally referred to school and workplace contexts when describing learning in this sense.

A pragmatic approach to "learning as application of concepts, theories or methodologies to real life situations" (Marton et al., 1993) was evident in approximately 66% of interviewees. Knowledge and skills were seen as important because they could be put to particular use. However, there were important differences between school principals, university administrators and system officials in this regard. Principals tended to focus more upon learning as a means to passing exams or obtaining degrees and this most probably reflects the dominance of examination systems in Chinese schools. Several maintained that the purpose of learning was "to pass the exams or obtain degrees" While sharing this utilitarian perspective, system officials tended to view learning from performative system perspectives like many of their western contemporaries (see Blackmore, 2004). They were more likely to focus upon "assessment and evaluation criteria" in terms of "mastering certain knowledge and skills." One even claimed in Chinese education "linguistic and logical-mathematical intelligences are emphasized", and "other intelligences are neglected." He added that "radical reform in assessment and evaluation systems," was needed if entrenched instrumental views of learning and knowledge were to change. Academics were more likely to perceive learning as mastery of a research field. One commented that "self-study, reading books or writing papers" was often limited to "learning disciplinary knowledge or conducting research work." Another claimed learning was mostly related to "studying disciplinary knowledge for the sake of work."

However, learning for instrumental purposes was a more complex concept than learning as rote memorization and reproduction (Marton et al., 1993), Rote learning or mechanical memorization was not so much conceived as an end in itself as cross-cultural theorists have commented, but as an instrument to achieve instrumental ends. It also moved beyond stereotypes of Chinese learners as passive rote learners (Watkins & Biggs, 2001). We are challenged to recognize the complex realities beneath the surface culture. The instrumental value of applied learnings in the workplace were also frequently mentioned. Both principals and academics spoke of "learning some useful knowledge and relating it to professional practice." Several focused upon how continued learning helped them to "solve dilemmas in the workplace."

It is interesting to note that system officials and university administrators seemed to attach more importance to theoretical knowledge than school principals. They tended to privilege theories as systematic and as static bodies of knowledge. A system official equated learning with "studying theories and application of theories into practice." Another emphasized "studying theories systematically and using them as guiding principles in practical life." A university administrator insisted that in China, emphasis was laid on "learning authoritative knowledge or a fixed model, memorizing it and then internalizing or applying into practice." This suggests that their beliefs about knowledge tended to be more oriented towards positivist concepts of universal, law-like precepts than the relativism of postmodern thought in contemporary Western discourses

However, almost one fifth of respondents lamented the discrepancy between theories and practice in Chinese education and emphasized the importance of contextualizing theories. A university administrator explained that "there are four basic types of knowledge, knowing what, knowing why, knowing how, and knowing who." He commented that in Chinese tradition more attention was paid to "knowledge per se," but its application was often neglected. A school principal commented upon a training course he had recently undertaken and lamented "there was often a missing link between lofty theories and practice" because he could barely apply what he had learned to his workplace. Some previous research has caricatured Chinese practice as "surface learning" (Van Rossum & Schenk, 1984). However, the insistence of respondents in this study upon the need to apply learnings to practice is a more complex concept than surface learning. The transformation of theories into working knowledge may be classified as a high level cognitive process, demanding a deep approach to learning (Fung, Carr, & Chan, 2001). Development of understanding and contextual awareness are integral parts of such applied knowledge.

Far fewer respondents (33%) regarded learning as a process to assist explaining phenomena or understanding the world. Those who held this conception typically spoke of making sense, discovering meaning or knowing the world. They were more akin to Marton's, Watkins, and Tang (1997) concept of higher order thinking involving *integrating, analyzing, and synthesizing knowledge, getting to know how things work and understanding reality*. Respondents from different sectors also continued to articulate conceptions from different angles. School principals tended to emphasize understanding the world through application of knowledge and inquiry strategies. One explained that "learning can be an abstract or a specific concept." She insisted that inquiry learning was needed to "make sense of the world" and "deepening our understanding about it."

System officials were more likely to value learning as "a new construction of understanding of the world based on a learner's prior knowledge." One commented that "the learning process is an active, proactive, emotional and inner experience." Academics showed greater interest in epistemology by tentatively exploring the nature of knowledge itself. One framed this interest from a positivist standpoint as exploring the general law of knowledge and "having a better understanding of the phenomena in the objective reality." Another posed the question, "how can we utilize the knowledge and perspectives learned to explain the phenomena occurring in our life?" This last response provides some embryonic evidence that Chinese academics were beginning to explore and explain the meaning of their worlds in ways consistent with the hermeneutic approaches which have developed in the West since the 1970s (Collard, 2000). Once again outmoded stereotypes are called into question.

ANALYSIS OF INITIAL CONCEPTIONS OF LEARNING

It should not be assumed that individual respondents adhered to one, solitary conception of learning at the beginning of this study. Indeed most held multiple conceptions of simultaneously. Table 11.1 reveals half of the respondents held three conceptions and the others held two conceptions simultaneously. Nor were individual conceptions mutually exclusive or independent of each other. For instance, one respondent held multiple conceptions of learning as passive acquisition of inherited knowledge but also believed other aspects of learning involved application of theories and attempted to develop unique understanding of the world. Conversely, another appeared to adhere to more complex and sophisticated conceptions. Nor can it be assumed that lower order conceptions are submerged or subsumed in higher order conceptions.

Table 11.1.   Frequency of Responses and Interviewees About Learning Conceptions Before and After the Course

Category	Before	Before	After	After
	Frequency of Responses & Percentage	Frequency of Interviewees & Percentage	Frequency of Responses & Percentage	Frequency of Interviewees & Percentage
L = acquiring knowledge and skills	17 (34%)	17 (85%)	3 (5.7%)	3 (15%0)
L = instrumental purposes	13 (26%)	13 (65%)0	1 (1.9%)	1 (5%)
L = applied knowlwdge	14 (28%)	14 (70%)	4 (7.5%)	1 (20%)
L = understanding the world	6 (12%)	6 (30%)	16 (30.2%)	16 (80%)
L = transformational and personal development	0	0	15 (28.3%)	15 (75%)
L = promoting organizational development	0	0	10 (18.9%)	10 (50%)
L = promoting social development	0	0	4 (7.5)	4 (20%)

Total interviewees = 20

It should be noted that studies in Western societies have revealed a much wider range of conceptions of learning than the four which emerged from initial interviews in this study (Marton et al., 1993; Marton et al., 1997; Pillay & Boulton-Lewis, 2000; Purdie, Hattie, & Douglas, 1996; Tang, 2001). A possible explanation for this is that the strong influence of Chinese learning traditions and conformity of thinking among the respondents have limited the range of conceptions prior to exposure to recent western conceptions through the course. If so, the limited range suggests that there was initially less diversity in concepts of learning amongst Chinese students than students from other cultures. They tended to be constrained and controlled by their inherited culture. However, the evidence of some already moving towards more complex conception suggests that such enculturation was not as absolute as cross-cultural theory would have us believe.

CONCEPTIONS OF LEARNING AFTER THE COURSE

The second round of interviews indicated that the four previous conceptions of learning had expanded to seven. The new ones were: learning as transforming perspectives and personal development; learning to promote organizational development; and learning to promote social development. The first category has been previously identified in phenomenographic studies (Marton et al., 1993) but the last two were new. The genesis of notions of learning for organizational and social development can be traced to recent leadership discourses (Argyris & Schon, 1978, 1996; Freire, 1976; Horton & Freire, 1990; Senge, 1990d). Some respondents indicated that exposure to the Western discourses had stimulated these conceptions.

Respondents did not necessarily abandoned previous conceptions but they appeared to have been modified, expanded and rearranged. Learning to understand the world became the most popular perspective (80%) and learning to promote organizational (75%) and social development (50%) had also become more popular. Learning for utilitarian purposes was only mentioned by one of the 20 respondents. By the end of the course there had been a shift from conceptions embedded in Chinese tradition to a new openness towards learning for personal growth, organizational and social development. Close analysis revealed that this was not a whimsical capitulation to Western discourses. Respondents carefully mediated and accommodated the new ideas into their preexisting cognitive frameworks.

By 2003 the proportion of respondents who emphasized that the purpose of teaching was to transmit knowledge had declined from 80%

to 15%. Two principals insisted that transmission of "basic knowledge and basic skills" should continue to play an important role in schooling but should not be the sole or primary purpose as they had previously assumed. They now placed stronger emphasis upon knowing "how to apply" It reflected a shift from inherited cultural thinking to more complex constructions after exposure to new discourses, "the knowledge in addition to what is knowledge." A system administrator now noted that acquiring knowledge and skills was only part of the learning process, while "knowing the world was more important." We cannot assume that respondents who did not mention this conception after the course had abandoned it. Rather, it was no longer as prominent as it had been before.

Fewer respondents argued for instrumental purposes for learning. The only explicit comment came from a principal who indicated that "learning is a means and need for one's professional development." Learning to apply knowledge also declined from approximately 70% to 20% of respondents. Several principals stressed they no longer viewed learning as knowledge acquisition and skills development but argued that the "application of knowledge in one's personal and professional life meant it became contextualized." A university administrator provided a rich insight into this shift:

> The concept of learning should be multidimensional, going far beyond the range of classrooms.... Learning should be an integrated and inseparable part of a human life. Learning can be several cycles from single loop learning to quadruple learning. In terms of organizational learning, the ultimate objective of learning is to maximize individual skills and abilities in order to better achieve organizational goals.

By the conclusion of the course a conception that the key purpose of learning is to understand the world was the most popular (80%). A principal argued that enhancing learning abilities like inquiry making and problem solving will enable us to better know and adapt to the changing world. A university administrator insisted "cultivating learning ability and creativity is essential," and through doing this "we can have a better understanding of reality and keep up to date."

There was also a new emphasis upon the role of personal experience and social interaction. One principal commented that, "the key elements of learning were practice, experience, inquiry, cooperation, and exploration." Another added that in addition to classroom learning, "social experience," "interaction with others" and "the process of accomplishing a task" were also important. When making such comments respondents' frequently referred to their interaction with peers in the course itself. They praised "classmates" as "wonderful learning resources" and claimed that exchanges with them deepened understandings about "professional practice" and "emergent issues in Chinese education."

By the second interviews approximately 20% of respondents classified themselves as *lifelong learners* and recognized the value of both formal and informal learning opportunities. This insight was shared by members from all three sectors. One principal stated "learning has become a lifestyle ... it represents one's quality of life." Another claimed that her notion of lifelong learning had been "extended by undertaking the course" and was related to her "constant professional development and personal growth."

Approximately 15% of respondents also revised their previous epistemological beliefs. University administrators were the most inclined to do so. One acknowledged that he had previously assumed that knowledge was "objective and single-dimensional" and that all knowledge was "transmitted from teachers." Now he realized that knowledge can be "subjective and multi-dimensional" and insisted that "everyone can have his or her opinion and interpretation about one issue." Another challenged the notion of sacred and authoritative knowledge:

> Now I believe learners are studying phenomena in a real world instead of merely learning theories or knowledge from books. Course materials or books can be used as aids to understand and explore the world in depth. If we identify and challenge assumptions behind a certain theory or body of knowledge, it means that an authoritative image of knowledge is shattered. Learning has moved from acquiring knowledge from books to inquiring the living world.

These respondents had moved from an absolute stance towards more relativistic frameworks. It is understandable that university personnel delved more deeply into epistemological issues than respondents from schools and bureaucracies. Academic cultures privilege knowledge creation and their workplace environments may have assisted in this regard.

The greatest change in the second interview round was the shift towards concepts of learning for transformational and personal perspectives (75%). Some argued that learning occurred when one formed new perspectives about both external and subjective realities. They spoke of "deepening the understanding," "opening the eyes," "extending the ideas" "broadening the horizons," and "widening the views." One university member claimed his beliefs about learning after the course were "deeper and more extensive," and he realized the concept of learning "had much richer meanings" than he had previously assumed.

Understanding of the role of reflection in learning processes also became more evident. A system official emphasized that learning was "creation and a process of innovation and transforming assumptions."

Another commented that knowledge involved "a continual process of thinking and reflection." He now viewed learning as "a continuous and dynamic process." He went even further to argue that "changing one's deeply rooted beliefs about learning also means changing one's thinking habits."

More than a third of respondents claimed that changes perspectives had provided them with "stronger self-awareness" "personal improvement," "empowerment," and "fulfillment." A principal indicated that he now paid "much attention to how to learn." He now viewed learning as "an experiential and reflective process" and criticized Chinese learning traditions for privileging "imitating and learning from teachers or supervisors." A system official agreed. She now understood "learning" as a process of "self-knowledge, self-exploration and self-development." For these individuals, exposure to contemporary forms of learning theory had actually displaced their previous allegiance to inherited practice.

Perspectives about teaching and professional practice also changed. A principal stressed the importance of "cooperative relationships between students and teachers." He insisted that learning required "interactive and two-way communication." He now saw the need for teachers to help learners "to construct knowledge based on their prior experience." A university administrator commented that "learning is related to a learner's sustainable development." Three respondents explicitly referred to learning as developing the affective as well as cognitive domains. One argued "learning should also be fun" and students should be "happy learners." Another linked "enjoyable learning experiences" to "insightful enlightenment." Yet another emphasized a learner may must develop "intellectually, psychologically and emotionally."

These new perspectives recall claims that reflections about learning produce change, transformation, and personal growth (Marton et al., 1993). In this study respondents tended to integrate these perspectives of "transformation" and "personal development" into one category and emphasize the interrelationship between them.

The concept of learning to promote organizational development was emphasized by half of the sample. They moved beyond previous conceptions of individual learning in isolated classrooms and formal institutions. One aspect of this shift was to value team and organizational learning and link them to sustainability in all three sectors. A principal commented that a person was not only responsible for personal learning, but also for "team learning and organisational learning." A system official indicated that he had not "associated learning with organizational development" in the past but now viewed it as inseparable. A university administrator insisted a "learning culture should be cultivated in an organisation by openly promoting individual learning and teamwork."

These respondents no longer viewed learning as the transmission of authoritative knowledge but as a dynamic "which makes individuals, teams, organizations, schools and families commit to a shared vision and achieve their goals." A tertiary educator contested concepts of knowledge as a static process of "acquiring defined knowledge at different stages in formal educational institutions" and argued for "a changing and dynamic process responsive to the rapidly changing world." Half of the respondents mentioned concepts of "a learning organisation" or "organisational learning" in the second interviews. It was. viewed as an integrating notion which linked learning and development at individual, team, and organizational levels. They argued that this cannot be achieved without effective personal development. system official insisted:

> Learning organisations will make sense only after we have deep understanding about learning. Organisational learning is based on a process of continual learning and reflection on the part of every member.... An organisation will maintain its sustainable development if everyone's potential can be fully tapped and personal development can be ensured.

He went on to say that "a flattened structure" is more appropriate than traditional hierarchies to realize such ideals. This suggests that more complex conceptions of learning have led participants in this study to develop new concepts about organizations themselves.

Learning to promote social development was mentioned by 20% of the respondents in the second interviews. It constitutes a higher order concept of learning consistent with emancipatory and liberationist theories (Friere, 1976; Habermas, 1971) which view educators as agents of social and political reform. A principal indicated a new-found commitment to "promoting a strong sense of social responsibility." He realized this would be "a long and incremental process." A system administrator now saw his role to include "transforming society," and "promoting social civilization." An academic declared that he would "consciously adjust his behaviors to social reform and development." Such rhetoric echoes past regimes of reformist effort and consciousness-raising in Chinese history, especially Mao's Cultural Revolution (1966–76). Another argued in more moderate terms:

> The purpose of learning is not to recite theories but to transform or develop learners emotionally, psychologically, and intellectually so that their perceptions about the world are expanded and problem solving abilities are promoted. I believe that the ultimate purpose of learning is to promote social progress through personal and organizational development.

The data from the second interviews indicates that most respondents continued to hold multiple conceptions of learning simultaneously. These included both higher and lower order conceptions. For instance, one respondent still valued knowledge acquisition as an important dimension of learning but now also saw its transformative potential. Conversely, another seemed to have abandoned lower order concepts in favor of more complex understandings of learning as personal and organizational development. We reiterate that these categories should not be viewed in a strict hierarchical order. They are interrelated and have a *loosely coupled* and *complementary relationship*. This study reveals that the lower order categories such as knowledge acquisition and application for instrumental purposes retain a legitimacy within a learning repertoire. If we view learning as a sequence of *steps* and *levels* within a person's life, lower order conceptions of learning may be necessary before individuals, organizations, societies and cultures can proceed to a higher levels of cognitive operations which promote personal, institutional, and social sustainability.

This study also attempted to classifiy the extent of conceptual change in individual actors. Respondents were asked to describe whether their concepts of learning had undergone large, moderate or small degrees of change by the end of the course. Interview data were reanalyzed to detect the movement across a number of categories. "Large change" referred to a respondent's conceptions moving across at least three categories. "Moderate change" meant a respondent modified his or her previous conceptions and this was signified by movement across one or two categories. "Small or no change" meant that an individual's conceptions remained constant between the two interviews. The self-reports were also linked to shifts from lower to higher level conceptions by the second interviews. Half the respondents reported large changes in their conceptions of learning. Seven (35%) reported modified or expanded conceptions and three (15%) reported no obvious change.

Past phenomenographic studies have argued that individuals' conceptions move from surface to deep constructions over time (Tang, 2001; Marton et al., 1993). This study also discovered a movement from inherited Chinese concepts to more complex perspectives which transcended a national inheritance. A system official indicated that the course, "changed my perspectives of myself and the whole system I am working in." Another explained that his initial conceptions of learning were "comparatively simple, limited and shallow" and that they had "undergone great changes and deepened." Others agreed that their previous beliefs were "limited and shallow" and products of traditional Chinese culture. The exposure to Western educational ideas, and participative pedagogy in particular, made them "think deeply and seriously about learning," Their conceptions were "transformed," "expanded" or "modified."

The emergent concepts of learning had "*much* richer meanings" than previous beliefs. The seven respondents who reported moderate change insisted that their conceptions were not "radically transformed" but "expanded or modified to some extent." Other beliefs were reinforced or confirmed. A university administrator noted that she used to simply view learning as "knowledge acquisition and application," but now emphasized "understanding and reflection as aspects of lifelong learning." A system official now viewed learning as "new construction of meaning" and "active creation." Such nuances illustrate that not all individuals respond to learning stimuli in the same manner. Some embrace change whole-heartedly, others have more cautious responses. Such distinctions indicate the need for sensitive concepts of cultural dynamics which can register different reactions within a population or cultural group.

Three respondents claimed that the course had "no obvious or only slight impact" on their conceptions of learning. Two indicated that although "the Western way of conducting class activities" was fresh they had already been "exposed to many advanced Western ideas." A system official insisted his understanding about learning "did not undergo signif-icant change" and asserted that "multiple perspectives from the East and West" were not sufficient forces of change" for him. A university adminis-trator struggled to make sense of Western concepts:

> We may have different interpretations and beliefs from those of the foreign teachers due to cultural differences. Sometimes it seemed that we were talk-ing the same concept but it was hard for us to understand them or vice versa. We tried to interpret with our understandings, come up with our views and then internalize what they have explained. We try to seek com-mon grounds in understanding certain concepts.

The combined data sets from both interviews suggest that respondents held more diversified and complex conceptions after the course. They had come to see learning as promoting personal, team, organizational, and even social development. School principals seemed to be the most receptive to the new ideas and system officials were the most cautious and conservative. This may well reflect the different locations in which they work as leaders. Schools are frontline organizations where the changing demands of society register directly and require "innovative responses." Conversely, educational bureaucracies are somewhat cushioned from the turbulence of schools. The position of system officials between authoritative directives from Beijing and the more responsive cultures of schools may well explain why their response to forces of change were more conservative.

DELIMITATIONS AND LIMITATIONS

The boundaries of the research were limited to understanding the participants' conceptions of learning and leadership and the perceived influence of the program upon their self-reported conceptual and practice change. The study compared the conceptions that participants brought to the course and their beliefs after the course. It investigated their initial conceptions and the influence of exposure to Western ideas on their understandings of learning. The study did not investigate the behaviors of the participants in their workplaces before and after undertaking the course.

Since it was a self-reporting study, real verification about changes in their workplaces would require different research methods which include data collection from other members of their work communities. That was determined to be beyond the scope of the study. It would be significant to investigate the long-term influence of the course upon the participants. The research has been limited to

- one leadership development program site in China, the Master of Educational Leadership program jointly conducted by University of Canberra and Hangzhou Normal University from March 2002 to December 2003. (However, four other cohorts have also repeated the course since then).
- educational leaders between the ages of 28 to 52 years, the majority (77%) of whom were male;
- leaders drawn from primary and secondary schools, to higher educational institutions, and local, municipal and provincial education departments;
- an economically developed region (Zhejiang Province) in East China, that is not typical of China today.

The study investigated the learning conceptions of a cohort of educational leaders in Zhejiang, China. As the sample was small in relation to the total population of educational leaders in the Province, results were specific to those in the sample. Consequently, there was no attempt to generalize findings to other educational leaders in China. However, the purpose of this research to explore participants' conceptions of learning and leadership and investigate the influence of the course upon their conceptions, is well suited to such a delimited focus and may be the springboard for broader research efforts. Although the greatest degree of change was related to conceptions of learning and knowledge, the following chapter will explore how these were linked to changing understandings of leadership itself.

REFERENCES

Akerlind, G. S. (2003). Growing and developing as a university teacher: Variation in meaning. *Studies in Higher Education, 28*(4), 375–390.

Argyris, C., & Schon, D. (1978). *Organizational learning: A theory of action persapective.* Reading MA: Addison-Wellesley.

Argyris, C., & Schon, D. (1996) *Organizational learning 11: Theory, method and practice.* Reading MA: Addison-Wellesley.

Blackmore, J. (2004). The emperor has no clothes: Professionalism, performativity and educational leadership in high-risk postmodern times. In J. Collard & C. Reynolds (Eds.), *Leadership, gender & culture; Male and female perspectives* (pp. 73–194). Philadelphia: Open University Press.

Bogdan, R., & Biklen, S. K. (1992). *Qualitative research for education* (2nd ed.). Boston: Allyn & Bacon.

Booth, S. (1997). On Phenomenography, learning and teaching. *Higher Education Research and Development, 16,* 135–159.

Boulton-Lewis, G. M., Wilss, L., & Lewis, D. (2003). Dissonance between Conceptions of learning and ways of learning for indigenous Australian university students. *Studies in Higher Education, 28*(1), 79–89.

Brock-Utne, B. (1996). Reliability and validity in qualitative research within education in Africa. *International Review of Education, 42*(6), 605–621.

Brookfield, S. (1986) *Understanding and facilitating adult learning.* San Francisco: Jossey-Bass.

Collard, J. (2000). *Figures and landscapes: Male and female principals in Victorian schools 1996-98.* Unpublished doctoral dissertation, University of Melbourne, Melbourne, Australia.

Conger J. A., & Kanungo, R. W. (1988). *Charismatic leadership: The elusive factor in organizational effectiveness.* San Francisco: Jossey Bass.

Fairholm, G. W. (1991). *Values leadership: Toward a new philosophy of leadership.* New York: Praeger.

Foley, G. (2000). A framework for understanding adult learning and education: In *Understanding adult learning and education* (pp. 7–22). Crow's Nest, NSW: Allen & Unwin.

Freire, P. (1976) *The practice of freedom.* London: Writers & Readers.

Fung, Y., Carr, R., & Chan, S. K. (2001) Conceptions of learning held by Bachelor of Education students at the Open University of Hong Kong. *Asia Pacific Journal of Education, 21* (1) 45-52.

Gu, M., & Meng, F. (Eds.). (2001). *Guoji Jiaoyu Xin Linian* [New international education ideas]. Haikou, China: Hainan chubanshe [Hainan Publishing House].

Habermas, J. (1971) *Knowledge and human interests* (J. Shapiro, Trans.) Boston: Beacon.

Horton, M., & Freire, P. (1990). *We make the road by walking.* Philadelphia: Temple University Press.

Knowles, M. (1978). *The adult learner: A neglected species.* Houston, TX: Gulf.

Knowles, M. (1980). *The modern practice of adult education* (2nd ed.). Chicago: Follett.

Knowles, M. S., Holton, E. F., & Swanson, R. A. (1998). *The adult learner* (5th ed.). Woburn, MA: Butterworth-Heinnemann.

Kolb, B. (1984). *Experimental learning: Experience as the source of learning and development.* Englewood Cliffs, NJ: Prentice-Hall.

Martin, E., Trigwell, K., Prosser, M., & Ramsden, P. (2003). Variation in the Experience of Leadership of Teaching in Higher Education. *Studies in Higher Education, 28*(3), 247–259.

Marton, F. (1994). Phenomenography. In T. Husen & T. N. Poslethaite (Eds.), *The International Encyclopaedia of Education* (2nd ed., Vol. 8, pp. 4424–4429). Oxford, England: Pergamon.

Marton, F., Dall'alba, G., & Beaty, E. (1993). Conceptions of learning. *International Journal of Educational Research, 19*, 277–300.

Marton, F., Watkins, D. A., & Tang, C. (1997). Discontinuities and continuities in the experience of learning: An interview study of high school students in Hong Kong, *Learning and Instruction, 7*(1) 21–48.

Mezirow, J. (1991) *Transformative dimensions of adult learning.* San Francisco: Jossey-Bass.

Orgill, M. (2000). *Phenomenography.* Retrieved 3 May 2004, from http://chemed.chem.purdue.edu/chemed/bodnergroup/frameworks/phenography

Pillay, H., & Boulton Lewis, G. (2000). Variations in conceptions of leaning in construction technology: Implications for learning, *Journal of Education and Work, 13*(2), 163–181.

Punch, K. F. (1998). *Introduction to social research: Quantitative and qualitative approaches.* London: SAGE.

Purdie, N., Hattie, J., & Douglas, G. (1996). Student conceptions of learning and their use of self-regulated learning strategies: A cross-cultural comparison. *Journal of Educational Psychology, 88*(1), 87–100.

Senge, P. (1990). *The fifth discipline: The art and of the learning organization.* New York: Doubleday.

Silverman, D. (2001). *Interpreting qualitative data: Methods for analysing talk, text and interaction* (2nd ed.). London: SAGE.

Tang, T. K. W. (2001). The influence of teacher education on conceptions of teaching and learning. In D. A. Watkins & J. B. Biggs (Eds.), *The Chinese learner: Cultural, psychological and contextual influences* (pp. 221–238). Melbourne: Australian Council for Educational Research.

Trigwell, K. (2000). *Phenomenography: Discernment and variation. Improving Student Learning, 7,* 133–158.

Van Rossum, E. J., & Schenk, S. M. (1984). The relationship between learning conception, study strategy and learning outcomes. *British Journal of Educational Psychology, 54,* 73–83.

Watkins, D. A., Biggs, J. B. (Eds.). (1996). *The Chinese learner: Cultural, psychological and contextual influences.* Melbourne: Australian Council for Educational Research.

Watkins, D. A., & Biggs, J. B. (2001). The paradox of the Chinese Learner and beyond. In D. A. Watkins & J. B. Biggs (Eds.), *Teaching the Chinese Learner: Psychological and pedagogical perspectives* (pp. 3–23). Melbourne: Australian Council for Educational Research.

Zhu, M. (Ed.). (2002). *Zoujin Xinkecheng: Yukecheng Shishizhe Duihua* [Step into New Curricula: A dialogue with curricula implementers]. Beijing, China: Beijing Normal University Press.

CHAPTER 12

CHINESE LEADERS AND WESTERN DISCOURSES 2002–2004

Ting Wang and John Collard

INTRODUCTION

The Australian academics involved in the Zhejiang program tender to privilege collaborative and distributed concepts of leadership drawn from Anglo-American discourses in recent decades (Gronn, 1999; Gronn, 2003; Lakomski, 2001) than the more hierarchical traditions emanating from Taylorism and bureaucratic-managerial traditions in the West. The same approach and research approaches outlined in the previous chapter were also used to study concepts of leadership both before and after the program. Those details will therefore not be reiterated in this chapter. However, at the outset, we would like to emphasize that, contrary to our expectations, the degree of change in the participants concepts of leadership was much less than in the area of their learning conceptions. Later in this chapter, we will explore some possible reasons for this and how it related to differenced between the domains themselves: one more experiential and the other more abstract or discipline-based in nature.

Leadership and Intercultural Dynamics, pp. 233–258
Copyright © 2009 by Information Age Publishing
All rights of reproduction in any form reserved.

Initial Conceptions of Leadership

> Traditional Chinese leaders are endorsed with official power and authority.
> They are often autocratic and patriarchal. Their wills and decisions are usu-
> ally imposed on the organizational members through the strict hierarchical
> structure. As a leader, how to manage the staff well is most important. Man-
> agers are expected to strictly implement plans according to the set rules and
> regulations. (A system official in this study)

This section explores the rich heritage of culturally-inherited
leadership concepts Chinese educational leaders brought to the Australian designed course. Five conceptions were identified prior to the course.
At the outset, it should be noted that the majority of these were of
national origin but there was also some evidence of the importation of
leadership traditions from other countries, especially traditions from the
Soviet regime of the previous century. Similarities were also noted in the
positivist legacy of Stalinist science on Chinese conceptions of specific
academic disciplines. This included education which is often called a
science! In this respect, this aspect of the study offers some interesting
parallels with the next one focus upon Belarus in the same period. The
conceptions included:

- Leadership as positional power
- Leadership as non-positional power
- Leadership as a practical art
- Leadership as teamwork with other leaders
- Leadership as vision and strategic planning

The first four categories tend to reflect traditional Chinese traditions
about leadership. They focus upon positional power, authoritative expertise, personal quality, leadership art. They emphasized task, directive
leadership, and teamwork among a group of leaders. Almost all of the
twenty interviewees (95%) held a conception of leadership as positional
power. More than half also held conceptions of it as non-positional power,
a practical art and as teamwork among leaders. This complex mix
accounted for 89.4% of responses. The finding suggests that most respondents conceived leadership as a directive act to accomplish specific tasks.

The concept of leadership as constituted by the power and authority of
a leader, usually male, at the top of a hierarchical pyramid has been
repeatedly noted by cross-cultural theorists. It reflects hierarchical,
bureaucratic, and patriarchal traditions which are deeply rooted in Confucian traditions which consider a leader to be a person who holds power
in a hierarchy, exercises it in a directive manner, and draws upon his/her

power base and authority to do so. Respondents from all three sectors placed strong emphasis on the authoritative and unquestioned role of leaders. They tended to be defined as one who "holds the official position," a "head of an institution who has power and privilege" or the "director of a formal organization." Another view saw a leader as "an organizer or a boss, who directs followers to accomplish certain tasks" Bureaucratic concepts of government officials who have "power ... at the top of the hierarchical structure" were also common. A more educationally-oriented concept viewed a leader as a "guide" and "director," who leads followers toward a set goal.

Approximately half of the respondents equated the role of a leader with that of a manager, or regarded leadership and management as similar concepts. They viewed leaders as individuals who possessed "abilities to determine the development of the organization." Leaders were therefore perceived to possess operational functions and only differed from managers in terms of levels of position in a hierarchical structure. In other words, they were often viewed as high-level managers whereas middle level managers were not regarded as leaders in the real sense. Although they may sometimes perform leadership roles, they were mainly regarded as line managers in functional departments, who were expected to carry out policies or implement plans issued from the top. In this respect they shared the conceptual confusion of much western discourse on these issues (Crawford, 2003). This view appeared to be shared across the three sectors.

One school principal considered himself to be an implementer or "transmitter" who receives the policies or instructions from higher administrative level, and then "transmits them to the teaching staff." This is akin to the self image government school principals have of themselves in government schools in Australia (Collard, 2003a). A divisional director from a university declared that in a strict sense he was not a leader but "a middle level manager or implementer." He insisted that only those who hold positions at top level, like university presidents, or school principals can be regarded as leaders. Such comments reflect a dominant paradigm for the accomplishment of tasks. Strict rules and regulations are imposed rigidly in a scientific manner.

The relationship between leaders and followers tends to revolve around control and obedience. Another principal emphasized, "control and strict management." Followers were defined as "implementers, who should carry out the plan faithfully." A university administrator stressed that a leader is expected to "manage and govern followers well." At least a third of principals and university administrators subscribed to the image of a leader or *a head*; an "awesome, authoritative and even fearsome figure who enjoys "great status at t the top of a pyramid." This concept was enmeshed with notions of power; "without power, one cannot be regarded as a leader." It should also be noted that few respondents saw themselves as authoritative leaders even though an outside observer would ascribe power and influence to them.

Bureaucratic system officials tended to be more critical of Chinese traditions of task orientation and disdain for the views of followers. One lamented, "the wills and wishes of leaders rather than followers are often emphasized." Another was more radical in her critique of position, power and authority; "people often hold negative attitudes towards leaders, who usually climb the ladder relying on nepotism and personal networks." This was a direct reference to the practice of *guanxi* in Chinese culture where favors are bestowed, traded and rewarded through generational and kinship networks. Many respondents tended to use terms such as "traditionally" or "generally speaking" to indicate these phenomena. This suggests that some were critical of their cultural inheritance, another nuance obscured by stereotypical national frameworks. They recognized the limitations of hierarchical concepts which overemphasized order and control in the same way as humanist theorists questioned Taylor's (1915) principles of scientific management in the decades succeeding World War II.

The complexity of *preexisting* conceptions of leadership becomes even more apparent when it is acknowledged that approximately two thirds of the sample also held notions of leadership as power or authority based on professional expertise and personal qualities, not just positional power. Descriptors such as "personal qualities," "professional knowledge," "professional expertise," "personal charisma," and "high morality" to inspire others, and establish role models for followers, were used in this regard. These conceptions can be traced to the moral authority of Confucian traditions and also share certain affinities with Western traditions of charismatic or transformational leadership (Bass, 1998; Bass & Avolio, 1993; Burns, 1978; Conger & Kanungo, 1988; Weber, 2002/1904).

Such respondents generally claimed that educational leaders possess profound professional knowledge and expertise, especially domain specific knowledge. This enables them to establish their authoritative status among teachers and provide appropriate supervision. Such a view permeated all three groups but was particularly prevalent among school principals and universities administrators. Again we can detect affinities with recent Western discourse about expert leadership (Leithwood, Begley, & Bradley-Cousins, 1992). For instance, one principal insisted that a leader should be "a subject expert so that he can instruct other teachers." Another emphasized the need for "profound knowledge and deep understanding about education and teaching." She went on to say that, besides qualities required by leaders generally, "an educational leader should be an authority in her field and a good instructional leader" if teachers are to regard her highly. A university administrator attached importance to "high academic qualities and research abilities" in addition to discipline specific knowledge. He commented that without these it will be difficult for him "to promote professional development and research activities among teachers."

In addition to authority derived from the leading role in specific subject/discipline domains or research fields, a leader's personal charisma or affinity derived from personal qualities or morality was also highly valued by respondents. This illustrates another dimension of Confucian traditions of the scholarly and moral leader (Lee, 1996; Wong, 2001). Such respondents commented that a leader should make full use his or her non-positional power to "influence," "inspire," "encourage" and "motivate" followers to achieve goals or accomplish tasks. Ideally a leader should be "a moral model" or "a charismatic hero" This insight was common across the school, system and university sectors.

In fact, some respondents claimed to be "charismatic leaders" themselves but accredited Confucian heritage rather than recent transformational discourse in the West with this quality. One principal explained that "morality and personal qualities of a leader" were emphasized in Confucian tradition. A good leader should be "a moral model and set good example for others." He regarded a leader as "a charismatic hero" whose individual qualities are important in achieving an organizational goal. A system official, who considered himself as "sort of a charismatic leader to some extent" believed that he seldom relied on his positional power to direct or order his followers. He insisted that he drew upon his "expertise, insight and self-confidence to influence others." A university administrator defined a leader needed to be "inspirational and demonstrating affinity." He went one step further by that "a gentleman is ready to die for his close friends." There was also a belief that improvement of one's leadership ability often required dedication to personal development and self-cultivation.

These non-positional concepts of leadership also share affinities with the trait and charismatic discourses which have been evident in Western cultures in the twentieth century (Conger & Kanungo, 1988; Stogdill, 1974; Weber, 1947). Trait theories have highlighted the exceptional qualities required by leaders while charismatic theorists have placed importance on the personal charisma or morality of leaders. Such a leader is assumed to be a directive individual with idiosyncratic vision and goals to which followers develop emotional and ideological commitments. However such conceptions amongst Chinese leaders are not derived from Western theory. They are a cultural inheritance which shares affinity with such theory and once again we see the simplicity of constructing polar oppositions between national cultures. Both of course reside within patriarchal traditions which locate power at the top and prescribe subordinate relationships between leaders and followers.

Approximately 50% of the respondents also regarded leadership as practical art. In this they considered leadership as a set of flexible strategies or tactics rather than a cluster of rigid rules or prescribed approaches. Particular emphasis was placed on the adaptability, applicability, and contingency of leadership. They argued that the choice of a certain leadership style or approach depended on the nature of the followers, different organizational conditions, and the wider social and cultural contexts. Such notions of leadership as practical art share some commonalities with Western contingency and situational leadership concepts advanced by Blake and Mouton, (1964), Fiedler (1967), Hersey and Blanchard (1979), and Vroom and Yetton (1973). According to these leadership concepts, the qualities, characteristics, and skills required by a leader are determined to a large extent by the maturity level of followers and the demands of the situation in which he or she functions as a leader. Leadership is perceived as an interactive phenomenon within groups. Leaders are expected to be self-conscious and reflective practitioners who adapt leadership styles to different situations and followers.

However, the respondents in this study were not privy to the humanist school of American leadership theory from past decades. About a third of them traced the concept of "leadership as practical art" back to Chinese culture and Confucianism. A university administrator made stated;

> Traditionally, leadership is considered as a practical moral art and ways of dealing with power and politics. For instance, many of Confucius' ideas have great influence in Chinese history and contemporary China. "The Art of War" by Sun Zi is an excellent example to show the importance of strategic planning and leadership art in Chinese history.

Others from the school systems believed their experience as teachers and an understanding of the nature of teaching staff determined their leadership styles. One principal argued that her style differed from that of a directive manager in an enterprise. Another female system administrator insisted that her previous experience as a teacher for ten years meant she regarded teachers as "intellectuals and professionals" and she believed it important to "consider the characteristics of the led and adopt their suggestions."

Approximately one fifth of the respondents commented that different stages of organizational development, culture and social contexts also decided their use of various leadership strategies. They tended to use terms like "artistic," "practical," "techniques" or "tactics" to describe their professional practice. This view was also shared across the three sectors. One principal insisted a leader must "adjust his or her leadership styles and practices according to different developmental stages of a school." She went on to explain that both of her previous principals were successful leaders who had different leadership styles. She warned against "a simple conclusion that a particular leadership style is the best" *but rather whether it was* "appropriate or beneficial to long-term development of a school."

A system official emphasized that a leader should consider "the qualities of followers and adapt his leadership styles to different situations and followers." As the leader of a large educational group comprised of various institutions, he stated he managed kindergarten teachers differently from university professors because "the natures of staff and organizational cultures are different." However, both school principals and university administrators were critical of bureaucratic and rigid structures at the system or provincial levels. They objected to official, top-down leadership approaches; "rigid bureaucratic systems and hierarchical orders are more obvious in educational departments than in schools or universities." An academic administrator who criticized "the hierarchical structure and strict power relationship in the administrative system is prevalent" argued that "schools and universities are much better." Such comments echo complaints we also hear in The West. It seems that the cries for changes to bureaucratic cultures in educational administrative systems are also prevalent in contemporary China.

The calls for contingency, flexibility, and adaptability in leadership approaches are therefore common across cultures. However, the Chinese leaders in this study were less likely to challenge high power distances between leaders and followers and the determination of organizational at the top. In this respect they confirm Hofstede's (1980) categories on this issue for they do not insist on the distribution of decision-making power in the same manner as Western communitarian and transformational theorists such as Bottery (1992), Chapman and Aspin (1997), or Gronn 2003).

However, team or collective leadership was popular with 80% of respondents. There was praise for leadership groups working as teams or cadres and relying on collective wisdom to achieve organizational goals. However, this was conceptualized as executive teamwork among leaders at official levels rather than democratic consultation of entire workforces. One explained that principals and deputies usually "have a clear division of labor and collaborated closely." For instance, the principal is responsible for "general administration of the school" and deputy principals are in charge of "teaching and learning, student management, finance and logistics respectively."

The term "democratic leadership" was employed but in a different sense than we would encounter in Australia, Scandinavia, or the United

Kingdom. A description of "principals and deputies meeting together regularly to make important decisions" really approximates to forms of executive teams in the West. System officials who insisted "decisions about important issues are usually made by a team of leaders" were similar. A university administrator also argued that collective leadership at high levels of the organization was important for sharing workloads.

Only a quarter of respondents, most of them school principals, extended their understanding of team leadership to seeking advice from teachers or Teacher Representatives Meetings. One maintained he relied on a team of leaders, middle level administrators, and teachers to manage the school well. Another indicated that before making important decisions he sometimes sought suggestions from teachers and the Teacher Representatives Meeting. Three respondents were critical and indicated that collective and team leadership in the real sense was far from a reality in Chinese schools. One insisted that the Teacher Representatives Meeting "should play a more important role in monitoring principals' work than currently practiced" and "a strict monitoring and evaluating system" should be developed.

System officials also suggested that team leadership was "an empty word," a tokenistic gesture rather than authentic collective leadership in schools. A university administrator concurred by explaining that "the notion of collective leadership" was often little more than "rhetoric." It seems that token collegiality can therefore be as superficial in Chinese institutions as it is in some Australian schools (Collard, 2004b). The same respondent also commented that administrators in Chinese universities often lacked the management skills and leadership capacities they required because of a naïve process whereby "good teachers or researchers were usually promoted to administrative or leadership positions." He complained that *"their leadership styles are usually autocratic and based on their prior experience,"* privileging *"control and obedience"* above personal charisma or professional development levels." Many of us who work in Western universities would share this perception about the inadequate training of university administrators. On this issue there may again be more commonality between organizational phenomena than assumed by cross-cultural theorists.

There was also some degree of ambiguity and dissonance in the comments of some respondents upon the issues of collective and directive leadership. Several suggested that "collective leadership may not always work in reality." They believed strong and directive leadership was needed to implement the radical educational reforms currently promoted by the Beijing Government. One university leader maintained that "a leader cannot be too democratic, making every decision upon extensive consultation." and insisted that "strong directive leadership is necessary when enforcing educational reforms." A school principal also commented:

> We pay much attention to team leadership and hold the Teacher Representatives Meeting twice a year to discuss important issues…. Even if the Teacher Representatives Meeting does not pass the motion, we can still implement it if it helps to promote educational reform. As you know, resistance from teachers to educational reform is often strong. We must be directive and assertive when necessary.

However, the same respondent also believed that "we must adopt democratic leadership approaches if they want to motivate teachers." Such comments are evidence of a tension in contemporary leadership discourse among Chinese educational leaders which we also hear throughout the world. It may suggest that they are searching for a balance between collective and directive modes and it could well be argued that this struggle has been recurrent throughout twentieth century China where strong directions from a central government require implementation at communal levels where the collective has been a hallmark of decision making.

It should be noted that the concepts of "team leadership" advanced by Chinese respondents were different from those found in contemporary western discourses about communitarian and transformational ideals. The latter frequently emphasize that all team members perform a leadership role in some ways. Leithwood (1992) employed the metaphor of the formal leader as a conductor who may recede into the band while an emergent leader leads a particular improvisation. Gronn's (1999) distributed leaders are recognized for their unique skills than their positional power within their organizations whereas Lakomski's (2001) contribute to collective cognitive horsepower rather than rely on the wisdom of a solitary authority. The respondents in this study were not so radical. When they refer to team leadership they meant that decision-making power is contained within a team at the top, and sometimes in the middle of an organizational pyramid. The concept sustains clear hierarchical divisions between senior, middle and lower level operators. Although some argued for a degree of consultation and empowerment, there was little evidence that they continued to think within paradigms of organizations which power and authority related to a small group people who hold official positions. There was no evidence of thought consistent with the organic and empowering paradigms which have characterized Western feminist discourse on leadership (Ozga, 1993; Porter, 1995; Shakeshaft, 1987) in recent decades. The research reveals nuanced differences rather than the absolute categories provided by cross-cultural theorists in the past.

The cohort's conceptions of strategic leadership centered around notions of having "keen insight," "vision," "forward looking," "an overall perspective," or "a big picture." Approximately one third, a minority of the sample commented upon the need to be "visionary and forward-looking." A school principal argued that good leaders must "think from an overall perspective and have a big picture first," *not merely* "a narrow perspective or particular point." He insisted this kind of "macro-level thinking really counts" when making important decisions. This view was shared by a university administrator who argued that leaders need "a proper understanding and grasp of emergent issues and the overall situation" as "a prelude or pre-condition to decision-making"

System administrators were more inclined to hold such views than organizationally-based respondents. One commented upon the need to "discern the emergent issues and urgent problems in educational development." Another insisted that an educational leader should be able to show himself in front of teachers and students "*as a professional educator and authority who knows education well*". Without this, he argued, a leader may "*lack his non-positional power*" and cannot be regarded as a good leader. Yet another believed a good leader "*must have keen insight and discernment about policies and plans, followers, and new issues in social development*". It is interesting that system officials were more vocal on this topic than principals and university leaders. However, when one recalls that educational reform in China is ordained by national committees and then dispersed through provincial and municipal systems it becomes comprehensible. System officials are frequently positioned as agents of change who have a responsibility to place macro level policies and issues before site-based leaders. In this respect they share much in common with officials in similar roles in Sweden (Davis & Johansson, 2004) or at state levels in Australia (Collard, 2003b). The nature of their leadership work fosters a more macro perspective than that of site-based leaders. This suggests that specific location in educational systems may be a more powerful influence on the way particular actors think than their national cultures.

At the micro or institutional levels respondents frequently expressed the need for strategic thinking and planning. One argued that broad vision must be supplemented by keen insight into emergent issues, "new key factors needed by organizational development." A university administrator insisted that a leader must "foresee the long-term effects of what he is doing today and consider what will happen in three or five years time." While both believed that strategic planning was an organizational leadership task the conceptualization of this was relatively impoverished. There was no evidence of strategies to consult or involve of organizational members in shaping the vision or planning implementation in the manner developed by school based management theorists in Western nations in recent decades (Caldwell & Spinks, 1988, 1998; Fullan & Hargreaves, 1991). We can therefore conclude that strategic planning skills were relatively underdeveloped in site leaders in schools and universities in Zhejiang Province in 2002.

The range of leadership conceptions held by the sample at the start of 2002 was therefore a mix of traditional thinking inherited from centuries of Chinese culture and some more complex perspectives. It was not possible to identify a single or dominant conception because respondents often expressed several conceptions concurrently. It appears that these conceptions were therefore not mutually exclusive or independent of each other. They were not in a strict hierarchical order or in a linear fashion. In other words, having sophisticated concepts was not incompatible with more basic assumptions. For instance, one female leader who was adamant about the importance of teamwork among leaders also adhered to notions of positional power. We are forced to conclude that Chinese educational leaders, like those in Western nations, hold complex cognitions about leadership which belie simple taxonomies. However, we can identify a range of concepts emanating from inherited traditions, workplace characteristics, and forces for change.

Conceptions of Leadership After the Course

The second round of interviews yielded data about respondents' conceptions of leadership and beliefs about themselves as leaders after they undertook the course. A this stage, six categories of conceptions of leadership emerged from the data analysis.

- Leadership as positional power
- Leadership as non-positional power
- Leadership as practical art
- Leadership as teamwork leaders
- Leadership as vision and strategic planning
- Leadership as consultation and collaboration.

The categories include the five identified in the initial interviews and one new category leadership as consultation and collaboration. The additional conception developed through the course tended to be more complex and focus on consultative and collaborative leadership. This and the concept of visionary and strategic leadership could be defined as higher level conceptions. As a group the cohort moved beyond inherited thinking which tended to focus on task and directive leadership. The scope and depth of the six conceptions after the course seemed to go beyond the five initial conceptions. This suggests that respondents' conceptions of leadership had been expanded by the course. Some interviewees may have held conceptions of consultative and collaborative leadership before the course. Some stated in the second interviews that this notion may have existed prior to the course but was reinforced or confirmed after the course. However, there was no evidence that interviewees stated this conception explicitly in the initial interviews. Therefore, in this study, conceptions consultative and collaborative leadership are interpreted as an expanded perspective after exposure to western discourses. Table 12.1 indicates that visionary and strategic concepts emerged as the predominant conceptions among 20 respondents after the course.

Other common conceptions reported by more than half of the respondents were:

- Leadership as non-positional power
- Leadership as practical art
- Leadership as consultation and collaboration

The responses from these four categories account for 92.4% of the total responses. The category with the lowest occurrence was Leadership as positional power, which was mentioned by only one respondent. This

Table 12.1.　Frequency of Responses and Interviewees About Learning Conceptions Before and After the Course

Category	Before Frequency of Responses & Percentage	Before Frequency of Interviewees & Percentage	After Frequency of Responses & Percentage	After Frequency of Interviewees & Percentage
L = positional power	19 (28.8%)	19 (95%)	1 (1.9%)	1 (5%)
L = non-positional power	13 (19.7%)	13 (65%)	10 (18.9%)	10 (50%)
L = a practical art	11 (16.7%)	11 (55%)	12 (22.6%)	12 (60%)
L = teamwork with other leaders	16 (24.2%)	16 (80%)	3 (5.7%)	3 (15%)
L = vision & strategic planning	7 (10.6%)	7 (35%)	15 (28.3%)	15 (75%)
L = consultation & collaboration	0	0	12 (22.6%)	12 (60%)

Total interviewees 20

conception was less dominant after the course than it had been prior to the course. An important finding is that conceptions of leadership held by the majority of respondents at the end of the course tended to be more focused on motivation and collaborative orientations.

Only one university administrator now adhered to the notion of leadership as positional power. He was critical of "Western leadership theories" which "do not emphasize positional power as we do." He demonstrated resistance to what he perceived as a foreign concept and held strongly to his Chinese inheritance of top-down, directive leadership:

> In China, it is hard to define leadership if we take out power. Decisions are made from the top and implemented through different layers. According to Western leadership theories, it seems that leaders rely more on consideration, communication and role models in order to achieve organizational goals.

Notions of student leadership or teacher leadership were unacceptable to him. He embodied critical rejection, as opposed to passive adaptation of Western leadership discourse. Others indicated that their initial allegiance to positional leadership had been modified by exposure to Western ideas. It became somewhat subjugated in their remarks and no longer held its previous the preeminence. This suggests a shift from inherited thinking to more complex and reflective thinking after the course.

Adherence to concepts of charismatic or trait theories of leadership also declined from approximately two thirds to half of the respondents by the second interview. There was evidence that many had adopted more organizational perspectives instead of relying on the inherent qualities of singular leaders. Whilst agreeing that personal qualities were still important, a system official argued that a leader must also be "a lifelong learner who can maintain sustainable development to adapt to changing contexts and educational reform." Another commented he now viewed "leadership from an organizational perspective rather than from a personal perspective." A university administrator appeared to have accommodated traditional concepts of positional and non-positional authority in China to a broader perspective where "leadership styles" and "personal charisma are all integrated parts of leadership" to achieve "organizational goals." Others continued to express allegiance to the Confucian conceptions of a leader as "a moral model" and "spiritual guide" but now insisted that such a leader should "influence and inspire others," *not just provide directive authority*:

> A leader should have stronger learning ability, higher spiritual level, higher moral standards, and more affecting emotion than others. He is a moral model, a spiritual guide, and an engine of an organization. He relies more on non-positional authority than power bestowed by an official position.

Such comments reflect active mediation between different cultures. Confucian tradition is repositioned within the framework of Western organizational discourses.

Some also questioned the relevance of Western ideas to Chinese contexts. A system official believed "moral leadership, emotional leadership, and substitutes for leadership or self-managing teams are desirable." However, he foresaw difficulties applying such notions in China. It should be noted here that contemporary Western concepts of ethical and moral leadership (Burns, 1978; Begley & Johansson, 2003; Hodgkinson, 1991) are frequently based on communitarian ideals and altruistic authority. The Confuscian heritage places greater emphasis upon the moral standards of a solitary leader. The two are potentially complementary but the transformation of followers into leaders (Burns, 1978) has had less cultural currency in China in the past. Western change agents would do well to note this before attempting to implement reforms in Chinese communities.

The proportion who viewed leadership as a practical art increased slightly between interviews but changed to a broader awareness which incorporated organizational cultures and wider social issues. Approximately a third maintained that cultural, economic, historical, and social realities in Western nations differed from Chinese contexts. Consequently, some argued that it would be inappropriate to "adopt Western leadership ideas indiscriminately." Ideas like distributed leadership, flattened structures and learning organizations were treated with some skepticism in this regard.

Some respondents extended such insights to the nature of followers in China. They suggested that strong bureaucratic cultures and a lack of "democratic and participative awareness" among Chinese teachers would inhibit the adoption of Western approaches. A principal commented that Chinese teachers were used "to following the orders from the top without asking any questions" and suggested "they may not know how to use democracy when you give democracy to them." He stressed the need to develop the maturity or acceptance level of followers before "promoting democratic decision-making." A university administrator agreed that China's "long history of autocratic feudalism" meant that ordinary people "lack democratic awareness or seldom actively participate in consultation or decision-making processes."

Several respondents thoughtfully argued the need to integrate Chinese traditions with Western leadership perspectives. A system official sought "a balance between democratic decision-making and scientific management." Another insisted that "management emphasizing control and strict regulations" *should be integrated with* "shared vision, consultation and empowerment." Another stressed:

> But we need to consider the qualities of organizational members. If their qualities are not up to the desirable standard, enforcing shared leadership or flattened structure may bring trouble to an organization.

Such comments are evidence of reflective responses and support the claims that educators from countries with strong inherited leadership traditions do not simply accept or import other cultural traditions without reflection. It remains to be seen whether seemingly conflicting philosophies and concepts embedded in these two perspectives can be brought into productive synergy.

Concepts of teamwork in the first interviews were limited to collaboration within elite cadres. By the second round they had developed broader parameters. They now embraced wider membership within organizations not just to those occupying positional power. Many insisted that theories of team leadership were not new to them but that their conceptions had been extended by Western discourses.

One believed it "involves teachers in decision-making." A system official insisted that "leaders are collaborators, service providers and coordinators in a team or organization." One university administrator claimed there were no fundamental differences between the tenets of Western and Chinese theories as both traditions contained similar values; "the purpose of leadership is to achieve a goal, and teamwork spirit is important." In this instance we see a positive synthesis constructed which bridges the differences so frequently assumed in cross-cultural approaches.

The proportion of respondents who linked leadership to vision and strategic planning had expanded to 75% by the end of the course. This probably reflected the priority given to these concepts in course readings and student assignments. There was an increased call for visionary leadership which could foresee organizational and social trends, be proactive, and plan strategically. A university administrator referred to leaders as guides or facilitators, "situated at the forefront of the complex environment and organization, and expected to respond quickly to the external environment." An official, who had previously viewed leadership as positional power insisted that "a leader is not a privileged person above others, but a visionary person ahead of others."

Approximately 40% indicated that they now regarded solitary visionary leader to be inherently limited. Involvement of organizational members in forming the vision or strategic plan was now considered equally important. An effective leader should "get staff involved in shaping the vision and make them own the vision." This reflects a major shift from singular concepts of charismatic or positional leadership towards a more collaborative, organizational construct. This insight was shared across school, system, and university sectors.

One principal emphasized teamwork and collective wisdom in leadership processes and now attempted "to solicit good ideas from organizational members, help them to reach consensus, and then commit them to the shared vision." Her view was echoed by a system official who previously regarded a leader as one "who has personal charisma and proposes encouraging slogans or goals at appropriate times so that others can follow." He now believed that this was insufficient; "the slogan should be a shared vision, which comes from followers, shared and owned by them."

There was also a new awareness that educational sectors possessed varied organizational cultures. A principal argued that system administrators were "line managers, who carry out policies from higher level administrators faithfully or modify them slightly according to the local contexts." He insisted they lacked opportunities to "sketch a blueprint for their organizations or commit the followers to a shared vision." He further argued that, school leaders have more flexibility than system administrators and believed he possessed the capacity to have "staff play an active role in creating a vision or mission statement for the school."

Approximately 20% of respondents demonstrated a more sophisticated understandings of the concepts of leadership and management by the end of the course. Principals tended to regard themselves as both leaders and managers who take on dual roles of visionary leadership and pragmatic implementation. System and university administrators continued to be more inclined to see themselves as "leaders at macro levels." A university administrator insisted "management is like putting a ladder against a wall in a right way, while leadership is like putting a ladder against a right wall." Another argued that management is a practical and technical competency whereas leadership requires higher order cognitions:

> Management is related to rules, regulations, accountability, control and obedience. Leadership has broader meanings in addition to control. It is mainly about creating a vision and making the team or organizational members commit to the shared vision. Leadership emphasizes strategic planning and management emphasizes tactics.

Three respondents indicated that they were also beginning to integrate elements of visionary, strategic and organizational leadership into a coherent philosophy by the end of the course. They employed images of the leader as a "conductor" or "facilitator." One principal believed a leader "was not necessarily the most intelligent or capable person in an organization," *but could* "create a cohesive organizational culture" by being "a coordinator of human relationships, promoter of problem solving, and facilitator of organizational learning." A system official began to place greater emphasis on a leader's influence upon the followers. He now argued "the main function of leadership has shifted from control and implementation to vision and motivation."

A new concept of leadership as consultation and collaboration was advanced by 60% of the respondents in second interviews. They illustrated their understandings from two perspectives; leadership as consultation and leadership as collaboration. Both concepts are committed to involvement and empowerment of staff in decision-making processes. However, there are also differences in the way they frame participation and power. Consultative leadership promotes "extensive consultation" but rarely couples this with power to make decisions (Collard, 2004b). Organizational members are given voice but not power. Some responses suggested "democratic consultation and consensus making" in contemporary China is restricted in this way. One principal placed a strong emphasis on "extensive consultation with teachers, students, and parents." A system official commented that from now on he would pay more attention to "consulting staff in his department or soliciting opinions from a wider circle" before making or implementing local educational policy. A university administrator considered "listening to teachers and raising their participatory awareness an important aspect of his role."

However none of these challenged the prerogatives of final positional power within their organizations. Soliciting feedback from constituents has undoubted capacity to inform decision makers and improve morale. However, if a positional leader believes it is his prerogative to decide whether or not to adopt their suggestions without transparent accountability it cannot be termed empowerment. One respondent commented "a leader should make decisions based on extensive consultation in the real sense, not a token." For him, truly collaborative leadership involved a transparent process of "constant reflection, feedback, modification and adjustment." He then went on to argue that authentic collaborative leadership involved "shared," "participative," and "distributed" power.

Confusion about consultative and collaborative leadership is not unique to China. It is shared by many school, system, and tertiary authorities in Western nations. This study reflects the relative inexperience of Chinese leaders with concepts of democracy and empowerment. Class participants would frequently comment "China is not a democracy, it is on the road to democracy!" This is true! Nor do they have a sophisticated understanding that American political discourse, with its emphasis upon individual rights in a capitalist economy differs markedly from Swedish concepts of a social democratic state. Western theories of distributed leadership are allied with notions of social equality and multiple levels of authority in organizations and polities (Gronn, 1999; Lakomski, 2001). Communitarian theorists assume that all constituents can participate in decision making according to their particular abilities, expertise, or skills (Barth, 1990; Burns, 1978; Chapman & Aspin, 1997). The key distinction between consultative and distributed leadership is the shared power to make decisions at multiple levels throughout organizations. Some respondents began to embrace shared and distributed leadership after the course. They insisted that ordinary organizational members should get involved in the decision-making processes and take on leadership roles. This included "teachers and students." This belief was more prevalent amongst principals and university administrators than system officials. Again this is understandable in that the latter have less direct contact with such constituents. A university administrator maintained "leadership means a leading process, a concept, a working style, or an awareness" and that it is possible for a "person who has no official position to play the role of leadership." He argued that "everyone including ordinary teachers may have leadership potential." This was a radical departure from previous assumptions about leadership as positional power.

Approximately 20% of respondents from all sectors understood that participative *leadership*, implies egalitarian ethics, not relationships characterized by "control and obey" or "order and implement." A university administrator insisted that "leadership emphasizes a relationship of cooperation and coordination." This view was echoed by a school principal who indicated he now held such a view:

> In the process of achieving organizational goals, leaders and followers are collaborators. My previous belief was that a leader is a pioneer or a fire fighter, who is at the front to guide followers or urge them with whips at the back. I now believe a leader should get involved in the process and become an organizational member.

However, others were cautious and stated "promoting democratic leadership" will be a long and incremental process in China. One principal suggested that Chinese educational leaders can incorporate some Western ideas, especially democratic ideas, to their practice. She believed "an integration of the essence of Western and Chinese ideas will be a desirable alternative for Chinese educational leaders to respond to the changing environment." She placed these comments within an awareness that "China is moving towards a democratic society, although it takes time."

The conceptions of leadership after the course extended across six instead of five categories. Individuals also continued to hold multiple positions simultaneously. Indeed there was some evidence that some held a contingency approach whereby they advocated various approaches in different contexts. There was evidence of a movement from inherited concepts towards more sophisticated and complex notions which incorporated some aspects of Western leadership discourses.

Self-reports about conceptual changes were again categorized as "large, moderate and small or no change." Five (25%) respondents reported no obvious change and their conceptions seemed to remain constant with their beliefs prior to the course. However, 75% reported large or moderate change in their perspectives about leadership.

Six respondents reported large changes in their conceptions. One principal indicated he did not expect to have "gained so much insight about leadership" because his major was educational management." A system official declared he "was different after taking the course in terms of leadership practice, strategies and plans proposed, ways of thinking and presentations at meetings." A university administrator reported his leadership perspective was now "more comprehensive and deeper than before." Others indicated that they had not previously "thought deeply or seriously" about the issue of leadership and had taken "traditional thinking" for granted. The exposure to Western leadership ideas, sharing perspectives with peers, and personal reflection had "modified, expanded or transformed" their previous assumptions. They had seldom associated learning with leadership before the course but some now viewed themselves as leading learners.

Almost half the sample reported moderate changes and modifications of their previous leadership concepts. A principal commented that his views underwent expansion and displaced strict adherence to scientific management with a more consultative approach. Others emphasized a new fidelity to strategic and visionary leadership. The five who argued that their fundamental conceptions of leadership had not changed demonstrate that resistance is a feature of intercultural dynamics. One university administrator reported "little change," found it hard to describe his understandings and even skipped this question during the second interview. Others from systems and universities argued that there are few fundamental differences between Chinese and Western leadership ideas. All of these were men over the age of 50. A senior official believed learning organization theories shared common ground with humanistic approaches currently advocated in China. However, it is interesting to note that there were no school based leaders or women in this category. This may suggest that they were more open to intercultural learning than those in other sectors. It may, in turn may be linked to the fact that school-based leaders and women in the sample were younger than the men in system and university administration.

The final conceptions of leadership did not cohere in a distinct or neat sequential order across the six categories. One principal subscribed to conceptions of leadership as positional power, leadership art, and teamwork. A system official had moved towards complex conceptions of visionary and consultative leadership after the course, but still adhered to conceptions of leadership as non-positional power and leadership art. This phenomenon is consistent with findings by Western researchers that individuals hold multiple or even conflicting conceptions and use them selectively, depending upon circumstances (Argyris & Schon, 1996).

Prior to the course most respondents held inherited assumptions about leadership as task oriented and directive in nature and 35% held more complex conceptions related to vision and strategic planning. None made any explicit references to concepts of leadership as consultation and collaboration. After the course the last conceptions had displaced the earlier ones in popularity. The data indicates that the perspectives of most of the sample were extended towards more complex constructions through the course. They had come to attach more importance to visionary and strategic leadership, and consultative and collaborative practice than previously.

Members from all sectors reported some large or moderate change. However school leaders were the only group whose total membership reported large or moderate change. Half of them reported large change in their conceptions whereas only one university administrator and one system administrator were in this category. Half of the system officials and school leaders reported moderate change while only one third of university administrators shared this perception. Indeed half of the university administrators and one third of system officials reported little change. Such findings suggest that school leaders were more open to new ideas than their counterparts from the other sectors. University administrators appeared to be most resistant to non-traditional approaches. We need to ask whether this was because school leaders possessed greater opportunities to develop expanded leadership approaches because of the smaller scale of their institutions? Alternatively, did university administrators and system officials have less discretionary power because they worked in larger, less flexible organizations?

Conclusions and Implications

This research reported in these two chapters was limited to understanding the participants' concepts of learning and leadership and the perceived influence of the program upon their self-reported cognitive changes. It did not investigate the behaviors of the participants in their workplaces. Verification about practice changes would require data collection from workplaces beyond the scope of this study. The long term impact of the changes over extended time would also require further investigation. The conclusions that can be drawn from this study are therefore limited to one leadership development program site in China, which involved leaders from schools, universities, and education systems in an economically developed region in Eastern China. The sample was a small slice of the total population of educational leaders in the Province. There is no attempt to generalize findings to other educational leaders in the province or throughout the nation. However, the purpose of the research, to explore participants' conceptions of learning and leadership and investigate the influence of the course upon them, is suited to such a limited focus and may be the springboard for broader research efforts.

The study shows that conceptions of learning and leadership are not necessarily as absolute, stable, or culture bound over time in the manner assumed by cross-cultural theorists. This is consistent with previous research which demonstrates that conceptions of learning can change or expand after specific interventions (McKenzie, 2003; Tang, 2001). This case study indicated that most of the participants developed more complex and expanded understandings of learning and leadership over a 1 year period. From a cultural perspective these changes reflect a movement from bounded Chinese beliefs already noted in the literature (Chan, 1999; Cortazzi & Jin, 2001; Kennedy, 2002; Zhu, 2002). Conceptions from after the course reflected their encounters with contemporary Western discourses. For the majority of subjects, this was not a matter of simple borrowing or rejection but a reflective mediation between diverse cultures. It constituted the development of an international perspective and critical thinking about the appropriateness of Western educational ideas to a Chinese context. As such the participants emerged as active learners mediating cultures rather than the passive recipients of inherited local traditions or puppets of global forces.

Most participants were positive about the changes in their understandings and welcomed expanding their views and strategies for leadership practice. They also exhibited caution about unmediated cultural-borrowing by emphasizing that accommodation of Western educational ideas must occur within an appreciation of local contexts and inherited cultures. Many recognized potential tensions between traditional Chinese assumptions and Western orientations. Such comments suggest that cultural adaptation to international perspectives will be an incremental and slow process. The majority recognized the differences between Chinese and Western cultures, and the consequent contextual constraints upon them. It would also be naive to assume that conceptual changes will auto-matically lead to dramatic shifts in the leadership practice of participants. Ho (2001) has suggested that some newly "espoused theories" take time before they are integrated into actual practice.

School principals appeared to be more receptive to learning new ideas and transforming their leadership practice than their counterparts from other sectors. They placed priority on relational and operational issues such as participative leadership, team learning and policy implementa-tion. System officials and university administrators tended to place more value upon inherited ideas. Two older men from these sectors could be described as resistant to Western ideas. University administrators tended to share their concerns about empowering, motivating, and involving staff. System officials were more interested in macro level issues such as strategic policy planning, and organizational structures.

The different cultures of the three sectors and the nature of their work may explain such variations. School principals were generally educational practitioners in small sites where intimate knowledge of learning and teaching issues are readily apparent. Staff management and morale issues are also more apparent in smaller scale organizations (Collard, 2004a). School leaders also appeared to possess greater autonomy and suffer less bureaucratic constraints than the other two groups. University adminis-trators were generally professional academics who had little direct experi-ence with the daily work of schools. They tended to privilege disciplinary knowledge above operational concerns. They also tended to be more reflective and inquiring about Western theories and more inclined to focus on controversial issues arising from the course. It appears that aca-demic university cultures may have been responsible for this difference. Members from local and provincial educational authorities were primarily bureaucrats and policy implementers. They focused on emergent, big pic-ture issues related to of educational reform in China and were more cau-tious, resistant, reflective, and inquiring about Western theories than the other groups. They also appeared more constrained by bureaucratic, hier-archical unabashedly political cultures, and therefore emerged as the most conservative in the cohort. Such findings are consistent with those of previous research in Australia which argues that sectorial and institutional cultures can generate important differences between leaders which essen-tialist theories obscure (Collard, 2000).

This study indicates that just as respondents may hold several concep-tions simultaneously; they may also utilize them selectively in different sit-uations. It therefore exemplifies the complexity and contingency of cultural variables as opposed to the law-like precepts of cross-cultural the-ories. These phenomena would provide an interesting theme for further research into the complexity of learning and leadership concepts within and between cultures.

It is important to reiterate that the categories of descriptions developed in this research do not form as strict a hierarchy as previous phenomenographic studies (Marton, Dall'alba, & Beaty, 1993; Tang, 2001). The tendency from lower order to higher order thinking is consistent with them but did not form a coherent hierarchy where each level subsumes the previous one. We therefore argue that the categories in this study form a loosely-coupled structure rather than the strict hierarchical sequence of previous research. This coupling includes clear logical overlaps and vague boundaries between categories. It suggests a more complex ontology than presumed by previous phenomenographic research. This issue has recently been raised by other researchers in the field (Ashworth & Lucas, 1998; Collin, 2002). As such, this research adds to the growing skepticism about the adequacy of categories in both cultural and phenomographic discourses. By uncovering two categories of learning previously unreported in phenomenographic studies it also alerts us to the limitations of the formal classroom as the research site. Significant learning occurs at organizational and social levels which has not been fully explored in this field.

The interviews revealed that participants were more impressed by their learning experience rather than the leadership content of the course. More participants reported large change in their conceptions of learning than in conceptions of leadership. This was an unexpected outcome. It suggests that the experience of learning may be a more powerful dynamic for change than exposure to new content. Conversely, leadership cannot be experienced as personally and directly as learning in a formal academic course. This may help explain why the impact upon their leadership conceptions was less profound. All educational programs comprise substantive content and pedagogy. The precise weighting of content and process in leadership education is relatively unresearched in this regard. A clear implication is that as much attention needs to be paid to the pedagogy as the content. Another is that courses may need to be expanded to include internship, simulations or scenarios in familiar and unfamiliar cultural settings.

The study indicates that the original learning conceptions of participants' emphasized authoritative knowledge and pedagogy and their leadership concepts stressed leader authority and follower obedience in hierarchical structures. These suggested an epistemological consistency or worldview. By 2003 a link between concepts of knowledge as provisional and contestable appeared to be aligned with preferences for constructivist knowledge claims, participative pedagogy, and collaborative or distributed leadership. The authoritative image of knowledge had been displaced by the view that it was socially constructed and mutable. The expanded leadership conceptions stressed the collective cognitive power and dispersed sites for decision-making within organizations. Individuals came to be viewed as active constructors of their own knowledge and effective organizations based on individual learning and team collaboration. Leaders were redefined as exemplary learners. The study hints at a link between constructivist conceptions of learning and participative leadership. Some participants stated explicitly that an understanding that leadership must promote learning in constantly changing contexts was the key outcome of the course.

REFERENCES

Argyris, C., & Schon, D. A. (1996). *Organizational learning II: Theory, method, and practice*. Reading, MA: Addison-Wesley.

Ashworth, P., & Lucas, U. (1998) What is the world of phenomenography? *Scandinavian Journal of Educational Research, 42*(2), 415–431.

Barth, R. S. (1990). Improving schools from within; Teachers, parents and principals can make the difference. San Francisco, CA: Jossey-Bass.

Bass, B. M. (1998). *Transformational leadership: Industrial, military, and educational impact*. Mahwah, NJ: Erlbaum.

Bass, B. M., & Avolio, B. J. (Eds.). (1993). Transformational leadership: A response to the critics. In M. M. Chemers & R. Ayman (Ed.), *Leadership theory and research: Perspectives and directions* (pp. 49–89). San Diego, CA: Academic Press.

Begley, P., & Johansson, O. (Eds.). (2003). *The ethical dimensions of school leadership*. The Netherlands: Kluwer Press.

Blake, R. R., & Mouton, J. S. (1964). *The managerial grid*. Houston, TX: Gulf.

Bottery, M. (1992). *The ethics of educational management, personal, social and political perspectives on school organization*. Trowbridge, London: Cassell.

Burns, J. M. (1978). *Leadership*. New York: Harper & Row.

Caldwell, B., & Spinks, J. M. (1988). *The self-managing school*. London: The Falmner Press.

Caldwell, B., & Spinks, J. M. (1998). *Beyond the self-managing school*. London: The Falmer Press.

Chapman, J. D., & Aspin, D. N. (1997). *The school, the community and lifelong learning*. London: Cassell.

Chan, S. (1999). The Chinese learner—A question of style. *Education + Training, 41*(6/7), 294–305.

Collard, J. (2000). *Figures and landscapes: Male and female principals in Victorian Schools 1996-98*. Unpublished doctoral dissertation, University of Melbourne, Australia.

Collard, J. (2003a). Principal beliefs: The interface of gender and sector. *The Alberta Journal of Educational Research, XLIX*(I), 37–54.

Collard, J. (2003b). The relationship of gender and context to leadership in Australian schools. In P. Begley & O. Johannson (Eds.), *The ethical dimensions of school leadership* (pp. 181–189). The Netherlands: Kluwer Press.

Collard, J. (2004a). Does size matter? In J. Collard & C. Reynolds (Eds.). *Leadership, gender & culture: Male and female perspectives* (pp. 73–89). Philadelphia: Open University Press.

Collard, J. (2004b). Steel magnolia & in velvet ghettoes: Female leaders in Australian girls' schools. In J. Collard & Reynolds, C. (Eds.), *Leadership, gender & culture: Male and female perspectives* (pp. 73–89). Philadelphia: Open University Press.

Collin, K. (2002). Development engineers, conceptions of learning at work, *Studies in Continuing Education, 24* (2), 133–152.

Conger J. A., & Kanungo, R. W. (1988). *Charismatic leadership: The elusive factor in organizational effectiveness.* San Francisco: Jossey Bass.

Cortazzi, M., & Jin, L. (2001). Large classes in China: "Good" teachers and interaction. In D. A. Watkins & J. B. Biggs (Eds.), Teaching the Chinese learner: Psychological and pedagogical perspectives (pp. 115–134). Hong Kong/Australia: Comparative Education Research Centre/Australian Council for Educational Research.

Crawford, M. (2003). Inventive management, wise leadership. In J. Bennett, M. Crawford & M. Cartwright (Eds.), *Effective educational leadership* (pp. 62–73). Thousand Oaks, CA: SAGE.

Davis, A., & Johansson, O. (2004). Gender and school leadership in Sweden. In J. Collard & C. Reynolds (Eds.), *Leadership, gender & culture: Male and female perspectives.* Philadelphia: Open University Press.

Fiedler, F. E. (1967). A theory of leadership effectiveness. New York: McGraw-Hill.

Fullan, M. G., & Hargreaves, A. (1991). *Working together for your school: Strategies for developing interactive professionalism in your school.* Hawthorn: Australian Council for Educational Administration.

Gronn, P. (1999). *Life in teams: Collaborative leadership and learning in autonomous work units.* Burwood: Australian Council for Educational Administration.

Gronn, P. (2003). *The new work of educational leaders: Changing leadership practice in an era of school reform.* London: SAGE/Paul Chapman.

Hersey, P., & Blanchard, K. H. (1979, June). Life cycle theory of leadership. *Training and Development Journal*, 94–100.

Hersey, P., & Blanchard, K. H. (1982). *Management of organizational behaviour utilizing human resources.* Englewood Cliffs, NJ: Prentice-Hall.

Ho, A. S. P. (2001). A conceptual change approach to university staff development. In D. A. Watkins & J. B. Biggs (Eds.), *Teaching the Chinese learner: Psychological and pedagogical perspectives* (pp. 239–254). Hong Kong/Australia: Comparative Education Research Centre/Australian Council for Educational Research.

Hodgkinson, C. (1991). *Educational leadership: The moral art.* Albany, NY: State University of New York Press.

Hofstede, G. H. (1980). *Culture's consequences: International differences in work-related values.* Beverly Hills, CA: SAGE.

Kennedy, P. (2002). Learning cultures and learning styles: Myth-understandings about adult (Hong Kong) Chinese learners. *International Journal of Lifelong Education, 21*(5), 430–445.

Lakomski, G. (2001). Organizational change, leadership and learning: Culture as cognitive process. *The International Journal of Educational Management, 15*(2), 68–77.

Leithwood, K. A., Begley P. T., & Bradley-Cousins J. (1992). *Developing expert leadership for future schools.* London: The Falmer Press.

Lee, W. O. (1996). The cultural context for Chinese Learners: Conceptions of learning in the Confucian tradition. In D. Watkins & J. Biggs (Eds.), *The Chinese learner: Cultural, psychological and contextual influences* (pp. 25–41). Hong Kong/Australia: Comparative Education Research Centre/Australian Council for Educational Research.

Marton, F., Dall'alba, G., & Beaty, E. (1993). Conceptions of learning. *International Journal of Educational Research, 19,* 277–300.

McKenzie, J. A. (2003). *Variation and change in university teachers ways of experiencing teaching.* Unpublished PhD thesis, University of Technology, Sydney.

Porter, P. (1995) The need for a spring clean: Gendered educational organizations and their glass ceilings, glass walls, sticky floors sticky cobwebs and slippery poles. In B. Limerick & B. Lingard (Eds.), Gender and changing educational management: Second yearbook of the Australian Council for Educational Administration (pp. 234–243). Rydalmere, Australia: Hodder Education.

Ozga J. (1993). *Women in educational management.* Buckingham, England: Open University Press.

Stogdill, R. M. (1974). *Handbook of leadership: A survey of theory and research.* New York: The Free Press.

Shakeshaft, C. (1987). *Women in educational administration.* Newbury Park, CA: SAGE.

Tang, T. K. W. (2001). The Influence of Teacher Education on Conceptions of Teaching and Learning. In D. A. Watkins & J. B. Biggs (Eds.), *Teaching the Chinese learner: Psychological and pedagogical perspectives* (pp. 221–238). Hong Kong/Australia: Comparative Education Research Centre/Australian Council for Educational Research.

Taylor, F. W. (1915). *The principles of scientific management.* New York: Harper & Row.

Vroom, V. H., & Yetton, P. W. (1973). Leadership and decision-making. Pittsburgh, PA: University of Pittsburgh Press.

Weber, M. (2002). *The protestant ethic and the spirit of capitalism.* New York: Routledge Press. (Original work published 1904)

Weber, M. (1947). The theory of social and economic organizations (R. A. Henderson & T. Parsons, Trans.). New York: Free Press.

Wong, K.-C. (2001). Chinese culture and leadership. *International Journal of Leadership in Education, 4*(4), 309–319.

Zhu, M. (Ed.). (2002). *Zoujin Xinkecheng: Yukecheng Shishizhe Duihua* [Step into new curricula: A dialogue with curricula implementers]. China: Beijing Normal University Press.

CHAPTER 13

SCHOOL LEADERSHIP IN CHANGING TIMES

The Case of Belarus

Niklas Eklund, Olof Johansson, and J. Theodore Repa

INTRODUCTION

The objective of this chapter is to examine the rhetoric and practices of educational leadership within a Belarus context, and to explore and understand the conditions affecting the work of their school leaders. Belarus became independent in 1991, there has been a clear trend towards liberalistic ideas with a focus on accountability, effectiveness, competition, and a new demand for local democracy. This trend seems to produce a certain level of homogeneity, but at the same time there is still a remnant of national and local culture from the older, traditional systems in Belarus.

The chapter asks questions about the support structures—both political and administrative—in place to assist Belarus school leaders. Interviews and to some extent reviews of the relevant research literature

Leadership and Intercultural Dynamics, pp. 259–277

shed light on the ways in which school leaders have responded to this new environment. Dilemmas, conflicts, and possibilities arising from the new situation, are explored and compared in order to be able to see more clearly the similarities and the differences from before.

It should not be surprising that school leaders across the countries have responded differently to changed policy circumstances. Local culture and distinctive aspects of national life will always tend to modify external influences such as those inherent in the philosophy and practice of school leadership. One could argue that the range of tensions and dilemmas facing teachers and their leaders are a direct result of the clash between generic public policy now being seen across the world, and the distinctive approach to life in Belarus. Leaders are, it seems, clearly in the middle of this clash, and must mediate between these two traditions.

The chapter has an evaluation focus. We collected information about the effects of two different international cooperation efforts in school leadership training. The first one, between Belarus and the United States, focused on developing new methods for preparing educational leaders. The second cooperation effort was between Belarus and Sweden. The program was constructed as a principal training program and our focus was to work with training modules which the participants later should be able to use. In the final stage of the program we constructed a leadership profile for good practice in Belarus. The profile was meant to be an instrument to be used in training activities but also in appraisal and evaluation discussions.

The research questions we address in this chapter are:

- What are the remaining effects?
- What impact has the training had on the persons involved?
- Have they been able to use the international experience in their work and professional development?

International Cooperation on School Leadership Development Between Belarus and the West: The Historical Context

Cooperation on school leadership development between Belarus and the West started innocently enough in the spring of 1991. Mikhail Gorbachev had come into power in the Soviet Union in 1985 and, as General Secretary of the Communist Party of the Soviet Union, introduced the new policies of *perestroika* (restructuring), *glasnost* (openness), *demokratizatsiya* (democratization), and *uskoreniye* ("acceleration" of economic development) at the 27th Congress of the Communist Party in February of 1986.[1] Five years later, Belarus, as did the other former Republics of the Soviet Union around this time, declared independence on July 27, 1991. The Presidents of Russia, Belarus, and Ukraine founded the Commonwealth of Independent States on December 8, 1991, declaring the end of the Soviet Union. Gorbachev resigned as President on December 25th and was replaced by Boris Yeltsin and the Soviet Union was formally dissolved the next day.

Initial Contacts Between Belarus and Western Educational Administration Educators

It was in this historical context that Iouri Zagoumennov, Professor of Educational Administration and Head of the Educational Administration Department of The Republic Institute for Upgrading Teachers of the Ministry of Education of the Republic of Belarus, convinced the Head of his Institute to fund a trip for a week in New York City in the Spring of 1991 to find out more about the tradition of democratic school leadership in the United States. Dr. Zagoumennov had only recently defended, in Moscow, his dissertation on Democratization of School Management in 1988, the first dissertation in the USSR focused on democratic governance of schools. Since *perestroika*, Dr. Zagoumennov conducted research and innovation activities in the USSR aimed at democratization of the management of schools.

Upon arrival in New York, Dr. Zagoumennov was referred to New York University through a contact at the Belarusian Consulate in New York City. There he met Theodore Repa, the new Chair of the Department of Administration, Leadership, and Technology and professor of educational administration. Dr. Zagoumennov spoke excellent English and he and Dr. Repa had a mutual interest in shared leadership and decision making in schools. Dr. Repa arranged for New York University's (NYU) faculty to give Dr. Zagoumennov some of the educational administration textbooks the NYU faculty used in their courses. Dr. Repa also invited Dr. Zagoumennov to accompany him in October in Baltimore to the annual convention of the University Council of Educational Administration (UCEA), the leading consortium of universities with doctoral programs in educational administration. At the conference, Dr. Repa introduced Dr. Zagoumennov to the leading scholars in educational administration from around the country, exposed him to the most recent research in the field, and showed him how to order free desk copies of books in educational administration from the publishers that were on display. NYU subsequently sponsored Dr. Zagoumennov's participation at UCEA in Houston and Minneapolis.

Dr. Repa next met with Dr. Zagoumennov during the spring of 1992 in Minsk, where Dr. Repa was a guest lecturer. Dr. Repa delivered two lectures to their graduate students (Repa, 1992a, 1992b). Additionally, Dr. Repa visited schools, met leading school administrators, spoke with representatives of the Ministry of Education, and became more familiar with how education of educators was organized in Belarus. Subsequently, Dr. Zagoumennov continued his education about Western educational administration preparation models by visiting Finland to learn about the Swedish models for the professional preparation of educational leaders.

International Educational Leadership Exchange Programs Between the Belarus and New York University 1992–1994

That fall semester Dr. Repa arranged for Dr. Zagoumennov to spend a sabbatical as a visiting scholar in NYU's Department of Administration, Leadership, and Technology. Dr. Zagoumennov co-taught a graduate level course, Leadership and Decision Making.

During the summer of 1993 Dr. Zagoumennov and Dr. Repa jointly taught an NYU Study Abroad course, Leadership and Decision Making in Minsk. Eight NYU students who were educators and nine Belarus educational administrators were enrolled for this 3 week experience. The U.S. educators stayed in the homes of their Belarus educators counterparts. In the course, they formed cross-cultural teams as they studied and practiced democratic leadership skills. Belarus students did not have to pay tuition for this course.

In 1994, funding from the Soros Foundation and NYU supported a 2-week visit to New York City by 12 Belarus educational administrators where they met and observed their counterparts modeling democratic teaching methods in urban and suburban schools. Dr. Repa and Dr. Zagoumennov were the lead faculty in this project.

International School Leadership Development Technical Assistance Program Between New York University and the Belarus Institute for Educational Administration 1993–1996

The next educational collaboration between NYU and Belarus was a 2-year collaborative project titled "The Newly Independent States Partnership: New York University and the Belarus Institute for Educational Administration." Funded by the United States Information Agency, the project included six NYU faculty specialists in educational administration, international education, higher education, social studies education, and educational telecommunications spending 1 month each summer in Belarus. Dr. Repa was one of the NYU faculty specialists that participated in this project. The NYU faculty partnered with faculty from the Belarus Institute, including Dr. Zagoumennov, and focused on facilitating the process of democratization in the Republic of Belarus through educational reform.

The approach was to engage in a mutual exchange of ideas and to transfer educational knowledge and technology from the United States to Belarus. The partnership focused on the following issues: the decentralization of education decision making in higher education and in schools; the development of a civic education curriculum that promoted democratic values as an integral part of good citizenship; and a computer-based telecommunications center through which educators in Belarus could have access on a continuing basis to electronic mail, computer-based conferencing, and online library resources in the United States and other developed countries.

Among the accomplishments were the following: the donation by the NYU School of Education of over 1,000 books on educational administration in Belarus, an extensive report on how to change the higher education system in Belarus to better meet international standards for degrees, the creating of a handbook to be used in in-service training on how to transform Belarus schools along democratic principles, the development of new social studies instructional materials focusing on Belarus and global history, and setting up and supplying the Institute with computers and modems to access the Internet.

The Spawning of Multiple Western Leadership Development Programs in Belarus

While a visiting scholar at NYU in 1992, Dr. Repa introduced Dr. Zagoumennov to Dr. Dale Mann, an educational administration professor colleague at Teacher's College, Columbia University. Dr. Mann invited Dr. Zagoumennov to be an observer at the Russian Educational Leaders for the 21st Century Program in St. Petersburg, sponsored by the Soros Foundation. George Soros also invited Dr. Zagoumennov to serve on the Board of Directors of the Soros Foundation in Minsk and to implement in Belarus with Dr. Mann the Belarus Educational Leaders for the 21st Century Program in 1993. In the Belarus educational leader program, six teams of administrators, one for each of the six administrative regions in Belarus, comprised of the regional superintendent of schools, two district superintendents, two principals, and a trainer from the regional in-service institute for school administrators, received 1 year of democratic training from world-class international experts in education and business. At the end of that training, the teams developed 5-year plans to improve the schools and democratic school leader preparation in their region.

Three other democratic educational leadership initiatives between Belarus and the West had their origin in 1993, although some did not start until some years later. The first began when Dale Mann introduced Dr. Zagoumennov to the Board of the International Congress for School Effectiveness and Improvement (ICSEI). This collaboration allowed Dr. Zagoumennov over the next 12 years to travel around the world to attend international conferences of ICSEI. In 1996 Dr. Zagoumennov hosted this conference in Minsk where Dr. Repa presented a paper that was subsequently published in Belarus (Repa 1996a, 1996b).

With the help of these international contacts Dr. Zagoumennov was able to secure funding to establish the Educational Center for Leadership Development (ECLD) in Minsk in 1994. Its accomplishments included:

- Initiating the first preservice course for educational administrators in the Minsk Region whereby 100% of the graduates were promoted to leadership positions in their schools and districts.
- Starting the publication of the first quarterly journal for school leaders in Belarus *Leadership and Management in Education*.
- Starting the first annual contest in Belarus for the "Belarus Educational Leader of the Year."

All these initiatives continued after being taken over by the Ministry of Education or regional and local educational authorities. They were extended to include:

- Facilitating the National Association of Educational Administrators in Belarus, a professional network of educational administrators.
- Securing funding to for 30 Belarus educators to visit the Spinoza Lyceum (a Dalton School) in Amsterdam, Holland, and to be introduced to the Dalton methodology.

Out of this last visit, a 4-year collaboration with the Spinoza Lyceum (Holland), the Belarus Ministry of Education, the Dutch National Institute of Development, and the Educational Center for Leadership Development (Belarus) was initiated in 1995. It established a network of schools in Belarus that adopted the Dalton School model. In addition to providing technical support to the adopting schools, a train-the-trainer model was used to prepare a group of independent Belarus educational consultants to support the newly established Dalton schools. The participants in the program established the National Association for Educational Inovations (NAEI) that is comprised of over 70 educational communities in all the Belarus administrative regions. Both schools that use the Dalton model as well as the NAEI continue today.

The next two Western collaborations developed out of meetings with two different scholars Dr. Zagoumennov met while attending an ICSEI conference. In Hong Kong in 2000, Dr. Zagoumennov met Dr. Olof Johansson, Professor and Director of Principal Development at Umeå University in Sweden. Dr. Johansson and Dr. Zagoumennov developed a joint project that focused on developing democratic educational leaders in Belarus. Their collaborative efforts produced two publications on educational leadership in Belarus (Johansson & Begley, 2001, 2003). The focus of the major project that led to these two publications was the *School Leadership Profile Project*, begun in 2001.

A profile is a two dimensional matrix that leads to a professional development plan based upon mutually agreed upon educational goals that are developed by writing team of representative practitioners and academics. Umeå University provided the professional development for the writing team that produced the profile for their school. Additionally, the collaboration organized two international conferences (Johansson & Begley, 2001, 2003).

In February of 2008, Drs. Johansson and Repa, along with the third co-author of this chapter Niklas Eklund of Umeå University, Sweden, spent a week in Minsk interviewing over 40 Belarusian educators who had participated in the various educational leadership development programs asking them to reflect on the impact of their particular experience.

Results From the 2008 Follow-up Interview With Dr. Iouri Zagoumennov

Dr. Zagoumennov was the central figure in the development of Western educational leader developmental activities in Belarus. He initiated contacts with Western experts in 1991 and over the years has been a lead contributor to various democratic educational leadership development projects in his country. Dr. Zagoumennov points to his initial exposure to Western educational leadership literature he found at NYU as a key factor in promoting his interest and expertise in educational leadership. Each contact with the West seemed to lead to the development of the next leadership project. Western technical support to establish Internet connections allowed Dr. Zagoumennov to find additional information about democratic school leadership, an idea not very well developed in Belarus before *perestroika,* as well as develop a cadre on international colleagues in educational administration, with which he could stay in touch and call upon. His international travel and ability to support other educational leaders in Belarus made him the leading educational administration professor in his country. However, it must be emphasized that without the initiative, cooperation, and navigational expertise of Dr. Zagoumennov, most of the leadership projects and successes in Belarus would have been extremely difficult, if not impossible.

Interviews and Survey Results From the Belarus and New York University Participants in the International Exchange Programs Between 1992–1994

Four Belarus educators and four United States educators that participated in the exchanges were interviewed or surveyed. All eight educators noted that they changed their views of education based upon their participation with the two international exchange programs. The Belarus educators focused on the helpfulness of observing and participating in democratic teaching methods within a classroom setting that could be used in their schools, e.g., teaming, exercises, simulations, task forces, and the like. They also noted that they became more self-confident educators by successfully completing an English taught course from an American university. All, but one, went on to take more educational leadership responsibilities in Belarus. The four American educators talked about using their new found international education experiences in their schools. They used examples they learned to help provide better multicultural experiences for their students. The thought they were better able to understand and meet the needs of their international students.

Interviews and Survey Results From the Belarus and New York University Participants in the Technical Assistance Programs Between 1993–1996

Three Belarus professors and three United States professors who participated in the 2-year technical assistance grant were interviewed or surveyed. The three Belarus professors all went on to assume important educational leadership positions. Dr. Zagoumennov continues to lead democratic, educational leadership development programs in Belarus. A second faculty member assumed a high ranking position in the Ministry of Education and helped Belarus move from a focus on knowledge-based education to competency-based education based upon international standards. The third faculty member spent a sabbatical at NYU and focuses her current efforts on educational reform in Belarus as a consultant. All three point to this 2-year project as being pivotal in broadening their vision about directions that educational reform should take in Belarus based upon an international perspective. And all three have assumed positions in Belarus that have allowed them to implement their shared vision.

The three New York University professors, while thankful for the personal, professional growth that resulted from their international education experience in Belarus, were more circumspect about the difficulties of cooperative, international educational reform efforts. Sustainability of and scaling up democratic educational reforms within the political context and history of a top-down educational management system in Belarus was seen as a challenge. Ultimately, the future life of the democratic educational reforms that were introduced were in the hands of the cadre of Belarus educational leaders who participated in the Western sponsored projects, as the Western experts moved on to other responsibilities and interests.

Interview Results From the Belarus and Swedish Participants in the Technical Assistance Programs Between 2000–2003

In an effort to assess the impact and utility of the Profile, Belarus school leaders were brought together in two separate groups to evaluate and discuss their experiences. In the group chaired by Prof. Olof Johansson and Dr. Niklas Eklund, seven participants (five female, two male) were asked to give an initial presentation of any professional changes linked with their work on the Profile a few years previously to discuss specifically how their views upon democracy, change, control, and knowledge in schools has changed. The presentations and ensuing group discussion went on for over 2 hours.

In the following, four separate sections trace the perceived changes among the seven participants starting with the personal level and regarding career, leadership styles, and the dissemination of democratic ideas and ideals. On the organizational level, it is related how participants view any regional or systemic effects in Belarus in addition to the personal development effects. Last but not least, an attempt is made to trace any lingering effects of the Profile in how the participants look at it today, any changes they would like to see given their past experiences, and ultimately to what extent they have or have not changed their ideas about what constitutes knowledge.

Career and Personal Changes

Out of the total seven participants, five have made significant career moves since 2003. One of them continues to work as a school principal, whereas another has returned to the role of school teacher. Generally, the Profile and related work and travel experiences have served as a source of personal inspiration for those who have moved on, over and above being a tool for teaching and administration in its own right. Professionally, those five participants who have moved up the career ladder have ended up in significant leadership positions in the Belorussian system of education. One female participant is now the head of the institute "Innovations in Education" which entails daily work in a section of the Ministry of Education in Minsk as well as on the one hand heading up coaching processes for teachers in local schools in Belorussian school districts and, on the other hand, doing and publishing research in Belorussian scientific journals. One of the male participants has taken up a higher administrative position and is currently involved in the building of a new university faculty. Another male participant is currently trying the entrepreneurial route, originally by starting up and running a private school in parallel with his old job as a school principal. His business increased rapidly over the first few years of activity, and he soon discovered that there was a market for new ideas and models of teaching and administration. Over the past few years, he has been able to build up extensive networks, both inside Belarus and internationally, which makes him confident that his school can be regarded as a regional resource center for education today.

One of the female participants has become an entrepreneur, currently working as an independent consultant to schools all over the Minsk region. Having become a consultant, she says, entails putting the ideas and practices of the Profile into action more or less every working day and although she finds herself struggling with both cultural resistance and institutional inertia in the educational system, she taps into a big market for models based on ideas about strategic goal setting, person-to-person communication, and the role of personal and group relationships in making strategic priorities. Last but not least, one of the female participants has become a manager in the Academy of Education in Minsk, at a teacher training institute. She too feels that the model thinking and strategic ideas of the Profile have been an immense help in identifying needs for change and being able to capitalize upon them. She adds that one of the more interesting aspects of the past 5 years of her professional experience has been to work in processes that have started out without budgets, in which she feels that the role of good leadership becomes a bigger, more crucial issue. Having risen to a higher administrative position in the Academy of Education, she still looks to the profile for inspiration when it comes to organizing seminars and conferences for new and younger school principals.

Leadership Styles and Ideas

There seems to be agreement in the group that the Profile, with its ideas about bottom-to-top processes of change and the pivotal role of democratic leadership, emerged at just the right time in Belarus. Consequently, it continues to play an important role not only on the personal level for participants and their respective co-workers, but also significantly as a critical source and check list in ongoing educational reform. All participants agree that the ideas about intellectual leadership, methodologies based on democratic principles, pluralism, and open-ended thinking continually inspire change on various levels of the system, although it has been particularly important to practices and communication processes in schools. Regarding the context of current educational reform in Belarus, however, opinions diverge. There is an optimistic outlook among the majority of participants, emphasizing the opportunities for change. But, conversely, there is also a more pessimistic under current, which insists the real opportunities for democratization in administration and teaching methods have come and gone.

The positive contextualization rests on the observation by some group participants that real changes have taken place in how school teachers, pupils, and managers interact. There is, as observed by one female participant, validation of democratic principles, such as soft measures and dialogue, to be found in how teachers address each other as co-workers. Furthermore, the more principals and other leaders increase their awareness and observance of democratic values, the more they are approached and addressed openly in return. The positive image also involves such practices as having more staff meetings and more seminars on a wide variety of issues related to education and work in schools. Another participant adds that concrete effects can be seen in how the dialogue between teachers and administrators has become livelier as critical, goal-oriented discussion even creeps into discussion over coffee or tea during the breaks. The idea, as set out in the Profile, to integrate individuals, institutions, and the relationship between them into model thinking needs to be illustrated by professionally successful individuals applying this perspective and becoming even more successful as a result. The key to such development, and taking a positive view of changes in Belarus, is for individuals to openly assume personal responsibility and to project a personal style which promotes commitment to tasks and to making things happen. In this view, role models are presently available in the educational system in Belarus, working as agents for change from below.

However two participants in the group paint their images of change in Belarus in far darker colors. There is, according to them, a cultural element in the process of change which is hard to grasp but at the same time impossible to circumvent. In stark contrast with the ideas behind the Profile, school leadership in Belarus tends to be hijacked by administrative and legal culture, or by outright institutional inertia. There is, according to one female participant, what she refers to as the "documents-first strategy." Indeed, she feels strongly that it has been an integral part of how administrators and managers are trained for decades and one that is deeply entrenched in Belorussian administrative culture. Individual examples of success, whether or not underpinned by efficient measures aimed at educational reform, always stand a good chance of becoming best practices even in such a system but, she concludes, the "document-first strategy" continues to be rewarded in Belorussian administration at large and, therefore, stands out as a formidable obstacle to change also in the educational system.

One of the male participants supports this negative view by saying that he believes it no secret that democratic leadership and principles are a hard sell in Belarus. With a background in both school and university administration, he feels it safe to say that authoritarian teaching methods are back in force in Belarus. However he also believes that the Profile has been very useful in providing keys to better management and conflict resolution among staff, he agrees that some significant democratizing effects can be observed in work places, particularly in individual leaders and administrators. Taking the bigger view, he is convinced that democratic leadership is possible regardless of what the overall political system looks like. At the end of the day, leadership is a direct part of every-day situations in schools and work places. But, on the systemic level, he too takes a dim view of both the scope and opportunities for change in Belarus since the space for individual leadership and success is, at best, limited.

Democratizing Schools

As the participants agree that pupils in Belorussian schools suffer from work overload, sometimes spending as much as 11 hours per day either in the immediate school environment or on assignments, there is little to evince that new ideas and ideals have penetrated the classroom. There is, as one participant puts it, simply not enough time for kids to worry about that. Conversely, for the individual teacher there is a similar problem with the work load, which gives little or no room for democratic experimentation in actual education. The group nevertheless agrees that there is a more pleasant tone between teachers and pupils in some schools, and that there is a positive correlation between the class room situation and the overall organizational culture of any given school. Differently put, the better the working place climate between teachers and other staff, the more likelihood of a positive spillover at the pupils' end.

The consensus in the group seems to be that the introduction of the Profile, its related ideas and subsequent practices has generated important organizational and cultural change in Belorussian schools as work places, that is, significant for leaders, teachers, and administrators. As competition between schools has increased as a result of educational reform in the past decade, the role and function of school principals as key actors has been greatly enhanced. In the wake of leaders' search for excellence and different sources of funding, new and more modern personnel and management policies have emerged. Again, the group agrees that the timing for the Profile was just right since, organizationally, the Belorussian education system was entering a new phase in its development. Both the financial and competitive autonomy of Belorussian schools have increased, and in the continuous struggle against institutional and administrative inertia in the system, schools have had to update and upgrade their human resource management. For example, one of the participants points to the increasing importance of international exchanges and networks as a significant sign of the times. Another participant adds that when focusing on the work place, it is possible to achieve results and to be productive even without any major educational reform in the country. On the whole, the group seems to be in agreement about the pivotal role which has been played by the Profile, both in the sense that it has altered the way individual leaders and administrators look at education and their own role in the system, but also in how the face of Belorussian school as a work place has changed. The general, cultural expectation is still for Belorussian officials and functionaries to keep a stiff upper lip in the light of economic or other shortages. They agree, however, that school teachers and administrators have made significant moves away from this stereotype among themselves. Today, it is far more likely that a school leader will be successful because of being liked as a leader, than it is because of being feared. Some ripple effects in Belorussian society are also obvious to the participants in this group, thus making them feel proud of a school system which can be not only creative, while adaptive, but also progressive, while productive. There are, in the words of one female participant, methodologies linked to democratic leadership and education which are readily available for people who are smart enough to realize and to use them.

Profile Impact Evaluated

The group agreed that the lasting effects of the Profile can be seen on two levels. On one level, working on the Profile and putting it to use in subsequent work has led to a number of critical realizations about the problems and opportunities of education in Belarus. The very act of producing a concrete document and bringing it back home has been a source of both pride and opportunities for technical learning. The group also agrees that over and above the relative merits and demerits of the document as such, it symbolizes the starting point of a process which is still ongoing. From the very beginning it seemed clear to the participants that they would not, indeed could not, go back home with a once and for all complete document and most of them have subsequently felt compelled to keep working on it, adding and subtracting, building from the Profile and out in the light of experiences and learning. Most participants currently do not feel a need to revise the Profile since this is what they have been doing anyway for several years. In some cases, participants have even published articles in journals which owe greatly to the Profile as an ideational compass and source of inspiration. Thus, on the first level of realization the Profile has served and continues to serve as a source of inspiration and a set of guidelines that continues to function among the group participants.

On another level, writing the Profile up, coming back home, and going about trying to put the new ideas and concepts to work in their home environment, participants seem to agree that difficult questions and critical perspectives have come to the fore over time. Impressions from visiting and working for a short while in Sweden have been the source of critical reflection. The group agrees, it was easy to be overwhelmed by how seemingly well organized and functional everything is in Sweden. To be a first-hand witness to how well Swedish children handle different forms of oral and visual presentation or to learn about the caring and inclusive psychology which governs Swedish schools was jolting. Another observation was the significance attributed to the development of individuality and personality, both as observed in school but also as observed among Swedish participants in the project. The group agrees that their participation in a conference in Sweden which was also attended by the Swedish queen was the pinnacle of this overall, overwhelming experience. At this conference the Swedish core attitude of equality was blatantly illustrated by how the queen entered and joined the conference not as a leader or person of state, but simply as one participant among the many. In the words of one group participant, "this was probably when the totalitarian stereotype in us died."

On this other level of realization, however, the memories of how Swedes seem to believe in their egalitarian model of democracy and how this belief produces a general sense of opportunity and can-do in schools gave the group participants a lasting belief in the merits of democracy. Over time, however, and working with similar ideals at home in Belarus, most of the group participants have at some point or other paused to reflect on how closely linked, not to say intertwined, that different models of democracy are with culture. This has given rise to some critical ideas, such as why the Swedes seemed so reluctant to criticize or problematize the hard side of democracy. In conversations, for example, some of the group participants tried to bring up such difficult issues as where the line should be drawn for how and when a democratic system is entitled to defend itself by forceful means. On reflection, this is interpreted by the group as a memento not to simply try to copy the Swedish model or to believe that any changes in such a direction can be realized quickly. The intersection between culture, historical experience, and teaching principles is simply too complex. Above all, it means to the group that some of the hard questions about democracy and egalitarian ideals that they have to face at home, in Belarus, in order to motivate their current beliefs they will have to face alone and without the support of any definite role model.

In answer to the question about what the group would have done differently if they were given the opportunity to rewrite the Profile today, there was significant agreement too. The benefits of new ideas and approaches, some that were set out already in the profile and some which have emanated from its later use, are simply seen as too great. The group participants are hard put to see any significant idea or concept that would improve the validity or utility of the Profile today. This is also given their several years' experience from working with the Profile in education in Belarus. They submit, however, that there is one significant gap between on the one hand the essentially Russian philosophical and educational tradition in which they work daily and on the other hand the pluralistic conceptual world of the Profile. The group would like to do more work on methodological aspects, or what they speaking with the Russian tradition refer to as "technological aspects." Such phenomena as networking, team spirit, on-the-floor leadership, competencies, and resource centers are clearly understandable on the conceptual level. But, the group participants currently feel a need to transform these and similar concepts into practical teaching and administration models for them to receive a better understanding among teachers and administrators in Belarus and, at the end of the day, to have bigger clout.

In answer to the second question, the group adds that there are 42 schools in the Minsk region alone, and in excess of 3,500 schools throughout the country. Bottom-up thinking and competence based career advancements remain yet to be implemented in most of them. According to the group the need is immense, but so is the institutional inertia. The group agrees that bureaucracy and heavy paper work is a Soviet legacy which does not seem to be going anywhere. School inspections and the activities of school inspectors are given as examples of how this works in

Belarus. The group is convinced that school inspectors for the most part are ambitious in trying to be objective. Also, for the most part, inspectors are neither friends nor enemies of any particular school, so from a certain angle the group can agree that the system of school inspection is set up pretty well. However, the combined experience of the group is also that inspectors for the most part simply do not understand the realities of life and work in the school system. Although they are professional and knowledgeable, they lack the specific experience and understanding that would permit them to look up from their documents and indicators to see the real world of education.

Recent Belorussian reforms aimed at increasing competition between schools have exacerbated the problem. The group goes on to give examples of how various forms of testing and the bases for comparison between schools are of dubious nature, how manipulation of national tests is an easy thing to do and how, as a result, national curricula are advanced on the basis of false information. Thus, in conclusion, the answer to the question about what the group participants would have liked to add to the Profile points to some of the systemic characteristics in Belorussian education. This particularly concerns the post-Soviet nature of education administration and evaluation, which is why the group constantly returns to their perceived need for methodological clarification and development.

In answer to if and how their view of the concept of knowledge has changed, the group wants to focus on the terms competencies and competence learning. They submit that school in Belarus for the most part is about learning facts and testing fact retention among pupils. Adding to that, they lament the fact that children in Belarus are laden with such heavy curricula and have so much learning by heart to do, that it is becoming a national health problem. "Our students never read novels, since they are not allowed to in school and are too tired to do it at home!" Another reinforced this point; "It is all papers, papers, and control!" At this juncture, the discussion gets very emotional and the general consensus is that teachers today feel sorry for the kids at school. For the most part, teachers are required to pump out facts and figures while regarding pupils as empty vessels to be filled with factual knowledge. Importantly, this methodology is underpinned by control mechanisms from the top and competitive evaluations. The group agrees that it is interesting how Soviet-style control mechanisms and ideas about learning have not only survived but, interestingly, been integrated with ideas about school autonomy and competition.

The combination of Soviet-style administration and control on the one hand, and autonomous competition on the other is lethal, according to the group. This is why they feel that every teacher in Belarus is currently fighting a battle uphill for a more individualizing and competence based view of education. Teachers, they say, know about how competence thinking is necessary in education. They can all more or less feel it after a few years on the job. "Facts belong to the worlds of religion and politics," says one participant in the group half-jokingly, and receives nods and smiles from the others. For the record, however, the group wishes to clarify that they think that their own sentiments on this issue are shared by the majority of teachers and a lot of school administrators in Belarus. Teachers, and by extension pupils, are forced to work according to curricula that completely substitute reflection and perspectives for quantities of fact retention. The group participants are sad to have to agree that school curricula in Belarus today are simply too massive for either pupils or teachers to find the time to pause and reflect upon what it is they are learning, how, and why.

Ultimately, the group reached a consensus on the overall positive impact of the Profile. It is agreed that both as an academic experience and as a source of new ideas and fresh thinking about education and school leadership in Belarus, the Profile has made a lot of difference. Eight years in retrospect, the group participants also see how it has impacted their individual career choices and the ways in which they go about practical work in education. The group is still wary of the many problems and pitfalls that remaining in post-Soviet politics and administration in Belarus. After all, they think that opportunities for international cooperation in a practical sense, as in the case of the Profile, aimed at concrete leadership and teaching tools and a joint publication, are few and far between for Belorussian educators. Despite this generally gloomy outlook on world and European affairs, however, they wish to emphasize that individuals and small groups can make a difference and how they feel that this is what they have been doing in Belorussian education for a number of years now. By way of conclusion, they wish to send a message to educators in other countries not to invest too much confidence in rigorous competition and control models, regardless of whether these are cloaked in pluralistic parlance, or not. It is, they say, the safest route to losing democracy.

Lessons Learned About School Leadership Development From the Western Assistance Programs in Belarus

Instead of drawing out some conclusions we would like to finish this chapter with reflections in the form of 10 reflection points from our different experiences. Our first reflection is that at the core of the all the activities stands a person, Dr. Zagoumennov from Minsk.

- A champion or champions within the country where technical assistance is being provided greatly facilitates efforts and supports continuity of interventions over time.
- Democratically determined, mutually agreed upon technical assistance goals between the Western providers and the recipients enhances the acceptability and implementation of those goals.
- Educator exchange and participation in Western grant programs that focused on school leadership development brought prestige and resources to the participants that allowed them to become more influential in their schools or institutions.
- Educator exchange and participation in Western programs created new visions about what democratic school leadership could be.
- Participation in international conferences led to new contacts that often led to the next technical assistance program.
- Successful initial technical assistance efforts focused on exposing participants to and providing them with Western literature on school leadership development.
- A second type of successful initial technical assistance effort focused on providing participants with access to the world-wide web in order to facilitate contact with Western experts and to keep abreast of new developments in democratic school leadership initiatives.
- Programs where democratic teaching and leadership techniques were modeled by Western experts provided behavior examples of the types of interventions to be emulated.
- School leadership in Belarus moved from knowledge-based education towards competency-based education and developed new school accreditation standards based international models, e.g. the Bologna and PISA standards for graduation and achievement respectively.
- Developing an internal network of like-minded supporters for democratic school reform efforts within Belarus provided for continuity of intervention efforts.

Finally, to be active in projects like these described above also gives back a lot to the Western experts. We have to think one more time about things we take for granted when they shall be explained and argued for as parts of something that can be called best practice.

NOTES

1. http://en.wikipedia.org/wiki/Mikhail_Gorbachev#Political_career

2. http://www.bologna-bergen2005.no/Docs/00-Main_doc/
    050221_ENQA_report.pdf
3. http://www.pisa.oecd.org/document/2/
    0,3343,en_32252351_32236191_39718850_1_1_1_1,00.html

REFERENCES

Repa, J. T. (1992a). *Organization of education in the United States.* Minsk, Belarus. The Republican Institute for Upgrading Teachers of the Ministry of Education of the Republic of Belarus.

Repa, J. T. (1992b). *Supervision of Teachers in the United States.* Minsk, Belarus: The Republican Institute for Upgrading Teachers of the Ministry of Education of the Republic of Belarus.

Repa, J. T. (1996a, May). *School transformation administrative preparation: An integration of a Belarus and United States models.* Belarus Institute of Educational Administration Conference, Minsk, Belarus.

Repa, J. T. (1996b). School transformational leadership: A comparison of Belarus and United States models. In Ministry of Education (Eds.), *New technology in systems of continuous education* (Vol. 3, p. 606). Minsk: Republic of Belarus.

Johansson, O., & Begley, P. T. (2001). *School leaders development in Belarus: In search of a new model.* Umeå, Sweden: Centre for Principal Development, Umeå University.

Johansson, O., & Begley, P. T. (2003). *School leadership in Belarus.* Umeå, Sweden: Centre for Principal Development, Umeå University.

CHAPTER 14

RIDING THE WAVES

Educators, Leaders, and Intercultural Practices in Overseas Schools

Elizabeth Murakami Ramalho and Jill Sperandio

INTRODUCTION

The fast pace of change to a global economy and a technologically interlinked world demands responsive leadership for P–12 schools everywhere. Educators and administrators find themselves challenged to evaluate these changes in contemporary world systems and to facilitate the preparation of students who are able to exist and thrive in situations demanding intercultural understanding and a global mind-set. Although these challenges exist for school leaders, educators, and students in national school systems everywhere, they are particularly acute for the growing number of educators and students in international schools worldwide.

In this study we examined two distinct and incremental stages in the transformational process from monocultural to intercultural educator:

Leadership and Intercultural Dynamics, pp. 279–296
Copyright © 2009 by Information Age Publishing
All rights of reproduction in any form reserved.

- the initial process when the educator lives and works abroad, in a new culture, leading him or her to become more internationally minded and interculturally competent,
- a second process when the educator's personal transformation translates into professional practice, especially when focused on helping students become international thinkers and global citizens.

It is also important to consider that most educational leaders begin their careers as teachers before taking on administrative roles. Therefore, many of the examples in this study reflect not only these educators' development, but also a continuum from teacher to administrator. The transformational process that occurs through intercultural exposure and development is the unit of analysis in this chapter. In this way, we hope to contribute to an understanding of the challenges facing educators who do not have the opportunity to undergo this transformation process by living abroad, yet must still find ways to develop a similar outcome of international mindedness in students with whom they share a common culture. A better appreciation of the factors encouraging and discouraging the identity-transformation process necessary to successfully live, work, and learn in foreign or multicultural environments may lead to the structuring of more realistic learning experiences for those who must gain international mindedness without leaving their home communities.

This chapter draws on the authors' experiences as international educators and administrators, in addition to data from a study of aspects of leadership in American international schools (Murakami Ramalho, 2005, 2008). We begin with a review of current discourse about preparing students for living in pluralistic societies, especially in the United States where we are presently preparing educators and school leaders. We consider the proliferation of international schools and the varying perceptions of their goals with respect to preparing internationally-minded and globally competent students, and the challenges these perceptions present to expatriate educators working in such schools. Using reflective data gathered from international school educators, we describe their perceptions of their personal transformations and the complex scenarios involving intercultural interactions that must be negotiated in international school settings. We conclude with a discussion of the ways in which international school experiences can help national schools that are struggling to implement intercultural practices.

Educating for Assimilation or Integration?

The corporate workplace, especially in the United States, places a high value on diversity training and intercultural exchange programs, yet schools in general seem to offer only ancillary opportunities for students to develop intercultural and interpersonal skills. Such disregard for multicultural or intercultural issues in U.S. schools originates from the historical perception that being culturally different equates with "deviancy," "pathology," or "inferiority" (Banks & McGee Banks, 2004; Nieto, 2004; Sue, Arredondo, & McDavis, 1992). Notions of cultural deficiency have permeated schools and perpetuated the idea that racial and ethnic minorities do not possess "the right culture," resulting in harmful practices in the preparation of both students and educators (Delpit, 1995; Dodd & Konzal, 2002; Giroux, 1995; Ladson-Billings, 1994; Valencia, 1991; Valenzuela, 1999).

Instead of valuing international and intercultural relations in schools, educators traditionally have been trained to convert students' international and intercultural social and cultural capital to monoculturalism, perceiving students with intercultural baggage as deficient and in need of "special education" unless they are learning a foreign language. Nowadays, educators are pressed to reexamine monoculturalism as a form of "maladjustment in a pluralistic society" (Szapocznik, Santisteban, Durtines, Perez-Vidal, & Hervis, 1983). So, how can educators and educational leaders shift from culturally deficient models and capitalize on students' social and cultural capital for a world that is increasingly pluralistic?

Some people may resist the idea of internationalism, yet provincialism is a deterrent to the advancement of intercultural practices. In countries like the United States, for example, focusing on the word *international* is problematic. Because the word *international* can convey a variety of meanings, from exotic to adventurous, it has numerous and controversial perspectives (Knight, 2004; Touraine, 2000). *International,* or internationalism as a movement, is defined by ideas of agreement, support, and cooperation (Liebeck & Pollard, 1994). However, the word also seems to generate ideas of differentiating the local from the foreign when people believe that international stands in opposition to national. *Internationalism* then conveys controversial overtones when used as a contrast to *nationalism,* which carries the idea of patriotism, a concept that favors resistance to external control because individuals might feel threatened when connecting ideas of outsiders and the nation. In such cases, internationalism ceases to have a supportive and collaborative tone, and begins to revolve around a political or nation-state tension. We are inclined to draw a line separating *us* from *others,* positioning ourselves on the local side of the line and placing everyone or everything else that is *different* on the international side.

Globalization may be seen as less meaningful in rural or less cosmopolitan areas, where modernization is still perceived as questionable, threatening nationalism and citizen loyalties (Burbules & Torres, 2000; Burbules, 2002). The danger of drawing a dividing line between national and international ideas in this case is that we are determining *who* and *what* should be considered when preparing students as citizens. By sorting out what counts, there is a risk of assuming that there is little to learn from exogenous knowledge. When making such a determination, we begin to create distinctive cognitive frames in which the line delineating *who* or *what* counts becomes discriminatory and endogenous.

In urban areas, people may be more exposed to the promise that globalization can generate a more prosperous and egalitarian world through education. In urban settings, the frequent presence of international visitors and the apparent success of cross-national negotiations are reminders that efforts to internationalize education provide students a positive opportunity for modernization through knowledge acquisition. Thus, education mirrors cosmopolitan movements, in which "education mirrors society in the sense that social change generates educational change" (Anderson, as cited in White, 1999, p. 168).

Nonetheless, students and their families are becoming increasingly international. Families are more mobile as a result of a global economy in which workers are often required to relocate abroad. Such mobility across nations expands rapidly as businesses branch out to different countries. Being prepared for international issues and intercultural relations is deemed a necessary skill for current and upcoming generations of students, those who prepare them, and especially educational leaders. Such preparation has important implications for the personal mind-sets and professional development of those who lead and teach students.

Intercultural dynamics contribute to preparing students for integration instead of assimilation. Intercultural or culturally sensitive pedagogy begins with an inclusive agenda, such as recognizing the mobility of people around the globe, and the need to be prepared to function in sociopolitical and economic transactions. In educational leadership, culturally sensitive studies increasingly are considered to make a significant contribution to the field (Greenfield, 1995; Hallinger & Leithwood, 1996; Heck, 1998), especially in the preparation of future citizens. Intercultural issues are especially important when considering the societal culture as the source of the values that shape the goals for the educational system (Hallinger & Leithwood, 1996). If the societal culture is becoming more diverse, our practices as educators and educational leaders then shift with regard to the way education is delivered. Educational leaders can improve diversity practices in schools by continuing to examine educational policies and practices

(Black & Mendenhall, 1990) that might hinder the preparation of students as citizens in a globalized society.

In the next section we explore the opportunities selected educators and administrators experienced while working in international schools as a means of understanding the ways in which intercultural development started from a shift in perspective—from local to global—in the way these educators perceived the world and applied these learning to their own educational craft. The fast pace at which these educators had to interpret and adapt information carried an added pedagogical value: From teaching in diverse contexts, to serving families in international settings, these educators and leaders recognized that "it's diversity that makes us strong."

International Opportunities for Educators and Leaders

Despite concerns about provincialism in educating students for a pluralistic society, a remarkable movement is occurring around the globe. Many international schools have been established in different countries. International School Services (2007), a nonprofit corporation providing educational services for international schools lists services in schools located in approximately 154 different countries. The United States Department of State Office of Overseas Schools alone lists 194 sponsored schools in 135 countries spread over all continents.

International schools include missionary or church-related schools, proprietary schools (day and boarding units), company schools (owned by large corporate entities doing business in remote areas of the world), not-for-profit schools (established by multinational groups and entities such as the United Nations), and, in the case of the United States, Department of Defense Dependents Schools (Vogel, 1992). A significant number of students and their families seek P–12 schools offering transferability of academic credits back to their home countries or from one country to another (Blanford & Shaw, 2001). Ownership and policy control can be local or organized by associations of parents of the children enrolled (U.S. Department of State, Office of Overseas Schools, 2007).

Even though international schools are perceived as interesting places to observe the intercultural preparation of students and educators, the proliferation of international schools has also generated debate across host nations. Host-country governments question whether international schools promote or hinder local cultural values. A few international schools promote solely American cultural values and isolate themselves from the host country's culture. Some countries then question whether these schools might be "diluting" the local children's culture, consequently disconnecting them from their national culture and values. This situation is perceived as detracting from the students' cultural and social capital, especially for local students who may be interested in acquiring an international education.

Korea, provides an appropriate example. The Korean government allows only those students who have foreign passports or have been educated abroad to attend international schools. Nonetheless, many Korean families express an interest in having their children attend international schools because of the perceived advantages this provides to their children's future education and careers. Despite local controversy, a recognized educational movement is under way, with the purpose of serving numerous families in intercultural transitions. These intercultural controversies are, in fact, valuable lessons for educators serving in intercultural contexts.

Educators Serving International Schools

Educators and educational leaders undergo a two-stage transformational process in their first year in an international school:

- the first stage when they define their identity in a foreign land (Who am I?)
- the second stage when they define their identity in a collective sense in relation to the school's identity in the international setting (Who are we?).

The first stage is more private and relates to the educators' initial years in a new culture abroad, which we identify as the process of becoming more "internationally" minded. The second stage is more public and relates to how the educators' personal transformation translates into new practice.

The educators' learning curve ranges from things to people, from getting acquainted with the new place where they are living and with the school facilities and community surroundings, to learning about the multiple roles educators must play (Mathews & Crow, 2003). Experiences once considered ordinary are now challenged and may be stressful, like getting groceries or asking for directions. In schools, the primary expectation is to have educators exemplify the best of American education abroad. However, educators often are challenged by the dichotomy of a somewhat familiar school setting, and simultaneous immersion in a not-so-familiar society. Adaptation to a new country requires that educators develop an understanding of what it means to live in and be part of an international setting. In their first year, educators who are neophytes in international settings must also become acquainted with the diverse school cultures.

Arguably, educators who choose to live and work outside the United States are ready to make necessary adaptations because living overseas was their choice. However, the transition requires that educators adapt rather quickly. Bennett (1986) suggested that there is significant growth when people become more culturally aware of experiences they once considered ordinary. The adaptation then involves reexamining one's values and habits and adapting them to the new milieu. Bennett claimed that this awareness is the first step in perceiving similarities across cultures, instead of focusing on differences.

The second and most important stage of the transformational process involves how the educators' personal transformation translates into new practice. A transformation occurs in educators' experiences between when they start as teachers and later become administrators. Educational leaders in international schools in many cases ascend from years of teaching experience in international settings, and may already have experienced the initial transformational phase. These educational leaders can therefore mentor and facilitate the progressive immersion of teachers who are neophytes to the new environment.

A number of intercultural challenges arise in the experiences of first-time school administrators (Alvy & Robbins, 1998; Daresh & Playko, 1997; Walker, Anderson, Sackney, & Woolf, 2003) as their umbrella of responsibilities unfolds (Lovely, 1999; Ubben & Hughes, 1997). Educational leaders, along with the teachers, are continuously challenged to revisit theories of action (Argyris & Schön, 1974), challenging inconsistencies between espoused theories, worldviews, and values that guide our behavior and theories-in-use worldviews and values that guide our actions. As Argyris and Schön posited, there is a disconnection between what we believe and what we do.

As educators and leaders are responsible for delivering quality education, at the same time, they are being challenged to revisit their beliefs during their assignments in international schools. They are pressed to adopt new practices that translate into the preparation of students as international/global citizens. For example, in our home countries, *international* may mean someone or something that originates anywhere but our home, our place. However, what happens when we move to another country? Will the new place still be international? Have we now become international ourselves? In the next section we provide individual and professional transformative processes of educators and educational leaders in international schools to examine how these transformative processes translate into intercultural practices.

Waves of Intercultural Transformation

In this study, we considered two distinct and incremental stages in the educators' intercultural transformation:

- the educators' initial years abroad working in a new culture, which led to their becoming more *internationally minded,*
- when this personal transformation translated into professional practice.

In this section we exemplify some of these stages with scenarios that reflect educators' and educational leaders' growing awareness of commonalities and differences among the different cultures to which they were exposed, including dilemmas and ethical issues involved in the intercultural transformation. Finally, we give examples of how the educators leaders incorporated these experiences into practice. The scenarios include experiences from a number of expatriate educators and educational leaders (names and locations masked) from different countries, and serving in different capacities. These educators had between 1 and 10 or more years of experience in international schools and included both educators we personally worked with during our experiences overseas and participants in research studies.

Growing Awareness of Commonalities and Differences

"Do you mean I am now an international, too?" asked a newly arrived teacher. By challenging old assumptions, this teacher seemed to have reframed her perspective now that she was removed from her own country. According to Bennett (1986), one's cultural understanding grows from his or her perception of cultural differences; from defensive to adaptative to integrative. In their new setting abroad, educators and educational leaders adjust to previously set paradigms. Adjusting to cultural differences often involves compromises. The need to compromise and the difficulties involved in doing so further prepare educators to develop intercultural practices. In fact, the challenge of personally negotiating previously held assumptions and biases and confronting *uncomfortable* situations is one of the most valuable assets acquired in developing culturally sensitive practices.

An interesting arena that brings to the fore cultural clashes in international schools is sports, and middle school principal, Terry Smith, attested to that. Mr. Smith was faced with a dispute between Latin American and Scandinavian middle school students. There had been constant fights on the football field. During the games, Scandinavian parents could be seen telling their children not to let themselves be goaded into fights and to get a school official or an adult to settle any differences. On the other hand, Latin American fathers were telling their sons that if there was a dispute, the children should settle it themselves—by force, if necessary. The fathers would tell their sons that they must always hit back, and if they did not, they (the fathers) would hit them (their sons), even though school policies made it clear that fighting would result in school suspension.

Mr. Smith quickly learned that finding the middle ground between diametrically opposed cultural paradigms was difficult but highly significant to his leadership. He learned that there was no right or wrong in the parents' attitudes when considering intercultural paradigms enabled Mr. Smith to explain to both groups of parents that they would probably be right in their respective countries. However, in the school, Mr. Smith needed not only to remind parents about the school policies, but also to find a compromise between the parents' perspectives, negotiating an acceptable middle way.

Headmaster Harry Weiland faced yet another challenge at one of the Dutch international schools in The Netherlands. Locally hired colleagues and teachers are protected by strong national labor laws that do not require them to conduct any after-school activities. However, in some international schools, sports are a significant part of student life. These schools recognize the benefit of intramural activities, especially for children experiencing high mobility and relative isolation from their extended families.

Netherlands' children usually go to community centers for sports. However, many international groups in Mr. Weiland's school—Koreans, Turks, and Japanese—had no access to the activities organized by local Dutch community centers. Mr. Weiland's negotiation involved asking teachers to reconsider the labor laws in order to introduce sports to the entire school community. If educators and educational leaders are not ready to compromise, they may not be fully prepared to help parents and students adjust to different rules and how they apply in various places. How can educators develop an understanding that different students and their families bring with them different social constructions?

As educators and educational leaders grow more comfortable with international schools and the new countries in which they are living, their cultural paradigms are challenged to incorporate pluralistic values. Bennett (1986) explained the process of transformation into pluralistic values: Characteristic of all pluralism is the internalization by one individual of two or more fairly complete cultural frames of reference. Because people at this stage are "identified" with the different world views, they simply experience cultural difference as part of their normal selves. The question of "respect for difference" that was a major factor in earlier stages here becomes synonymous with "respect for self." (p. 55)

Once educators and educational leaders became more comfortable with the new environment, they perceived that the parameters of their individual realities were challenged. An administrator at one of the American schools located in the Middle East was driving around the city and stopped to observe some youths in a school yard playing basketball. It occurred to him that he had never actually been in a local school, so he decided to stop and pay a visit. The local school administrator welcomed him, showed him around, and then, later in the office, told him how glad he was to have an American visit the school. He said he felt tremendous guilt about the September 11 event; he had been at his office when he learned about the collapse of The Twin Towers. He could still remember the horror of watching people leaping from the building, and thinking how terrible that someone could have committed such a crime. The local school administrator shared that there had been no one with whom he could share his sympathy. The American was very touched by the experience and the genuine show of emotion from such an unexpected quarter.

Ethical Considerations and Dilemmas

International schools have been recognized as promoting "unity in diversity" (Hayden & Thompson, 1996). However, students, parents, and educators also experience intercultural clashes, as evidenced by Mr. Smith's and Headmaster Weiland's experiences presented above. These clashes have a high value in the incremental acquisition of intercultural values. Ethical considerations are a significant part of this process, and once incorporated in educators' and educational leaders' considerations, these may be carried over into professional practices, as exemplified below.

New teachers and administrators in a school in Southern Asia had an opportunity to discuss the way the cleaning staff were treated. In that particular country, a local class/caste system was part of the societal behavior. Was it acceptable to see local teachers and local students treat these employees in a way that would be perceived as mistreatment in Western cultures? What international school teachers and administrators perceived as an ethic of care and respect for all people, regardless of their jobs, would be challenged by the local students, parents, and teachers as showing disrespect for their culture.

Many school administrators in international schools also wrestle with the unequal payment policies between internationally and locally hired teachers (Hardman, 2001). The local teachers are usually well qualified (U.S. Department of State, 2003), but they do not receive the same salaries as internationally hired teachers. Even though the academic preparation of internationally hired teachers may be similar to that of some locally hired teachers, local teachers are paid less for doing essentially the same job as their expatriate counterparts, even when the former have more years of experience. This practice has been perceived as perpetuating inequalities in the workplace, intensifying cultural tensions, and intercultural clashes among teachers who often are teaching the same discipline next to each other, with the same load. Local staff members often are satisfied with their salaries because they usually are much better paid than they would be in local schools, but evidently there is tension about salary disparities within the schools. In addition, the international teachers often might not want to acknowledge that local teachers have the same degree of excellence as they do, but at the same time they feel uncomfortable when they feel that the school is exploiting local staff.

Some of these examples do not provide a sense of justice having been served. However, the scenarios share the notion that ethical considerations are culturally sensitive and context specific. Intercultural clashes can occur from the moment one attempts to shake someone's hand when the protocol is to bow and never touch the other person. By being exposed to different points of view, international educators acquire intercultural awareness. Especially for educational leaders, ethical considerations are paramount as they establish the organization's culture. For example, most international schools develop interactions with local communities through social service projects. The goal of such projects is to promote connections with the local community. How can educators and leaders use these opportunities to prepare students for rich intercultural exchanges?

Power and privilege are a dangerous combination when devoid of culturally sensitive practices. Bialakowsky (2002) said that our traditional way of looking at society from a single legitimate side that we, in hegemonic societies, identify as the "us" may be caustic if educational leaders choose to educate for assimilation, instead of for integration. As Strike and Ternasky (1993) affirmed, "Nothing erodes community more quickly than a pervasive feeling that an organization is routinely unfair" (p. 4). Therefore, a concern for professional ethics as immersed in culture and politics (Giroux, 1992) is a significant aspect of school life that educators and educational leaders need to instill to encourage the healthy participation of all stakeholders.

Incorporating Intercultural Practices

As educators' perspectives change in relation to commonalities and differences in international values, their new environments motivate them to adopt new practices. In fact, Dewey (1938/1963) declared that experience does not occur in a vacuum and that "there are sources outside an individual which give rise to experience" (p. 39). However, these experiences seem to turn into meaningful lessons only when educators incorporate them into their personal and professional practices. Cole and Wertsch (2004) recognized connections between bio-sociocultural processes and human development. Educators at this point would recognize that their new experiences have transformed them. As one of the teachers in this study highlighted, "I would probably be more of a foreigner in my own country if I moved back to my hometown in Ohio." Building a bridge between reframing old assumptions and including newly constructed notions seemed to represent a large part of the educators' adaptation to the international environment.

The importance of focusing on similarities instead of differences, or the concepts of "us" and "other," was one of the highlights included in this chapter. One of the educators in a larger study of organizational dynamics in international schools (Murakami, 2008) indicated the need to focus on similarities as "the need to learn to exist with one another, where barriers of differences begin to drop and commonalities have to be brought into alignment" (p. 92). Bennett (1986) indicated that focusing on similarities results in the advancement of individuals from the minimization of differences toward an acceptance stage in the development of culturally sensitive behavior. The acceptance stage is, according to Bennett, "the first step toward ethnorelativism, or the assumption that cultures can only be understood relative to one another" (p. 46). Acceptance depends on respect for differences and an acknowledgment that one's world view is but a relative cultural construct.

Maria Westbrook, an elementary teacher in an international school in Asia, suggested that "Teachers need to look beyond the subject being taught and relate to other people—and come out of their bubbles. Students can learn so much from the interaction with others, but unfortunately many schools do not back that up." Assistant principal Jerry Gonzales, working in Eastern Europe, illustrated his learning and growing process:

> You're plucked out of your world, and we are all dropped into this place. We have the choice to learn from one another and make the world a better place or just put it aside and ignore it. The sense of security of different nationalities being together forces the door open, and we have to relate to one another in building a relationship because those who don't relate don't survive here, and they don't stay here for long. So you are in a world inside a world, kind of thing, and the interrelationships that you develop in here can make you grow so much. I think you give and take with one another, more like a huge family, and that's the beauty of a system like this.

Maria's approach was to link and acknowledge who everyone is (including herself) on a daily basis and not try to ignore commonalities and differences, or treat the students like they are something else or something different. She affirmed, "Because I have this diversity I use it as a motivation to prepare students as lovers of learning." In addition, Mr. Gonzales said that when he stepped out of the classroom to serve in an administrative capacity, his focus included mentoring teachers and parents through intercultural matters. He linked the intercultural responsibility to the obligation of schools to provide a sense of safety to staff, faculty, parents, and the community-at-large:

> If I should talk about diversity and the power of walking in the hallways here, where five or six different languages are being simultaneously exchanged ... the power of us looking through all of that to a common direction and goal has been just a sense of personal empowerment, that my beliefs did align with what needs to be done for every child.

Mr. Gonzales also reflected on his experiences as a teacher back in the United States. His perception was that highlighting diversity based on language in his previous job was seen as weakening the fabric of the local culture. This fear in U.S. schools, he stated, "makes educators afraid that students are not able to participate in the school system until they become more English proficient, giving reason to xenophobic attitudes."

Unarguably, first-hand experience in an intercultural setting seems to make a difference in terms of influencing practice. Many of the educators and educational leaders in this study seemed to start with their own growth—an understanding of "how" one becomes international—followed by several episodes that challenged their local social constructions and invited an internationally minded paradigm. Educators in international schools seemed to more frequently recognize students for "who they are" when they were also able to identify themselves with the students, which in this case included the country of origin and identity issues.

DISCUSSION

Intercultural transformation was perceived as being developed through waves of different interactions. Intercultural understanding seems to be gained in the initial years in which educators join international schools. While living in an international community, teachers get a sense of the rhythm of life for educators and educational leaders living abroad, and experience the interactions among people of different cultures. With time, those interactions become part of a society based on "unity-in-difference" (Giroux, 1995), one that values unity and respects differences. When this all becomes second nature, educators and educational leaders develop the confidence to embrace a wider repertoire of intercultural patterns with which to carry out their roles. The more cultures with which they become familiar, the more quickly educators and leaders can adjust. In so doing, they develop a much wider range of intercultural patterns that seem "normal" or "ordinary" rather than different.

Developing intercultural relations will always include a degree of discomfort. Here's a final example: An international school administrator related the story of a teenager from the Southern part of the United States whose parents reluctantly enrolled her in an international school in Azerbaijan whose students came mainly from the mid-Western United States and the United Kingdom. Her parents were employed in the oil industry, and this was her first experience living outside the United States. This student was horrified by what she considered an alien (Azeri) culture, and she had difficulty relating to the cultures of her peer group at the school. The girl was a skilled guitar player, and in an attempt to help her adjust to the school, the Azeri music teacher encouraged her to write a song about her feelings and unhappiness. The teacher thought this would be a form of therapy for the girl, and would also gain her peers' appreciation for her music skills. The girl did indeed write the song and, clearly pleased with the result, performed it for the teacher and her Azeri colleague. In the song the girl criticized the local custom of gold-plating one's teeth seen as an attractive feature in the society. Her reference to this custom proved very upsetting for the Azeri teacher, who scolded the teenager for being demeaning and demanded that the song be changed immediately. The incident left the teenager, the music teacher, and the Azeri staff upset and confused. It demonstrated to the administrator that teaching the local culture was not enough; both students and teachers often learn lessons in cultural sensitivity the hard way.

For those questioning how educators can become inclusive in their practices without living abroad, we considered that one of the significant lessons provided by these scenarios is the acknowledgment that most intercultural experiences do not provide closure. Feeling uncomfortable with unresolved situations is the norm, and a mid-way resolution often might involve feelings of only partial accomplishment. Nonetheless, these unresolved feelings as they are negotiated at a personal level are the ones that will be conducive to the development of best intercultural practices. In addition, ethical considerations were deemed significant in the development of new intercultural practices because we are invited to revisit and analyze our own practices that may contain monocultural or xenophobic ideas.

We questioned whether intercultural sensitivity can be achieved only when educators and educational leaders experience the same cultural challenges as do their students. When educators identified themselves as being international, they were able to relate to the students' experiences of discrimination. The challenge then becomes helping students in international schools to gain this sensitivity too, even when parents expect international schools to promote only "Western" culture and values. Educators and educational leaders then must learn rapidly about intercultural sensitive practices, a situation not dissimilar to that of principals in multi-ethnic schools in the States.

Can lessons from international schools inform other schools in the implementation of inclusive practices? We considered provincialism to be one of the deterrents to the advancement of inclusive practices. Until we determine whether education should indeed be provided to every child, the implementation of inclusive practices will be challenged by parents, teachers, and educational leaders. In reality, many children, including immigrants, migrants, first-generation students, students of color, and students connected to poverty, currently are considered not deserving of quality education. Abandoning deficiency models that consider who does not deserve education is of utmost significance in creating inclusive practices and preparing students for a successful future.

By observing the inclusive perspectives of educators practicing internationally, we were able to recognize the deep knowledge these educators and educational leaders had developed. The experience was changing educators living overseas from looking at differences from the standpoint of "Oh … you are different" to "Wow! You are different." This does not mean, however, that the opportunity to teach abroad is the key factor in educators' becoming interculturally sensitive. It may mean, though, that inclusive practices are woven into the day-to-day routines of international schools. Educators' and educational leaders' perceptions of intercultural issues seemed to develop through new perceptions of leadership for diversity. Reflecting on her experience, Maria noted:

> When you tune in CNN and you're sitting at home, it doesn't seem real. It seems surreal because it's happening out there. Now, I am "out there," and I am learning to exist with other cultures. How many times can we sit down and talk with an Angolean child about what's happening in their world, and later that day visit a Saudi Arabian student's family for dinner and experience no alcohol and women that won't touch you when you want to shake their hand?

As the scenarios in this chapter illustrated, the preparation of educators as world citizens may take an awareness of self, a personal transformation from old realities and ethical considerations and, most important, intercultural and pedagogical training. In addition, educators may need to become interested in intercultural issues even when there is no opportunity to travel abroad, in order to effectively and affectively exercise leading and teaching toward diversity. It seems significant, then, to ensure that schools address marginality and social exclusion in their personal, empirical, and epistemological character in order to prevent students' disengagement and lack of aspirations as contributing citizens. A commonality of purpose is needed to prepare educators and educational leaders to become interculturally-minded in order to, in turn, prepare students as citizens to be part of the refinement and enlightenment of future societies.

REFERENCES

Alvy, H., & Robbins, P. (1998). *If I only knew ... success strategies for navigating the principalship*. Thousand Oaks, CA: Corwin.

Argyris, C., & Schön, D. (1974). *Theory in practice: Increasing professional effectiveness*. San Francisco: Jossey-Bass.

Banks, J. A., & McGee Banks, C. A. (Eds.). (2004). *Handbook Of Research On Multicultural Education* (2nd ed.). San Francisco: Jossey-Bass.

Bennett, M. J. (1986). Towards ethnorelativism: A developmental model of intercultural sensitivity. In M. Paige (Ed.), *Cross cultural orientation* (pp. 27–69). Blue Ridge Summit, PA: University Press of America.

Bialakowsky, A. L. (2002). *Marginalization and exclusion: The hemisphere's number one problem. The challenge of the social, educational and health policies. Analysis and institutional proposals*. Toronto, Canada: York University [Online]. Retrieved from http://www.yorku.ca/robarts/archives/institute/2001/pdf/bialakowsky.pdf

Black, J. S., & Mendenhall, M. (1990). Cross-cultural training effectiveness: A review and a theoretical framework for future research. *The Academy of Management Review, 5*(1), 113–136.

Blanford, S., & Shaw, M. (2001). *Managing international schools*. New York: RoutledgeFalmer.

Burbules, N. C. (2002). The global context of educational research. In L. Bresler & A. Ardichvili (Eds.), *Research in international education: Experience, theory, and practice* (pp. 157–169). New York: Peter Lang.

Burbules, N. C., & Torres, C. A. (2000) *Globalization and education: Critical perspectives*. London: Routledge.

Cole, M., & Wertsch, J. V. (2004). Beyond the individual-social antimony in discussions of Piaget and Vygotsky. Kentucky: Vygotsky Project, Murray University. [Online]. Retrieved from http://www.massey.ac.nz/~alock/virtual/colevyg.htm

Daresh, J., & Playko. M. (1997). *Beginning the principalship: A practical guide for new school leaders*. Thousand Oaks, CA: Corwin.

Delpit, L. (1995). *Other people's children: Cultural conflict in the classroom*. New York: The New York Press.

Dewey, J. (1963). *Experience and education*. New York: Macmillan. (Original work published 1938)

Dodd, A. W., & Konzal, J. L. (2002). *How communities build stronger schools: Stories, strategies and promising practices for educating every child*. New York: Palgrave McMillan.

Giroux, H. A. (1992). Educational leadership and the crisis of democratic government. *Educational Researcher, 21*(4), 4–11.

Giroux, H. A. (1995). National identity and the politics of multiculturalism. *College Literature, 22,* 41–56.

Greenfield, W. D. (1995). Toward a theory of school administration: The centrality of leadership. *Educational Administration Quarterly, 31*(1), 61-87.

Hallinger, P., & Leithwood, K. (1996). Culture and educational administration. *Journal of Educational Administration, 34*(5), 98–116.

Hardman, J. (2001). Improving recruitment and retention of quality overseas teachers. In S. Blanford & M. Shaw (Eds.), *Managing international schools* (pp. 123–134). New York: RoutledgeFalmer.

Hayden, M. C., & Thompson, J. J. (1996). Potential difference: The driving force for international education. *International Schools Journal, 16*(1), 46–57.

Heck, R. H. (1998). Conceptual and methodological issues in investigating principal leadership across cultures. *Peabody Journal of Education, 73*(2), 51–80.

International School Services. (2007). Retrieved August, 20, 2007, from www.iss.org

Knight, J. (2004). Internationalization remodeled: Definitions, approaches, and rationales. *Journal of Studies in International Education, 8*(1), 5–31.

Ladson-Billings, G. (1994). *The dreamkeepers: Successful teachers of African American children.* San Francisco: Jossey-Bass.

Liebeck, H., & Pollard, E. (1994). *The Oxford Dictionary.* Oxford, GB: Oxford University Press.

Lovely, S. (1999). Developing leaders from within. *Trust for Educational Leadership, 29*(1), 12–13.

Mathews, L. J., & Crow, G. (2003). *Being and becoming a principal: Role conceptions for contemporary principals and assistant principals.* Needham Heights, MA: Allyn & Bacon.

Murakami Ramalho, E. (2005). *Leadership from an integrative perspective in American international schools.* Unpublished doctoral dissertation, Michigan State University.

Murakami Ramalho, E. (2008). Domestic practices in foreign lands: Lessons on leadership for diversity in American international schools. *Journal of Studies in International Education, 12*(1), 76–95.

Nieto, S. (2004). *Affirming diversity: The sociopolitical context of multicultural education* (4th ed.). New York: Pearson Education.

Strike, K. A., & Ternasky, P. L. (Eds). (1993). *Ethics for professionals in education: Perspectives for preparation and practice.* New York: Teachers College Press.

Sue, D. W., Arrendondo, P., & McDavis, R. (1992). Multicultural counseling competencies and standards: A call to the professions. *Journal of Counseling and Development, 70*(4), 477–486.

Szapocznik, J., Santisteban, D., Durtines, W., Perez-Vidal, A., & Hervis, O. L. (1983, November). *Bicultural effectiveness training: A treatment for enhancing intercultural adjustment in Cuban American families.* Paper presented at the Ethnicity, Acculturation, and Mental Health Among Hispanics Conference, Albuquerque, NM.

Touraine, A. (2000). *Can we live together? Equality and difference*. Stanford, CA: Stanford University Press.

Ubben, G., & Hughes, L. (1997). *The principal: Creative leadership for effective schools*. Needham Heights, MA: Allyn & Bacon.

U.S. Department of State, Office of Overseas Schools. (2003). *American-sponsored elementary and secondary schools overseas* (Overseas Schools Advisory Council Worldwide Fact Sheet—2003–2004). Washington, DC: Government Printing Office.

U.S. Department of State, Office of Overseas Schools. (2007). *American-sponsored elementary and secondary schools* (Overseas Schools Advisory Council Worldwide Fact Sheet—2006–2007). Accessed September 12, 2007. Retrieved from http://www.state.gov/m/a/os/1253.htm

Valencia, R. R. (1991). The plight of Chicano students: An overview of schooling conditions and outcomes. In R. R. Valencia (Ed.), *Chicano school failure and success: Research and policy agendas for the 1990's* (pp. 204–251). London: Falmer Press.

Valenzuela, A. (1999) *Subtractive schooling: U.S. Mexican youth and the politics of caring*. Albany: State University of New York Press.

Vogel, K. R. (1992). *A longitudinal study of selected characteristics of chief administrative officers in American-sponsored overseas schools*. Unpublished doctoral dissertation, University of South Carolina.

Walker, K., Anderson, K., Sackney, L., & Woolf, J. (2003). Unexpected learning by neophyte principals: Factors related to success of first year principals in schools. *Managing Global Transitions: International Research Journal, 1*(2), 195–213.

White, C. (1999) *Transforming social studies education: A critical perspective*. Springfield, IL: Charles Thomas.

CHAPTER 15

SHIFTING LANDSCAPES/ SHIFTING *LANGUE*

Qualitative Research From the In-Between[1]

Maricela Oliva

INTRODUCTION

I take the concept of *langue* as a starting point from which to begin the discussion of an alternative method for research in education, one that I call dialogic educational criticism. Use of the term *langue* is rooted, as we know, in the structuralists' development of a binary distinguishing between the necessary and available building blocks of language (*langue*) and the use of these for communication (*parole*). This understanding of *langue* as the "system of linguistic possibilities shared by a speech community at a given point in time" (Hirsch, 1971, p. 1187) assumes that the shared linguistic possibilities are finite and unambiguous. Thus, *langue* was understood in structuralism as the rules-based components of language such as grammar, syntax, phonemes, and the accepted possibilities for how these could be put together to enable communication (Eagleton,

Leadership and Intercultural Dynamics, pp. 297–323

1996; Hirsch, 1976; Ricoeur, 1979). Speech events themselves were called *parole*, these were made possible only as a result of the commonly held *langue* of language users.[2]

Given *langue* as structuralism's point of departure, "all [communicating] minds looked pretty much alike" (Eagleton, 1996, p. 95) theoretically, even when they connected to the world in widely divergent ways. Just as others have critiqued the positivist foundation of validity criteria (Garratt & Hodkinson, 1998; Lather, 1993) or the sameness of these criteria across multiple paradigms (Scheurich, 1996), it is my contention that an uncritical embracing of *langue* as a type of authoritative metadiscourse about discourse undergirds much educational research. Researchers have largely assumed that language and the meanings that it communicates have a type of reified and unambiguous concreteness. In so doing, researchers also have assumed that components of language mean the same thing and are used in the same way by individuals from different communities. Research based on this view, even much research seeking to critique and to empower, uncritically assumes a correct meaning in discourse in much the same way as *langue* is assumed to authoritatively undergird discourse. Consequently, it is quite possible and worth exploring whether, this is linked to a predominantly monolingual and trenchantly monocultural perspective within U.S. culture and society. However, it is not my aim to explore or develop that issue here; instead, my aim is to challenge and move beyond a foundation of *langue* in educational research.[3]

The research method that I propose here is necessitated by our increasing understanding in the postmodern moment (Lincoln & Denzin, 1994) that the structuralist conception of *langue* is illusory (Bruns, 1987; Clifford, 1986; Foucault, 1973). Not only is our communication about the world through language limited by our bounded rather than all-encompassing perceptual horizon, but it also is destabilized by highly differentiated experiential schemata. We know that life experiences are influenced by gender, racial, cultural, and other differences but we have not always translated this awareness into an acknowledgment that communication in parole can itself be influenced by such differences. This has implications for research in education that we have yet to fully explore. Elliot Eisner (1991) is one author whose work discusses the transactive space of research. However, he does so primarily to argue against the subject-object separation of the researcher and the researched that is valued by traditional research. He does not fully exploit the implications and possibilities for research when it is conducted from such a transactive space. I argue that doing so would situate researchers-as communicative-subjects not directly within particular cultural, linguistic, epistemic, theoretical, or research communities but rather in between them. This does not mean, however, that they end up with a view from nowhere. A positionality strategically enacted at the margins of or between communities is different and (to some) new, but it is not necessarily less valid than positionalities at the "center" of national, cultural, or discourse communities.

In this chapter, I propose a new method for qualitative research that explicitly heightens the importance of a researcher's "dwelling" in the transactive space alluded to by Eisner and others. However, it is important to note that the terms *method* and *methodology* are used from a constructivist epistemological perspective. I acknowledge, as described by Garratt and Hodkinson (1998), that individuals reading the terms from a positivist or non-constructivist perspective will find their use here ingenuous or even wrong. Nevertheless, as numerous authors already have amply demonstrated (Denzin & Lincoln, 1994; Eisner, 1991; Fish, 1980; Foucault, 1973; Gardiner, 1992; Garratt & Hodkinson, 1998; Lather, 1993; Scheurich, 1996; Smith, 1997; Wolcott, 1994), once we let go of traditional criteria for assessing research and validity, it is still possible to think with reflection and in nontraditional ways about method and validity.

What I propose is a research practice in which participants produce "meaning ... through a Third Space, which represents both the general conditions of language and the specific implication of the utterance in a performative strategy of which it cannot 'in itself' be conscious" (Bhabha, 1994, p. 36). As I discuss later, I also contend that such an approach embodies and performs a culturally Chicano way of being and knowing.

METHOD AND MEANING MAKING

The methodological considerations outlined above were prompted for me by research that I conducted on a case of North American higher education cooperation. This research involved government and higher education representatives from Mexico, Canada, and the United States. My initial goal was to determine the underlying purpose of a collaborative international group composed of representatives from three countries and then to discover the manner in which articulated goals were accomplished. I quickly determined that this initial research objective was inappropriately grounded in an assumption that a singular univocal *langue* governed the interaction (parole) of participants. That assumption was challenged by my increasing awareness of the sometimes obvious and sometimes subtle ways in which differences in culture, history, socialization, ideology, and national identity were enacted in the interaction of the participants, even when those interactions were conducted in the same (English) language. This realization was akin to the problem of the ambiguity of meaning that Eagleton (1996) posed as a hypothetical question:

> If I had a concept, fixed a verbal sign to it, and threw the whole package across to someone else, who looked at the sign and rifled through his own verbal filing system for the corresponding concept, how could I ever know that he was matching up signs and concepts in the way that I was? (p. 100)

Structuralism assumed *langue* to be just this type of a verbal filing system, one embedded with cultural, value, and other codes that made communication between speaker/writer and listener/reader something akin to matching elements of the same code. By contrast, I contend that even communication in the same language is embedded with different cultural, value, and other codes. It is my view that living and growing up in a multilingual and multicultural environment along the Texas-Mexico border contributed to providing me with this awareness. That environment then led me to acquire skills that made me aware not only of Eagleton's question but also of the need to be versed and adept in the use and transformation of multiple codes, of shifting *langue*.

Growing up in such an environment made me conversant in multiple languages and cultural codes as well as in their use. Without even thinking about it, I internalized process knowledge about how multiple codes could be concurrently in play during communication and about how a transgressive use of them could result in more creative or effective communication. At the same time, I also learned how the lack of familiarity with multiple codes and with their creative and transgressive use could lead to "communicative packages" (to use Eagleton's term) that did not successfully make it from sender to receiver.[4] When years later I sat in as an observer in international collaboration meetings, this Chicano way of knowing gave me a particular type of "enlightened eye" (Eisner, 1991) with which to take in what was happening. It caused me to listen for and attempt to identify the distinct communicative codes being used by speakers and then to recognize or "hear" when, as a result of this, communicative "meaning packages" were transformed on the path from sender to receiver. I resolved to explicitly account for this unstable *langue* in my research but soon found that methodologies tended instead to assume a unitary or coherent communicative code. I concluded that existing methodologies did not provide adequate space for working with and valuing multiple communicative codes in the way that was necessary to explicitly account for this heteroglot discursive engagement. The question for me became how, instead of privileging a particular cultural communication code or *langue*, I might allow the various codes to be and stay in play during research, at least until their representation in my own discursively situated research product.

Positionings and Frameworks

I addressed the challenges posed by the lack of an appropriate methodology by positioning myself in three distinct ways. First, I decided to posit a distinct form of "connoisseurship" (Eisner, 1991) arising from my experiences and socialization as a Mexican culture-origin person living in a border area of the United States (Anzaldúa, 1987; Bruce-Novoa, 1982; Cervantes, 1981; Chabram, 1994). That is, although Mexican by cultural tradition and American by birth and citizenship, my multilingual skills and self-described identification as a Chicana locate me in the interstices (Bhabha, 1994) of these or in between them. This positionality provides me with culturally unique skills and insights (Eisner, 1991) from which to conduct North American collaboration research that acknowledges and values the multiple discourses embedded in it.

Second, I incorporated the theoretical ideas of Mikhail M. Bakhtin (1981a, 1981b, 1981c, 1986; Crapanzano, 1995; Gardiner, 1992; Holquist, 1981, 1990; Mandelkar, 1995; Morson & Emerson, 1989) with Eisner's (1991) conceptualization of connoisseurship. Bakhtin's theoretical ideas explicitly resist the assumption of one "authoritative" discourse to allow for the existence of a plurality of voices and perspectives. This principle of polyvocality was important to this research as a strategy for resisting the national and cultural hegemony of any of the three countries (Mexico, United States, or Canada).This allowed for heteroglot, or polyvocal, perspectives on international collaboration, including my own, to be nonhierarchically accounted for and acknowledged.

Third, my experience as a participant in international collaboration meetings involving governmental, higher education, and philanthropic representatives from Mexico, the United States, and Canada provided an important warrant for engaging research in the emerging domain of North American higher education collaboration. Not only was I experienced in international collaboration work, but I was interested in conducting research on it from a particular border Chicano positionality. This last positioning was particularly important for me because my perspective and voice are not typically heard in academe. The perspectives that I bring are different in a number of ways including that I am female and Chicano,[5] the product of a particular geography (Texas) and academic preparation (Ivy League, literature); I am also multilingual in a predominantly monolingual society, have particular commitments to social justice, an ethic of care, international education), and have been socialized in a U.S.-Mexico border environment that creates an "interstitial"/"borderlands"/"third" space (Anzaldúa, 1987, p. 3; Bhabha, 1994, p. 4; Bruce-Novoa, 1982; Crapanzano, 1995; Pastor & Castañeda, 1988) that is epistemologically situated not in one country or the other, one

culture or the other, one reality or the other, but another.[6] The conver-
gence of these socializing experiences not only drew me to a study of
international cooperation but also enhanced my ability to conduct it by
providing me with multiple "stabilizing authorities" (Crapanzano, 1995)
from which to critically engage subjects, data, and my own interpretations. With this last perspective in mind and with no small amount of
trepidation, I chose to affirm my desire as a Chicana in academe "to stand
and chisel my own face" (Anzaldúa, 1987, p. 22) methodologically, choosing to "trust ... what I have built with my own hands" (Cervantes, 1981, p.
14).

Bakhtin and Dialogic Educational Criticism

Dialogic educational criticism is the method that evolved from available theory, practice, and my own experience and that I now offer here as
an alternative research approach. However, understanding dialogic educational criticism requires an awareness of several theoretical concepts
from the work of Bakhtin such as his concepts of *dialogism, zones of influence*, and *refraction*. Although these are discussed in additional detail later,
it is enough here to say that dialogism is interaction that values all the
discourses in communication. The discourses of distinct communicators
create particular zones of influence that then interact with the zones of
influence of others. Through the interaction of language (discourse's primary medium) through zones of influence, the meaning of language is
refracted in ways that bend and distort the meaning of communication
packages arising out of different zones. Although Bakhtin did not go so
far as to discuss what results from this process, I contend that something
new, an Other to all, can result from the integration and transformation
of multiple discourses. That Other parallels the Other of a Chicano positionality. For this reason, I incorporated a conceptual term, *the third*, to the
Bakhtinian concepts. As I will indicate later, *thirdness*, both as a way of
being and as an outcome, is the necessary and epistemologically Chicano
part of dialogic educational criticism.

Theoretical Concepts

In *The Dialogic Imagination* (Holquist, 1981), a presentation and discussion of his ideas, Bakhtin contrasts the concept of dialogism (polyvocality
and openness to multiple discourses) with a monologic (unitary and
closed) orientation. Bakhtin elaborates both concepts in his studies of the
novel, the genre that he preferred. He contends that although the novel
has an author, the genre's characters enact multiple "unmerged con-
sciousnesses" and a "mixture of valid voices" (as cited in Gardiner, 1992,

p. 24) that give the novel a dialogic, not monologic, discursive freedom. In describing dialogism, Bakhtin makes it clear that he is referring to more than simple communication; he is talking about the particular social relation that is existence or being in the world. Dialogism is about the "simultaneity" of "Self/Other" (Holquist, 1990, p. 19) in the moment when:

> meaning ... comes about ... as a result of the relation between two bodies occupying *simultaneous but different* space, where bodies may be thought of as ranging from the immediacy of our physical bodies, to political bodies, and to bodies of ideas in general (ideologies). (pp. 20–21, emphasis in original)

As in the "transactive" space of research (Eisner, 1991; Jansen & Peshkin, 1992), dialogic interaction transcends the traditional Self-Other dichotomy by replacing it with a historically overlapping (same time/space) relation between Self and Other. Thus, "Bakhtin's observer is also, simultaneously, an *active participant* in the relation of simultaneity. Conceiving being dialogically means that reality is always experienced, not just perceived, and further that it is experienced from a particular position" (p. 21, emphases in original). In contrast to dialogism, Bakhtin views monologic discourse as outside of the relational transactive space, as "privileged language that approaches us from without ... more akin to retelling a text in one's own words, with one's own accents, gestures, modifications" (Holquist, 1981, p. 424). At its extreme, an insular and removed monologism;

> denies the existence outside itself of another consciousness with equal rights and equal responsibilities ... manages without the other, and therefore to some degree materializes all reality. Monologue pretends to be the *ultimate word*. It closes down the represented world and represented persons. (Gardiner, 1992, p. 27, emphasis in original)

Bakhtin's position, then, is that discursive dialogism, although not the default mode of either human or literary interaction, nevertheless is to be valued and self-consciously enacted. But that can be done only by first acknowledging the unique and distinct discourses that the characters and individuals bring to their engagement with others. He writes about those distinct discourses as zones of influence that are "both a territory and a sphere of influence.... In Bakhtin's view, there are no zones belonging to no one.... There are disputed zones, but never empty ones" (Holquist, 1981, p. 434). Bakhtin's elaboration of zones of influence serves as a warrant for researchers who choose to acknowledge and value the distinct discourses at a given research site. These discourses include even the researchers' own perspectives,[7] which connect to but are distinct from the cultural, national, organizational, and actor discourses engaged there.

By describing this nonhegemonic discursive engagement as dialogism-via-zones-of-influence, Bakhtin also was able to name and describe *refraction* as the process by which multiple discourses were mutually influenced and changed. Through refraction, "a semantic 'spectral dispersion' occurs, but not *within* the object ... but [rather] before the word reaches the object, in the 'occupied territory' surrounding the object" (Holquist, 1981, p. 432, emphasis in original). Thus, for Bakhtin, words and discourses do not convey fixed meanings. Words are loaded with meanings from prior use, with those understandings that the author tries to use and with those understandings that readers bring from their experience—all of which shape the interpretation of the speech event. In this way, refraction underlines the instability and opaqueness of meaning resulting from the distortions to which words are subject on the way from author to reader or from speaker to listener.

In applying the concept of refraction to research, wider understandings of refraction can be useful. Scheurich (1994), for example, argues that "social regularities" (a type of zone of influence) shape and constrain the way in which policy issues are identified as well as the policy solutions offered in response to them. Just as Scheurich does in his policy discussion, researchers using dialogic educational criticism we can also ask what it means to acknowledge zones of influence without being inordinately limited, constrained, and captured by them.

Nevertheless, those not used to or unskilled in such a process tend to think of common understandings as a necessary prerequisite for discursive engagement. Crapanzano (1995), for example, contends that a stabilizing authority[8] or common linguistic, experiential, social, and symbolic ground to which interlocutors appeal is necessary to communicate. In his view, the lack of such a "stabilizing authority" unavoidably impedes communication, and the absence of these at discursive sites makes communicative engagement impossible. He writes, for example,

> In some extraordinary exchanges—cross-cultural exchanges before they are routinized ... or exchanges during periods of crisis or, less well understood, creative fervor—there is no mutually acknowledged Third to whom rhetorical appeal can be made. When the Third is simply an empty function, there can be no communication. (p. 140)

The view expressed here profoundly reflects our overwhelmingly taken-for-granted reliance on *langue* in our thinking about the limits and possibilities of such engagements. In real-world interactions and research, however, the theoretical assumption that a common foundation for understanding is required disregards the existence of multiple meaning-making systems and the implicitly hegemonic effect of privileging one meaning system over another. It further discounts the possibility that new language and meaning systems can be created out of discrepant languages or communication mechanisms. Not only is this something that Chicanos and multicultural groups practice routinely and about which they are unselfconsciously aware, but a Chicano lived experience, especially in explicitly border areas, has enabled many to recognize doing so as a valued and pragmatically useful way to be and to know.

This way of knowing involves the dialogic relation of two or more bodies, such as bodies of language, culture, nationhood, and sociohistorical ideologies, in what Bhabha (1994) calls a third space. This is another way of saying that in a Chicano way of knowing, meaning making occurs from the interstices of meaning systems, from a creative "third" or newly "other" space as opposed to from one or another pole of a binary interaction (Bhabha, 1994). If accounted for in research, this Chicano worldview allows researchers to think about where and how speakers' a priori stabilizing authorities (Crapanzano, 1995) engage each other in communication, regardless of whether that communication occurs in domestic or international contexts. Because the Third and the discourses made possible by/in it are, thus, implicitly created by contingently positioned, shifting, speakers and listeners, neither discourses, meaning systems, nor our own position vis-à-vis others are predetermined and they are unavoidably tenuous and unstable.

What is at the center of this way of knowing, then? Bhabha (1994) argues that from the interstices or in-between spaces such as those described here as Chicano, discourse is "performative rather than experiential" (p. 181). The moment before enunciation and the blank page before writing, for example, are prediscursive moments in which individuals must act (p. 183). The space of that disjuncture or "time lag," as Bhabha calls it, is the always-negotiated rather than predetermined space before action:

> The agency implicit in this discourse is objectified in a structure of the negotiation of meaning that is not a free-floating time lack but a time lag— a contingent tmoment—in the signification of closure.... The time lag between the event of the sign ... and its discursive eventuality ... exemplifies a process where intentionality is negotiated. (p. 183)

Dialogic educational criticism, thus, assumes that sites have multiple meaning systems embedded in them. Rather than settle a priori on the epistemological lens to be used in research, this way of knowing seeks to identify, learn, and make use of multiple discourses and meaning systems so as to resist privileging any one of them. Those can exist at group, individual, cultural, national, theoretical, goal, or other levels. Doing this is coupled with a measure of comfort about and trust that new, contingent, and jointly constructed meaning systems can emerge from the interaction of multiple discourses and that these are preferable to exogenous ones. Although some common ground is helpful, as Crapanzano (1995) right-fully asserts, dialogic educational criticism does not go so far as to assume that all communicative meaning and knowledge must be held in common to communicate and engage each other. The reason is that such an assumption could not be made without first hierarchizing the discrepant discourses and meaning systems based on a priori and implicitly hege-monic assertions of their value and usefulness. The process of doing so, as we unselfconsciously and routinely do in this country, is a process that is anathema to a Chicano way of being and knowing.

Acknowledging the existence and interaction of zones of influence in the dialogically refracting engagement of multiple discourses clearly com-plicates a research design and analysis. But it also is more likely that, in this way, the complexity of issues, variables, and contexts can be accounted for in the same way in which practitioners would account for them. One is prompted, nevertheless, to ask the validity question, that is, whether research conducted in this manner produces worthy results?

> Communication permits—indeed, demands—that shareable and non-idiosyncratic understandings and meanings be constructed through rules of grammar, syntax, and orderly formats of expression. The communication form, like all formats of communication, makes the invisible visible, repro-ducible, and memorable. (Altheide & Johnson, 1994, p. 493)

> In poststructuralist terms, the "crisis of representation" is not the end of representation but the end of pure presence.... It is not a matter of looking harder or more closely but of seeing what frames our seeing. (Lather, 1993, p. 675)

Altheide and Johnson (1994) confidently express the expectation that a common foundation of "tacit" understandings will authoritatively "press content into its shape" (p. 493) after research has been conducted. Or, to rephrase the quote, responsible researchers produce valid research results because they tap into a preexisting, if unstructured, wealth of knowledge about and conceptualizations of the world they share with those they study. Lather's (1993) quote, on the other hand, speaks to what she calls the "limit question" of research (p. 674) that marks the boundary of acceptable research practice beyond which transgressions produce nonvalid and unreliable results. Lather resists the regularizing influences imposed by such limits and by legitimated validity criteria, asking "What might open-ended and context-sensitive validity criteria look like?" (p. 674). In the method proposed here, I clearly am beyond a reliance on shared tacit understandings. Am I beyond the border that separates what is acceptable and unacceptable, what is valid and invalid, in research? Or, am I providing one of the possibly innumerable responses to Lather's and others' yearnings? This is a critical question for any new or hybrid practice.

Earlier sections of this chapter have demonstrated that traditional concepts of validity are not appropriate for or congruent with dialogic educational criticism. At the beginning, I described how a problematized confidence in common discursive meaning prompted me to turn away from a structuralist concept of *langue* as a foundation for my own research with communities of national and cultural difference. From a poststructuralist perspective, then, this discussion of validity is an effort to "imagine what kind of argument it would take to decisively convince the "other side" (Smith, 1997, p. 6) to accept the research practice proposed here. I discuss this later by describing dialogic educational criticism as a method with one new and three preexisting validity criteria that are to be applied with the method. Before doing that, and to create a context for that brief discussion, I briefly review what several researchers have said about validity.

Reconstructing Validity

Although one view of validity in qualitative research is that the concept is inappropriate and should be rejected (Wolcott, 1994) or at least reconceptualized (Garratt & Hodkinson, 1998; Lather, 1993; Scheurich, 1996), I take a less critical position for research with this method. Research conducted through dialogic educational criticism can convey important new information and images for use by researchers and practitioners. Dialogic educational criticism is *about something*, even if it now is about how the meaning of events is interpreted, about the transactive relationship created between participants and about the different points of view from which all involved speak from, act in, and interpret the world. A reasonable position vis-à-vis validity for this method, then, is to work from the view that "validity, in a broad sense, pertains to this relationship between an account and something outside of that account, whether this is something that is construed as objective reality, the constructions of actors, or a variety of other possible interpretations" (Maxwell, 1992, p. 283).

Eisner (1991, pp. 107–120), suggests three measures of validity to be used with his method: structural coroboration, consensual validation, and referential adequacy. *Structural corroboration* is similar to triangulation or the "means through which multiple types of data are related to each other to support or contradict the interpretation and evaluation of a state of affairs" (p. 110). *Consensual validation* (pp. 112–113) is agreement by competent individuals that, on one or several levels, description, interpretation, evaluation, and thematics, the educational criticism is convincing or sound. This validity claim is either bestowed by competent readers because the evidence presented is consistent with the assertions being made or inferred when two competent researchers preparing an educational criticism of the same case note similar or overlapping issues. *Referential adequacy* exists when the educational criticism of a given case, guided by the unique and exploited insight or skill of the researcher, results in "more complex and sensitive human perception and understanding"(p. 113) and when "readers are able to see what they would have missed without the critic's observations" (p. 114).

To these, I add another method-congruent criterion for dialogic educational criticism that I call *dialogic validity*. The dialogic validity criterion stems from how, following Bakhtin (1981a, 1981b, 1981c, 1986), this particular adaptation of educational criticism makes it possible to "proliferate and appreciate difference" (Scheurich, 1996, p. 58). It falls into the category that Schwandt (1997) calls non-epistemic validity, one in which:

> validity is made into something other than an epistemic criterion. Validity maybe interpreted as a criterion of good communication or dialogue; the focus shifts from whether an account is true to how the account was formed in conversation between inquirer and participants. (p. 170)

Given that dialogic educational criticism values and searches for multiple perspectives, it is appropriate to assess whether these have been surfaced, how that has been accomplished, and what it means to succeed or fail at that effort. To assess dialogic validity, two questions need to be asked by those who apply dialogic educational criticism. First, as a researcher, have I looked beyond the end-point coherence of the authoritative discourse of discursive products, both the case's and my own, to tell a story of the dialogues from which they emerge? Second, was my manner of collecting data and developing interpretations, to the extent that this requires a relationship with others, *dialogic*, that is, *open, creative, respectfully intentional* rather than *mono-logic*: *closed, power laden, predetermined*? If a researcher has not presented an artificially coherent interpretation of the research site, its data, and research findings, and if the researcher has been open, creative, and respectfully intentional in conducting a study, then the dialogic validity claim can be made.[9]

In this way, dialogic educational criticism performs a paralogic validity claim that "recognizes the multiplicity of language games and the 'temporary contract' of any consensus" (Lather, 1993, p. 679). By valuing a Chicano positionality grounded in resistance to the metadiscourse of *langue*, it also enacts a voluptuous validity "of the marginalized, unwilling to stay out of 'the center,' who ... behaves, in this moment, as though she or he has a right to lay claim to a place in the discursive spotlight" (Lubiano,

1991, p. 150, as cited in Lather, 1993, p. 682). Again, this occurs through dialogic educational criticism's positioning of the Chicano, an ethnically marginalized *other* (Parker, Villenas, & Deyle, 1998) in traditional research, as a process expert, a connoisseur (Eisner, 1991) at knowing in between.

APPLYING DIALOGIC EDUCATIONAL CRITICISM

Adding new cultural competencies does not require abandoning old ones. (Wolcott, 1994, p. 324)

The method proposed and described here is a combination of old practice and new thinking about research. What would this hybrid dialogic educational criticism method look like in practice? What attributes and circumstances of the research site compel a researcher to use such an approach? In this section, I illustrate how dialogic educational criticism was used with research on North American higher education collaboration to account for the multiple perspectives inherent in that project as well as those emerging endogenously (wholly in thirdness) from it. As argued previously, doing so notes the shifting rather than stable *langue* of dialogic and refracted discourses. Such refracted discourses either produced new stabilizing authorities through contingent and endogenous *thirds* or resulted in missed communicative "packages" (Eagleton, 1996), the latter made apparent only by paralogically "fostering heterogeneity, refusing closure" (Lather, 1993, p. 679) in a way that embraces heteroglot and multiple rather than singular or coherent communicative discourses.

The Site: A Case for Dialogic Educational Criticism

During 1992, in the throes of the political and social debate over whether to ratify the North American Free Trade Agreement (NAFTA), governmental representatives of the United States, Mexico, and Canada informally commenced a trilateral collaboration project of their own. This project brought governmental and higher education representatives together to talk about how colleges and universities in the three countries could work together on collaborative trilateral projects.

These governmental representatives laid the groundwork for the beginning of the initiative with behind-the-scenes discussions about what such a project could mean and do. Ultimately, they focused their attention on four areas of joint activity: creating a common information database to be used by educators in the three countries, addressing how the mobility of students and scholars could be enhanced in North America, discussing how the particularly unique attributes and strengths of higher education in the three countries could be optimized, and discussing and conceptualizing how unequal educational partners' national identities (United States-Mexico-Canada) could, nonetheless, be sustained to promote better mutual understanding. With foundation and limited government support, they then identified a small group of key academic leaders in the three countries to participate in meetings that would create the new initiative (Oliva, 1997). All activities of the collaboration group were informal, with implementation of project goals in the three countries depending on the use of existing structures; participants' creative management, funding, goodwill; and actors' particular discursive positionalities (Oliva, 1997).[10] Despite this, in the context of North American economic integration, interest in U.S.-Mexico and U.S.-Mexico-Canada higher education collaboration was like a viral bug in the air, and it was catching. In the United States, the Kellogg Foundation supported some activities, as did the Ford Foundation. Racine, Wisconsin, was the location of the first trilateral collaboration meeting for educators and policymakers. In individual states such as Texas and Arizona, educators prevailed on their legislatures to eliminate administrative and financial obstacles to U.S.-Mexico-Canada student exchanges.[11] In Canada, the government contracted for and convened conferences on North American identity. It also conducted a foreign policy review in which the higher education sector's capacity to work with parallel sectors in Mexico and the United States was deemed critical.

South of the United States, Mexican government officials and educators created an organization to encourage and support the development of international education administrators in that country's higher education sector. That organization (Asociación Mexicana para la Educación Internacional) and the Western Interstate Commission on Higher Education of the United States jointly developed leadership seminars to bring together higher education administrators from North America. These seminars served to create a North American network of international higher education practitioners and to "teach" higher education administrators what they needed to know to develop international or trilateral projects (Oliva, 1997).

Unstable *Langue* of Collaboration

This spreading ferment of North American higher education collaboration activity was not widely apparent to most educators at that time. Few people at the institutional level and fewer outside of these collaboration activities were aware that higher education in the three countries was being affected by these developments. However, a participant with an *enlightened* and a *reflective* eye could see, even then, that the trilateral engagement called into question the taken-for-granted communicative adequacy of language. In meetings, Mexican and U.S. Anglo participants interacted as if they were communicating from a transparent and stable foundation of *langue*, although my multilingual proficiency and multicultural being/knowing skills indicated that they were doing so without a common stabilizing authority. Furthermore, their lack of awareness of this miscommunication also meant that they did not attempt to create endogenous discourses in the trans-active third space of their interaction. A few examples illustrate how, as I participated in and otherwise researched U.S.-Mexico and U.S.-Mexico-Canada collaboration, a singular coherent positionality was problematized for me in such heteroglot interaction.

Despite the fact that participants spoke in a common language (English), this created a false confidence about their ability to communicate and understand each other. The use and misinterpretation of false cognates was one obvious way in which it became clear that parole was based on an unstable *langue*. For example, the English word *faculty* (professors) was refracted in Mexicans' understanding of the word *facultad* (professional schools) in ways that interfered with understanding. A Mexican educator might interpret an American or a Canadian statement about teaching staff (faculty) as one having to do with particular higher education organizational units (*facultades*) and vice versa.

Furthermore, when educators talked about collaboration in higher education across national and education system borders, they brought their own culturally and socially constructed understandings of higher education to the discussion. For example, Mexican participants often were unaware that U.S. and Canadian universities grounded in general education were not organized in the same way as Mexico's profession-oriented public institutions (Gill & Alvarez, 1994). Different tacit and unspoken images of higher education, thus, were instantiated by participants, with few questioning whether speakers and listeners were communicating with or about the same ones.

Similarly, in Mexico, a postrevolutionary "democratizing" and "service" higher education ethos was embedded in much of the work and legitimated mission of the public higher education sector. U.S. participants often were unaware of this embedded value, and they easily dismissed or discounted it as they advocated for other priorities and projects. Increased student enrollment from Mexico was appealing to the U.S. institutions, for example, and they tended to focus on recruiting from Mexico's private universities. Because those are expensive and have graduation requirements that differ from those of public institutions, undergraduate students there were much more likely to be wealthy and to not contribute the social service duty that public universities require of their students. The U.S. strategy, thus, tended to be perceived as undervaluing the participation of public university students that Mexican participants wanted U.S. institutions to recruit as well. Mexican participants, by the same token, sometimes focused their attention exclusively on elite U.S. universities as collaboration partners. Their image of educational "excellence" was institutional, and they did not recognize that in the United States excellence might be assessed at the departmental or program level. All of these variable assumptions reflected broader organizational and social differences in the three countries including the extent to which higher education systems were centralized or decentralized and the nature of federal government involvement in each case.

But perhaps the clearest example of what I have been describing occurred when Mexican participants disappointedly expressed their belief that the U.S. commitment to the collaboration project had not equaled Mexico's. They referred to this variable commitment in comments describing and assessing the implementation of the project in the United States, Mexico, and Canada. In a face-to-face interview, two participants described the implementation of the joint project to me in this way:

First Mexican Participant:
It was much more formal in Mexico because in Mexico there was a representative from the Secretariat for Public Education [Ministry of Education] as a direct authority over universities in Mexico. So, they could say, "This is going to happen" and "You have to make a commitment to this."

Second Mexican Participant:
And, "We'll find the money."

First Mexican Participant:
"We'll find the money" …. But not the United States.

Second Mexican Participant:
There was never that countenance. And Canada, … well, in between. (Oliva, 1997, pp. 201–202)

These statements were particularly striking in light of statements by U.S. and Canadian participants that their personal and governmental commitment to the project was high.

Fortunately, rather than attempt to determine whether Mexican or U.S. and Canadian statements were true in the conventional sense, the research orientation I had chosen compelled me to ask how the conflicting discourses about commitment and implementation could all be true.

By thinking of each of the distinct statements as emerging from culturally, nationally, and socially differentiated zones of influence, I decided to look more closely at from whence they came to better understand how they were refracted through the mutually influencing interaction of the three zones. I concluded that three important factors were embedded in each of the discursive zones (United States, Mexico, and Canada) but that their differential characters across educational systems provided credible evidence for the truth of the discrepant perspectives. Those factors included (a) the goals of the collaboration project as differentially constructed by participants, (b) the different higher education structures in the three countries, and (c) the coordination mechanism chosen independently by the leadership of each country for implementation of the project in each.

Three Tables 15.1, 15.3, 15.4 from a report of findings (Oliva, 1998) illustrate how participants from the three countries could have discursively different perspectives about what was happening in the project. The first of these (Table 15.1) shows that participants had in mind different populations of students to be served by the collaborative project and also had different ideas about which education sectors would be affected.

Table 15.2 shows that participants from the three countries had different assumptions about education itself that were shaped by their particular (national) experiences and by their governments' roles in it. Mexican participants, for example, consistently came from the governmental education sector. Of the three countries, theirs also had the most centralized educational system. They brought this image and related assumptions about education to the work of the collaborative. Their thinking about the project was unavoidably framed by their experience and view of education as a centralized ministry activity in which the government has a strong, if not controlling, role.

This was in sharp contrast to the *somewhat* decentralized and the *very* decentralized images and assumptions about education held by U.S. and Canadian representatives, respectively. When these national higher

**Table 15.1. Embedded Spillover:
Steering Committee Assumptions**

	Student and Functional Domains	
Country	*Students to Be Served*	*Domains to Be Addressed*
Mexico	Native students	All education domains
Canada	Native and foreign students	Foreign affairs through higher education
United States	Foreign students	Higher education/ research exchange

Table 15.2.   National Higher Education Structure

	Mexico	Canada	United States
Centralized[a] +/–	+		
Decentralized +/–		+	–

Note: + = strong; – = weak.
[a]Defined by whether there is a federal higher education coordinating agency or other presence.

Table 15.3.   Coordination Strategy Within Countries

	Mexico	Canada	United States
Formal[a] +/–	+	+	
Informal[b] +/–			+

Note: + = strong; – = weak.
[b]Table assumes that there is no constitutional standing along integrationist (European Union) lines.

education contexts were coupled with a description of the coordination mechanisms used by participants in the three countries (Table 15.3), it became apparent that notwithstanding identification of the same project outcomes, differences among the three countries were prompting different participant views of the collaboration.

Depending on their own embedded assumptions and a priori images of educational goals, student populations, and structure, participants differentially assessed the effectiveness and outcomes of the project.[11] From the positioned perspective of each group, their assessments and judgments did, indeed, have merit. Looked at from a dialogic space accountable to but outside of each, it was possible to see that each of the discrepant statements could be true. These factors and characteristics of the three countries could then be displayed visually as a matrix (see Table 4) that accounts for the level of centralization of education within the countries as well as their internal coordination mechanisms.

Together, this made it possible for me to consider, from a conceptually third space that was other to each, how the three groups of representatives arrived at their discrepant views (discourses) about each country's commitment to the project. This could not have been possible without the dialogical engagement of these multiple discourses that was made possible by research conducted via dialogic educational criticism.

Once attended to, these examples became rich fodder for thinking about research in culturally and discursively heteroglot sites such as this

**Table 15.4. Implementation of North American
Higher Education Cooperation**

	Coordination Within Country			
Structure	Formal +	Formal –	Informal –	Informal +
Centralized +	Mexico			
Centralized –				
Decentralized –				United States
Decentralized +	Canada			

Note: + = strong; – = weak.

project. In thinking about and conducting research on the collaborative initiative, important questions included the following:

- If an unstable *langue* results in competing possibilities and interpretations of meaning, is one more correct than others?
- As a researcher, how do I account for the invisible and unspoken bending of communicative intent that might be more apparent, or only apparent, to a practiced multi-perspectival social/social/cultural/linguistic (Chicano) knower?
- Where does a Chicano researcher position herself to both acknowledge personal commitments and still remain critically conscious of the distinct national/cultural/epistemic communities and their discourses so as not to hierarchize them?

On this last question, I had in mind Fish's (1980) contention that we all communicate to and from particular communities. But what happens when the community as constructed is heteroglot, as in this North American higher education collaboration? To which national/cultural/epistemic or social/cultural/linguistic community do researchers pledge first allegiance? Which one has preeminent value and authority? The questions, notwithstanding Fish's guidance, are important because the answers serve as the advance organizers and choices of *langue* from which a researcher-of-heteroglot-sites knows the world.

As a Chicano researcher, I concluded that too much of the richness and complexity of the case would be lost in choosing one community from which to speak and know. This would have been like choosing to think from a mainstream U.S. or mainstream Mexican perspective when the Chicano way of being and knowing is in the transactive space between them. The only remaining place from which to know was from the interstices between discursive perspectives, those unstable and shifting locations on the margins of particular discourses. I sought to situate myself in a researcher positionality at the intersection of discourses that is implicitly a type of connected knowing (Thayer-Bacon, 1993).

Procedurally dwelling in the transactive as an in-between positionality is a Chicano way of knowing, but in heteroglot research sites, it is not in and of itself a Chicano positionality. Thus, it is important to explicitly note that the hybrid method I have called dialogic educational criticism is a methodological orientation that addresses two compelling objectives. The first is to embrace a Chicano way of being in and knowing the world as a type of epistemological connoisseurship for research in heteroglot sites. The second is to value, on the blank page that is the time lag (Bhabha, 1994) or figurative moment before the research act, the dialogue of heteroglossia and polyvocality rather than the authoritative discourse of the researcher or a particular community. In so doing, dialogic educational criticism "minimizes the suppression of difference while capturing the complex, dynamic, and relational nature of real-world collaboratives" (Oliva, 1997, p. 229).

It is not my intent to imply that this method can be used only in international sites such as this North American higher education cooperative initiative or even only by Chicanos and border-landers. Rather, research in the explicitly multinational and multicultural international collaboration foregrounded the need to acknowledge and account for difference in more inclusive and respectful ways than have been readily available. A dialogic educational criticism method allowed me to better accomplish this in research. However, we should be able to productively turn a magnified Chicano oriented dialogic educational criticism lens on our own intranational and local sites of difference and polyvocality.

CONCLUSION

The method I have described was fashioned out of the need presented by a case of cross-cultural, multinational, and multi-perspectival research that initially assumed a foundation of *langue*. Because the collaborative project involved an arguably homogeneous group (leadership, governmental, and education elites) and was formally conducted in a common language (English), the initial taken-for-granted assumption was that everyone was or would be working from the same cultural, epistemic, and knowledge page. The assumption was that participants' surface commonalities reflected common "rules of grammar, syntax, and orderly formats of understanding" that discursively made "the invisible visible, reproducible, and memorable" (Altheide & Johnson, 1994, p. 493) in communicative and cultural discourse. Because it quickly became clear this was not the case, a more appropriate non-foundational approach was fashioned from existing practices (Eisner, 1991), my Chicano way of knowing, and the theoretical and conceptual vocabulary of M. M. Bakhtin (1981a, 1981b, 1981c, 1986).

Embedded in this new dialogic educational criticism method is a willingness on the part of the researcher to suspend and contingently shift, if only temporarily, membership in the site's heteroglot discursive communities. Those not used to this type of engagement with others might be at a loss as to how exactly this might be done. Dialogic educational criticism cannot and should not attempt to remedy this by presenting itself as a normative process for legitimating knowledge and making validity claims. Instead, to dialogically account for multiple discourses and shifting *langue*, it must work against the discursive "privilege of those who have so skillfully carved that privilege into the foundation of the nation. We will have to adopt a position of consistently swimming against the current. We run the risk of being permanent outsiders" (Ladson-Billings, 1998, p. 22). In so valuing its non-epistemic project (Schwandt, 1997), dialogic educational criticism presents itself as a positioned Chicano dialogic process and way of knowing that makes it possible for thirdness to arise out of multiple and divergent discourses.

Although dialogic educational criticism is not a "normative" or predetermined approach, some readers might nevertheless find it useful to have the approach described again in brief. Thus, when conducting research via this method, researchers would:

- Seek out research in sites about which they have unique skills and knowledge, where they have a level of connoisseurship as defined by Eisner, 1991) that allows them to contribute new images and knowledge.

- Assume the existence of multiple unstable discourses and meaning-making systems at those sites that are both exogenous (a priori) and potentially endogenous (generated in thirdness).

- Consistent with connoisseurship precepts, value their own researcher perspectives, especially if they are perspectives that are absent or marginalized in current practice.

- Identify, value, and interpretively account for the key multiple discourses in the research site. Depending on the focus of the research, these could be evident in discursive variations among groups, languages, nationalisms, cultures, genders, and a variety of other domains.

- Accept and value the researcher perspective as one mediated in the transactive space between researcher and the research site and context, between researcher discourses and other discourses, and so forth. Established mechanisms (member checks and constant comparison methods could help to achieve dialogic meaning making if applied non-hierarchically and in a manner consistent with an assumed possibility of thirdness.

- In making validity assessments, determine whether research has dialogic validity because it was conducted in a manner that accounts for and is inclusive of discrepant discourses and worldviews.

If conducted in this way, dialogic educational criticism research is antifoundational in the manner argued for by Lather (1993) but also is polyvocal and contingent in the manner argued for most forcefully by Bakhtin (1981a, 1981b, 1981c, 1986). Consistent with a Chicano way of knowing, it also does not exclude or undervalue perspectives that might be absent or marginalized from mainstream disciplinary discourses.

Thus, conducting dialogic educational criticism is, in Bakhtinian terms, to epistemologically position oneself in distinct and shifting zones of influence, both to attempt to cognitively know from those positions and to refract discourses and have them refracted from those positionalities. It is not only attuned to but also values multiple meaning systems and the possibilities that arise when space is made for them to interact, to be juxtaposed, or to be creatively transformed. Given the prerequisite awareness of multiple meaning systems, such a positionality is able to assert itself in the intersection of these to resist the closing off of creative possibilities. Such a closure would result from privileging one or another of the available meaning systems at the expense of others.

This process not only helps researchers to better understand the particular perspectives at a given site but also makes it possible for them to become the creative (thirdness) site at which distinct perspectives are integrated via a transactive, Chicano-oriented meaning-making representation. In this way, this approach is different from other research practices, namely, those designed to speak, know, and research from particular communities, standpoints, and even paradigms. In explicitly suspending practiced ways of being in and researching the world, however, the method helps new possibilities to come into being from the transactive third space. It allows for the production of new images and enlightened representations that might help us to see educational sites and educational issues in new ways. For how effectively inclusive is research in sites of cultural, linguistic, racial, ethnic, gender, or economic difference when we assume the existence of "shareable and non-idiosyncratic understandings and meanings" that make "the invisible visible" (Altheide &Johnson, 1994)?

My experience has been that in tethering ourselves to a metadiscourse of *langue* by unproblematically assuming discursive homogeneity at such sites, we potentially do not so much research heteroglot sites as construct them with the particular biases and frameworks that we take there. Dialogic educational criticism is not a panacea to doing this, but it is one step toward producing new images and knowledge about communities and groups that are otherwise silenced and marginalized. In the manner posited by Eisner (1991), this method presumes topical (education, higher education, other) and process (Chicano) connoisseurship; a researcher's willingness to other the Self with her community and other communities; and a flexible, creative, and multidiscursive way of being in research. When researchers resist a foundation of *langue* in their research design and practice, they position themselves, as do Chicanos, not so much within discursive communities as flexibly between and among them. In so doing, we better understand how, notwithstanding discursive dividing lines and borders, we might nevertheless connect. This is my goal, one that I call on more of us to take on as a challenge.

NOTES

1. This chapter is based on an earlier version presented at the annual conference of the American Educational Research Association, San Diego, April 1998. It is a revised version of an article published in *Qualitative Inquiry*, March 2000, pp. 33–57. All permissions to adapt this article have been granted by the Editor, Professor Yvonna Lincoln and by SAGE.

2. This avowed characteristic of *langue* (Hirsch, 1976) is what I am critiquing here as the false and unproblematized premise on which many of our research methods are based. Eagleton's (1996) more thoughtful discussion and critique of *langue* reflects the view of it that I am espousing in this chapter.

3. The alternative I propose serves as the place for conceptually willful *dwelling* between locations through which a researcher accounts for, acknowledges, and juxtaposes multiple positions, including her own.

4. The first type of miscommunication was possible in nearly any exchange because we did not always share tacit understandings of the language we used. The second was most likely when language was being creatively transformed, as in when the resources of multiple language and meaning systems are employed in communication. One has only to consider academic discussions of code switching and *caló* for examples of creative and linguistically transgressive communicative processes.

5. The terms *Chicano* and *Chicana* are used in this article, but not interchangeably. Chicano refers to a politically informed Mexican American cultural identity, whereas Chicana is a noun or an adjective for a Chicano

female. In other circumstances, Chicana might refer to a feminist cultural perspective.

6. In a recent book chapter, Chabram (1994) quotes a 1987 interview with Bruce- Novoa. The topic is where and how to locate the culturally interstitial products of authors (Chicanos) whose heritage is Mexican but who live and write in the United States: "I saw the binaries as anti-Chicano; as soon as we adopt binaries, we're in trouble.... I talk about the Chicano as an interspace, that is, neither one of the poles.... It's really a synthesis ... a constant dialectic that can never be achieved until death.... I really do believe in this other space ... where [the literary object] has it's own subject."

7. Researcher identities are not unitary and unambiguous but can be thought of as heteroglot. Eagleton (1996), among others, critiques the idea of a unified and stable identity when he writes, "Since language is something that I am made out of ... the whole idea that I am a stable, unified entity must also be a fiction" (p. 112). See also Alarcón (1994) and Anzaldúa (1987).

8. National standpoints often are assumed to be mono-cultural standpoints, as Crapanzano (1995) seems to do. For a clearer example of this, see Hirsch's (1988) *Cultural Literacy.* However, it is my view that cultures legitimated as "national" really are unavoidably partial and constructed through the suppression or denial of non-legitimated cultural discourses.

9. There is insufficient space here to report on the conclusions and dialogic validity claims of this research, but results have been presented elsewhere (Oliva, 1998).

10. In the research, these are broadly categorized as actor preferences There is insufficient space here to report on the conclusions and dialogic validity claims of this research, but results have been presented elsewhere (Oliva, 1998).

11. For more information on these international exchange policies in Texas, see chapter 21, subchapter AA, of the Texas Higher Education Coordinating Board rules. The section can be found at http://www.thecb.state.tx.us/rules/21/21_aa.htm. Subchapter AA began as permissive legislation for Texas institutions' organized student exchange programs with Mexico; Canada was added later to support North Americanization efforts. Subsequently, the authorization in this chapter also was opened up to exchanges with other countries.

REFERENCES

Alarcón, N. (1994). The theoretical subject(s) of this bridge called my back and Anglo-American feminism. In H. Calderón & J. D. Saldívar (Eds.), *Criticism in the borderlands: Studies in Chicano literature, culture, and ideology* (pp. 28–39). Durham, NC: Duke University Press.

Altheide, D. L., & Johnson, J. M. (1994). Criteria for assessing interpretive validity in qualitative research. In N. K. Denzin & Y. S. Lincoln (Eds.), *Handbook of Qualitative Research* (pp. 485–499). Thousand Oaks, CA: SAGE.

Anzaldúa, G. (1987). *Borderlands: La frontera*. San Francisco: Aunt Lute Books.

Bakhtin, M. M. (1981a). Discourse in the novel. In M. Holquist (Ed.), *The dialogic imagination: Four essays by M. M. Bakhtin* (pp. 259–422). Austin: University of Texas Press.

Bakhtin, M. M. (1981b). Epic and novel. In M. Holquist (Ed.), *The Dialogic imagination: Four essays by M. M. Bakhtin* (pp. 3–40). Austin: University of Texas Press.

Bakhtin, M. M. (1981c). Forms of time and of the chronotope in the novel: Notes toward a historical poetics. In M. Holquist (Ed.), *The Dialogic imagination: Four Essays by M. M. Bakhtin* (pp. 3–40). Austin: University of Texas Press.

Bakhtin, M. M. (1986). Toward a methodology for the human sciences. In E. Emerson & M. Holquist (Eds.), *Speech genres and other essays* (pp. 159–172). Austin: University of Texas Press.

Bhabha, H. K. (1994). *The location of culture*. London: Routledge.

Bruce-Novoa, J. (1982). *Chicano poetry: A response to chaos*. Austin: University of Texas Press.

Bruns, G. L. (1987). On the weakness of language in the human sciences. In J. S. Nelson, A. Megill, & D. N. McCloskey (Eds.), *The rhetoric of the human sciences: Language and argument in scholarship and public affairs* (pp. 238–262). Madison: University of Wisconsin Press.

Cervantes, L. D. (1981). *Emplumada*. Pittsburgh, PA: University of Pittsburgh Press.

Chabram, A. (1994). Conceptualizing Chicano critical discourse. In H. Calderón & J. D. Saldívar (Eds.), *Criticism in The Borderlands: Studies in Chicano literature, culture, and ideology* (pp. 127–148). Durham, NC: Duke University Press.

Clifford, J. (1986). Introduction: Partial truths. In J. Clifford & G. E. Marcus (Eds.), *Writing culture* (pp. 1–26). Berkeley: University of California Press.

Crapanzano, V. (1995). The postmodern crisis: Discourse, parody, memory. In A. Mandelkar (Ed.), *Bakhtin in contexts: Across the disciplines* (pp. 137–150). Evanston, IL: Northwestern University Press.

Denzin, N. K., & Lincoln, Y. S. (1994). Introduction: Entering the field of qualitative research. In N. K. Denzin & Y. S. Lincoln (Eds.), *Handbook of Qualitative Research* (pp. 1–22). Thousand Oaks, CA: SAGE.

Eagleton, T. (1996). *Literary theory: An introduction* (2nd ed.). Minneapolis: University of Minnesota Press.

Eisner, E. W. (1991). *The enlightened eye: Qualitative inquiry and the enhancement of educational practice*. New York: Macmillan.

Fish, S. (1980). *Is there a text in this class? The authority of interpretive communities*. Cambridge, MA: Harvard University Press.

Foucault, M. (1973). *The order of things: An archaeology of the human sciences*. New York: Vintage Books.

Gardiner, M. (1992). *The dialogics of critique*. London: Routledge.

Garratt, D., & Hodkinson, P. (1998). Can there be criteria for selecting research criteria? A hermeneutical analysis of an inescapable dilemma. *Qualitative Inquiry, 4*, 515–539.

Gill, J., & Alvarez, L. (1994). *Understanding the differences: An essay on higher education in Mexico and the United States*. Boulder, CO: Western Interstate

Commission on Higher Education and Asociación Mexicana Para la Educación Internacional.

Hirsch, E. D., Jr. (1971). Objective interpretation. In H. Adams (Ed.), *Critical theory since Plato* (pp. 1177–1194). New York: Harcourt Brace Jovanovich.

Hirsch, E. D., Jr. (1976). *Validity in interpretation*. New Haven, CT: Yale University Press.

Hirsch, E. D., Jr. (1988). *Cultural literacy: What every american needs to know*. New York: Vintage Books.

Holquist, M. (1981). *The dialogic imagination: Four essays by M. M. Bakhtin*. Austin: University of Texas Press.

Holquist, M. (1990). *Dialogism: Bakhtin and his world*. London: Routledge.

Jansen, G., & Peshkin, A. (1992). Subjectivity in qualitative research. In M. D. LeCompte, W. L. Millroy, & J. Preissle (Eds.), *The Handbook of Qualitative Research in Education* (pp. 681–725). New York: Academic Press.

Ladson-Billings, G. (1998). Just what is critical race theory and what's it doing in a nice field like education? *International Journal of Qualitative Studies in Education, 11*, 7–24.

Lather, P. (1993). Fertile obsession: Validity after post-structuralism. *Sociological Quarterly, 34*, 674–693.

Lincoln, Y. S., & Denzin, N. K. (1994). The fifth moment. In N. K. Denzin & Y. S. Lincoln (Eds.), *Handbook of Qualitative Research* (pp. 575–586). Thousand Oaks, CA: SAGE.

Lubiano, W. (1991). Shuckin' off the African American native Other: What's "Po-Mo" got to do with it? *Cultural Critique, 18*, 149–186.

Mandelkar, A. (Ed.). (1995). *Bakhtin in contexts: Across the disciplines*. Evanston, IL: Northwestern University Press.

Maxwell, J. A. (1992). Understanding and validity in qualitative research. *Harvard EducationalReview, 62*, 279–300.

Morson, G. S., & Emerson, C. (1989). *Rethinking Bakhtin: Extensions and challenges*. Evanston, IL: Northwestern University Press.

Oliva, M. (1997). *Zones of influence and discourses of preference in North American higher education cooperation*. Unpublished doctoral dissertation, University of Texas at Austin.

Oliva, M. (1998, April). *Educational co-operation in North America: Findings from recent research*. Paper presented at the annual meeting of the American Educational Research Association, San Diego, CA.

Parker, L., Villenas, S., & Deyle, D. (Eds.). (1998). Critical race theory [special issue]. *International Journal of Qualitative Studies in Education, 11*(1).

Pastor, R. A., & Castañeda, J. G. (1988). *Limits to friendship: The United States and Mexico*. New York: Knopf.

Ricoeur, P. (1979). The model of the text: Meaningful action considered as text. In P. Rabinow & W. M. Sullivan (Eds.), *Interpretive Social Science: A reader* (pp. 73–101). Berkeley: University of California Press.

Scheurich, J. J. (1994). Policy archaeology: A new policy studies methodology. *Journal of Education Policy, 9*, 297–316.

Scheurich, J. J. (1996). The masks of validity: A deconstructive investigation. *International Journal of Qualitative Studies in Education, 9*, 49–60.

Schwandt, T. A. (1997). *Qualitative inquiry: A dictionary of terms*. Thousand Oaks, CA: SAGE.

Smith, J. K. (1997). The stories educational researchers tell about themselves. *Educational Researcher, 26*(5), 4–11.

Thayer-Bacon, B. J. (1993). Caring and its relationship to critical thinking. *EducationalTheory, 43*, 323–334.

Wolcott, H. F. (1994). *Transforming qualitative data: Description, analysis, interpretation*.Thousand Oaks, CA: SAGE.

PART V

IMPLICATIONS FOR FUTURE THEORY AND PREACTIVE

CHAPTER 16

"ISN'T IT RICH?"

From Past Practice to New Horizons!

John Collard

When Sondheim wrote these lyrics about troubled lovers plagued by different assumptions and miscommunication, he labeled it a kind of "farce." I want to explore this paradigm in relation to what confronts us today in the field of cultural diversity, interpersonal and international growth, and hope for a better future.

We carry inheritances from Eurpoean and American nation states who practiced colonialism in other territories. My work with educational leaders in small nations such as Bhutan and The Maldives in the past decade has also alerted me to how even a colonized nation like India has subsequently colonized education systems among its less powerful neighbors. The worldviews of colonizing predecessors were frequently monocultural and imperialist in intent. Ethnic and indigenous cultures were perceived as something to be assimilated, conquered, converted, exploited, marginalized and subordinated. Even contemporary international capitalism still operates out of an assumption that "I thought that you'd want what I want."

Leadership and Intercultural Dynamics, pp. 327–340
Copyright © 2009 by Information Age Publishing

The current massive expansion of middle class consumer markets in China and India seems to attest that things have not changed very much since the colonial regimes. A consumerist hegemony ethic is a core component of the current internationalist hegemonies. However, at the margins of these expanding markets there are still marginalized cultures and communities who are condemned to poverty and injustice because they do not possess the skills or assets to join the mainstream. International aid and education programs are frequently undertaken with a philosophy of "capacity development" to help impoverished communities develop the "human capital" and "economic resources" to join the mainstream culture

Despite the most noble of personal intentions, educators and aid workers are still enmeshed in a form of *farce*. Our academies, companies, and governments continue to send in "emissaries" to deliver ideologies and practices with "usual flair" which may not be always in the best interests of the communities to which they are directed.

The emissary frequently suffer from forms of cultural myopia. They often assume that a Western leadership program developed in "advanced democracies" will automatically transfer effectively to other nations. Indigenous communities are persuaded to barter their sacred sites for economic gain. Even in China where well over 95% of the population come from the same ethnic group (Han Chinese) we hear forlorn protests from Burmese and Islamic minorities on the borderlands while Tibetans campaign against an oppressive and unjust occupation of their land.

We need to broaden the lenses of the emissaries to see beyond their own cultural frameworks. They need to develop lateral sensitivities and skills to even begin to understand the cultures and terrains they are entering. Of course such skills would also stand them in good stead in their metropolitan states to help them comprehend the needs of displaced indigenous communities, the pain inside ethnic ghettoes, and the anguish of displaced refugees who are only offered hope if they can assimilate without causing disturbance to mainstream cultures.

We fail to see that cultural diversity is, in itself, a great "richness!" Giroux (1992, 1995) made this point over a decade ago when he contested notions of "the right culture" and posited the alternative of "unity in difference." Policymakers in Canada and Australia seemed to have understood such notions in the 1970s when they declared their nations to be multicultural states which tolerated ethnic differences among national citizens. The last decade has seen the erosion of such enlightened tolerance in many Western democracies (Collard, 2002). Refugees have been transformed into threats to national security in Australia and the United States. The policy response has been one of "offshore detention" or "internment camps" in nations which are themselves products of refugee settlement. Consequently government funds which could have been devoted to refugee settlement have been callously redirected to border security! In France and the United Kingdom we witness national backlash against citizens whose skin color and religious affiliations do not match the traditional mainstream.

The remainder of this chapter will chart the territory our authors have researched and contested. It will argue for a new theoretical perspective to inform educational leadership in an increasingly diverse world. We will advance alternative research methodolologies to the traditions which initially informed anthropology, sociology and cross cultural theory. These will be based on dialogical and interactive modes capable of capturing the subjective and complex realities of actors in our institutions and societies. We will argue the relevance of critical and constructivist pedagogies which allow space for students and educators to reflect upon and reconstruct their world views. This is allied to a commitment to place social justice issues at the center of curricula and to teach critical literacies to those who need help to challenge unjust structures and traditions.

Leaders are conceived as part of the target audience for such praxis for they must be lifelong learners equipped to analyze and reflect upon the needs of the diverse communities they serve. And they must embrace the struggle to develop a leadership praxis which is inspired by the ethics of compassion and social justice. Finally, we will argue that the time has truly come for an authentic ethic of internationalism which respects and privileges the interests of diverse nations and communities. We believe that these are the qualities needed in the education systems of the future to both redress the damage of past intolerance and to create future citizens and leaders for a diverse global community.

REVISING THEORIES

Our understanding of the concept of culture has evolved considerably since the colonial era. Anthropologists initially viewed culture as a static and coherent reality; something akin to the sepia prints with which they illustrated their accounts of exotic primitives for metropolitan audiences. Early sociologists tended to paint essentialist portraits of cultural and gender regimes. Parsons and Bales (1956) scripts for male and female gender roles were a prime example of the reductive impact of such thinking which obscured the complexity which truly existed at the time. Cross cultural theorists have played an important role in sensitizing us to differences in national cultures in recent decades but their units of analysis (nation states) and research methods (broad scale questionnaires) have only produced panoramas which obscure the complex differences which operate inside national cultures. Court's point that the Pakeha habit of treating Maori individuals as a homogeneous group and that even though an ethnic group may share some common characteristics, it is naïve to assume it is homogeneous. Even indigenous cultures contain "borderlands and binaries" and generalized portrayals of ethnic minorities are likely to obscure important differences within them.

The fundamental problem with cross cultural theories is that they assume cultures are monolithic, static realities. They fail to comprehend that culture operates at multiple levels within a nation state. Even if there is a coherent national culture in existence, there will be geographic and regional variations within it. When we come to areas such as education, health and welfare, we inevitably encounter the culture of systems which may work in harmony or even be a source of dissonance. The repeated failure of Australian Commonwealth Governments to introduce national policies for schooling in a federation, where education was determined to be the jurisdiction of separate states and territories is testimony to this. Conversely nations such as Norway, Sweden, and The Netherlands which have national and municipal structures have operated very efficient national school systems for decades. Oliva's account of how Canadian, Mexican and U.S. officials perceive implementation of policy at tertiary levels is another clear example.

Sectoral cultures also modify national cultural maps. Collard's (2003, 2004) analyses of how Catholic, government, and independent school principals perceive schooling and leadership differently in Australia clearly indicates the need for more precise roadmaps. The research from Zhejiang Province reported in this book is further evidence that the precise sites where leaders work shape different approaches to educational praxis. The same case study also indicates that generational differences influence response to change. School leaders who were younger were more responsive to Western leadership discourse than older male system bureaucrats and academics. There was also an interactive effect with gender here too as the younger cohort contained more females than the older cohort. The changing roles and opportunities for women in China was therefore another factor which modifies cross cultural portraits of a monolithic Chinese culture. Such examples firmly support Hart's (1998) distinction between studies which compare and contrast generalized characteristics of two or more cultures and a more dynamic approach which studies what happens at the individual, group, organizational, systemic, or institutional levels when agents from different cultural platforms interact.

The assumption that settler societies like Australia, Canada, New Zealand, and the United States have a monolithic mainstream culture is both misleading and mythical. Assimilationist ideologies have been particularly harmful to both indigenous and immigrant groups in such nations. Murakami-Ramahlo and Sperandio have clearly indicated that the equation of cultural difference with deviance, pathology, and inferiority in U.S. schools have had harmful effects on both students and educators. However, If we view Oliva's personal revelations as a case study we can also see another side as a young Chicano woman learned to see from the third space between interlocking cultural realities.

I myself encountered how misleading generic ethnic portraits can be when I conducted research with educational leaders in San Antonio, one of the most multicultural cities in the United States in 2007. I initially accepted the official statistics that the population in the schools was 60% Hispanic, 30% Anglo-American and 10% Afro-American. I consequently structured my interview and focus group samples to reflect these proportions. I soon learned how inadequate these labels were when my first Afro-American interviewee proudly proclaimed herself to be Caribbean American. My Hispanic sample also included two self-proclaimed Latinos and a voting member of an Indian community. Velez clearly illustrates in his chapter that such ethnic confusions permeate U.S. mainstream culture. My response to a misleading sample selection was to expand it to be more inclusive. Luckily, I asked if there were other leaders I should interview who did not fit the original three demographic descriptors. I am pleased to report that my expanded sample ended up including a Filipino-American and a Hawaiian-American. (see Collard, forthcoming). Of course my conclusion was, if a select sample of educational leaders was so much more diverse than the official statistics, how much more complex was the student and parent populations they were serving?

Consideration of settler societies would be radically incomplete if we fail to acknowledge the destructive impact of the violent displacement of indigenous populations in The New World. Explorers, traders, settlers, and missionaries blithely assumed they possessed a cultural imperative to destroy and alter preexisting cultures. Christian missionaries followed closely on the heels of traders and settlers filled with zeal to convert *heathen populations* to *the truth!* They never questioned how appropriate the assimilate or perish strategies they employed in mission stations and schools were. The removal of indigenous children from their mothers by patriarchal Australian authorities even until the 1960s constitutes one of the most flawed manifestations of a distorted worldview. Johansson Fua's chapter clearly illustrates how Christian culture has impacted upon leadership in Tonga to produce a composite culture. Normore's references to priests using the confessional to gather information which was then used to divide indigenous communities provides a more insidious insight.

Sondheim's song recognizes the need for apologies; "Sorry, my dear!" Fortunately, the settler societies have come to a similar realization in recent decades. However, words are never enough and formal apologies continue to be inadequate if programs in education, health, and welfare for displaced indigenous populations continue to operate from monocultural and assimilationist assumptions. Court's case study alerts us to the seductive deception which can occur when liberal democratic discourses promote tolerance of difference at a rhetorical level but actually marginalizes Mere because she does not conform to their routines and assumptions. She also acknowledges that in such contexts silence and withdrawal are forms of resistance and self-protection by minority group members. In this case bicultural tolerance actually masked unequal power relationships amongst teachers who were not going to change their own individual practice. Mere was stigmatized and eventually withdrew from the conflict by moving to an all Maori school where she would not feel so ostracized. We can interpret this in two ways: did she move to an appropriate comfort zone or was she forced to a ghetto where she could not disrupt the dominant professional culture of Telford School?

Normore's point that real progress requires new sets of leadership skills and knowledge which are responsive to the cultural needs of the target population is indisputable. Giroux (1996, p. 128) called for the *courage* to "make despair unconvincing and hope practical!" In advancing these points both scholars are really challenging leaders and researchers to remove their culturally-conditioned monocles and recognize the need for liberational advocacy, to challenge political, economic, and social structures that privilege some and disadvantage others. There is a need to understand that even clinics and schools characterized by unequal power relationships and systems of oppression continue to violate the rights of minority peoples. Our future leaders must be trained to sensitive to the social and equity issues, culture, history, and economic challenges of First Nations schools and surrounding communities. Of course such qualities are desirable in the leaders of all institutions and locations where human beings suffer various forms of disadvantage. The case study provided by Garza and Merchant illustrates one such approach to this issue.

A final point about cultural theory is that all cultures contain internal tensions and are capable of generating resistance and rejection when dominant traditions are challenged. The U.S. professors who worked in Minsk were conscious that their reform efforts met some resistance from established administrative practices inherited from the Soviet Regime. One of the beneficiaries of this international cooperation insisted that a documents first strategy was a formidable obstacle to change. The eagerness of school based Chinese leaders to adopt Western discourses about learning and leadership was not matched by their respective system officials and academic leaders. At least two members of the cohort were explicitly opposed to the collaborative leadership modes they were exposed to. So just as we have to avoid stereotypes about national cultural traits, we must be equally cautions not to assume that all intercultural interactions produce uniform responses in target groups.

The theoretical resolution we offer to the need to understand and be responsive to the needs of indigenous, ethnic, and international groups is an awareness of intercultural dynamics allied with critical pedagogies and ethical leadership committed to social justice. We seek to transcend the quick fix, recipe approach to leadership whether it be clothed in the rhetoric of charismatic, emotional, strategic transformational discourses. Instead we wish to resurrect the concept of the leader as reflective practitioner (Schon, 1988). However, our ideal leader will possess the skills of cultural awareness and intercultural dynamics. He or she will perform a role as a cultural mediator in complex intercultural contexts and the praxis will be guided by the ethics of compassion and social justice. Paige (2004, p. 13) expressed it succinctly when he called for a theory which recognizes the diverse cultural origins of knowledge and values, incorporates multiple frames of reference into knowledge construction, learns from and with people from other cultures and applies ethical choices which recognize the complexities of cultural interaction.

RESEARCH DIRECTIONS

The central argument in chapter 2 was that while quantitative studies may have yielded broad descriptors of national cultures in the past, they are incapable of illuminating the precise and nuanced interactions between cultural actors. Communication theorists have accepted this point for over two decades now. Instead I advanced alternative forms of qualitative enquiry to comprehend the microlevel realities of intercultural dynamics. Other authors in this book have pushed the boundaries a little further. In particular they point to the value of discourse analysis in assisting us to develop more precise understandings of complex demographics and verbal interactions.

Velez's research is particularly poignant in that it points to how ethnic descriptors are used imprecisely and for different purposes in U.S. public discourse. It points to the likelihood of confusion in the use of terms like Hispanic and Latino in institutions like schools and welfare agencies. His case study of a Latino Professor supports the claims Oliva advances that the United States is a heteroglot linguistic community. Her discourse analysis of actors at a North American Higher Education gathering has implications, as she points out well beyond that specific event or the borderlands of U.S. society. It suggests that dialogical analysis can become a key too to help us better understand the assumptions constructions embedded in the discourse of actors in intercultural interactions. The longitudinal case study presented by Garza and Merchant highlights the value of such investigations for their deliberate privileging of the student voice enables us to understand the process whereby their cohort of educational leaders came to embrace the ethic of social justice as the primary rationale for their professional lives.

Consideration of dialogical and discourse research methods also raises the key question of the role and voice of the researcher. Court raises this when she acknowledged:

> As the researcher, I am, of course, embedded in this study, both in terms of its design and its "findings," which have been constructed within and filtered through my own subjectivity as a middle class, Päkehä academic researcher, who has grown up and been schooled in the mainstream education system in Aotearoa New Zealand.

Wang acknowledged a similar point when reporting that she was both teacher and researcher with the Zhejiang cohort and that this may have had a Hawthorn effect upon some of her respondents. Of course her status as a bilingual researcher also meant that she was in an excellent position to understand and interpret the differing assumptions conceptions her cohort brought to contemporary Western discourses about learning and leadership. In this respect she was addressing Oliva's dilemma; "to which national/cultural/epistemic or social/cultural/linguistic community do researchers pledge first allegiance? Which one has preeminent value and authority?"

We would argue that the first step is to recognize and respect the multiple cultural backgrounds operating in intercultural contexts whether they be with indigenous, ethnic, or international populations. The research methods must be inclusive and respectful and encourage dialogue, reflection and reconstruction. And finally, the outcomes do not necessarily have to be presented in the mode of the omniscient author/researcher which has been privileged by cross cultural theorists. Rather, the author needs to orchestrate polyvocal accounts which capture the realities they have studied. Shah does this when she allows her adolescent Muslim youth to talk freely about how he felt about being suddenly labeled Bin Laden by his school colleagues after 9/11. She allowed him to tell us how such labeling both hurt and marginalized him in a school environment where he had previously felt comfortable. We can see that such experiences could well plant the seeds of the home grown terrorism which the U.K. experienced shortly after.

However, as Court acknowledges there is still a place for the voice of the researcher. Yvonna Lincoln has helped me immensely in moving to a standpoint where I am prepared to momentarily shed the carefully honed voice of the objective researcher and share my understandings in a personal voice. One of my great disappointments in collating this collection has been my inability to deliver research by an indigenous Australian about their situation. Two started to write but the realities are still too painful for them to complete their accounts. And so I offer my own insight of what is still happening in *The Lucky Country* where educational and health statistics indicate that our native inhabitants are still largely condemned to Third World status;

> parrots scream obscenities at dawn,
> tear timid shoots from drought-struck gums
> and drop them carelessly to earth
> where warlike ants drain the sap
> from their withered forms.
>
> a black girl wails in the tattered shade
> knowing her baby will not survive this summer day.
> he already has the eyes of a dying man
> looking to a dreamtime beyond the hard-baked earth.
>
> weathered farmers stare into horizons
> which fail to promise any rain,
> shake their heads
> and retreat into cavernous kitchens
> where wives brew constant cups of consolation.
>
> at evening the land exhales a slender breeze
> in union with the last breath of the dying child!
> the farmers tune flickering screens
> in search of better fortunes,
> medicate despair with alcohol
> and slumber towards another dawn.

Sutherland's case study of her work in a binational school in Australia is unabashedly personal. She reflects upon the inheritance she brought from her previous leadership experiences and then deconstructs her professional identity to create a new one more suited to the cultural complexity she now has to manage on a daily basis. She then sought broader perspectives by studying similar schools in other national settings and presents us with an emergent framework for leadership in bicultural sites. In this sense her work, like that of Oliva, are virtual case studies in themselves. They illustrate how researchers in this field must be self-reflective learners engaged in an ongoing project of redefining their standpoints and voices. The latter is a voice of hope when she offers her "magnified Chicano oriented dialogic lens" to others to help understand on our own "difference and polyvocality."

CRITICAL PEDAGOGIES

In discussing this topic we need to recall that its remit goes well beyond the students in our institutions. Our framework is one of lifelong learning (Chapman & Aspin, 1997) and, in this respect, institutional and political leaders are viewed as continuing learners. Normore has addressed this issue for intercultural contexts in his chapter:

> the development of culturally relevant pedagogy is contingent upon critical reflection about race and culture of educational leaders, teachers, and the students. It's a process for improving practice, rethinking philosophies, raising self-awareness, and becoming effective leaders for today's ever changing student populations.

However, he takes us one step further when he links critical pedagogy to social justice whereby "school leaders envision the classroom as a site where new knowledge, grounded in the experiences of students and teachers" is developed. He argues that such strategies are "empowering" and contain a political potential towards collective struggle to create more egalitarian societies. The Belarus cohort seemed to be seeking such developments when they eschewed the Soviet tradition of regarding educators as technological experts and called for *practical teaching and administration models* to enable them to contest the regime of facts and testing facts which makes schooling so arduous for their pupils. The Zhejiang leaders expressed similar frustration with the stranglehold examination systems have over Chinese students and teachers. Ironically the San Antonio leaders I interviewed in 2007 were critical of the test regimes which have subordinated broader curriculum goals in Texas in recent years.

Normore's version of critical pedagogy in intercultural contexts is built on a premise that the educator "makes sure she understands the students' preexisting conceptions and guides activities to address and build on them." This was also the premise which guided the design of the Educational leadership course in Zhejiang province in 2002. To paraphrase Normore "creating meaningful educational experiences and lifelong learning environments for both the youth and adults" requires "a language and cultural context that supports the traditions, knowledge, and languages" of the target groups "as the starting place for learning new ideas and knowledge." And for educators themselves "the hope is that the history and culture that is powerful," will support them as reflective practitioners who understand "what it means to teach, learn and lead across cultures while simultaneously honoring the integrity of those cultures."

The outcomes of critical-constructivist pedagogy are glimpsed in the study of the Zhejiang educational leaders. The course was designed in such a way as to acknowledge and respect the long and rich traditions of

Chinese learning and leadership. Initial activities sought to surface pre-existing inherited assumptions and beliefs. There were difficult moments when it was clear that adult learners who had been previously educated from a strongly theoretical and recall pedagogy were somewhat uncomfortable with the more discursive modes of Australian educators. When these were surfaced and discussed it emerged that the core issue was that the two groups operated from different epistemic platforms about the nature of knowledge and, subsequently, the most appropriate learning and teaching strategies. The interview data indicates that this neutralized resistance but it did not mean that the Chinese leaders simply capitulated and accepted contemporary Western discourses. Instead, they mediated the new knowledge in the context of their understandings of Chinese traditions and realities. Some new ideas were accommodated into their cognitive repertoires, others were rejected as in appropriate.

Critical pedagogy is the polar opposite of what Marakami Ramalho and Sperandio have noted as standard practice in some international schools where educators "have been trained to convert students' with international and intercultural social and cultural capital to monoculturalism." A colleague with over 2 decades of experience in internmational schools in Hong King confirmed their analysis:

> My experience of international schooling leads me to believe that they are not really the guide to 'international mindedness".... International schools are set up to keep expatriate citizens in the correct pond for their education, and to lead them to tertiary admission.... International schools are also fee paying institutions so other locals who join are there because their parents can afford it and it is perceived as a route to a "good" university.... The international secondary schools are governed by the exams that sit waiting at the end of the line and the choice of materials is often confined by the syllabus.... The challenge for School Leaders is to establish a culture within their own schools based firmly on inclusivity, tolerance, and understanding.[1]

Do such comments imply that some international schools are sites of contemporary Western cultural imperialism and privileged pathways to sandstone or ivy league universities? What of the plethora of offshore courses now delivered by "advanced academies" in developing contexts. Are some of our colleagues guilty of delivering contemporary forms of intellectual cargo culture on populations for whom they may well be inappropriate?

LEADERS, LEARNING, AND ETHICS

It should be clear by now that the authors in this collection are not supportive of leaders playing a simple transmissive role as cultural agents.

Nor are we comfortable with concepts of them as line agents of political and bureaucratic regimes as Sutherland confronted when working with French educators. Instead we favor a notion of leaders as sensitive reflective practitioners, committed to serving the needs of the populations they deal with and guided by an ethical compass where two of the key reference points ate compassion and social justice. We align ourselves with Hodgkinson (1991) and his successors who view leadership as a moral art! More recently Bogotch (2005) has challenged educational leaders to refocus their educational work towards social justice. This has been particularly difficult in recent decades when Western political regimes have viewed education as an economic investment strategy whether they be in local or international delivery sites. Blackmore (2004) has pointed out that the system officials wearing Armani suits and padded shoulders have been more interested in performative regimes than social justice. Such economic regimes have placed scant value on critical reflection, critical and culturally relevant pedagogy and frequently turned to a blind eye to the growing inequalities in education in developed nations. Instead they have espoused the neoliberal concept of market forces instead of critically examining which social and ethnic group members are falling through the cracks of decaying systems.

Those who have espoused cross cultural competencies in the past have frequently been focused upon communication skills and technologies. Johansson Fua's work in The Pacific reminds us that communication and relationship skills continue to be as important today as when US theorists added them to the task oriented discourse of scientific manageralism in the decades after World War II (see Hersey & Blanchard, 1982). Intercultural, if not all educational endeavors requires highly developed relationship repertoires.

These relationship dimensions are also inevitably intertwined with the praxis of power. The Zhejiang cohort initially viewed positional power as the essence of leadership. Some of the Belarus cohort were frustrated by how bureaucratic power and accountabilities subordinated and hijacked their efforts to improve relationships in schools, especially with their students. Sutherland has noted how French authorities view educators as implementers of government policy and how this in turn impacts upon interpersonal relationships in binational sites. Court has highlighted how unequal power structures at Telford School sabotaged the neoliberal project of improving race relationships within a small institution. Maori participation in decision making was not a genuine option in its apparently progressive shared leadership structures.

Educational leaders inevitably possess a degree of power and privilege in their workplaces. However, if they deploy it through a singular, myopic lens that assumes the dominant hegemonies in societies and systems possess incontrovertible legitimacy they will be failing the diverse populations they are meant to serve. The assimilationist ideologies of the twentieth century are no longer ethically or practically viable. Contemporary leaders have an ethical responsibility to see outside the box or beyond the habitas they have inherited (Habbermaas, 1990). As leaders they must practice continuous, reflective, and reconstructive learning.

Marakami Ramalho and Sperandio have questioned whether this can only occur in intercultural domains if teachers and leaders are removed from familiar territory and exposed to similar challenges as their students. However, the outcomes of the Zhejiang cohort seem to belie this immersion philosophy. It is interesting that exposure to contemporary discourses on both learning and leadership had differential impacts within the cohort. The changes in leadership conceptions were less marked than those about learning. This suggests that direct pedagogical experience may be a more powerful instrument of change than theoretical constructs. It may also suggest that there is more space for change in the personal domain of learning than in the public domain of leadership. The Belarus participants may have noted something similar when they argued that although the bureaucratic traditions subverted their democratic intentions, their interpersonal relationships within schools improved and became more egalitarian.

If these reflections are true then they continue to provide enormous hope for the educational profession. We know how to generate engaged learning in classrooms and leadership workshops. Such experiences have the power to unfreeze the inherited cultural assumptions which Schein (1985) and Senge (1990) have characterized as impediments to change.

We can facilitate new learning and, in addressing issues about mainstream, minority and indigenous cultures we can displace outmoded mono-cultural lenses. Thank you Mr. Sondheim but we do not need clowns, nor grease paint, and we should certainly not indulge in farce! We need sound ethical praxis based on an appreciation of the richness offered by multiple cultures and we also need to continue to learn how to work with them. Only then can we begin the healing which will help to construct a more just and harmonious world at all levels in the coming century. That is the ethical imperative we are charged with at this point in human history! Isn't it rich!

NOTES

1. Personal e-mail correspondence from Janine Tai (Hong Kong) September 3, 2008.

REFERENCES

Blackmore, J. (2004). The emperor has no clothes: Professionalism, performativity and educational leadership in high-risk postmodern times. In J. Collard & C. Reynolds (Eds.), *Leadership, gender & culture: Male and female perspectives* (pp. 73–194). Philadelphia: Open University Press.

Bogotch, I. E. (2005, November). *Social justice as an educational construct: Problems and possibilities.* Paper presented at the annual meeting of the University Council of Educational Administration, Nashville, TN.

Chapman, J. D., & Aspin, D. N. (1997). *The school, the community and lifelong learning.* London: Cassell.

Collard, J. (2002). *Hobart, Adelaide and the New Millenium: Shifting goals for Australian schooling 1989–2001,* Unicorn, Online Refereed Paper, No 19. 1–10.

Collard, J (2003) Principal beliefs: The interface of gender and sector. *The Alberta Journal of Educational Research, XLIX*(1), 37–54,

Collard, J. (2004). Steel magnolias in velvet ghettoes: Female leaders in Australian girls' schools. In J. Collard & C. Reynolds (Eds.), *Leadership, gender & culture, male and female perspectives* (pp. 75–89). Philadelphia: Open University Press.

Giroux, H. A. (1992). Educational leadership and the crisis of democratic government. *Educational Researcher, 21*(4), 4–11.

Giroux, H. A. (1995). National identity and the politics of multiculturalism. *College Literature, 22,* 41–56.

Giroux, H. A. (1996). *Fugitive Cultures: Race, violence and youth.* New York: Routledge.

Habbermaas, J. (1990). *Moral consciousness and communicative action* (C. Lenhardt & S. W. Nicholson, Trans.). Cambridge, MA: MIT Press.

Hart, W. B. (1998). What is intercultural relations? *The E-Journal of Intercultural Relations,* 1-8. Retrieved February 20, 2006, http://www.interculturalrelations.com

Hersey, P., & Blanchard, K. (1982). *Management of organizational behaviour: Utilizing Human Resources.* Englewood Cliffs, NJ: Prentice-Hall.

Hodgkinson, C. (1991). *Leadership: The moral art.* Albany: State University of New York Press.

Paige, R. M. (2004, August). *The intercultural in teaching and learning: A developmental perspective.* Paper presented at University of South Australia.

Parsons, T., & Bales, R. F. (1956). *Family socialization and interaction process.* London: Routledge.

Schon, D. A. (1988). *Educating the reflective practitioner.* San Francisco: Jossey-Bass.

Schein, E. H. (1985). *Organizational culture and leadership: A dynamic view.* San Francisco: Jossey-Bass.

Senge, P. (1990). *The fifth discipline: The art and practice of learning organizations.* New York: Doubleday.

ABOUT THE AUTHORS

Anthony H. Normore is associate professor and program development coordinator of the doctorate in educational leadership, graduate education division, College of Education, at the California State University-Dominguez Hills in Los Angeles. His research focuses on leadership development of urban school leaders in the context of ethics and social justice. His book *Leadership for Social Justice: Promoting Equity and Excellence through Inquiry and Reflective Practice* was published in fall, 2008 with Information Age Publishers. His research publications have appeared in national and international peer-reviewed journals including *Journal of School Leadership, Journal of Educational Administration, Values and Ethics in Educational Administration, The Alberta Journal of Educational Research, Canadian Journal of Education Administration and Policy, International Journal of Urban Educational Leadership, Educational Policy, International Electronic Journal for Leadership in Learning,* and *Journal of Research on Leadership Education.*

Betty Merchant is dean of the College of Education and Human Development at the University of Texas, San Antonio (UTSA) where she also served as chair of the department of educational leadership and policy studies. Dr. Merchant received her PhD in policy analysis from Stanford University in 1991. Before going to Texas, she was an associate professor in the Department of Educational Organization and Leadership at the University of Illinois Urbana-Champaign. Dr. Merchant has taught in public schools, preschool through high school, and in tribally controlled, Native American schools in the Southwest. Her research interests focus on educational policy, equity, student diversity, and school leadership within American and international contexts. In 2007 Dr. Merchant was a consultant to a professional development program for Swedish School principals.

Carlos Martin Vélez was born and raised in Lima, Perú. He pursued his undergraduate and graduate studies in education at Universidad Nacional de San Marcos in Lima before migrating to the United States. He received his MA in Spanish from Michigan State University, and pursued his initial doctoral studies in language education at the University of Iowa. He obtained his PhD in culture, literacy, and language from the University of Texas at San Antonio in 2007. He is a first-year assistant professor of Spanish and ESL at Brescia University in Kentucky. His research focuses on the critical discursive construction (both in English and Spanish) of the transcultural, fragmented, and contextual identities of silenced, marginal, and resistant Chicana/o and Latina/o in/migrant groups and individuals in educational and popular discourses in the Americas and Spain. He is interested in transdisciplinary research on the ideologies associated with these identities in university-community based studies.

Elizabeth Murakami-Ramalho comes from Brazil and is now an assistant professor in educational leadership in the Department of Educational Leadership and Policy Studies at the University of Texas-San Antonio. She teaches graduate level courses in school leadership, applied research, organizational theory and change, and principal preparation, with an emphasis in the promotion of learning communities. Her research focuses on urban and international education, including a critical examination of organizational learning and ecology, leadership dynamics, globalization, hybrid identities/communities, social justice, race, and gender. She is the author of articles in international education to include: *Domestic Practices in Foreign Lands: Lessons on Leadership for Diversity in American International Schools* (Journal of Studies in International Education, 2008); *Globally Mobile: Talking with Ruth Useem and Ann Baker Cottrell about Cross-National Educational Experiences* (International Educator, 2002). She is the past editorial assistant (2003–2006) of the American Educational Research Association's leading educational journal, *The American Educational Research Journal: Section on Social and Institutional Analysis.*

Encarnación Garza, Jr. is the son of Mexican born parents who came into the United States in the late 1940s. Encarnación is a former migrant farmworker and worked in the fields until he graduated from college. He has extensive experience working with students with backgrounds very similar to his own. Throughout his career he has served students in various capacities. He has been a teacher, counselor, director of an alternative education center, elementary school principal, and school superintendent. Encarnación has also worked with migrant programs in the states of Colorado, Ohio, New York, Maine, Montana, Florida, and Washington. Currently Encarnación is an Assistant Professor at the University of Texas at San Antonio in the Department of Educational Leadership and Policy Studies. His major focus is the preparation of school leaders that will serve minority children. His book, *Resiliency and Success: Migrant Children in the U.S.* (2004, Paradigm Publishers) was co-authored with Professors Pedro Reyes and Enrique Trueba.

J. Theodore Repa is a professor of administration and instructional leadership at Touro College, New York. After earning his PhD from Stanford University's School of Education, he served as professor and chair of the Department of Administration, Leadership, and Technology at New York University for 30 years. His research interests focus on equity and excellence in education. Since perestroika, Professor Repa has traveled extensively in the Commonwealth of Independent State countries and worked to help reform their preparation of their educational leaders.

John Collard FACE was appointed convenor of graduate programs in the School of Education and Community Studies at the University of Canberra in 2004. A past secondary school teacher and principal, John has also worked in state and national programs in areas such as leadership, professional development, strategic planning, curriculum design, program evaluation, and futures planning. His specific research interests are in the fields of leadership, gender studies, public policy and intercultural dynamics. He has published books and refereed articles in all these areas. He teaches graduate programs for the university both in Australia and Asia and is well known as a speaker at international conferences in Australia, Europe, and North America. In 2007 he was visiting international professor at the University of Texas where he has worked with school districts, superintendents and masters and doctoral students in a diverse multicultural context and is currently preparing the research outcomes as a companion study to his earlier work in China. His previous book was *Leadership, Gender & Culture; Male and Female Perspectives* (OUP/McGraw Hill 2005). He is also a published poet and has recently been writing Irish-Australian cultural history in the form of film scripts.

John Tippeconnic III, PhD, is a professor in the Educational Leadership Program at The Pennsylvania State University. He is also the director of the American Indian Leadership Program and co-director of the Center for the Study of Leadership in American Indian Education. He has over 30 years experience in education at the national, state, local, and tribal levels. His research interests include educational policy, leadership, school reform, higher education, and American Indian education. He is a member of the Comanche Tribe.

Judith Chapman AM is professor of education and director of the Centre for Lifelong Learning at Australian Catholic University. Judith began her career as a teacher in secondary schools in Australia and Europe before undertaking postgraduate studies in the United States. She was formerly dean of the faculty of education at ACU (1998–2003), professor of education and associate dean (teaching and learning) of the combined faculties of economics, commerce, education and law at The University of Western Australia (1993–1998), and director of the Centre for School Decision Making and Management at Monash University (1979–1993). She has undertaken extensive research and consultancy for international and national authorities, including OECD, UNESCO, the World Bank, I.D.P., and the Australian Commonwealth Government. Her publications include: *Values Education and Lifelong Learning* (Dordrecht: Springer 2007); *Lifelong Learning, Participation and Equity* (Dordrecht: Springer 2006); *The International Handbook on Lifelong Learning* (Dordrecht: Kluwer 2001) and *The School, Community and Lifelong Learning* (London: Cassell 1997).

Kate Sutherland is an experience educational leader within the government sector of the Australian Capital Territory (ACT), Australia. She currently occupies the position of deputy principal, Telopea Park School/Lycée Franco-Australien de Canberra, a binational and bicultural French-Australian Kindergarten to Year 10 school where she has been since May 2005. Her interest in intercultural leadership was initiated by her leadership experience at this school. Prior to this position she had been deputy principal in a government high school and manager of the ACT Australian Quality Teacher Program. She has held leadership positions in local and national professional associations. Kate was awarded her master's in education leadership at the university of canberra in 2003 and is currently preparing to undertake a PhD investigating intercultural leadership within bicultural schools.

Marian Court taught for many years in primary, intermediate and secondary schools and worked briefly as an EEO reviewer with the New Zealand Education Review Office before taking up a position at Massey University, where she coordinates and teaches in the educational administration and leadership programme. Her research and publications have drawn on feminist, poststructuralist and Kaupapa Maori approaches in explorations of social justice issues in education. Recent writing has focussed on the impact of new public management accountability regimes in education; intersections between gender and ethnicity in teachers' work and leadership; and innovatory approaches to sharing school leadership, including a study with Hine Waitere of a bicultural co-principalship.

Maricela Oliva is a faculty member in the Department of Educational Leadership and Policy Studies at the University of Texas at San Antonio, with an emphasis in higher education. Raised in the predominately Latino Texas/Mexico borderlands and the first in her family to attend college, Oliva sees students' college readiness, access, and graduation as necessary for a more equitable, socially just society. She has over 22 years' experience in higher education--including administration and policy work with the Texas Higher Education Coordinating Board—and serves on the editorial boards of the *Review of Higher Education, International Journal of Qualitative Studies in Education* and the *Journal of Hispanic Higher Education (JHHE)*. Other publications forthcoming in 2009 include *Leadership for Social Justice: Making Revolutions in Education,* 2nd edition (Allyn & Bacon) and a special issue in the *JHHE* on "Actualizing school-university collaboration: Moving from theory to practice in a partnership context.

Niklas Eklund is a senior lecturer/associate professor in the Department of Political Science at Umeå University in Sweden. He teaches courses in Russian and post-Soviet politics, public administration, international relations, and civics for teacher education. Dr. Eklund's doctoral dissertation, *Sweden and Poland Entering the EU-Comparative Patterns of Organization and Cognition* (2005) reflects his interest and expertise in organizational and cognitive aspects of political and administrative reform. More recently, he was co-editor of and authored two chapters in the *Handbook of Administrative Reform-An International Perspective* (2008). He currently serves on the editorial board of the journal *Statsvetenskaplig Tidskrift*, on the electoral board of the Swedish Political Science Association, and as a delegate to the association's section for international politics. Dr.Eklund earned his bachelor's of social sciences at Umeå University, where he also earned his licentiate and PhD degrees in political science.

Dr. Olof Johansson is professor of political science, and head and director of the Department of the National Head Teachers Training Programme at Umeå University, Sweden. He is also an international associate of the Centre for the Study of Values and Leadership and a member of the Board of Governors of the UCEA: Willower Centre for the Study of Leadership and Ethics located at Penn State University in the United States. His research interest has over the years been focused on political culture, public policy making, and administration. During the last years the focus of his research interest has been on educational leadership. He is at present involved in two different comparative research projects: The International Project on Successful School Leadership in Australia, Canada, England, Hong Kong Sweden and the United States and Leading Schools Successfully in Challenging Urban Context: Strategies for Improvement in Greece, Spain, Portugal, Poland, Ireland, England, Finland and Sweden. The Swedish platform for these projects is the Swedish research project "Structure, Culture, Leadership: Prerequisites for Successful Schools" with Dr Johansson as the main researcher and grant holder. This project is financed by the Swedish Research Council and has six doctoral students and three additional researchers.

Saeeda Shah has been working at the School of Education, University of Leicester since 2003. Previously, she has worked in higher education in Pakistan, holding senior management posts with both academic and administrative responsibilities, her last post being professor and dean of faculty at the University of Azad Jammu & Kashmir, Pakistan. Her research interests include educational management and leadership with a focus on faith, culture, gender, and power issues. She has presented widely in international conferences, and has published extensively in the areas of educational leadership, gender, Islam and society, diversity and identity/ethnicity. Saeeda is actively involved in the voluntary sector. She has participated many times in the United Nation's Human Rights Commission's sessions in relation to her work for human rights, particularly for the rights of marginalised groups including women and youth.

Seu'ula Johansson Fua is currently working at the University of the South Pacific's Institute of Education as the Fellow for Research and Leadership in Education. She has worked on various leadership and research projects in Tonga, Cook Islands, Tuvalu, Nauru, and Marshall Islands and leadership trainings with USP students and educational leaders from around the region. It has indeed been an exciting journey of discovery about Pacific personhood and about regional identity. Seu'ula is Tongan and grew up on the island of Tongatapu having gone to a local government primary school and later Tonga High School. She was subsequently educated in New Zealand and later in Canada where she completed her PhD. She I was a civil servant for the Tongan Government and has taught at Tonga College and at the Community Development Training Centre.

Susan C. Faircloth is an enrolled member of the Coharie Tribe. She joined the faculty of The Pennsylvania State University (Penn State) in the Fall of 2003. She is currently an Assistant Professor of Educational Leadership, having recently completed a three-year joint appointment in Special Education. She earned both her master's and doctoral degrees from Penn State where she was a fellow in the American Indian Special Education Teacher Training Program and the American Indian Leadership Program. After earning her doctoral degree, she served as the Director of Policy Analysis and Research with the American Indian Higher Education Consortium. Dr Faircloth's research focuses on the education of American Indian and Alaska Native (AI/AN) students with disabilities. She is specifically interested in the factors that account for the referral and placement of AI/AN students in special education programs and services in the early grades, the role of Head Start programs and services in the education of young AI/ANs, the preparation of school leaders, and the moral and ethical dimensions of school leadership. Her work has been published in *Harvard Educational Review*, *The Journal of Special Education Leadership*, *International Studies in Educational Administration*, *Values and Ethics in Educational Administration*, the *Tribal College Journal of American Indian Higher Education*, the *Rural Special Education Quarterly*, and the *Journal of Disability Policy Studies*.

Ting Wang is course convenor of The Master of Educational Leadership (China) and Co-ordinator of Offshore Education Programs in the Faculty of Education at the University of Canberra, Australia. She received her PhD in education from the University of Canberra. She has many years' experience of teaching in transnational leadership development programs. Her research interests include leadership in cross-cultural settings, higher education in an international context, Chinese learners, professional development of educators, and intercultural studies.

Printed in the United States
144450LV00002B/32/P

9 781607 520061